CW01563409

ALCHEMY AND PSYCHOTHERAPY

Alchemical symbols are alive in popular culture, as recently popularised in the Harry Potter books and films. Alchemy intrigued Carl Jung, the founder of analytical psychology. It inspired him as he wrote *The Red Book* – the journal of his voyage of internal discovery. He devoted much of his life to it, using alchemical symbols as metaphors for unconscious processes. *Alchemy and Psychotherapy* explores the issue of alchemy in the consulting room and its application to social and political problems. This book argues against the dominant discourse in contemporary psychotherapy – scientific materialism – and for the discovery of spiritual meaning.

Alchemy and Psychotherapy has four main parts:

'Alchemy and Meaning' looks at the history of alchemy, particularly the symbol of the coniunctio – sacred marriage – as a metaphor for the therapeutic relationship.

'The Symbolic Attitude' explores working with dreams, fairytales, astrology and the body: each of which is, itself, a symbolic language.

'The Spirit and the Natural World' discusses 'burn-out' of therapists and our ecological resources – the mystical aspects of quantum physics and the philosophical underpinning of symbol formation.

'Clinical Applications' shows alchemy's use with victims of abuse, with those struggling to secure gender identity, in anorexia and in 'social healing' – atonement and restorative justice – applying the idea of the coniunctio.

Alchemy and Psychotherapy is illustrated throughout with clinical examples, alchemical pictures and poetry to emphasise that alchemy is both a creative art and a science. Bringing together clinicians from different analytical psychology schools in the UK, contributors show that the consulting room is their alchemical laboratory, and that research is their creative engagement.

Alchemy and Psychotherapy will be a valuable resource for practitioners, students at all levels of psychotherapy, analytical psychology, psychoanalysis and creative, art-based therapies, and for creative practitioners (in film, literature and performing arts) who draw on Jung's ideas.

Dale Mathers is a member of the Association of Jungian Analysts. He teaches analytical psychology in the UK and Europe and is in private practice in South London.

ALCHEMY AND PSYCHOTHERAPY

Post-Jungian Perspectives

Edited by
Dale Mathers

Routledge
Taylor & Francis Group

LONDON AND NEW YORK

First published 2014
by Routledge
27 Church Road, Hove, East Sussex, BN3 2FA

and by Routledge
711 Third Avenue, New York, NY 10017

Routledge is an imprint of the Taylor & Francis Group, an informa business

© 2014 Dale Mathers

British Library Cataloguing in Publication Data
A catalogue record for this book is available from the British Library

Library of Congress Cataloging in Publication Data
Alchemy and psychotherapy : post-jungian perspectives / edited by
Dale Mathers. – First Edition.
pages cm
Includes index.
1. Jungian psychology. 2. Psychotherapy. 3. Alchemy.
4. Archetype (Psychology) I. Mathers, Dale, 1955–
BF175.A5494 2014
155.2′644–dc23
2013035422

ISBN: 978–0–415–68203–9 (hbk)
ISBN: 978–0–415–68204–6 (pbk)
ISBN: 978–1–315–81327–1 (ebk)

Typeset in Times
by Keystroke, Station Road, Codsall, Wolverhampton

THIS BOOK IS DEDICATED TO OUR FRIENDS
AND COLLEAGUES AND TO OUR BEST TEACHERS –
OUR PATIENTS.

CONTENTS

CONTENTS

ILLUSTRATIONS

ABOUT THE CONTRIBUTORS

Maryann Barone-Chapman, MSc, Dip Psych, Member of AJA. PhD candidate at Cardiff University's School of Social Science researching unconscious processes in late motherhood. In 2005, whilst training, she won first prize for her unpublished research at a joint academic conference of the IAAP and IAJS. She is in private practice in London. Her publications include: 'The Hunger to Fill an Empty Space: an investigation of primordial affects and meaning making processes in repeated use of ART' (2007), *Journal of Analytical Psychology:* 52:4, 479–501; 'Pregnant Pause: procreative desire, reproductive technology and narrative shifts at midlife' in Raya Jones (ed.), *Body, Mind and Healing After Jung: a Space of Questions* (2011) London: Routledge.

Antonia Boll, MA (Cantab.) She is a professional member of AJA and former Chair. She teaches on the AJA training and until recently was a trainer and supervisor at Re.Vision, London and the Psychosynthesis Institute, Gothenburg, Sweden. She contributes to the Hereford Jungian seminars and runs post-graduate workshops in Sweden. Antonia is a visiting supervisor on the IAAP Developing Group Training, Kiev, Ukraine and she is in private practice in London.

Catherine Bygott is a supervising member of ASA and a senior member of the Independent Group of Analytical Psychologists (IGAP), serving on their council and training programme. She lectures and leads seminars and conference workshops on the *Red Book*, structure and dynamics of the psyche, and its amplification through alchemy, fairytale and active imagination. She was born in Canada and is in private practice in Somerset, UK. Her publications include: 'The Red Book and Clinical Practice' (2012) *Journal of Analytical Psychology*, 57:4, 455–461 London: Wiley-Blackwell.

John Colverson, BSc, Biology, John Moores University, Liverpool; MA in Jungian and post Jungian studies, Essex University; MA in Integrative Psychotherapy, Middlesex University. John trained in integrative psychotherapy at the Minster Centre, London. He is a professional member of the Association of Group and Individual Psychotherapy (AGIP) and a member of AJA. He worked in therapeutic communities, homeless hostels, and hospitals and has an interest in eating disorders which he developed particularly while working at Capio Nightingale hospital, London, and later at the Priory hospital, Chelmsford. Website: www.jungianpsychoanalysis.co.uk.

Adele Davide, formerly in private practice as a Jungian analyst from 1985 to 2010: training analyst, supervisor and lecturer for AJA; supervisor and lecturer at the Centre for Psychological Astrology from 1985 to1996. Adele lectured in creative writing and literature in higher education from 1974–1983, in drawing and composition at Plymouth College of Art 1964, and in drawing at Chelsea College of Art. In 1963 she received a medal for painting from the Regent St. Polytechnic; in 1978 she won a prize at the Caernarvon Poetry Festival and in 1993 she won the Cheltenham festival Appleby Cup for poetry. Adele continues to paint, write and publish on mythological and psychological themes. Her publications include: poetry in anthologies, newspapers and journals in Great Britain, USA, Canada, Sweden and Japan, translations into Swedish and Japanese; *Becoming* (1980) London: Migrant Press; *The Moon's Song* (2001) London: Katabasis.

Nathan Field trained as a Jungian analyst with the British Association of Psychotherapy and retired in 2002 after over 30 years in private practice. Nathan taught, supervised, and lectured widely and was a former chair of training and later chair of council at the London Centre for Psychotherapy. His publications include: *Breakdown and Breakthrough: Psychotherapy in a New Dimension* (1996) London: Routledge; *Ten Lectures on Psychotherapy and Spirituality* (ed.) (2005) London: Karnac.

Rabbi David L. Freeman, Rabbinic Diploma and Honorary Fellow, Leo Baeck College, London. David was ordained Rabbi in 1967 and served congregations in London and Birmingham; Jewish Chaplain to the Universities of Birmingham, Nottingham and Aston. He was a member of the Religious Liaison Panel of Amnesty International and a Hospice Chaplain. Rabbi David trained with the Association of Jungian analysts, with whom he is a supervisor and ex-Chair. He is also a member of the Independent Group of Analytical Psychologists (IGAP) and has lectured and taught in various analytical trainings. Past Chair and Fellow of the Guild of Pastoral Psychology. He is in private practice in London.

Phil Goss, PhD, MSc, Member of AJA, Senior Lecturer and Course Leader for MA Integrative Psychotherapy at the University of Central Lancashire. Phil teaches and leads workshops on gender, contra-sexual influences, and Jungian perspectives on learning difficulties and education. He is in private practice in Cumbria and his publications include: *Men, Women and Relationships: a Post-Jungian approach* (2010) London: Routledge.

Birgit Heuer, BEd, PhD candidate, Jungian analyst with the British Psychotherapy Foundation, and previously trained in body-oriented psychotherapy. Birgit has been in private practice for 33 years. She served on the BAP training committee and worked as clinical supervisor at Kingston University. She teaches in several Jungian-analytic trainings: on the body in analysis, the theme of forgiveness and on the experience of the holy in the consulting room. Publications include: 'Clinical paradigm as analytic third. Reflections on a century of analysis and an emergent paradigm for the millennium.' In Christopher, E. and Solomon, H. (eds), *Contemporary Jungian Clinical Practice* (2003) London: Karnac; 'Buddha in the depressive position. On the healing paradigm.' *Proceedings of the sixteenth International Congress for Analytical Psychology* (2004) Barcelona Einsiedeln: Daimon; 'Discourse of illness or discourse of health'. In Huskinson, L. (ed.), (2008) *Dreaming the Myth Onward*. London: Routledge; 'The experience of the numinous in the consulting-room'. In Stein, M. (ed.), (2010) *Jungian Psychoanalysis*. Chicago: Open Court.

Gottfried M. Heuer, PhD, is a training analyst and supervisor with the Association of Jungian Analysts, Neo-Reichian body psychotherapist, and has worked in clinical practice for 40 years in West London. Dr Heuer is an independent scholar with over 65 published papers on the links between analysis, radical politics, body psychotherapy and spirituality as well as on the history of analytic ideas in *The International Journal of Psychoanalysis*, *The Journal of Analytical Psychology*, *The International Journal of Jungian Studies*, *Harvest*, *Psychotherapy and Politics International*, *Spring*, etc. He is also a graphic artist, photographer, sculptor (one-man and group-shows in the UK and abroad), and a published poet. Publications include: *A Translucent Turtle Ascends to the Stars* (London/Berlin 1984); 10 congress – and symposium – proceedings for the International Otto Gross Society (www.ottogross.org/) (which he co-founded); *Sacral Revolutions. Reflecting on the Work of Andrew Samuels: Cutting Edges in Psychoanalysis and Jungian Analysis*, London: Routledge (2010); *Sexual Revolutions: Psychoanalysis, History and the Father*, London: Routledge (2011).

Carola Mathers, MB, BS, MRCPsych, Supervisor with AJA. Formerly a consultant psychotherapist at the Southwest London and St. George's NHS Trust, Dr Mathers is now in private practice. She analyses, teaches and supervises for psychotherapy and Jungian analytic trainings in England, Poland and Russia. She is also an artist, working with watercolours, oils and mixed media: www.carolamatherspsychotherapy.co.uk.

Dale Mathers, MB, BS, MRCPsych. Dale is a supervisor with AJA, and a psychiatrist. He teaches analytical psychology in the UK and Europe and is in private practice in South London. Dale is interested in creative writing and his publications include: *An introduction to meaning and purpose in analytical psychology* (2001) London: Routledge; *Vision and Supervision* (2009) London: Routledge (ed.); *Self and No Self* (2009) London: Routledge (ed.).

Karin Syrett, MA, MSc (Psychol). Karin is a training analyst and supervisor with AJA; former chair of the training committee. She practised as an astrologer in the 1980s and trained with the Westminster Pastoral Foundation. She was an honorary psychotherapist at Guy's and Charing Cross Hospitals. Karin worked as a part-time psychotherapist at the Charter Clinic, London, where she researched patients' expectations of treatment. She is interested in the arts, divination, spirituality, literature and typology. She travels extensively in search of the ancient mythologies and mysteries and has been in private practice in West London for the past 30 years.

Richard Wainwright, MA, member of AJA and psychoanalytic member of the Foundation for Psychotherapy and Counselling (FPC) for whom he is a supervisor. He is a principal supervisor on the IAAP training programme in Kiev, Ukraine. Richard comes from a background in theatre and theatre research and was formerly a senior lecturer in Drama Therapy at the University of Hertfordshire. He is well known for his work as a teacher and a dramaturg in making theatre arts and poetics accessible, leading seminars and workshops internationally which evoke the interface of artistic and analytic practice. He is presently working on a series of essays and is in private practice in South London.

Michael Whan, MA, analytical psychologist with the Independent Group of Analytical Psychologists, the Association of Independent Psychotherapists, and the College of Psychoanalysts. Michael is in private practice in St. Albans and London. His previous publications include contributions to four books; articles in the journals *Spring*, *Chiron*, *Harvest*, *Dragonflies*, *Existential Analysis*, *The European Journal of Psychotherapy*, *Counselling*, *Health*, and *The International Journal of Jungian Studies*.

Ruth Williams, MA. Ruth is a member of the Association of Jungian Analysts and a practising Jungian Analyst–Analytical Psychologist, integrative psycho-therapist and supervisor based in London. Chair of the Confederation for Analytical Psychology, she is also a delegate to the Council for Jungian Analysis and Psychoanalysis and the Psychotherapy Council, the strategic body of the UK Council for Psychotherapy. Publications include: 'Analytical Psychology' (2012) in the *Sage Handbook of Counselling and Psychotherapy*, London: Sage; a number of entries to *The Encyclopaedia of Psychology and Religion*, Eds. D. A. Leeming, K. Madden, S. Marlan, (2009) New York: Springer. www.RuthWilliams.org.uk.

FOREWORD

John Beebe

This book links alchemy, a complex subject with deep historical roots, with a type of depth psychotherapy that is just a century old. In so doing, it follows the lead of C. G. Jung, whose psychological interpretation of alchemical texts has already become canonical and, not least for that reason, controversial. It was Jung who first made the case for regarding alchemy as the true precursor, not just of chemistry, but of analytical psychotherapy. In an epilogue to his final book on that subject, *Mysterium Coniunctionis* [The Mystery of the Conjunction], he wrote:

> Alchemy, with its wealth of symbols, gives us an insight into an endeavour of the human mind which could be compared to a religious rite, an *opus divinum*. . . . The conventional devaluation of alchemy on the one hand and of the psyche on the other had first to be cleared away . . . [before we could] see how effectively alchemy prepared the ground for the psychology of the unconscious, first by leaving behind, in its treasury of symbols, illustrative material of the utmost value for modern interpretations in this field, and secondly by indicating symbolical procedures for synthesis which we can rediscover in the dreams of our patients. We can see today that the entire alchemical procedure for uniting the opposites, which I have described in the foregoing, could just as well represent the individuation of a single individual, though with the not unimportant difference that no single individual ever attains to the richness and scope of the alchemical symbolism.
>
> (CW 14, paras 790, 792)

Because the clinical accounts supplied in this book have been offered by contributors who have drawn upon Jung's insights to inform their own observations, it is necessary to unpack what Jung claims for alchemy before we can understand how it applies to psychotherapy as practised by analytical psychologists today. The authors of these chapters are hard-working mental health professionals used to being paid for their work, and they would not conceive what they do as a cult practice. Yet they too have observed how for their clients what transpires in an analytical setting can be a religious experience of the kind that would not have been unfamiliar to people living in the ancient world who chose to participate in one of the Mysteries then available. The factor in common with those rites would be transition from a state of being that sees itself as at the mercy of fate, having been born with a particular delimiting character into a set of circumstances that have even further restricted that character's options. Luther Martin's *Hellenistic Religions: An Introduction* has shown that, as one reviewer of that remarkably clarifying text has put it, 'the common, universal theme in mystery religions is encountering and, in some sense, "transcending" deter-minism, Fate, or Necessity' (Hoffman, 2002). This is not so different from the attitude toward self of the contemporary analytic patient who is all too aware of the repetition compulsion driving repeated enactment of a set of deep-seated complexes.

Not a great many educated people in the West today accept the astrological world view that was universal in the ancient world of late antiquity – informing, for instance, the Magi that hurried to Bethlehem to celebrate the birth of Christ. The Chaldean astronomers had long since demonstrated that five planets and two lights (sun and moon) held visible, measurable positions in space, and everyone, by the time of Christ, believed that the pattern of these heavenly bodies, visible from earth, controlled, not just the character of the individual, from the horoscopic time of birth forward, but even the life experiences that would be, in this incarnation, significant for that individual. Destiny therefore meant not just the basic quality of the person's life but also the time and circumstance of the person's death. Alchemy appeared as an experimental, magical, and philosophical tradi-tion in the West at a time when astrology had held for at least six centuries its hegemony over the Ancients' psychological vision. In introducing for psycho-logical discussion what is sometimes described as the oldest Western alchemical text, the visions of Zosimos of Panopolis, Egypt, Jung describes Zosimos as 'an important alchemist and Gnostic of the third century AD' (CW 13, para. 85). But by then, when the technique was already thriving, it would have been impossible to understand the practice of alchemy, and why it was needed, without grasping that it was a method for gaining liberation from one's otherwise foreclosed astrological destiny.

Alchemy was not in this respect essentially different from other mystery religions, including Christianity, for all of them sought release from the 'depen-dence of character and destiny on certain moments of time' (CW 12, para. 40) such as the time of birth that (as the horoscopes revealed) bound the nature of one's personal spirit to the matter of the cosmos. The brilliance embedded in alchemy was that it took this correspondence seriously and began to work on the spirit at the material level, starting with metallurgy, the mining and mixing of metals. Elemental minerals such as mercury, copper, iron, tin, lead, were regarded, accord-ing to the theory of correspondences then prevalent, as the representatives of the planets Mercury, Venus, Mars, Jupiter, and Saturn. It was understood that if their earthly forms could be manipulated successfully, then the law of correspondences expressed by the alchemical maxim, 'As above, so below' could work in human favour if reversed, for 'As below, so above' had, according to the same law, to be equally true. In other words, if the astrological, heavenly pattern could be transformed through laboratory operations performed by the alchemist working on base, earthly metals, the very character of the person on whose behalf this experiment had been practised might be changed sufficiently to create for him or for her an entirely new fate.

Depth psychotherapy often has held a similar ambition when it comes to work on psychological complexes. Even today, despite decades of experiment with the symbolic attitude recommended by Jung, the level at which a psychotherapy commonly starts is literal and material, psyche projected on the matters at hand. The correspondences that a psychotherapist must deal with involve the ways lives are governed by the circumstances of one's money, sexuality, parents, relationship status, and political position in society. Such issues, which are archetypal in the sense that they are inevitably going to be faced by all humans, are at the heart of the complexes that are brought by a patient to a psychotherapist, and work on them in therapy can free up unexpected energy. What has up to now simply governed the person's life seems to evoke agency, rather than anxious reaction. The process of the therapies in which this happy outcome emerges is usually as messy, individual, and filled with esoteric instruments of change as any that might have occurred in a successful alchemical laboratory. We cannot claim for psychotherapy the regularity of a science, any more than alchemy ever achieved the status of true science, even in its richest period, the Renaissance, just before the Scientific Revolution pre-empted its momentum.

Psychotherapy today, like alchemy in the early seventeenth century, has the advantage of being still on the cusp of becoming a science. It can be practised and conceptualized in many ways, each rich in its potential to enhance transformation. By comparing itself to alchemy, Jungian analysis has distinguished itself from other schools mainly in recognizing the symbolic thrust of its enterprise, and in producing practitioners willing to be candid about what they have experienced rather than rushing to codify their craft into a science. I admire the courage of the contributors to this book in sharing just how they mix the materials brought to them by present-day clients who are en route to discovering how their complexes may be unsnarled sufficiently to enable the flexible tension that propels transformation. Though the goal of the individuated patient may turn out to be as elusive as the liberation of the human spirit via the Philosopher's Stone, the discoveries patients in analytical psychotherapy have made about their own alchemical energies retain the potential to generate new transformative practices in all of us. The reader of this book, whether psychotherapist, patient, or amateur *aficionado* of the soul, will benefit from what it tells us is being done on this Jungian ground. I hope, particularly, that sophisticated readers already accustomed to perusing the psychotherapy literature can rise above the complacency that attends being introduced to new developments within an established discipline and pursue what is to be freshly discovered here with a sensibility naïve enough to consider, as if for the first time, what real change within the self may require.

John Beebe,
Jung Institute of
San Francisco

References

Hoffman, Michael (2002) Review of Martin (1987). Online www.amazon.com/Hellenistic-Religions-Introduction-Luther (consulted February 3, 2013).

Jung, C. G. (1963–1968) Except where indicated, references are by volume and paragraph number to *The Collected Works of C. G. JUNG, 20 vol.* London and Princeton, NJ: Routledge and Princeton University Press.

Martin, Luther (1987) *Hellenistic Religions: An Introduction.* Oxford and New York: Oxford University Press.

FOREWORD

Susan Rowland

Alchemy is not true. It is not possible to transform lead into gold through a series of chemical additions, subtractions, distillations and cooking operations in a rudimentary laboratory as was practised in medieval and Renaissance Europe. No wonder that 'alchemist' became a byword for 'con-man' as demonstrated in Ben Jonson's 1611 play of that name. Jonson's work, *The Alchemist*, concerns a pretend practitioner of the alchemical or hermetic arts who extorts large sums of money from gullible clients until he himself loses everything. This play marks a cultural turning point. From this era alchemy begins to give way to its successor, chemistry, in which mystical approaches to matter are firmly banished in favour of scientific experimentation that will inexorably culminate in the discovery of the periodic table of the elements.

And yet in the early twentieth century, psychoanalyst C. G. Jung became fascinated with Renaissance books of alchemy. At least three volumes of his *Collected Works* are wholly devoted to alchemy and its symbolism in relation to psychotherapy. In the twenty-first century, a National Theatre production of Jonson's *The Alchemist* portrayed the titular anti-hero as a fake guru with a Californian twang. Is it a mistake for a psychotherapist to promise golden success from the leaden problems of today's complex world? Do analysts risk the danger of falling into the historic trap of alchemy: offering a ready way for the unscrupulous to coin money from those after a quick fix?

No, I am not suggesting that Jung or Jungians are false gurus. Nor am I suggesting that alchemy was simply a way to obtain money by duping a credulous public. Rather, Jung's symptomatically counter-cultural valuing of alchemy speaks to his courage and insight into digging up what had been lost when the modern scientific paradigm reinvented alchemy as chemistry. For the false alchemists paradoxically succeeded. They really did 'obtain' gold from the (worthless) dross or lead that they offered; they made money! While alchemy proper had cultural currency, false alchemists coined it. In that ability to manipulate desires and fears, they point to something significant that their con-artistry fails to enact: real transformation. What can be done with desire that drives people beyond their common sense or the precepts inhabiting their conscious minds?

So what was it about alchemy that permitted such economic success in its exploitation? Clearly the basic premise of turning a cheap and plentiful metal, lead, into a rare and precious one, gold, had commercial viability – but surely its chemical improbability would have quenched it as a practice long before it actually ceased to operate? As Jung quickly realized, alchemy persisted in the face of its apparent ineffectiveness for two reasons: it originated in a world view very different from the modern notion of human physical and psychic separation from the world and, second, it was a process of *working on the alchemist him or herself.*

For alchemists, spirit and matter were not separate realms; spirit and matter were of one order, interconnected. Matter contained spirit and spirit had a material dimension. Hence, divine spirit could indeed transform or be extracted from lowly, base, leaden matter. Moreover, if spirit and matter are together then they both inhere in the human body. The alchemist does not only manipulate substances in glass test tubes; he uses what they called the *imaginatio*, like the modern sense of imagination but significantly different. Where spirit and matter exist together, the *imaginatio* is a spiritual force with material penetration, to be part of the transforming process. Therefore, what was known as 'the Great Work' of alchemy was a spiritual, intellectual, imaginative, scientific and even artistic multi-media operation.

Bringing all these activities together was the symbol. Encoded in the alchemist's writing, visually represented in drawing and woodcuts, the symbol was an image that also was occurring in the alchemist's body and psyche. An image in the modern psychological sense of the earliest stage of cognition, the alchemical symbol was very definitely what Jung called a symbol in distinction from a sign. To Jung both symbols and signs are types of image. Whereas a sign points to something known and wholly conscious, the symbol points to the unknown, not yet known or partly unknowable. Put another way, the symbol joins embodied immanent experience to the unconscious populated with the capacity for archetypal transcendence.

In Jung's modern world, characterized by divisions and specializations, the notion of knowable images, including words, is part of the architecture of who we believe we are. In the world of medieval and Renaissance alchemy in which divine spirit infused matter and nature, images were more *natively* symbols. They did more than just point to the unknowable collective unconscious. Alchemy symbols, as Jung himself stated, were themselves both imagination and reality, 'real and unreal' (CW 12 para. 400).

With such a sense of alchemy, Jung realized that its practice manifested a different type of consciousness; one more connected to matter, unconscious, body and spirit. For after all, alchemy was the manifestation of a holistic universe; for alchemists human consciousness was co-created in relation to divine spirit imbued in all of nature. Of course, as Jung also noted, his Renaissance alchemists had become partly Christianized in a way that was about to propel them into the scientific revolution and their radical turn into chemistry. He discovered that Renaissance alchemy texts were predicated on a narrative of *rescuing* the divine imprisoned in matter. God wanted his transcendence to become as mainstream Christianity portrayed him: the immaterial divine being who created matter, body and nature as separate from himself. Renaissance alchemists were hurrying to join the dominant religious ethos; one which was just about to institute its transcendent God in science by focussing on matter as without soul: for alchemy to chemistry!

C. G. Jung had an acute sense of paradigm shifts and recognized that by excluding soul from matter, post-Renaissance chemists were also excluding psyche. The alchemy he found in Renaissance books was to have a major influence upon his psychotherapy both conceptually and culturally. Conceptually, Jung said that alchemy worked because it was a work of psyche. Without realizing it, alchemists projected their psyches into the matter in their laboratories. The lead was their heavy depressed souls. The quest for gold was a desire to experience the divine or in Jung's terms, to be connected to the major archetype of wholeness, the self. Alchemy was fascinating and satisfying because it was a means to individuation in the sense of becoming a more 'whole' person feeling connections to matter, spirit and the cosmos. Culturally therefore, alchemy was Jungian psychotherapy before Jung. It provided a historical and epistemological validation of Jung's ideas.

The very strangeness of the world of alchemists and their symbols made it a psychically activated language. This is what we see in this fine book, edited by Dale Mathers. In these chapters by practising psychotherapists, alchemy mobilizes, provokes and enables transformation and healing. It is an embodied, aesthetic mode of being that fuses and de-fuses, unites and fragments, dissolves and coagulates psychic states both within one person and between therapist and patient. The unfamiliar terms allow a suspension of everyday entanglements in conventional ideas. More importantly, alchemy is a language of im/possibilities where fantasy can be expressed, even embodied, yet remain symbolic and metaphoric. By considering the therapeutic session as a temenos, a vessel for transformation and rebirth, therapy can bathe the troubled soul in the wisdom of an-other age.

Jung did not quite stick to his 'modern' translation of alchemy as psychic projection onto matter. In later work he developed his notion of synchronicity in which something happening in the psychic real is effected by, or itself affects, something material with no rational cause. Such 'meaningful coincidences' infer that psyche and matter is not as wholly divided as alchemy as projection implies. Put another way, the transferences and counter-transferences of alchemical conjunction in the consulting room may not be where alchemy ends. Adding synchronicity to the mix would make alchemy as therapy into something else as well; not just training to live in the world in a new way, but training to make the world new.

I commend this fine book for opening the door into the riches and imaginative inspiration of alchemy in psychotherapy.

Susan Rowland PhD,
Pacifica Graduate Institute, California.
January 2013

Reference

Jung, C. G. (1968) Except where indicated, references are by volume and paragraph number to *The Collected Works of C. G. Jung*, 20 vol. London and Princeton, NJ: Routledge and Princeton University Press.

ACKNOWLEDGEMENTS

Adele Davide for kind permission to print 'Water and Stone' and reprint 'The hours of the day' and 'Hermes' from *The Moon's Song*, London (2001) Katabasis Press. Princeton University press for permission to quote from the collected works of C. G. Jung; and for the following illustrations, *The Coniunctio* and *The Green Lion eats the Sun* (from CW 16 and CW 12). Foto Deutsche Museum and Rosekilde and Bagger Ltd., Copenhagen, for the plate *Rosinus ad Sarratantam. Artis aurif.* from *Alchemy* by Johannes Fabricius. Diamond Books Ed. (1994). Karin Syrett drew Jung and Freud's astrological charts. 'Strangeland' by Tracey Emin (2005), reproduced by permission of the publisher Hodder and Stoughton Limited. Springer Press for permission to reprint part of Ruth William's entry on atonement in *The Encyclopaedia of Psychology & Religion*, eds D. A. Leeming, K. Madden, S. Marlan, Springer (2009). Open Court Books for permission to reproduce the *'Calcinatio'* diagram from Edward Edinger's *Anatomy of the Psyche* (1994). Ruth Williams drew the gestalt diagram. Thanks to Jerome Bernstein for permission to quote his letter on the Navaho. FLB for her illustration in Chapter 12, 'The Exorcism' (oil on canvas). The *'Wilhelm Reich Sigil'* is drawn by Dr Gottfried Heuer, who gave kind permission to print his poems, 'Transubstantiation' and 'Alchemy'.

Cover art: 'Phoenix' by Carola Mathers
www.alternativeartsales.com

INTRODUCTION

Dale Mathers

You remember that I also stressed, perhaps the most important point, that the alchemists, in observing and experiencing their symbols and in their written descriptions, worked without any conscious religious or scientific programme, so that their conclusions are spontaneous, uncorrected impressions of the unconscious with very little conscious interference, in contrast to other symbolic material which has always been revised.

Marie Louise von Franz (1980, p. 40)

Lead into gold?

Medieval alchemists tried making gold in their crucibles and failed – unless they'd put gold in at the beginning. Today we can take a copper atom, atomic number 29, a tin atom, atomic number 50, and push them together very quickly. This makes gold, atomic number 79. To do this all you need is a large hadron collider, a particle accelerator. At CERN, Geneva, the alchemical vessel is a tunnel of magnets and hardware, 27 kilometres long and 4 metres high. It cost over 3 billion pounds. A gold tooth filling made here might ruin a Sheikh. It *is* possible, but it isn't necessary or wise. Appropriate technology is a key theme in our book. What discourse do we need to turn leaden experience to creative gold?

Our text is a version of 'Aladdin and the Genie'. Instead of 'new lamps for old', we're offering 'old lamps for new'. We'll use an old light to look at the creative psyche, to show how the language and ideas of an ancient art, alchemy, a forerunner of science, illuminate contemporary struggles at wresting the gold of meaning from the collisions of our over-accelerated lives. Alchemy is a poetry of science. I hope it may help you to find both gold and the philosopher's stone – that is, how to form and use symbols in new, creative and healing ways.

Alchemical language can work as a 'particle decelerator'. Symbols of transformation, of holding and containing, speak about changes resulting from work and by prayer (as in the alchemical motto, *Orando Laborando*). Alchemy, like analysis, depends on work and prayer: to reflect, to 'be with' as well as 'to do'; to 'not know' as well as 'to know'; to allow the natural chaos and uncertainty of any

1

creative process. It includes 'the Spiritual', however that may be understood. Alchemists are often seen as grandiose, bombastic, charlatans and mountebanks, or humble, poor and perhaps a little crazy. This rings with our experience as counsellors/therapists/analysts, recipients of similar, 'magical' projections. Are we, like alchemists, taking gold from people, only to give them a little of it back?

What do counsellors/therapists/analysts do? We certainly cannot force change on anyone by shouting the magic word 'change!' Unconscious processes don't respond in the long term to the 'McTherapies' on the market – cheap and cheerful, acronym-based and full of toxic additives. A better way to approach the creative unconscious is to allow it to approach you; that is, to enter its discourse. And to do that, you have to share its language, its poetry, which is neither ego-based nor rational. This is why each section begins with a poem.

The poetry of dreams is a language we all speak to ourselves every night. Interpretation of dreams cannot be done using a dictionary of images, because symbols, by definition, contain an unknown; sometimes, an unknowable. Alchemical language is a dialect of the language of the collective unconscious; rich in positive connotations, 'there's gold in there!' and paradoxical injunctions, 'if you don't work, it works' – methods still valued today by family therapists. Alchemists might also be pioneer 'post-modernists' – they too were experts at using long words in ways ordinary people do not quite grasp, and at deconstruction (of base metals to make gold). Of course, they didn't only deconstruct; sometimes their retorts blew up.

The quest

Our text deconstructs three stories/myths/discourses used in contemporary counselling/therapy/analysis: the alchemical, developmental and neuroscientific.

A discourse is a *way of writing*: say, a cookery book – Delia Smith, 'cooking with mother'; Jamie Oliver, 'cooking with attitude'; (Clement) Freud, 'cooking with humour,' or Gertrude Stein, writing as Alice B. Toklas, 'cooking with panache'. A discourse is not '*what* we talk about' (content) – that is a narrative – it is '*how* we talk about' (form), and it is 'a talk in order to achieve a result . . .' Discourses have a political purpose beyond merely conveying information.

Like a political spin doctor, a discourse seeks to shape our perceptions, to encourage us to think in certain ways, rather like a 'dress code' for the psyche. A discourse uses premature closures – 'X means what I want it to mean': for example, in a red-top tabloid newspaper, 'Jung? Mystic spanks patient!' . . . 'Freud? Cocaine junkie!' Or whatever. A discourse can turn a golden narrative into lead. This discourse analysis of the analytic discourse looks at *how* language is used in three theories about the psyche, comparing 'old for new'. We contrast a medieval post-modern discourse, with two unashamedly modern ones. Our preferred discourse, post-modern alchemy, is playful; a magical and poetic language. How?

When we talk about 'gold' or 'the philosopher's stone' we are using a language we *know* is not real – not attempting a description of things 'as they really are'. It is a myth, useful in understanding the myths we make about ourselves. The American sage Mark Twain is supposed to have said 'faith is believing in what you know ain't so.' We *know* we are doing that, talking in symbols, in a language of interpretation.

Modernist discourses often take as facts what we'd call 'faiths'. To mistake symbols for facts, as well as being a philosophical category error, is a premature closure which stifles creativity. Developmental psychology and neuroscience are useful, if not essential, attempts to describe 'things as they really are', but they capture what it is to be human as successfully as reading a cookery book captures the taste of real food. Too often, these discourses are used as recipes. For example, 'depression' – existential angst and spiritual pain – is distilled into a disease with an ICD4 definition, treated with medication and ten sessions of cognitive behavioural therapy.

All three discourses – by encouraging us to think in certain ways, rather than for ourselves – involve power dynamics. In alchemy, this is clear enough. The male adept does the magic, the female helper, the *soror mystica*, does the work and gets dirty. There is obvious gender power in the discourse. And analysis/therapy/counselling is hierarchical. Power is skewed. *We* do the magic, *they* do the work and get dirty. If this were not so, it would be like trying to teach a person to cook by never letting them near a saucepan. Medieval alchemy was hierarchical, secretive, 'tainted with the black mud of occultism'. Yet the true power did not rest in the adept (the one), the soror (the two) or the vessel (the third), but in the shared, mysterious, hidden fourth – the magic of 'what is going on in the retort'.

Or, 'what is going on in the intersubjective space where our unconscious minds overlap?' This is the magic land of transitional objects, a *between* place: threshold, liminal; where the language of symbols is spoken. We don't live here. We can watch as unknowables arise from 'not-knowing'. And 'not knowing' is not from lack of skill or theory, but because we can't *know* the unconscious ... 'the unconscious is unconscious is unconscious', to misquote Gertrude Stein's 'a rose is a rose is a rose'. The unconscious is collective, a discourse shared by all of us, across all cultures.

In 'the Visions Seminars' given to analytic candidates from 1930 to 1934, Jung presented an image of the blind 'million-year-old man'. Wondering why he was sightless, Gerhard Adler answered, 'he is blind because he is the collective unconscious which does not promote consciousness. Seeing is consciousness.'

To which Jung answered:

> I think that would be the most concise answer to my question. This figure quite certainly represents the collective unconscious, and the fact that the unconscious is blind, that it does not see, is in its definition. If the unconscious could see, there would be no unconscious, and we would be entirely superfluous. Everything would be foreseen, we would have predestination with no freedom whatever, no chance of free will.
>
> (1998, pp. 1021–1022)

Developmental psychology and neuroscience are determinedly modern; materialist-based discourses about 'doing'. They seem to accept a logic of cause and effect, of determinism. But we can't know the unconscious, particularly the collective unconscious, not just because we haven't found out enough about it yet. These discourses offer not gold, but a Utopian future . . . 'one day we will know all about the brain and its development, and then . . .!' These discourses risk becoming inappropriate technologies, particularly in the more fundamentalist, reductionist versions. They share a fascination with big science and social Darwinism, where the 'fittest' survive and the 'unfit' are discarded. These two dominant discourses in counselling/therapy/analysis risk losing a sense of scale and a sense of wonder by valuing knowledge over wisdom, and 'results' over 'acceptance of what cannot be changed'. 'Real gold' (materialism) is valued over 'alchemical gold' (spiritual values).

Calling something 'a discourse' invites a difficult question: not 'what does it mean?', but 'what is it for?' A discourse *shapes a mode of perception*. Discourses about the unconscious which attempt to know that which cannot be known, which reduce us to atoms then tell us we are in a 'Scientific Utopia', are more of a nonsense than alchemy. The Victorian satirist Samuel Butler, in his novel *Erewhon* (1872, 1970), takes a young traveller to a Utopia to deconstruct Victorian society, its appalling criminal justice system, gross inequalities in wealth and health, the tyrannies of imperialism. Butler's world is much like ours, particularly after the banks performed negative alchemy on behalf of advanced global capitalism.

In *Erewhon* ('nowhere' backwards – almost), criminals are treated as ill and offered therapy. The sick are criminals, 'made to pay' with musical money. With the symbol, 'musical banks', Butler attacked both organised religion and Victorian capitalism. In his day, churches exchanged street currency for coins they minted themselves. A wise idea, as many counterfeit coins were in circulation. 'Musical banks' gave dead signs in exchange for living symbols. Any discourse has a currency, its 'magic words'.

Alchemy is full of magic words, like *magnum opus, massa confusa, prima materia, coniunctio* . . . grand-sounding, Latin, reeking of mystery and chemicals. Alchemy parodied itself. Not a grand but a grandiose narrative. A con trick, as in Ben Jonson's play *The Alchemist* (1610). In it, three crooks – Captain Face, Subtle and Doll the prostitute – gull Sir Epicure Mammon, the greedy plutocrat, out of his gold. If he gives them all of his, they'll make more . . . Butler and Jonson satirise greed-induced credulity. We all need to believe what we do is 'gold'; that is, ethical. Language reflects our ethic, and our ethic reflects our language. But if we say, 'I want a thing to be true, then it is true', that's magical thinking. This is common to all three discourses – with one crucial difference: *when* we use alchemical metaphors, *then* we know we are 'making up a story'.

We know a phrase like *massa confusa* (the muck in the retort at the start of an alchemical operation) is simply a metaphor for the confused mess in the psyche of a patient, which we meet with the, hopefully slightly less confused, mess in our own. We know we are going to distil, dissolve, coagulate, sublime, reflux and incubate whatever emerges. Alchemical metaphors signify processes of trans-formation, are 'process metaphors', not 'facts'. They can't be mistaken for facts. This reduces the danger of reification, of turning an idea into a thing, of turning counselling/therapy/analysis into a 'musical bank'.

Any creative process involves an investment. You can't get gold out of this text unless you 'give us the gold' of your time. You are interested . . . perhaps hoping this book will give 'mystical insights', rather than question cherished, and financially rewarding, beliefs. In developmental discourse, phrases like 'mother–infant dyad', and 'anxious attachment' are the kind of theoretical gold a counsellor/therapist/analyst expects to find. Therefore, they find them. They go in at the beginning, so they come out at the end. In neuroscience, phrases like 'amygdalo-thalamic circuits' and 'fMRI imaging' become exciting signifiers. To see difficulties in living only in terms of science, whether fact or fiction, and science as the gold standard for truths about being human is hubris.

A discourse is a social construction with political implications. Social con-structivism:

> denies that our knowledge is a direct perception of reality. In fact it might be said that as a culture or society we construct our own versions of reality between us. Since we have to accept the historical and cultural relativism of all forms of knowledge, it follows that the notion of "truth" becomes problematic. Within social constructivism there can be no such thing as an objective fact. All knowledge is derived from looking at the world from some perspective or other, and is in the service of some interests rather than others.
>
> (Burr, 2003, p. 6)

Using a mythic language to speak of and with the unconscious is in the interest of the unconscious. Using a language to speak of the psyche in terms of reductive science is in whose service? It may contain truth, be insightful, be 'things as they really are', but is it creative? Can it show us how to make the philosopher's stone? Does it help us form and use symbols?

Philosophically, 'science is the gold standard' is a problematic discourse. The first problem is false attribution: the *post hoc, ergo propter hoc* fallacy – *after this, therefore because of this* – (common to superstitions and religious beliefs); assuming that just because B follows A, A causes B, without looking at counter arguments or the possibility that A and B are both caused by the same thing, C. What if both (developmental) and (neuro-scientific) are caused by (spiritual)? The modernist discourses have a second problem: infinite regress . . . if we define a creative choice as one caused by an act of will, then if acts of will are themselves choices, they too were caused by a previous choice, and so on. If 'it's your mother . . .', then 'it was her mother . . .', and so on. If 'it's your brain . . .', then 'it's all brains before yours . . .', leading to 'milk causes crime because criminals drank milk as babies'.

Alchemy, of course, is spectacularly fond of serving both errors, far earlier, sauced with magical thinking. Scientific metaphors are not symbols, they are knowns pointing to knows. Babies have mothers; we all know that. If mother isn't a symbol, she's a sign. There is no 'added value'. French psychoanalyst Andre Green knew that when analysts talk about 'breasts and penises' they ought to remember they are using the words as metaphors:

> the fiercest partisans of the reference to the loss of the breast in contemporary psychoanalytic theory, the Kleinians, now admit, humbly watering down their wine, that the breast is just a word to designate the mother, this, to the satisfaction of non-Kleinian theoreticians who often psychologise psychoanalysis. One must retain the metaphor of the breast, for the breast, like the penis, can only be symbolic.
>
> (1980, pp. 147–148)

Green's criticism has little impact on dominant discourses in the UK. They seek hegemony – power exerted by a small dominant group over the majority, often requiring their collusive co-operation (see Casement, 1995). Alchemical metaphors give us symbolic language. A sign (a word or phrase) plus an unknowable creates gold – the process *is* the philosopher's stone, an ability to be with not knowing, to form and use symbols. Gold might be a sensation recalled, an intuition sparked, a new thought, a deeper feeling.

When putting gold into a creative act, an initial assay is essential: how much gold do I have, how much can I put in? The gold is likely to be found in an existing life full of uncertainty: knowing this results from developmental traumas and is understandable in neuroscientific terms does not help it change.

Gold in, gold out?

An adage amongst analysts is 'insight does not equal change'. Alchemical metaphor, put in as gold, leads to far more uncertainty about what we do as a counsellor/therapist/analyst, as a creative person. Alchemists 'seeded the vessel', putting gold in at the beginning. They carefully dissolved the patron's gold in *Aqua Regia* – 'Royal Water' – a dangerous mix of concentrated sulphuric and nitric acids. As 'like drew like', gold would, almost always, be found at the end of the *Magnum Opus*, the Great Work, provided the alchemist had not kept too much, for expenses.

Fortunately, neither they nor their patrons knew much about measuring: there was no medieval equivalent of *Systeme International* units (metres, kilogrammes and seconds). Like counsellors/therapists/analysts, and those who work creatively, they didn't precisely know what they were doing; it 'just happened . . .'. The 'gold seed' in this text is 'a language that is no longer spoken which lets us say things about that which cannot be known'. If alchemy is like any contemporary science, it is most like quantum physics (see Chapter 9). It depends upon uncertainty.

Gold needs a measure of its purity; to 'prove its truth' an alchemist would say. How can we, as participants in our observations, do an assay? Can we evaluate one socially constructed discourse over another? Can we choose what model of being human we have? Alchemical metaphors offer a 'quantum' approach, including the unknowable, the unconscious itself. In mathematics, indeterminate numbers, (I) are used in quantum mechanics. Descriptions of fundamental particles can be in terms of their charge, velocity or mass. The more known about one of these three, the less can be known about the others. Alchemical terms are also indeterminate. They are myths: forms of speech which evoke the unconscious and carry a multiplicity of meanings. Symbolic language allows an 'open system' approach to problems which block creativity in living. Our book is about playing with meaning, and the models we have for how we make meaning. Perhaps the best reason for using alchemical symbols is that they are intrinsically playful.

Analytical psychology holds that ego exists as a potential in the newborn. Ego names a set of reality-testing functions rather than a thing. It is that with which we make meaning, through interactions with the unconscious, personal and collective. It is not 'meaning in itself'. To be creative is to allow our reality-testing functions to play with the unconscious.

Though Jung used the language of experimental psychology to begin describing the unconscious, he learnt through wrestling with contradictory inner feelings that science was not the right bottle to contain the spirit. His *Red Book* (2009) is full of painful, repetitious, often tendentious dialogues between him as 'a spiritual seeker' and him as 'a scientific realist'. Here he sketched maps of the unconscious, trying to reconcile conflicting emotions and spiritual needs. The *Red Book* is his negotiation on behalf of the creative self, arguing with the developmental and neuroscientific side of his mind. It was a gold mine for his collected works.

Alchemy: a symbolic language

Jung deconstructed alchemy to create a new language to talk about that which cannot be known. He did not write a dictionary of alchemy in which one medieval term, say *Aurum Verum* – the true gold – always translates as 'the true self'. '*Massa confusa*' – the muck at the start of the process – does not always equal 'id'. Jung imagined meaning-filled parallels between the processes of 'making gold' and 'making the self', individuation. He found open-ended metaphors about what being creatively human might be. Precisely because the language of alchemy is, to a modern scientific mind, clearly 'nonsense' – 'money from a musical bank' – it gives us a freedom to say things which can't be said. Old stories can be 'born again', rather than being trapped by repetitive compulsions, complexes seeking hegemony in the psyche or dominant discourses.

Our text is not against 'scientific discourses'. It is *for* the appropriate use of technology. In planning our book, we agreed the word 'spiritual' seemed closest to that which we wished to share – we are not going to define this term; we couldn't agree on a definition. We will explore what 'spiritual' means and hope you can see that we refer to 'an open system', rather than to any religion-bound dogma; to an attitude based in experiential learning, rather than an escape into transcendence. Our hypothesis is that alchemical metaphors give greater freedom, allow more creative space.

A map

Our book has four parts: Alchemy and Meaning, The Symbolic Attitude, The Spirit and the Natural World, and Clinical Applications. Rabbi David Freeman, once a chemist, introduces Jung's alchemical studies, considering the paradoxical nature of self, the theory of opposites and its regulating function in the psyche. He reminds us that 'we have to leave our heads behind', as alchemical metaphors are non-rational. He gives a preliminary outline of the individuation process, focussing on the *putrefactio* – by which that believed to be worthless becomes that of most value.

Catherine Bygott looks at Jung's 'difficult' master work, *Mysterium Coniunctionis* (CW 14). Alchemy is a living symbolism reflecting archetypal dynamics. Jung felt his psychology was for people seeking to give meaning to the second half of life. By looking at the symbolism of the sun and moon, '*Sol*' and '*Luna*', in earlier developmental stages and the spiritual changes following midlife, an underlying process of unfolding consciousness appears: the separation and combining of opposites.

Dale Mathers explores 'the Rosarium Philosophorum': a set of alchemical pictures Jung used in *The Psychology of the Transference* (CW 16) as metaphors for transference and counter transference. The material in the alchemist's vessel begins as male mercury and female sulphur – an amalgam, the sterile hermaphrodite. It becomes gold as they join together to form the fertile androgyne. This idea of a mystic marriage in the psyche is illustrated by clinical work with a male transvestite. The Rosarium offered containing symbols for analyst and patient during a shift in sexuality and gender identity.

In Part 2, The Symbolic Attitude, Carola Mathers examines the symbol's containing functions seen in 'the Queen–Servant fantasy'. A fantasy of the Queen (analyst) and Servant (analysand) who appeared in a session, transformed via dreams and fantasies to emerge as real objects at the end of this analysis. This involved *meditation*, *imagination* and *amplification*: spiritual exercise, as well as an uncovering of developmental history.

Antonia Boll explores alchemical symbolism in fairytales. Many conclude with a wedding; the couple then 'live happily ever after'. As a feminist, she challenges these endings, examining differences between fairytales with male heroes and female heroines using Jung's theory of an inner partnership between Animus and Anima. No real relationships exist without heroic struggles, yet we take these childhood stories as 'truths' about 'what ought to happen'.

Karin Syrett uses astrology as a clinical tool. Like alchemy, astrology is an open system. She explains some of the shared symbolism, including typology. Jung's theories about type were not new: astrologists, alchemists and philosophers had used them for thousands of years. She explores 'typological discourse' as a discourse of control.

Richard Wainwright shows how 'the concept of *imaginatio* is perhaps the most important key to the understanding of the *opus*' (CW 12, para. 396). The consulting room and theatre laboratory are compared as alchemical vessels, containing projective identification. In both, two strangers come together, allowing the excluded and despised to be reclaimed. Improvisation is an appropriate technology. It provokes the unforeseen.

In Part 3, The Spirit and the Natural World, we move out into the collective. Gottfried Heuer takes 'burn out' as a metaphor for global exploitation. Too many counsellors/therapists/analysts join the dominant 'Overwork Culture' discourse, becoming part of the problem rather than the solution. The dilemma of multi-level exploitation – a traditionally masculine attitude towards the world – is contrasted with a traditionally feminine realm of relating, offering the idea of 'Radical Hope'.

Transformation is a conceptual fulcrum at the heart of alchemy, argues Birgit Heuer. Deeply felt experiences in clinical reality depend on our views of the nature of reality. Drawing on quantum physics and the paradoxical nature of light, which behaves both as a particle and a wave, she explores the emergence of the spiritual in the midst of empirical science. The quantum paradigm of transformation allows for the emergence of an analytic attitude inspired by meditative and prayerful states.

Michael Whan looks at how alchemical images, for many Jungians, can be a defining gesture, yet sometimes a defensive discourse. Merely *applying* alchemical language to the individual, private condition of a person's psyche can reduce Jung's alchemical psychology to a 'grand narrative'. Drawing on Wilhelm Giegerich, he suggests that alchemy is a psychological language, not a rhetorical ornament. The 'philosopher's stone', the transformational key as well as goal of the alchemical quest, is a paradox: 'the stone that is no stone'; we do not have to turn a metaphor into a thing.

Part 4, Clinical Applications, looks inside and outside the consulting room, at social conflict, sexual and gender identity, self-starvation, and wonders how Jung progressed in his own individuation. Ruth Williams reminds us that the image of the Coniunctio symbolises atonement. This word means forgiveness, reconciliation, remorse, repentance and reparation. The symbol of the union of opposites elucidates this, bringing a transpersonal perspective. Maryann Barone-Chapman shows how the body can act as a container for conflict. She describes work with abused patients, with unstable gender identities, and describes drawing out the sulphuric acid of their anger.

The alchemy of redefining the masculine is the focus for Phil Goss. He points out distinctions between the imbibed social and the embedded, archetypal *masculine*. Language for talking about male experiencing arose, fleetingly finding verbal and non-verbal expression.

John Colverson looks at how alchemical metaphors express concretely in the self-starvation in anorexia. Anorexia seeks to split the spirit from soul and matter – often with fatal results. It is not just a problem for the individual; it presents a mirroring image for the starvation of our social soul due to its dislocation from nature. He argues that anorexia is the latest in a series of 'cultural shadows' – the witch prefigured the anorexic. The persecution of witches as evil 'earthy' women, and the demonisation and imprisonment of the spirit by reductive science go together.

To conclude, Nathan Field explores individuation, particularly in Jung's life. The word is analogous to self-realisation, self-actualisation, transcendence and enlightenment. First, he looks at a vivid account of a case where, bewildered by the emergence in his patient of a range of bizarre symptoms, Jung recognised his patient was enacting a Kundalini experience. He discusses the relationship of numinous experiences to healing, sexuality and spirituality in the context of Jung's life.

The philosopher's stone

Four themes illustrating the quest for the philosopher's stone spontaneously emerged in our collaboration. First, the concept of the *unus mundus* – 'one world' – seems primary. This imaginal space is where archetypes and synchronicity relate. Second, meaningful coincidence, or synchronicity, occurs when both the observer and the phenomena observed come from the same place in the unconscious. The *unus mundus* is the alchemical vessel holding the opposites, which come together in the *coniunctio* or mystic marriage. Third, opposites are transformed, gradually changing one into the other. This may require innocence and cunning, as shown in the story 'the Spirit in the bottle' (CW 13, para. 239 ff.) in which a boy tricks the trapped spirit Mercurius into giving him valuable gifts. And fourth, the myth of Pandora – whose box released suffering, yet had hope hidden at the bottom (Thomas 2009 pp. xxiii–xxxi). Hope is essential for any creative operation that 'makes gold'. We feel alchemy is a language of hope, and hope you enjoy the alchemical quest.

References

Burr, V. (2003) *Social Constructionism*, London: Routledge.
Butler, S. (1970) *Erewhon*, London: Penguin.
Casement, A. (1995) 'A brief history of Jungian splits in the UK', *Journal of Analytical Psychology* 40: 327–342.
Green, A. (2005) (trans. Katherine Aubertin) *On Private Madness*, London: Karnac Classics.
Jung, C. G. (1963) *Memories, Dreams, Reflections*, London: Collins.
—— (1998) (ed. Claire Douglas) *Visions Seminars*, vol. 2 London: Routledge.
—— (2009) *The Red Book*, New York: W. W. Norton & Company.
Thomas, G. (2009) *Healing Pandora*, Berkeley, California: North Atlantic Books.
von Franz, M. L. (1980) *Alchemy*, Toronto: Inner City Books.

Part I

ALCHEMY AND MEANING

WATER AND STONE

As in emotion, as in ever-living law,
the golden sands of spring
become pebbles in midlife.
The Chinese say
the clearly enlightened
always fall into the well;
another upgrade, another improving
ten thousand illusions to wrestle
to resist.

                                    Adele Davide

1

THE STONE THAT THE BUILDERS REJECTED

Rabbi David L. Freeman

Introduction

Western education teaches us to think in terms of cause and effect and to proceed logically through any argument or discussion. Where alchemy is concerned this presents an immediate difficulty, if not an impossibility. There is an old French alchemical maxim that teaches what you must do if you want to find out who you are: you must go to the forest (which represents the unconscious) and before entering you must take a sharp clean knife and cut off your head, then place it beside a tree and carefully make a note of where it is because it will need to be put back on again on leaving the forest: you cannot live without a head! Now enter the forest without your head and you will be able to find out who you are. Having done that, return to where your head was left and take some honey (good for bringing body and soul together) and stick it back on again. Obviously this is not to be taken literally but it demonstrates the alchemist's firm belief in the crucial need to suspend thinking before embarking upon any alchemical endeavour. This is an extremely difficult thing to do and some may find it impossible, but without being able to do it the world of alchemy will simply seem to be an ancient irrational pursuit with little or no relevance to the present-day practice of psychotherapy.

The centrality of alchemy in Jung's psychology is clear. At least three volumes of his *Collected Works* are devoted to it. I will look at the ancient art of alchemy examining the archetype of the self, fundamental to the Jungian model for understanding the psyche. This leads on to the concept of the individuation process as mirrored in the experiments and processes of the alchemists. Jung saw these as a most profound metaphor whose symbolism he felt was closer to the unconscious than any other. The search for the philosopher's stone, the gold, from base metal demonstrates the stages in the archetypal journey of the ego towards its acknowledgment of and final submission to the central archetype that Jung called 'the self'.

Alchemy as a process metaphor

The Hebrew verse, '*even ma'asu habonim hay'ta le-rosh pina*' translates as, 'The stone that the builders rejected is become the chief cornerstone' (*Tenach* Psalm 118, verse 22). This is one of the famous celebratory Psalms of the Hebrew Bible and is generally understood to refer to the foundation stone of the first Temple built by King Solomon in Jerusalem in approximately the tenth century BCE. Some commentators have found the verse mystifying and various meanings have been suggested. However, a symbolic interpretation might be, 'the stone that the builders rejected was the stone chosen as the best of all the stones for the highest possible honour of being the chief cornerstone of the Temple'. This may be compared to the story of Cinderella, the rejected sister but the one chosen at the end of the tale to marry the prince. Many myths and fairytales contain these same elements. Another is referred to by Marie Louise von Franz:

> In a beautiful and well-known Russian fairy tale the story of a king and his three sons is told. The two elder sons ride out from their father's stable on the most wonderful magnificent horses, but the youngest takes a little shaggy pony and sits on it the wrong way round, with his head towards the horses tail and goes off derided by everybody. He is of course the one who became the Great Russian hero and the one who inherited the kingdom.
>
> (von Franz and Hillman, 1975, p. 6)

In some versions of this story the youngest is a fool, a coward or a poor peasant boy but always the rejected one. Many hero stories carry the same pattern of the humble birth of the hero contrasting with the highest and most elevated position reached at the end. This is a clear mythologem, namely that which has the lowest value is ultimately that which comes to have the highest. Joseph Campbell (1904–1987) was known for his work on comparative mythology. He described this mythological adventure of the hero as following a specific pattern that is reflected in initiation rites:

> A hero ventures forth from a world of common day into a region of super-natural wonder: fabulous forces are there encountered and a decisive victory is won: the hero comes back from this mysterious adventure with the power to bestow boons on his fellow man.
>
> (Campbell, 1973, p. 30)

Examples of this mythologem are found in the traditions and stories of all peoples and cultures throughout human history.

The Hebrew midrash consists of many collections of parables, stories and commentaries, which elucidate and complement Biblical texts, as old as and sometimes even older than the text itself. The collective noun is midrash and this word also denotes each story or parable, which is referred to as 'a midrash'. In one such midrash we find the story of the patriarch Abraham who, when a newly born baby, was hidden in a cave to protect him from the Babylonian King Nimrod who sought to kill him (Anon, *Bet Hamidrash*, 1820, II, 118–196). The Hebrew Bible tells the story of the greatest Jewish prophet Moses who, as a baby, was hidden in the bulrushes from the Pharaoh who sought to kill all babies (*Tannic* Exodus, Chapter 2, verse 3) and the New Testament tells how baby Jesus was born and hidden in a stable from the King Herod who wanted to destroy him (Luke, Chapter 2). All these myths and tales universally depict an inner human pattern; that which was once the lowest and most despised in the end is that which has the highest value. That paradox where the lowest is potentially the highest and vice versa is the essence of alchemy and is an archetypal process and pattern.

Archetypes are the part of the psyche inherited and therefore common to all peoples. They cannot be seen but exist as potential patterns of behaviour in the collective unconscious of humanity, similar to instincts, and can only be observed as they manifest in behaviour patterns and in imagery. They are potential as outlines for future behaviours, innate structures in the psyche waiting to be lived out, seen in the myths and stories of all mankind. Archetypes carry a powerful affect which, when experienced, is numinous – a feeling of something other, much greater than oneself. During a lifetime there is a process of natural psychological development and maturity, a becoming whole. Archetypes are fundamental to that process which we call individuation. More will be said about this through the book, particularly in Chapter 15. Alchemy is about paradox; gold is found in base metal and individuation is a process where the archetypal and personal gold is found in the unfolding life journey of an individual. It is extremely difficult to describe this process because of its paradoxical nature and because it is something experienced rather than explained. For example, Jungians often refer to 'The gold in the dung heap' but it is far from easy to comprehend the full significance of these words.

I saw this strikingly illustrated some years ago at an annual conference of the Guild of Pastoral Psychology, an organisation in the U.K. formed to explore the interface between religion and the psychology of C. G. Jung. The poet, David Caccia, was invited to read to us. His audience contained many religious people well versed in Jungian theory. David himself was a deeply spiritual man, sadly dying from an inoperable brain tumour. Through his poetry he struggled hard to find the meaning of his terrible pain. This brought him to a personal confrontation with the blackest of depressions and was reflected in his poetry. When he read the words,

> When G-d and shit are easily confused,
> Then both are much less easily abused,
> (Caccia, 1975, p. 7)

together with other poems of similar nature, people got up and walked out; others were extremely angry. (*In accordance with the fourth of the Ten Commandments*

[Tannic Exodus, Chapter 20, verse 7] Jewish law forbids writing the Divine Name in full. Therefore I shall use 'G-d' in all cases.)

These people simply could not bear to hear those words or listen to the deepest of human truths, which this man knew first hand from immediate personal experience. He was the living embodiment of these truths yet sadly and inevitably some could only hear it as bad language and heresy. Here is a clinical example: Jane, a businesswoman in her late forties came seeking analysis as her life had been reduced to ruin. She was suicidal having lost her job, husband, friends and self-respect. She had been an alcoholic for four years but now her physical condition had become critical. Early in the analysis she brought the following dream:

> I work for London Transport. My work is in the deepest tunnels under the streets of London. It is my job to go down into the sewer every day. The stench is nauseating and each time I go I fear I shall die from asphyxiation, but it is my job to shovel away the daily shit from the whole of London. This is my task and it is truly foul and momentous.

Jane awoke in terror, unable to explain why, yet she could see her dream was telling how her life was at rock bottom. She felt without any value. What she could not see was how the dream indicated that, on a much deeper level, a process had commenced, an initiation, the start of a *rite de passage* back into life. From the depth and blackness of the sewer, from the dung and excrement of ten million people, new life was offered. Now there was a compost heap, rotting could commence and who knows what beautiful flowers it might later grow. Her unconscious offered her the hope and promise of new life from the shit.

This is what alchemists called putrefactio: exactly as in this dream, vile and disgusting, repulsive and putrefying with so utterly foul a stench no one can bear to be anywhere near it. It is the most sickening of places yet also the place where there is found the gold, the universal panacea, the elixir of life, the philosopher's stone.

The alchemical process

The alchemists carried out a series of procedures by which they believed they could extract gold from base metal. However, one very important fact needs to be remembered: it was much more than a series of tasks to be performed in their laboratories. Alchemists lived their work in body and soul, totally committed and dedicated to their task and identified in body and mind with what took place in the flask. Some became seriously ill, some died. Like all mystical processes and the unconscious itself, alchemical work can be very dangerous if approached without proper knowledge and preparation.

The process consisted of three works. Paradox must be kept in mind through their entirety. For the first, *ignis innaturalis* ('the secret fire' or 'the dry water') had to be prepared. Following this, a mysterious substance called the *prima materia* had to be found. This is described as something right under your nose, yet you might have to spend your whole lifetime searching to find it. It is that which you reject and despise and it may require a long perilous quest to find it. Once the alchemist had the *prima materia* he placed it in a mortar, pulverised it with a pestle, mixed it with the *ignis innaturalis* and then left it out all night to be moistened by the morning dew. There would then be an extremely long period of waiting for the right moment to proceed. Whilst waiting for however long it took, the alchemist would recite prayers and take astrological readings. It was crucial that he waited until it was the right time; forcing it or becoming impatient destroyed the whole procedure. Alchemists were certain in their belief, as with any venture, however good the procedure it will not work if it is performed at the wrong time.

Once the alchemist found the right time he would enclose the resulting substance in 'the philosopher's egg', a hermetically sealed vessel strong enough to contain the chemical reactions and exactly right for the purpose. More waiting could then be necessary in order to obtain the exact vessel and this also must not be rushed. He then placed the egg inside the *athanor* – a furnace capable of maintaining an even temperature. Alchemists understood there were two opposing principles at work inside the philosopher's egg. These he described as the sulphur and the mercury, also called the solar and the lunar, the hot and the cold, the male and the female. Today we might call them the masculine and the feminine, the animus and the anima. He applied the heat most carefully and gradually these two principles separated. Following this, there is a long process of decay and putrefaction without which no transformation is possible. When this eventually ended it was the conclusion of 'the first work'.

After this followed 'the second work', known as 'the death'. The couple dissolve into black, called the *nigredo*. It is said they produce a perfect child and this process continues until all is totally putrefied and the opposites are dissolved in the liquid, often illustrated by the terrifying imagery of dismemberment and dissolution, giving meaning to the phrase 'no generation without corruption'. It is called 'blacker than black', a time of indescribably vile suffering, truly, 'the dark night of the soul'; all hope is lost and despair takes over. The decaying and putrefying continues seemingly without end until a stage begins which may or may not actually be visible. The tiniest speck of light appears in the black followed by the appearance of many colours. This is called *cauda pavonis*, 'the peacock's tail'. It is comparable to the Christian story of the night sky in Bethlehem at the moment of the birth of Jesus and the Christian ritual of Advent, a ritual process leading up to Christmas. Each day gets darker and darker until all the light is gone. Then new light begins and the child is born.

There is a star spoken of in the Jewish mystic tradition which illuminated the whole sky at the moment of the birth of the patriarch Abraham (Anon, *Bet Hamidrash*, 1820, II, 118–196). The *Zohar* (lit. the book of splendour) is popularly the most well-known of the Hebrew mystical texts. In it is a story of how, at the moment of the birth of Moses, everything was filled with the brilliance and radiance of primordial light, the special light created before the beginning of the world and all that is in it. G-d first made this light and then everything was created from it. Shortly after its creation G-d hid this light, a light of immense brilliance equal to the power of both the sun and the moon together in the sky (*Zohar* II, 11b). The Christian New Testament describes an eastern star which appeared over the birth place of Jesus (Matthew, Chapter 2, verse 9). The second alchemical work came to an end when a white colour appeared in the egg, the *albedo*.

The third work is to repeat the first two as many times as it takes until 'the ultimate perfection', is reached; and there appears, 'the Red King who is reunited with his Queen in the fire of love'. At this point the third work is completed. Great patience and fortitude is called for throughout as the three works had to be repeated countless times before the gold was formed, hence the alchemist's motto *orare et laborare,* 'work and pray'.

Gnosticism and the discovery of the metaphor

For Jung the alchemical *opus* was the closest possible metaphor for the unconscious. He searched to find objective evidence for what he had discovered himself and came on it by accident, which he might have called synchronicity.

> As my life entered its second half, I was already embarked upon the confrontation with the contents of the unconscious. First I had to find evidence for the historical prefiguration of my inner experiences. That is to say, I had to ask myself, 'Where have my particular experiences already occurred in history?' If I had not succeeded in finding such evidence, I would never have been able to substantiate my ideas.
>
> (Jung, 1997, p. 226)

He found this evidence in two sources, Gnosticism and alchemy.

> The experiences of the alchemists were, in a sense, my experiences and their world was my world. This was, of course, a momentous discovery. I had stumbled upon the historical counterpart of my psychology of the unconscious. The possibility of a comparison of Alchemy with the uninterrupted chain back to Gnosticism, gave substance to my psychology.
>
> (Jung, 1977, p. 231)

Traditionally Gnosticism is thought of as an ancient heresy which arose from second-century Christianity and then died out. This is not the case. It was pre-Christian and existed throughout the whole ancient world. It would be more accurate to say it encompassed Christianity rather than Christianity encompassed it. A simplified description of Gnosticism is of an antithetical dualism between immateriality (deemed to be good) and materiality (deemed to be evil). A portion of immateriality (or spirit) is trapped in the human body and to reach the highest spiritual value has to be liberated. When this immaterial spark is liberated it unites with the g-dhead. Liberating the immaterial meant the releasing of the highest value from that which is the lowest.

The Gnostics were persecuted by the Church yet, according to Jung, were able to survive by taking on another form: 'In spite of the suppression of the Gnostic heresy it continued to flourish throughout the Middle Ages under the disguise of alchemy' (CW 11, para. 160). He saw the process by which alchemists imagined they could make gold from base metal as continuing the Gnostic belief in the freeing of the fallen sparks of spirit from matter. These apparently outward processes portray inner processes, the transformation from the lowest value of sheer ego consciousness to the highest value of all, namely the recognition by the ego of the unconscious and its reintegration with the self.

Many Gnostic myths are creation myths. Viewed psychologically they can be seen as describing the progression of the human psyche. Jung saw Gnosticism and alchemy as the same but many scholars debate this; some defend his view, others think he was mistaken (Segal, 1992, p. 31). Professor Gilles Quispel, Dutch theologian and historian of Christianity and Gnosticism who died in 2006, had a long correspondence with Jung and supported his view; Father Victor White, a Dominican priest who died in 1960 who also corresponded with Jung, did not. In a paper on Gnosticism presented to the Guild of Pastoral Psychology in London in 1948, he was most critical of Jung on this whole issue (White, 1952, Chapter 11). He thought Jung was biased in his views about Gnosticism and alchemy and accused him of being trapped in a dualism more like the ancient Manichean religion. The discussion continues today, as does the question of whether Jung himself was a Gnostic. Whatever scholars and critics may argue, it is important to remember Jung's interest in alchemy and Gnosticism was that both describe processes where the highest value is reached from the lowest.

In 1945, in Upper Egypt, a collection of 13 ancient codices was discovered. These contained over 50 Gnostic texts which constituted the Nag Hammadi Library, the discovery and translation of which was completed in the 1970s. It gave a vast amount of information about early Gnostic thinking and theology. This was largely unknown to Jung; most of his work was done before this discovery. In his forward to the second edition of his commentary on, 'the Secret of the Golden Flower', he pointed out he had depended upon Christian opponents of Gnosticism for information (CW 13, p. iii). There is no doubt he considered alchemy more important than Gnosticism as a prefiguration of his psychology; the entire *Collected Works* contain only one small essay on Gnosticism where he discussed its parallels with alchemy:

> the Gnostics were too remote for me to establish any link with them in
> regard to the questions that were confronting me. As far as I could see,
> the tradition which might have connected Gnosis with the present seemed

to have been severed and for a long time it proved impossible to find any
bridge that led from Gnosticism . . . to the contemporary world. But when
I began to understand alchemy I realised that it represented the historical
link with Gnosticism, and that continuity therefore existed between past
and present. Grounded in the natural philosophy of the Middle Ages,
Alchemy formed the bridge on the one hand into the past – to Gnosticism
and on the other into the future, to the modern psychology of the unconscious.

(Jung, 1977, pp. 226–227)

Projection of the self

Alchemists believed in a process by which gold could be produced from base
metals; Gnostics believed immaterial sparks of spirit could be released from the
body to enable them to reunite with the g-dhead. Psychologically, that which is
sought after is not in the outer world but in the inner world of the psyche; an inner
human process was simply projected onto the outside world, the process Jung
called 'the individuation process', which is why alchemy became the core of his
work.

In Jung's model of the psyche the highest value is the self. We are entirely
unconscious at birth and consciousness emerges slowly as we grow older. The
unconscious is the natural state which Jung called 'Reality *in potentia*' (CW 9i,
para. 498), all that we could be and have ever been. Consciousness is the awareness of oneself as a subject, an 'I', separate from the world and the unconscious.
Jung called that first centre of consciousness the ego. Also, just as there is an 'I',
which is the centre of consciousness, there is also a greater 'I', namely the 'I which
is unconscious'. This is the central archetype, which Jung called the self. Edward
Edinger (founding member of the C. G. Jung Foundation for Analytical
Psychology in New York) followed on in the line of his predecessor Eric Neumann
(who studied with Jung at Zurich in the 1930s and wrote extensively developing
Jung's ideas). Edinger described it:

> The self is the ordering and unifying centre of the total psyche . . . the ego
> is the seat of subjective identity while the self is the seat of objective
> identity. The self is thus the supreme psychic authority and subordinates
> the ego to it. . . . It is identical with the *imago Dei* [the image of G-d.]
> . . . it is expressed by certain typical symbolic images called Mandalas.
> (Edinger, 1992, p. 3)

The Mandala is an important symbol of the self; a wonderful expression of the self
as the highest value, the philosopher's stone of the alchemists. It is often called
numinous which means it is charged with an enormous amount of psychic energy
and can occur as an overpowering religious experience.

At birth the ego and the self are one, like a small circle inside a large circle. At this stage the new baby knows little separation between itself and its mother. As life proceeds the ego begins to separate and moves out from the self along what can be called 'the ego/self axis' (ibid., pp. 4–7). This is an excruciating experience, as Klein described in the moving from the Paranoid/Schizoid to the Depressive position (Klein, 1980, p. 34). This movement can be described in many ways, as the first of the many *nigredos* of life, as the commencement of a hero myth, as the start of that process already described in which the ego must recognise and indeed be defeated by the self as the higher authority.

How can one possibly describe the self except perhaps symbolically, words are inadequate. It is the divine spark within us, terrifying and wonderful. It is not extinguishable but yet it is capable of extinguishing us. It is numinous and contains all possible opposites. It has been called 'the quintessence of all'. It is unique, it is the total person and the higher authority to which the ego must submit. There is often unspeakable suffering in this process as the ego resists surrendering its autonomy, but that suffering can ultimately lead to transformation, as takes place in alchemy. In an essay Jung wrote with Kerenyi (a Hungarian classicist who lived in Switzerland, one of the founders of modern study in Greek mythology), the subject they were discussing was the archetype of the Divine Child (not to be confused with the personal child) about which Jung said:

> we have a similar modulation of themes in alchemy – in the synonyms for the *lapis*. As the *materia prima*, it is the *lapis exilis et vilis* (stone poor and vile. Jung takes this from an alchemical work called The Rosarium Philosophorum, a famous series of 20 woodcuts first printed in 1550). As a substance in process of transformation it is *servus rubeus* or *fugitivus* (lit. Red man/slave. Red being the rubedo); and finally, in its true apotheosis it attains the dignity of a *filius sapientiae* (lit. Child of wisdom. Sometimes this is equated with the philosopher's stone, for Jung the essence of the Individuation Process) or *deus terrenus* (The image of the sun in the earth, the image of G-d appearing in gold), a "light above all lights," a power which contains in itself all the power of the upper and nether regions. It becomes a *corpus glorificatum* (The incorruptible body of resurrection in the Christian tradition) which enjoys everlasting incorruptibility and is therefore a panacea (bringer of healing).
>
> (Jung and Kerenyi, 1969, p. 90)

This brings to mind the primordial light described by the Hebrew mystics, mentioned earlier. It was a light with the power of both sun and moon in the sky, from which everything was created, hidden by G-d shortly after its creation only to reappear for the tiniest fragment of time at the birth of Moses.

The ego is called upon to surrender to the self but fights and struggles against relinquishing any of its power and autonomy. It does not want to let go; its function is to control. We resist letting go and finding the panacea, the light for which we search. The motif of the archetype of the Divine Child expresses this particularly well. It can be seen in the many stories where a king has an intuition or dream of the imminent birth of a new king or redeemer. He sends out all his armies to destroy this threat to his authority. The Divine Child is a symbol of the awakening of the self in all its tremendous potential. It is the paradox of the trauma of dying and living where it is the dying that makes the living.

Auroleus Phillipus Theostratus Bombastus von Hohenheim, immortalised as Paracelsus, was born in 1493, the son of a well-known physician described as a Grand Master of the Teutonic Order, from whom he took his first instruction in medicine. At 16 he entered the University of Basle where he studied alchemy, surgery and medicine. In alchemy he is often referred to as Paracelsus the Great and is quoted extensively by Jung. Paracelsus expressed this very simply:

> Decay is the beginning of all birth.
>
> (Jacobi, 1995, p. 143)

> For as putrefaction in the bowel reduces all foods into dung, so also without the belly, putrefaction in glass transmutes all things from one form to another . . . since then, putrefaction is the first step and commencement of generation, it is of the highest degree necessary that we should understand this process.
>
> (Anon, 1992, p. 120)

Hermes Tristmegistus was a legendary sage and eponymous patron of Hermeticism. He is regarded by tradition as the author of the Emerald Tablet, a book said to be the bible of the alchemists. He often appears in alchemical works as an old man sitting with the Emerald Tablet open on his knee. After the conquest of Egypt by Alexander the Great in 332 BCE, the Greeks in Egypt mixed their own gods and culture with those of the Egyptians. Hermes Tristmegistus was a coming together of the Egyptian god Thoth and the Greek Hermes. 'Tristmegistus' means 'thrice great'. In the Emerald Tablet he says:

> and also the seeds of the fruit and of every work of art will perish, but will be increased by necessity and renewed by the gods and the course of nature's measured cycle. The whole blending of the cosmos renewed by nature is of G-d.
>
> (Anon, 2004, Book 3, verse 4)

This is the paradox of the self.

Paradoxes speak deeply within us and can stir us without any conscious thought at all. They are charged with numinosity, like poetic images which reach our depth without first touching the surface. A paradox is a different form of truth, a truth of opposites, as in the saying of Lao Tzu, 'those who know don't speak and those who speak don't know', or 'What is below is like that which is above, and that which is above is like that which is below' (Tuby, 1982, pp. 20, 22).

Jung's theory of opposites was more than a theoretical model of the psyche, it was fundamental to his understanding of the nature of life. Hester Solomon, past president of the International Association for Analytical Psychology (IAAP), holds that both Freud and Jung were steeped in Hegel's dialectical vision concerning the process of change. She suggests this permeated their theories, thoroughly immersed as they were in the same German culture (see Chapter 10 for further discussion). Hegel's theory is about how two opposing structures (thesis and antithesis) define each other first by negation, then by moving towards integration (synthesis). He saw this dialectical logic applied within any system, including the psychological (Solomon, 1991, pp. 307–308).

Jung found what for many might be a great religious, philosophical and psychological understanding of the nature of being, namely the paradox of the self. His life's journey led him to see that there is no such thing as uniformity of meaning; all meaning rests upon paradox. For many this is a great gift, an answer to the question of the meaning of our lives; the opposites we endure and enjoy, the nature of the Divine and the question of suffering.

Conclusion

The alchemists regarded alchemy as the greatest unknown and the greater the unknown the more it will attract projections. Alchemists projected the deepest layers of their unconscious into their experiments and processes. For this reason Jung understood its symbols to be closer to the unconscious than any other expression, dream or myth. We owe a debt to him for many discoveries and insights, but it seems to me we owe him most for his discovery of alchemy as the metaphor for life in all its mysteries and struggles, its beauty and its ugliness, its pleasures and its pains – in other words its paradox.

Of course we all know that no one could make gold from base metal, but at the same time it is equally true and certain that in our ability to form and use symbols we can make gold – and we do.

References

Anon (approx. 200–160 CE) *Sefer Hazohar*. Traditionally attributed to Rabbi Shimon bar Yochai.

—— (1820) *Bet Hamidrash* (Ed. E. Jellineck). Publisher unknown.

—— (1961) *Tanach (Mikraot Gedolot)*. Tel Aviv, Israel: Pardes Publishers.

—— (1961, 1970) *New English Bible*. Oxford: Oxford University Press and Cambridge University Press.

—— (1992) *Hermetic and Alchemical Writings of Paracelsus the Great* (Trans. A. E. Waite). Edmonds, WA: The Alchemical Press.

—— (2004) *Corpus Hermeticum. Hermes Tristmegistus* (Trans. C. Salamon, D. van Oyen and W. D. Wharton) in *The Way of Hermes* London: Gerald Duckworth and Co. Ltd.

Caccia, D. (1975) *Poems and Aphorisms*. London: Interprint.

Campbell, J. (1973) *The Hero with a Thousand Faces*. Princeton, NJ: Princeton University Press.

Edinger, E. (1992) *Ego and Archetype*. Boston, USA and London: Shambhala.

Jacobi, J. (1995) *Paracelsus, Selected Readings*, Bollingen Series XXVIII. Princeton, NJ: Princeton University Press.

Jung, C. G. (1953–1977) Except where indicated, references are by volume and paragraph number to *The Collected Works of C. G. Jung*, 20 vol., London and Princeton, NJ: Routledge and Princeton University Press.

—— (1977) *Memories, Dreams, Reflections*. London: Collins.

—— and Kerenyi, C. (1969) *Essays on a Science of Mythology*, Bollingen Series XXII. Princeton, NJ: Princeton University Press.

Klein, M. (1980) *Envy and Gratitude and Other Works 1946 to 1963*. London: The Hogarth Press and The Institute of Psycho-Analysis.

Klossowski de Rola, S. (1973) *Alchemy: The Secret Art*. London: Thames and Hudson.

Segal, R. E. (1992) *The Gnostic Jung*. London: Routledge.

Solomon, H. (1991) 'Archetypal Psychology and Object Relations Theory', *Journal of Analytical Psychology*, vol. 36, 3, pp. 307–341.

Tuby, M. (1982) *The Search and Alchemy*. London: Guild of Pastoral Psychology, Lecture pamphlet no. 210.

von Franz, M. (1980) *Alchemy. An Introduction to the Symbolism and the Psychology*. Toronto, Canada: Inner City Books.

—— and Hillman, J. (1975) *Jung's Typology* Zurich: Spring Publications.

White, V. (1949) *Some Notes on Gnosticism*. London: Guild of Pastoral Psychology, Lecture pamphlet no. 59.

—— (1952) *G-d and The Unconscious*. Zurich: Spring Publications.

2

MYSTERIUM CONIUNCTIONIS
Fabric of Life

Catherine Bygott

Oh mask of man,
From what deep source do you draw your voice?
(Catherine Bygott)

Introduction

Alchemy reveals what is shrouded in mystery. It mirrors deep life processes, providing a symbolic language of perception for some and a vehicle through which to engage with mystery for others. For Carl Gustav Jung it reflected a profound journey to establish a relationship with the archetypal psyche through encounter, discrimination and incorporation.

Drawing on the work of sixteenth-century alchemist Gerhard Dorn, C. G. Jung and Pythagoras, the Jungian analyst Edward Edinger conceived of life as a process of differentiation from magical identifications through stages of conscious re-integration (1995, pp. 277–279). In this chapter, I want to develop his view further by suggesting that alchemy is a living symbolism reflecting archetypal dynamics of the psyche which can enter our experience directly through the forces of nature or through a relationship between the conscious and unconscious mind via the logos. The first is simply personal experience and development as it is lived and refined. The second unfolds through challenging confrontation with oneself and conscious endeavour to develop a deep, objective relationship with oneself and with all it means to be human.

The ancient language of alchemy is dynamic and symbolic, having the capacity to enrich the full spectrum of psychoanalytic theory and practice. To my mind, it offers the possibility of a shared, cohesive foundation for conceiving of and engaging with psyche psychotherapeutically whether through the amplification of dreams and images or through transference/counter-transference interpretation (CW 16, Foreword, pp. 164–166).

A question of mindset

Any discussion of the mystery at the root of alchemical philosophy begins with recognising that we live in a Western culture founded on 'scientific materialism' and all share this fundamental orientation to a greater or lesser extent. At its core, 'scientific materialism' is a value system which does not recognise mystery as a dimension of life. By its very nature, mystery defies reason. Carl Johan Calleman, a Swedish biologist working internationally, sees biology and Darwinism as central to 'scientific materialism':

> To question Darwinism is absolutely taboo. Many radical thoughts in many areas of science may be proposed, but not this, that human beings have been created by God ... if Darwinism does not hold, the most important pillar upon which today's materialist philosophy of science is built would collapse ... proposals have been advanced to create a more spiritually oriented world view, often based on ... new physics, but the effects on academic science have only been minor. This is because the critical pillar of today's science is not physics, but biology ...
>
> (Calleman, 2001, p. 97)

Materialistic philosophy extends well beyond the bounds of science to many aspects of life. As a social collective, we are enthralled by the miraculous feats of technology. From birth, our skills, perceptions, expectations and self-reflections are developed within a collective mindset which gives preference to the intellectual and conceptual over the imaginal and symbolical. There is a basic assumption that the ego and its life in the world, our capacity to orient ourselves in relation to time, place, person and the 'here-and-now', are synonymous with the greater objective psyche. With this misconception, we cut ourselves off from our own mysterious depths.

Two dimensions of psyche are present in all of us: personality and the true inner nature. In psychotherapy, reductive techniques are used to tease out the unique individual personality from internalised environmental influences of earlier life in the hope of releasing blockages to the natural, instinctive flow towards ego development. Reductive psychotherapeutic techniques have evolved out of a scientific rationalism which supports ego development. Initially, the unconscious was viewed as a kind of philosophical concept. Through Freud's discoveries it became grounded as a practical medical concept. Psychotherapeutic methods developed from the medical paradigm support patients in forging an ego strong enough to be able to participate effectively in our everyday world. From this perspective, the ego may be seen through the lens of 'scientific materialism' as an objective thing, having supreme value in the psyche. The true self, in contrast, holds knowledge gained and passed on over the generations from earliest human beginnings. The development of our true deeper nature is much like creating a sculpture from a living tree. The sculpted form gradually emerges as wood is chipped away to reveal the true individual essence. We can see this impulse towards manifesting a true inner essence in young people's instinctive urge to live life for its own sake and in so doing, become rooted in reality, their limits and their abilities.

Our collective world is out of balance. Continuing advances in technology and encroaching materialistic influences disrupt authentic patterns of human life. Some people perceive the era of scientific rationalism as wakening humanity from an age-old dream state, as if the power to distinguish 'real' from 'unreal' is itself subject to biological evolution (Burckhardt, 1974, pp. 7–8). Far from taking us into an increased capacity to differentiate 'real' from 'unreal', scientific rationalism leads us into a parallel world.

> Television, video cassettes, video tape-recorders/players, video games and personal computers all form an encompassing electronic system whose various forms 'interface' to constitute an alternative and absolute world that uniquely incorporates spectator/user in a spatially de-centred, weakly temporised and quasi-disembodied state.
>
> (Sobchak, 1996 cited in Briggs, Asa and Burke, 2002, p. 321)

Against this bleak backdrop, a cry is rising from the human soul, the *cri de Merlin* – a cry for water in the desert of dehumanisation.

Jung pioneered the way beyond the biological and medical when he separated from Freud. What followed was a profound encounter with the unconscious recorded and published as the *Red Book*. This pivotal work is the foundation of his unique psychological orientation and all his later writings. He began by asking himself, 'Why is myself a desert?' and answering, 'I have avoided the place of my soul' (Jung, 2009, p. 237). He endured the death of the heroic ego and emerged into a new reality – a psychic reality mirrored by the ancient art of alchemy. Jung's methodology can be criticised for being nearly non-existent when perceived only through the lens of rationality with its blindness to the ways of mystery. However, Jung and his methods belong to a new post 'scientific materialism', 'Weltanschauung', and can best be accessed and understood within this new world view, as the subtle mysteries of new physics cannot be perceived from within a Newtonian paradigm.

To cultivate an empathic grasp of how medieval alchemy resonates with the psyche, it is necessary to set aside post-Enlightenment rationality and pre-conceived notions about the nature of things. Imagine being a medieval alchemist. You see all things in the universe as inter-related following the Hermetic law of correspondences described in the Emerald Tablet (Hauck, 1999, p. 51):

> That which is Below corresponds to that which is Above,
> and that which is Above corresponds to that which is Below,
> to accomplish the miracles of the One Thing.

Chemistry and alchemy, astronomy and astrology live together infused by the presence of God. Symbols, images and rituals mediate between the macrocosm and the microcosm, between the inner, spiritual world and the outer, physical world. Some alchemists, such as Michael Maier (1568–1622) and Gerhard Dorn (1530–1584), worked with physical substances in their laboratories, whilst being aware that the alchemical process went well beyond the material. They aimed at an experience of 'transmutation', or metamorphosis, of base substance into the illumination of self-knowing through direct experience. These alchemical trans-mutations were perceived as occurring within the psyche on levels of reality not ordinarily accessible in everyday life.

Everyone experiences a mysterious moment at least once in life – an uncanny, out-of-the-ordinary moment which has a disorienting effect. It is not easily forgotten no matter how many years pass. Values, priorities and one's whole perception of life and meaning may be changed. Ego maturity and circumstance influence whether this moment is perceived to be creative or destructive, welcome or threatening. We have different reactions to mystery ranging from outright denial through rationalisation to simple acceptance. If you reflect back over your life, you may recall an uncanny experience of your own and how you reacted to it. Alchemists like Maier and Dorn were profoundly aware of mystery and much of their work can only be understood from this perspective.

The subtle medium partaking of both mind and substance is the soul realm referred to by the alchemists as 'Mercurius' – the subtle soul-form of the chemical element mercury, sharing many of its properties. The work of alchemy takes place in this liminality where visible time-bound, and invisible timeless worlds meet and something is born in us. To access the insight and knowledge of the mysterious philosophy of the alchemists we have to be willing and able to hover between manifest life and its subtle essence through metaphor and symbol. Indian Vedic philosophy describes it as the eternal dance between Shiva (essence) and Shakti (form). Chinese Taoist philosophy pictures it as the Yang/Yin symbol which provides the fundamental structure of the 'I Ching (Book of Changes)' (Wilhelm, 1951). Alchemists describe it as the *Mysterium Coniunctionis*, the sacred marriage of *Sol* and *Luna*, the solar and lunar principles. Jung's analytic psychology describes it as the masculine/feminine *Dance of Opposites* resolved through the *Transcendent Function* (CW 8, paras 131–193).

To contemplate *Lady Alchemia* and her place in contemporary psychothera-peutic practice requires us to step apart from the busyness of daily life to a place of quiet, of inward openness and alert, receptive stillness. This is a place of poetry, a place of soul, a place of mystery. Alchemical references, images and experiences incorporate this poetic, soulful dimension. The intellect alone cannot gain entry to this world: medieval alchemists who tried to practise their Art with only a rational, worldly focus were called 'puffers'. Their efforts were like the air from bellows that fanned flames in the alchemical fire but never transformed anything.

What is alchemy?

Symbolic alchemy is an art of imagination. Like imagination, it functions as a soul bridge of image, metaphor and living symbol, having both tangible form and inexplicable essence. In Jung's psychology of the unconscious, images are perceived as substantial entities within the psyche having the same degree of reality as physical anatomy. Jung described this anatomy of psyche when he wrote, 'Mind and body are . . . the expression of a single entity . . . This living being appears outwardly as the material body, but inwardly as a series of images of the vital activities taking place within it' (CW 8, para. 619).

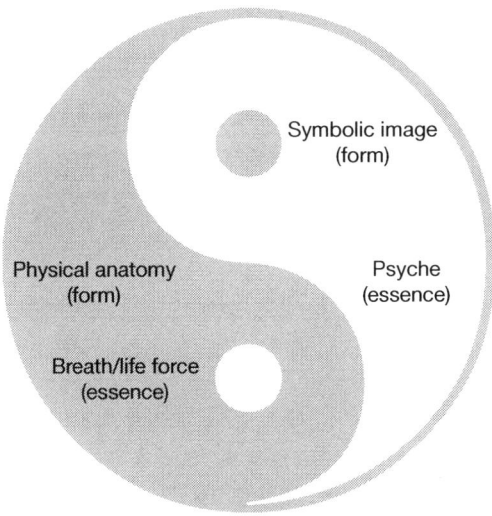

Figure 2.1 The dynamic dance of essence and form in Jung's psychology

Distilled down to its most fundamental elements, symbolic alchemy is comprised of symbol, process and journey. *Mercurius*, an over-arching alchemical symbol, represents the base metal (*lead*) and the transmuted metal (*gold*) – the beginning and end of the opus. It is also the catalyst of transmutation. Its active aspect is symbolised by the alchemical sun (*Sol*), the recapture aspect by the alchemical moon (*Luna*).

The fiery solar principle, *Sol*, finds expression psychologically as the motive/desire nature. It is the bright, golden sun and its opposite, the dark, black sun. When we speak of passion, desire and the instinctive driving force of life which Dylan Thomas writes about in his poem, 'The force that through the green fuse drives the flower', we are speaking of *Sol*. Pause for a moment and consider your own passionate drives and will power. How and where are these energies expressed in your life? Recall a moment of achievement, your motivation for getting something you want, a desire to do things your own way. What feelings were involved? Consider frustrating situations when you felt thwarted, blocked by people, events or your own limitations. Reflection on these experiences will give you a taste of *Sol*'s rays shining through your personality.

Situations beyond our control bringing challenges, woundings and failures forge and refine our will in the fires of life – alchemical processes experienced through the passions and force of human nature. Alchemy, as it mirrors conscious encounter with the archetypal layers of psyche, needs laboratory conditions. Jung used the technique of 'Active Imagination', a dialectic confrontation between his strong ego and the unconscious, to achieve this.

Sol's companion, *Luna*, symbolises the diffuse quality of the watery lunar principle in both its dark and light aspects, expressed through the moral nature. Traditionally, the moon represents the feminine mysteries through which the seed essence, desirous impulse or creative inspiration finds form. It may be as subtle as an intuitive hint becoming a fully formed thought, or as concrete as a sexual impulse creating new life in the form of a child. Symbolically, *Luna*'s light is a reflection of *Sol*'s light, emphasising the fundamental importance of self-reflective thought in refining the moral nature. As with *Sol*, *Luna* engages us on the stage of life while the alchemist engages *Luna* in the alembic of the laboratory.

Difficulty, frustration and wounding are life's means of refining our motives and desires. Feelings wash through us slowly dissolving hard-hearted self-centredness. Guilt and grace cultivate our empathy and compassion. Gradually our moral nature is purified. Has your will ever tempted you to break a moral boundary to satisfy desire? On reflection, did the experience leave you feeling fuller or emptier? Contemplating your innermost thoughts and feelings with self-honesty works on instinct and heart. By taking responsibility inwardly and outwardly, a little bit of alchemical *lead* may begin a process of transmutation.

The ever-changing relationship and refinement of these two principles, *Sol* and *Luna*, is the essence of spiritual alchemy. The leaden *Mercurius*, also known as the *prima materia*, undergoes a journey of transmutation, beginning with the blackening of the *nigredo*, through the whitening of the *albedo*, and finally to the reddening of the *rubedo* and fulfilment in the mystery of sacred marriage that is the *unus mundus*.

The colours reflect the inner psychological experience at each stage of the work through which the raw material of our true individuality is forged. Black is an expression of the initial melancholia; white descends like a sacred dove bringing hope and vitality of spirit to the suffering soul; red re-engages the red-blooded vitality of the initiate in the everyday world, with the task of applying all that has been learned. This reddening is a transmutation involving mystery: life begins to unfold on the basis of synchronicity, or meaningful coincidence – conscious and unconscious dancing together creatively. The key process activating these trans-mutations is *solve et coagula* (dissolve and coagulate) – dissolve the body/form and coagulate the spirit/essence. The *solve* phase aims at dissolution, separation or death, *mortificatio*. The *coagula* phase aims at the birth of a new form arising from a union, or *coniunctio*, of *Sol* and *Luna*.

How does alchemy reflect archetypal events in the mundane world?

In the spring/summer of 2011, two events took place in the UK. They provide a place of entry to the alchemist's laboratory – no value judgement is implied. Both events were motivated by passionate desire, symbolised by *Sol*, but the moral ground into which the seed was planted, symbolised by *Luna*, was quite different.

Event 1: The phone hacking scandal arose from greed and hubris at the *News of the World* newspaper. Staff invaded people's privacy to scoop sensational news stories with no regard for emotional cost or moral integrity, and little consideration. Hundreds of victims, witnesses and statements were heard by the Leveson Judicial Inquiry into the culture, practices and ethics of the British Press. The newspaper itself died in the flames of controversy. Scandal spread beyond the *News of the World* to other newspapers, senior members of Scotland Yard and the British Government. The crisis went beyond the invasion of personal privacy, undermining public trust in law enforcement and political neutrality.

Event 2: The Royal Wedding of Catherine Middleton to Prince William arose from an alluring dress modelled at a university fund-raising event. The couple met and a relationship between them unfolded gradually. They endured a period of separation followed by a long courtship which allowed time for love to mature, trust to become established and problems to be resolved. There was a wish to grow beyond the bitterness and suffering of previous Royal marriages. The lovers were given necessary emotional and mental support. Press and public alike wished Catherine's and Prince William's personal and public integrity to be respected.

The qualities of self-discipline (*Sol*) and moral integrity (*Luna*) being brought to bear on instinctive motivation played a significant role in determining the dramatically different outcome of these two events. In the alchemist's retort, the first event illustrates the *prima materia* undergoing *nigredo* processes of blackening – the dark aspect of *Sol* and *Luna*; the second event, *albedo* processes of whitening – the rising sun and waxing moon.

A holistic vision of alchemy

When viewed from the deeper perspective of the archetypal layers of psyche, the apparent conflict between developmental and archetypal psychology may be perceived more holistically through the mirror of alchemy. For example, maturational processes of self-transformation, such as puberty, are archetypal unfoldings of human development initiated in us by the unconscious. They are threshold crossings evoking the 'tremendum' of life's mysteries: the elemental, beautiful, terrifying, illuminating archetypal forces of the numinous. We experience them as happening to us as if we are being carried along by a strong current not under conscious control, will or desire. These threshold crossings can be conceived of alchemically as a *coniunctio* of *Sol* and *Luna* bringing death to an old order and birth to a new.

The 'alchemist' as a force of nature lies in the unconscious as the consciousness-promoting instinct which gives birth to and supports the development of the ego. Adaptation to the external is the main task of the first half of life. The laboratory is the world stage; the alchemical operations are catalysed by unconscious projective mechanisms and the *gold* aimed at is the mature, integrated ego. This is the territory of developmental and humanistic psychology. The second half of life confronts us with the need to limit outer activity in favour of inner activity to discover meaning in life – a most difficult challenge in our extraverted Western world. For most people, instinct as 'alchemist' continues its influence from the archetypal depths of the unconscious. For some, the crisis of midlife initiates a 'second birth' in the subtle realm of the inner world. Conscious endeavour, the logos, takes on the work of spiritual alchemy. It was in the context of this conscious endeavour that alchemy had meaning for Jung and his depth psychology.

Instinct as alchemist

Our first breath begins a journey from chaos into order largely through the bond with the mother, or mother-figure. Islands of growing consciousness in an infant gradually merge into larger islands until a tremendous moment arrives when conscious and unconscious unite, a *coniunctio*, like a lightning bolt connecting heaven and earth; the child refers to itself as 'I'. The birth of ego is at the same moment a death of being at-one with all life, the alchemical *mortificatio*, bringing completion to a *solve et coagula* alchemical process.

> Life in itself is nature, and nature has no conscious history. It is consciousness that creates time and thereby creates history . . . the processes of nature are in an endless circle. It is only the conscious ego which makes it possible to step outside this circle and by contemplating it from outside, so to speak, recreate it anew. Such is the enormous achievement of human consciousness.
>
> (Adler, 1966, p. 130)

Childhood unfolds with 'the gradual shelling out of the delicate germ of individuality from the various layers of identifications and magical participations' (Adler, 1966, p. 136) as the nascent ego is forged in *Sol*'s fire, the primal forces of desire, rage and will to power. Warmth in the early environment gives the child an experience of *Sol*'s fire mediated by human relationship, the softer reflected light of *Luna*. Psychologically, any primal feeling not subjected to *mortificatio* may be split-off and repressed into shadow to be revisited later, or may cling to the developing ego after this developmental phase and be acted out in socially inappropriate ways. For instance, outrage may be perceived as a justified motivation for committing an act of theft or violence (dark *Sol*). The ego is always potentially at the mercy of any primal force which has yet to be mediated by human relationship.

Separation from identification with primal emotions brings an expansion of consciousness, opening the way for the second *coniunctio*, a *mortificatio*, of *Sol* and *Luna*, and the expression of warm-blooded instincts and challenges of puberty. The primary psychological task of adolescence is to cut a psychic umbilical cord which connects growing individuality to the psychic womb of the family – to integrate the containment found within family, or family-like social grouping, by discovering the capacity for self-containment. The third union of *Sol* and *Luna* arises through separation from dependence on outer sources of containment, a *mortificatio* of the warm-blooded instincts. The Father world is entered and a self-reliant, rational, discriminating ego is gradually established.

Attainment of an integrated, socially adapted ego-consciousness is the main task of the personality and is brought to fulfilment through the *mortificatio* of concrete thinking – the task of mid-life. This means separating from an identification with archetypal images of Father as lawgiver and spirit – the power of word and intellect. With this transmutation, the alchemical work of the consciousness-promoting instinct within the unconscious is complete. The ego has been forged and established as *Sol*'s representative in consciousness. *Lead* has been transmuted into *gold*. Conscious and unconscious are polarised. The tension of opposites is at its greatest and the ego experiences itself as the powerful ruler of its realm. This is a black and white world. One's point of view is simple, direct and one-dimensional. Dreams with images of walls, locked doors or gates and imprisonment characterise this polarisation.

The problem of how to integrate opposites now arises: how to mediate judgements of oneself and others which imprison aspects of the psyche from finding free expression. Jung's psychological approach makes a significant and unique contribution to this task:

> The dominant must contain them both, the standpoint of ego-consciousness and the standpoint of the archetypes in the unconscious. The binding force that inevitably attaches to a dominant should not mean a prison for one and a carte-blanche for the other, but duty and justice for both.
>
> (CW 14, para. 517) (also see Chapter 11).

Part of the common crisis at mid-life is a discovery that ego development no longer leads to creative living. Pursuing more of the same creates an imbalance in the psyche and begins to hollow-out earlier achievements. Ego psychology is of limited value to people who have a well-established ego. If this is not understood, therapist and patient risk cultivating regressive attitudes which look back to the outer-oriented solutions of youth. This default approach unwittingly inverts the natural unfolding of psychic growth beyond the ego towards the subtle, inner mystery. 'The representation of instincts in consciousness . . . their manifestation in images, is one of the essential conditions of consciousness . . . and [consciousness] is decisively bound up with this reflection of the unconscious psychic process in it' (Neumann, 1963, p. 5). The treasure now lies in the chaos, the dregs left behind as the ego was distilled. As shown in Chapter 1, the *putrefactio* journey leads into a dark, disgusting place. The ego will try every trick it can to retain its dominance and very often succeeds with the 'alchemist' remaining in the unconscious.

Conscious endeavour as alchemist

At mid-life, Jung took a step which didn't make rational sense; he stopped collaborating with Freud, moved away from the dominant 'scientific materialist' cultural attitude and from many of his professional involvements to turn inward and engage directly with the unconscious. He was confronted with the need to subject the heroic attitude of his ego to the alchemical *mortificatio* process without also destroying his ego. The separations he had effected outwardly also had to be undertaken inwardly. In his *Red Book*, Jung records and reflects on the 'active imagination' encounters between his ego and personified figures of the unconscious from this period of his life (Jung, 2009). His pioneering act opened the way into a psychic territory beyond the ego with its linear conditions, cause/effect principles and time/space boundaries (see Chapter 9).

Sometime after mid-life, the ego is called upon to sacrifice its power and position as sole authority and accept relative authority in the psyche. This turning of the tide threatens the ego with death, catalysing significant conflict between conscious and unconscious. The struggle frequently manifests in the body through illness or injury and/or in shame-generating life events. Experiences of vulnerability, limitation and defeat arise engendering humiliation or humility depending on the degree of willingness to acknowledge the greater force of the unconscious – the mystery.

The transition is a disorienting time of chaos and confusion. One of the most difficult aspects of this crossing is the awareness of stepping out of the natural, collective flow – leaving the 'road of the many' to step onto the 'path of the few' into the deeper mystery and ways of the non-rational. Apocalyptic dream images may appear. For several years, a man in his mid-fifties sensed he needed a change. He'd reached the top of a successful business career and supported a wife and teenage children. The prospect of a career change was threatening; he was stuck. He dreamed:

> Another man and I are told by scientists that people haven't taken enough notice of ecology. As a result, it is the end of this human race – a kind of mass genocide. Everyone is to be gathered into trucks and crushed. The trucks begin arriving. I look around at all the smart cars and hotels and wonder whether this had all happened before and that in a million years the human race would have evolved again and something from our epoch might be found. The scene changed. I'm with others. We realise we had been in a dream. I say the scientists were right, we deserved this end. One

man challenges me demanding logical reasons, others join in. I find my
voice for the first time and everybody starts to agree with me.

On reflection, the dreamer became aware that if he didn't co-operate with his
deeper knowing, circumstances beyond his control could force 'crushing' change
on him.

During ego development, our socially adapted personality and essential nature
become separated. Between personality and essence lies the shadowland of self-
deception, lies, anger, rejection, resentment, self-aggrandisement, shame, unacknowledged virtue and achievement, childish fantasy, secret desire, variance from
social norms and broken taboos. This shadowland is symbolised by *Mercurius*
in its initial state of alchemical *lead* – trickster and chameleon shape-changer.
When the unconscious activates a thrust towards greater conscious awareness,
this subterranean world rises into consciousness. If the ego can catch hold of
something from this elusive shadowland and hold it in awareness, and if the ego
is at the same time itself caught by the deeper psyche, the *prima materia* will have
been found and the work of alchemy through conscious endeavour can begin. As
alchemist, it is for the ego to work with what emerges through dreams, symptoms,
images and the strong affects of inner/outer conflict.

The work of psychological alchemy

The inter-relationship of the material and spiritual is at the heart of alchemy. The
word 'laboratory' is itself an expression of this unification; it contains both the
Latin word 'laborare' (to work) and 'orare' (to pray). Alchemy is sacred work. In
the laboratory, an alchemist's first task is to work with *lead*, the blackness. Jung
describes this psychological situation:

> Introversion, introspection, meditation and careful investigation of
> desires and their motives . . . a turning away from sensuous reality, a
> withdrawal of the fantasy-projections that give "the ten thousand
> things" their attractive and deceptive glamour . . . the soul "stands
> between good and evil", the disciple will have every opportunity to
> discover the dark side of his personality, his inferior wishes and
> motives.
>
> (CW 14, para. 673)

As psychic contents free themselves from their projected attachment to the body,
to outer objects and to the world, the spiritual alchemist suffers encountering the
chthonic spirit, dragon or devil on the *night sea journey* of the *nigredo*.

After two years of analysis, the dreams of a middle-aged man, successfully
established in the world, changed in character. Dream figures revealed themselves
and began beckoning him to go deeper. One day he commented that it was the
imaginal which made life worth living:

I zoom along on the one hand with all the tasks of work and family, and then there's this "other" down here when I stop. I'm so literal, this is so subtle, a feeling – no, a way of seeing, pervasive.

He described the experience as being like 'going for a walk over the hills on a sunny day and coming across a dead sheep! It's not what you want to find with all the blowflies and everything'. We explored the symbol of a dead sheep. It became apparent he was being confronted with the death of his 'follower' mentality, someone who was free to roam but needed the warm security of the herd. This image illuminated his feeling of not understanding anything any more:

> I've never had so many questions about everything. It used to be simple. I understand less than at any time in my life. I experience something and expect to get a certain outcome based on the experience and yet it turns out to be something quite other, totally unexpected and disorienting.

He had lost his sense of agency, of feeling he was the determining factor of his own experience. As if in response, Dorn once wrote:

> Learn from within thyself to know all that is in heaven and on earth, and especially that all was created for thy sake . . . thou wilt never make from others the One which thou seekest, except first there be made one thing of thyself . . .
>
> (1602, p. 466 ff., cited in CW 14, para. 685)

The *nigredo* introduces an extended period of melancholy and depression as the soul struggles in darkness with a chaos of inner and outer experience. Psychotherapy often begins under its influence. Jung's interpretation of a relevant alchemical text provides guidance:

> contemplate your lack of fantasy, of inspiration and inner aliveness, which you feel as sheer stagnation and a barren wilderness, and impregnate it with the interest born of alarm at your inner death, then something can take shape in you, for your inner emptiness conceals just as great a fullness if only you allow it to penetrate you.
>
> (CW 14, para. 190)

Contemplation gradually shifts the focus from perceiving the cause of one's difficulty as lying in the objective, outer world towards experiential knowledge that this complex interplay of inner and outer experience originates in the subjective, inner world.

Psychotherapeutic process encourages discussion and reflection on dark passions and strong feelings. With patience and perseverance, moments of self-recognition arise. Difficult emotions are revisited again and again until the lighter atmosphere of self-awareness is able to be sustained. This circular process was known to the alchemists as the *circulatio*. Through the harsh, elemental processes of burnings, mortifications and cold-rejections, and the self-reflective, human processes of discrimination, distillation and circulation, bright *Sol*'s scorching heat of high summer – the rational clarity and control of a kingly ego – is moderated and dark *Sol*'s frozen, winter-solstice landscape of repression is warmed. It requires an unusual degree of objectivity to question the illusory impressions we have of our own personality. Deep resistance may arise in the process as it involves the *mortificatio* of natural, unconscious living and the birth of conscious self-reflection, logos as the guiding light of the psyche (see Chapter 10). As long as shadow is not recognised, there can be no healing and no salvation. This word 'salvation' belongs to the naturally religious language of the deep psyche. Jung recognised this; the medieval alchemist lived it. In Sonnet 53, Shakespeare raises the question at the heart of the *nigredo*,

> What is your substance? Whereof are you made,
> That millions of strange shadows on you tend.
> (West, 2007, p. 172)

With sufficient integration, the chaos of *nigredo* gives way to the *albedo* – an ordered polarisation of opposites, the *coincidentia oppositorum*. The upper realm of spirit and soul separates from the lower realm of body and earthly instinct. Desire once fulfilled brings disappointment, whether for a fast car, stylish shoes, a glamourous partner or ambitious promotion. The glittery illusion of soul projection drops away draining the desired object of its colour and appeal, leaving only aching awareness of inner emptiness. In the *albedo* phase, the soul's purposes are symbolic ones not to be given lasting, concrete form. In Jung's words, the disciple:

> will learn to know his soul . . . who conjures up a delusory world for him. He attains this knowledge with the help of the spirit . . . the higher mental faculties such as reason, insight and moral discrimination. But, in so far as the spirit is also a "window into eternity" . . . it conveys to the soul a certain "divine flux" and the knowledge of higher things wherein consists precisely its . . . animation of the soul.
> (CW 14, para. 673)

The ego identifies with this marriage of soul and spirit, *Luna* and *Sol*. Untransformed shadow elements are left unawakened, repressed in the body or projected onto the world.

In his interview with Stephen Black for the BBC in 1955, Jung spoke of the psychotherapeutic journey as having:

> many stages or levels. If you take an ordinary case of neurosis, it may only go as far as healing the symptom or giving the patient such an

attitude that he can deal with his neurosis . . . other cases take very long, and you can't send them away because they won't go. They want to know more, to make the whole process of development, which goes from stage to stage, a widening out of the mental horizon . . . to get . . . rounded out [from one-sidedness], or mentally more developed, more conscious.

(McGuire and Hull, 1977, p. 255)

The self-knowledge in the *albedo* phase is not a knowledge of the ego in '*the spirit of this time*', but knowledge of the self, which Jung understood as an inner image of God hidden within the body, '*in the spirit of the depths*' (Jung, 2009, p. 229). This is the self-knowledge of the full heights and depths of our own character. Sulphuric, solar heat from the battle of opposites first forges, later refines, the place of ego within the greater psyche. The hotter the fire and the greater the pressure, the stronger the metal of consciousness and objectivity forged. Humility awakens a creative interplay between the transpersonal, objective psyche and a personal, receptive ego. With this ego refinement, life unfolds increasingly through synchronicity, a factor existing outside the ego's realm.

After a long analysis, a single woman in her early fifties had already made the journey into her shadowlands where she found the necessary inner resources to obtain a higher education and establish a creative, professional career. She found redemption through a relationship with a man, both a physical and spiritual communion. The *albedo*, inner marriage, could not be fully embodied in outer marriage – he was already married. By accepting this restriction, she was left with a problem: how could she integrate this redeeming experience? She suffered the deep pain of sacrificing a relationship which could not be fulfilled to go deeper into her own journey. The profound knowledge of bitter-sweetness, ecstatic-agony born of conscious sacrifice infused her body, soul and spirit.

She described waking with anxiety one Sunday morning aware of a profound stillness; she lived alone. 'By feeling it, it is already letting go of it. Just to stay still and breathe it.' She dropped down into her anxiety without judgement. When she reached the bottom, it turned and there was a sense of light. She surrendered to her anxious feeling to find what was needed, to pay homage to the unconscious:

On the threshold is where I tremble. The dark mother is so strong. It takes every ounce of strength to mediate that threshold. I have to be not so afraid of new opportunities that come, not judge them in expectation of repeating the negative that's known. You have to go down deep enough to stop your world turning on the same old axis.

Understanding the truly paradoxical, ambiguous nature of our humanity re-unites separated elements into a unified third thing, known alchemically as the *filius philosophorum*, or, psychologically, as the *transcendent function*. Jung records his own experience, 'Opposing me, the God sank into my heart when I was confused by mockery and worship, by grief and laughter, by yes and no. The one arose from the melting together of the two' (Jung, 2009, p. 244).

In his book, *Thresholds of Initiation*, Jungian analyst Joseph Henderson describes the dream image of a woman crossing this initiatory threshold of paradox. The image resembled

> an ancient temple or maybe just seven great steps hewn out of stone. The lowermost step represented the mating of man and woman. Then there were ascending levels of "yearning" and on the topmost level "God's Image", which represented the uppermost level.
>
> (Henderson, 1967, p. 198)

Paradoxically, the human and divine are simultaneously present. The tension of opposites is reconciled in the transcendent symbol of a bridging stairway which is also a temple.

Solve et coagula processes dissolve the literal, material experience of unconscious living to reveal knowledge of its spiritual essence. In place of simple, natural instinct there is a self-awareness and a profound experience, deeply rooted in paradox, of having become oneself. The *rubedo*, or reddening stage, transforms the ideal state into the 'red-blooded' instinctive vitality of fully embodied experience. Spiritual essence is, once again, coagulated in worldly form. Shadow no longer acts autonomously. Its integration creates a unity of psyche, where the established habit of self-reflection becomes a natural characteristic of the personality. Life unfolds as if carried forward by both human endeavour and a 'magic carpet' of synchronicity. The alchemical transmutation of *lead* to *gold* corresponds to the developmental journey from non-ego to ego and the psycho-spiritual, archetypal journey from ego returning to non-ego as the self-image. T. S. Eliot captures the essence of the alchemical opus with his words, '*to arrive where we started and know the place for the first time*' (1990, p. 222). It appears deceptively simple. In reality it is difficult, sometimes dangerous psychological work requiring years of treading a path that always leads into the unknown. The alchemist subjects his or her soul and spirit to fire, water and air: forging in fire, refining through washing and distilling over and over again, until they are purified.

The mysterious union of all psychic factors, the *unus mundus*, is the culminating transmutation, the *mystical marriage*. For most, this moment, if it arrives, comes with the end of life. Jungian analyst Marie Louise Von Franz cites the near-death dream of an 80-year-old woman where the 'alchemist' is working from the instinctive unconscious:

> She saw a cross; at the centre stood a radiating sapphire. She knew in the dream she was experiencing a moment of heavenly existence . . . the cross signifies the union of all opposites. In the medieval tradition the

sapphire was considered to be the "foundation stone" of Heavenly Jerusalem and an image of Christ.

(Eldred, 1982 cited in Von Franz, 1998, p. 134)

Founded on a lifetime of conscious endeavour as alchemist, Jung describes his experience of the *hierosgamos* while also in a near-death state, 'At bottom it was I myself: I was the marriage. And my beatitude was that of a blissful wedding . . . There was a pneuma of inexpressible sanctity in the room, whose manifestation was the mysterium coniunctionis' (Jung, 1983, p. 326). He also describes his experience psychologically in his *Collected Works*:

> The coronation, apotheosis, and marriage signalise the equal status of conscious and unconscious that becomes possible at the highest level – a coincidentia oppositorum with redeeming effects . . . The union of opposites is a transconscious process and, in principle, not amenable to scientific explanation. The marriage must remain the "mystery of the queen", the secret of the art . . . and in [the royal] art and its allegories the drama of [the alchemist's] own soul, his individuation process, is played out.
>
> (CW 14, paras 540–543)

Jung opens his magnum opus, '*Mysterium Coniunctionis*' with the words, 'The factors which come together in the *coniunctio* are conceived as opposites, either confronting one another in enmity or attracting one another in love' (CW 14, para. 1). The truth of this statement becomes manifestly visible in the events of the *News of the World*'s demise and the Royal Wedding referred to earlier. This magnification of archetypal, psychological dynamics in world events helps us to glimpse more clearly invisible dimensions of these same psychic processes as they unfold on the subtle planes of our own inner world. The ego is forged from the primal sea by the 'alchemist' as a consciousness-creating instinct in the unconscious. When the time is ripe, the psyche activates an opportunity to embark on a journey of re-uniting through conscious endeavour, logos, those factors previously separated. The self-serving ego is subjected, again and again, to a process of being re-forged in fire, washed by tears and divine grace, and dried in airy self-reflection until it serves something greater than itself. The *albedo* process, or *lesser coniunctio*, re-unites soul and spirit. The *rubedo* process of the *greater coniunctio* integrates mystical dimensions of soul and spirit with the body and its physical life in the world. Dedication, self-discipline and humility marry head and heart, generating wisdom and deeply human relatedness towards all life. Alchemical symbols and processes weave together the threads of developmental and archetypal psychologies – just as the fabric of life is woven – through Mystery.

Acknowledgements

My thanks to the three analysands referred to in this chapter. Thanks also to Peter Bygott, Adele David, Josephine Evetts-Secker, Susan Harrison-Mayor and David Mayor for their comments.

References

Adler, Gerhard (1966) *Studies in Analytical Psychology* London: Hodder and Stoughton.

Burckhardt, Titus (1974) (Foreword by Jacob Needleman) *Alchemy* Baltimore, Maryland: Penguin Books.

Calleman, C. J. (2001) *The Mayan Calendar* Basingstoke: Garev Publishing International.

Dorn, G. (1602) *Theatrum Chemicum* Vol 1. 'Philosophia meditativa' pp. 466 ff. cited in C. G. Jung, CW 14 (eds Herbert Read, Michael Fordham and Gerhard Adler; trans. R. F. C. Hull). London and Princeton, New Jersey: Routledge and Princeton University Press.

Edinger, E. (1995) *The Mysterium Lectures* Toronto: Inner City Books.

Eldred, David. (1982) *The Psychodynamics of the Dying Process: An Analysis of the Dreams and Paintings of a Terminally Ill Woman* Dissertation, University of Michigan. Unpublished. Cited in Von Franz, Marie Louise (1998) *On Dreams and Death* Chicago and La Salle, Illinios: Open Court.

Eliot, T. S. (1990) *Collected Poems 1909–1962* London: Faber and Faber.

Hauck, D. W. (1999) *The Emerald Tablet* London: Arkana, Penguin Books.

Henderson, J. L. (1967) *Thresholds of Initiation* Middletown, Connecticut: Wesleyan University Press.

Jung, C. G. (1953–1977) except where indicated, references are by volume and paragraph number to the *Collected Works of C. G. Jung*, 20 vol. (eds Herbert Read, Michael Fordham and Gerhard Adler; trans. R. F. C. Hull). London and Princeton, New Jersey: Routledge and Princeton University Press.

—— (1983) *Memories, Dreams, Reflections* London: Fontana Paperbacks.

—— (2009) *The Red Book* New York: W. W. Norton & Company.

McGuire, W. and Hull, R. F. C. (eds) (1977) *Jung Speaking* 'The Stephen Black Interview, July 1955'. Princeton, New Jersey: Princeton University Press.

Neumann, E. (1954) *The Origin and History of Consciousness* Princeton, New Jersey: Princeton University Press.

—— (1963) *The Great Mother* Princeton, New Jersey: Princeton University Press.

Richards, Cerri (1980) *Drawings to Poems by Dylan Thomas* London: Enitharmon Press.

Sobchack, Vivian (1996) *The Persistence of History* cited in Briggs, Asa and Peter Burke (2002) *A Social History of the Media: From Gutenberg to the Internet* Cambridge: Polity Press.

West, David (2007) *Shakespeare's Sonnets* London: Duckworth Overlook.

Wilhelm, R. (1951) (trans: Carrie F. Baynes; foreword by C. G. Jung) *The I Ching: Book of Changes* London: Routledge & Kegan Paul.

3

THE ROSARIUM
PHILOSOPHORUM

Dale Mathers

The important part played in the history of Alchemy by the heiros-gamos and the mystical marriage, and also by the *coniunctio*, corresponds to the central significance of the transference in psychotherapy on the one hand and in the field of normal human relationship on the other. For this reason, it did not seem to me too rash an undertaking to use an historical document, whose substance derives from centuries of mental effort, as the basis and guiding thread of my argument . . . to give any description of the trans-ference phenomenon is a very difficult and delicate task, and I did not know how to set about it except by drawing upon the symbolism of the alchemical opus.

(CW 16, para. 538)

Introduction

I'm going to look at a set of alchemical pictures which Jung used to structure ideas about transference and counter transference – repetitions in the present of relational patterns learnt in childhood which are projected in analysis – to show how these symbols allowed imagination and creativity into a closed system: the troubled psyche of a transvestite. Through analysis, Robert began to re-name and re-claim himself as a person. He was, to his mind, both male and female yet neither male nor female. As he pointed out, 'the problem with "being a trannie" is that no one wants to do it with you'. His analysis, like the Rosarium pictures, was a symbolic journey from what I'll call 'the hermaphrodite' to 'the androgyne': the hermaphrodite being sterile, 'neither/nor' male or female; the androgyne being 'both/and', a creative union of opposites.

Transference is a fluid, multi-gendered experience. We may feel, as analysts, at times like a patient's mother, father or lover – regardless of our gender. This can be disturbing, especially when strong erotic feelings arise; perhaps equally, if these are next to impossible. We may find ourselves spontaneously fantasising about 'doing it' with our patients – which, if acted out, is unethical (see Chapter 15). However, imagining 'doing it', if consciously examined, can give invaluable insights about capacities to relate, and which obstacles, which complexes, make relating difficult.

Andrew Samuels, my former supervisor, explored the symbolic dimensions of Eros in the transference and counter transference (1985). Once, with a difficult female patient, Betty, who I felt unable to like, he suggested active imagination – perhaps like this:

> for a moment, Dale, suspend your own sexuality and gender, your age, your background – now relax, go inside and try to imagine what sex and gender you and the patient might have? Who is the man, who is the woman? Who would ask whom to "do it"? What would you actually "do", if you physically made love?

Imagining the act gave me symbolic information, a map for a journey, like the Rosarium itself. With Betty, I found myself imagining we'd be girls romping naked together in an open field, like a French 'sixties soft porn movie. This helped me realise her inner conflict with her own homosexual feelings, her fear of Eros towards her feminine side, stemming from relating to a mother who had no Eros for her. My counter transference active imagination might have been a compensation for this. Likewise, doing therapy with a young lad who sold himself to buy heroin, I imagined picking him up in a gay bar, realised when we came to 'do it' how desperately he'd rather be cuddled: be loved by a man who was not his physically violent father, nor to be raped again (as he was at boarding school). With a straight businessman, I imagined being one of the many women he couldn't stop bedding, realising his inability to 'take in' intimacy . . . and so on. Most analysts have had similar symbolic experiences. But I could not imagine what I might 'do' with Robert.

It was not easy to empathise. I found it increasingly hard to symbolise intimacy. My counter transferential experience was of confusion – was I a man or a woman for him, both or neither? My experience mirrored his isolation, his feeling unlovable.

Moments of intimacy are pictured in the Rosarium as physical intercourse, the *coniunctio* (Figure 3.1). This symbolises the sacred marriage, the heirosgamos – an idea I discuss later.

But can we have intercourse if we don't know what gender we are, as happened in this transference? What might it be repeating? Would it help to know? In classical psychoanalytic narratives, naming transferential patterns as they appear is believed to produce insight, believed to permit change. There are other narratives about 'restorative experiences in the transference': as an analyst repeatedly survives a patient's anger, offering recognition rather than retaliation, so the patient is able to work through buried feelings, to reflect consciously – to symbolise rather than unconsciously repeat and act out. Jungian analysts narrate change not only as 'resolution of the transference', but also as the development of an ability to form and use symbols. This happens as the analytic pair learn to hold

Figure 3.1 The *coniunctio*
Source: CW 16, p. 237.

and combine opposites, tolerate uncertainty and imagine possible futures – as well as reconstructing the past. To show Jung's idea of the *coniunctio* as central to this process, I will describe the Rosarium pictures, my work with Robert and ideas about transvestism, and how symbol formation gradually emerged, leading to an image of what we might 'do' if we 'did it'. This allowed us both to move on.

The Rosarium philosophorum

The Rosarium pictures describe the union of opposites. The word 'Rosary' does not mean a string of prayer beads but a rose garden, a popular medieval metaphor for any collection of wise sayings. The alchemical treatise they illustrate was first published in 1550 in Frankfurt. Jung selected ten woodcuts (some versions have as many as 20) to create a process metaphor, a symbolic sequence representing the union of opposites – of archetypal male and female. He believed the masculine and feminine archetypes, Animus and Anima, as well as guiding physical maturation and physical love, have a spiritual dimension (CW 9, paras 36–41). They refer to the unknown and unknowable. We do not, maybe cannot, truly know the embodied world of another gender. We can share social constructions – symbols and actions which a culture names masculine or feminine – such as dress. We can share the mystery of looking into the eyes of mother for an infant, or a beloved at their beloved, and expecting a sparkle, a gleam of gold. This is the moment of *coniunctio*, merger, intercourse – real or symbolic.

Analytical psychologists and alchemists use symbol to describe processes by which a complex process became simplified – 'gold is extracted from the *prima materia*' (as meaning is from a complex). For alchemists, 'gold' meant both a real metal and the spirit trapped in matter; a symbol, 'philosophical gold'. A symbol is a sign plus ×, where × is uncertain, and sometimes unknowable. A sign stands for something known, a symbol stands for something which cannot yet, and may never have, a precise meaning (Mathers, 2001, pp. 171–173). Suppose 'transference' is a symbol and not a sign: this is perhaps why Jung chose to talk about it using a medieval allegory. Transference is not a material fact, like real gold. It is a symbol – philosophical gold.

For we cannot know if any behaviours seen in a consulting room repeat past experiences with a parent, or mirror those in the present with a close friend – as in the 'triangle of person' described by psychoanalyst David Malan (1979, p. 80) – 'other, transference to analyst, parent'. We assume this happens, but assumption is not 'real gold'. Assumptions risk collapsing the symbolic into the signifying, an anxious yielding to a need to know rather than to 'be with not knowing'. We have difficulty forming and using symbols when there is too much uncertainty. And if we use 'transference' simply as a noun, rather than a verb, we risk enshrining a psychic function, making an experience into a thing – reifying. Decoding a symbolic journey like the Rosarium occurs at different levels, as the symbols in a transference appear and dissolve. Rather than 'resolving a transference', suggesting an impossible fairytale ending in which all projections are withdrawn and magically transformed into gold, what actually happens is a gradual change in the rate at which projections are recognised, and at which symbols form. The Rosarium pictures suggest this is a natural and loving process.

Analytical psychology developed its theory of mind from Jung's notion of enantiodromia, which, like Marx's dialectical materialism, comes from Hegel (Solomon, 1994). There is a thesis, antithesis and synthesis. Enantiodromia, a Greek word, means to run round in a circle (from *dromos*, to run – as in velodrome – and *enantio*, opposite, as in enantiomorph – a mirror image). Jung found the idea in Plato, who said: 'Everything arises in this way, opposites from their opposites' (1966, Vol. 1, sect. 71a). The Rosarium story is a romance between opposites, a King and Queen: representing (traditionally and respectively) father, Animus and consciousness; and mother, Anima and the unconscious. (Alchemy, being medieval, did not trouble with feminism or political correctness.) The ten pictures are:

1 *the mercurial fountain*
2 *king and queen*
3 *the naked truth*
4 *immersion in the bath*
5 *the* coniunctio
6 *death*

7   *the ascent of the soul*
8   *purification*
9   *the return of the soul*
10 *the new birth*

From Mercury's fountain flow the four elements: air, fire, water and earth. These represent the four humours in medieval medicine: sanguine, choleric, phlegmatic and melancholic. These, in turn, represent the four functions of the psyche: thought, intuition, feeling and sensation. I find it more useful to think of these as 'perceptual preferences' rather than 'types' – as saying 'I'm a thinking type' (or whatever) carries the danger of reification and limiting one's perceptions.

Succinctly, in the Rosairum story, the king and queen meet, fully clothed, offering flowers. A bird, the spirit, holds a third flower, forming a six-pointed star, representing the union of spirit and matter. In alchemy, a triangle pointing up represented the spirit, and down, matter. The couple undress, share a bath and make love – the *coniunctio*. Their bodies die and ferment. The spirit, shown as a bird, leaves, and the two, conjoined, are purified by rain. The spirit returns. The journey ends with the crowned figure of the androgyne, both male and female, standing beside a flowering tree. Each flower has a face – perhaps these are persona, faces we show the world (or 'sub-personalities'). The quest brings masculine and the feminine into one body. As analytical psychologist Lionel Corbett describes, the journey creates 'glue' to bring about unification: the 'glue' is imagination (1997, pp. 125–159). A summary cannot do justice to the symbols, it merely points to signifiers.

The narrative is of a heirosgamos (Greek: 'holy marriage'). In Ancient Greece, and other cultures, sexual rituals were enacted. Humans coupled as god and goddess to bring fertility. These enactments also had a political function, to reconcile differences between small, war-like kingdoms, to reduce 'animosity'. Jung suggested we carry in our psyche an image of the opposite sex: over-simply, the man in the woman is the Animus, the woman in the man is the Anima. Remember Jung's thinking was shaped by the social constructions of 1920s bourgeois Western Europe. His conceptions of 'male' and 'female' may, to us, seem stereotypical – men being strong and logical, women weak and emotional (Jung, 1998, pp. 126–127, 614–615, 955, 962).

Contemporary analytical psychologists might understand Animus and Anima differently, as genetically coded programmes for gendered activity: 'born-with software' whose installation is mediated by physical maturation, parents and culture. They are concerned with sex: again, over-simply, a boy falls in love with his Anima, projected onto his girlfriend (or boyfriend), and vice versa. This is a transference, as our sense of gender and unconscious choice of targets for projection (falling in love) depend on sensual and sexual relating learnt from infancy onward. Animus and Anima can be inspirational, the artist's muse; or destructive, ruthless and lethal, if thwarted – hence 'animosity'. Together, they are called the syzygy, Greek for a married couple. Here, the King and Queen coming together in a primal scene creating a child, a union of body and spirit.

In Jung's time, it was held that only a man 'has an Anima' and only a woman 'has an Animus' – as if archetypes were things, rather than functions. I think men and women have both: the Animus of a man being his un-lived masculine, the Anima of a woman her un-lived feminine – relational potentials. Male is not the 'shadow of female' or vice versa. With Betty, the difficult female patient mentioned earlier, being gay was an unlived potential. For Robert, an unlived potential might be a long-term relationship as a man with a woman. The conflict which led to his first seeking analysis arose when this opportunity occurred.

Clinical example

Robert, in mid-life, came back to analysis complaining of long-standing depression. He previously had a ten-year Kleinian analysis, which he felt saved his life, for he'd become suicidal about cross-dressing, a comforting behaviour since early boyhood. He was born just under a year after the sudden death of his older sister, Roberta, aged four. He was supposed to be her, a 'replacement child', at which he failed. Robert (also known as Rachel) was short, stocky, strongly built, dark haired. He often wore black. When he wore shorts and a T-shirt I noticed he shaved his arms and legs. In his mid-forties, he was a successful lawyer. An ebullient, mercurial extrovert with a strong sensation function, he loved music, art, cooking, carpentry and dressing up as a woman. He hated having impulsive rages, the habit of animosity. He often raged at himself. Desperate after another pointless conflict, he wanted to see his first analyst, but she had retired. He was furious about 'mummy not being there for me, again!'; understandably puzzled I did not know everything she knew, without being told.

There were sulphurous stormings out, mercurial stormings back, salty tears of rage and remorse. The transference, he interpreted, was simple: I was 'bad mummy' because I was 'daddy'. In his first analysis he discovered he'd always believed his mother hoped for a girl to replace Roberta. He felt met by his first analyst, a 'good enough' mother, 'but boys need fathers too'. As I'd just been wrong for being a father, I was puzzled. Whatever gender I was, it would be wrong.

His own father was over 50 when Robert was born: a loving, generous, old-fashioned man who married late. As a teenager, he'd served at the end of the First World War. He was not able to rough and tumble like Robert's friends' younger fathers. Robert enjoyed verbal fights with me. When we began, mother was denigrated, father idealised (the clothed King and Queen). Yet, if 'father and son' dynamics emerged, he'd rage. We could not stay as 'King and Queen' without it becoming unbearably painful. My ease with being either had to be enviously attacked, for he was easy with neither. He'd find opposites to rage at, assuming from my accent I must be 'a country-bred Tory toff', whilst he was a lower-middle-class London boy, and a good socialist. 'It must have been easy for you', he grumbled. I was tempted to tell him my parents were in the Party, but didn't.

In his inner world, Robert insisted men be men and women be women, as if his Edwardian, Tory-voting father spoke. Robert brought the image of 'angels in marble' – a quote from the Tory prime minister Benjamin Disraeli, referring to the aspiring working class whom he saw as natural conservative voters. Robert found parallels between his family's social position and transvestism: they were neither workers nor 'toffs'; they aspired to something they could never attain. I thought of his dead sister, and imagined a real marble angel on her shrine.

As a boy, Robert was active, sporty, mischievous; a keen scout, an enthusiastic jazz musician. Early memories include finding his sister's name on all his coat hangers, in his Beatrix Potter books and seeing her picture enshrined on the mantelpiece. He remembers being held between his mother's knees to get his hair combed, 'like a girl' (he always messed it up on the way to school). He didn't pass his eleven plus: mother was a school teacher, another disappointment. 'She did all the practical things a mother had to do', he said, 'but there was no joy in her'. He began trying on her silk underwear aged about seven. In his last year at primary school, he and friends enjoyed pre-adolescent sex play, shared their first orgasms and perhaps a stolen cigarette afterwards. He'd dress up, put on makeup and play the girl. During adolescence, he had happy sexual relationships with girls; later, at Oxbridge, he had a 'steady'.

He found a Chambers to practise law (barristers and judges get to dress up). Robert found a motherly prostitute who'd employ him as a 'French Maid' – to tidy up, make cups of tea and be rewarded with sex at the end of a busy day. He attended S and M parties in this role: though neither a 'top' nor a 'bottom', the scene, with its clubby friendliness, rules and codes, was seductively like the boy scouts: dressing up, ropes and knots. He knew where he was. Despair at his continuing compulsion to cross-dress brought him to his first analysis, as he wanted to be committed to a girl. Inability to maintain a sense of gender – or sexuality – brought him to his second.

I often wondered about his inner world. What did it feel like to be touched like a girl by your mother, when you are a boy? What did it feel like to have a father too old to play football? To always feel, no matter how hard you tried, that you never get anything right for anyone, ever? Despair and rage will be ordinary. Envy of those with 'good enough' parents led to envious attacks and Robert often had fights as a boy. Good things were easily spoilt, whether possessions or relationships; but once he had a good thing it was impossible to let go. It took many years for him to give his late father's carpentry tools to a charity. Perhaps he enshrined his fathers 'tools' (penises) as father symbolically failed to transmit his potency?

Robert easily got lost in details. Choosing a new dishwasher took six months, there were so many choices. This became our first symbol. We coined 'to dishwasher' as a new verb to describe circular, concrete, obsessional thinking: a defence against 'getting it wrong again', and against shame. Washing up is a stereotypic couple activity, 'you wash, I'll dry' is a non-gendered, open negotiation. 'Dishwashering', like dressing up, defends against symbol formation, and is an envious attack on the Self – a refusal to enter its open system. An obsessive bachelor lawyer buys a dishwasher he doesn't actually need because he lives alone. The dishwasher washes and dries behind its closed door, just as his sexual activity is 'behind closed doors'. As he said, 'being a trannie is a wonderful way of finding disapproval, because nobody wants to "do it" with you'. And, though cheerfully celebrated by practitioners on websites such as 'tvChix', transvestism nearly always draws shaming and stigmatising reactions. A transvestite looks both male and female, yet may feel neither male nor female. No one, straight or gay, is attracted. I wondered if that was Robert's purpose, enacting an unspoken parental wish. I'd not wish to generalise this idea and make it a 'law'.

The law, Robert felt, is creative – it brings order to chaos by making up particular sorts of believable stories – at which he excelled. He has an Irish gift for story, and before his first analysis he had great difficulty separating fact from fantasy, particularly sexual fantasy. You could drown in the mercurial fountain of his stories. They were sad rather than titillating, with images of people, including himself, going to great lengths to avoid intimacy whilst achieving orgasm. He'd learnt the term 'part object' relating from his previous analyst, intellectually understood this was what he did, but the insight brought little change.

To help him symbolise part-object relating, I told the story of Trickster, the hero of the Winnebago Native American myth cycle. Though called 'Elder Brother', he is both male and female, and neither male nor female. He can make himself a vulva out of a deer's liver, and carries his penis on his back in a box. Trickster sees the chief's beautiful daughters bathing on the far bank of a river. He sends his hard penis across for *coniunctio*, but the girls see it coming and flee. He tries again, weighting his penis with a stone. Alas, it sinks. The third time he gets it just right. His penis enters the prettiest girl. Unfortunately, it gets stuck. The wise woman has to be called to pull it out (Radin, 1972, p. 57). The penis is both a part object and a bridge (Gordon, 1993, pp. 69–84). Robert laughed at the story, and identified with Trickster. Like Trickster, he could penetrate, but only while remaining on the far bank.

He would stay far away from me by repeating trivial domestic details for weeks – 'dish washering'. It felt like playing 'mummies and daddies'. To avoid getting washed away myself in a deluge of feelings (for I'd begun to wonder if I was a girl, a boy or any kind of object), I began to look at the Rosarium pictures, badly in need of a map. Was I to be King or Queen, or both? If Robert feels both male and female, is this an androgynous experience or a hermaphroditic one? I became as confused in my theorising as I did in my clinical experience: so, at the same time as studying alchemy, I looked at psychoanalytic theorising around cross-dressing.

Transvestism

If parents and culture cannot provide settings where archetypes of gender and sexuality, Animus and Anima, install adequately then a complex forms – a repetitious compulsion, a habit of concretisation. Normally, in the transference and counter transference, feelings and thoughts flow in a third area, a 'between', held by clear boundaries. The analytic frame is 'an alchemical vessel', which, if strong enough and the emotional temperature is right, lets gold form: the gold of the Self. For children, the vessel is the family, society and culture. Children need affirmation of their gender and sexuality to form reality-testing functions (an ego), personae (faces to show the world) and a mature, fluid adult identity (individuate). Depth psychologists all agree problems in early life impact on adult relating. Psychoanalysts and learning theorists suggest transvestism develops if gender identity is poorly established. Transvestites may or may not believe they are the wrong gender, but rarely wish for gender change. They are not transsexuals (like Bree, played by Felicity Huffman in Donald Tuckers Academy Award nominated film, *Transamerica*, 2005).

The German physician and pioneer gay rights campaigner, Magnus Hirschfeld, coined the word 'transvestite' in 1910, from the Latin 'trans' (across) and 'vestitus' (dress). He found transvestites could be male or female, heterosexual, homosexual, bisexual or asexual (Hirschfeld, 1910/1991, pp. 147–148). He noted the transvestite *coniunctio* involves a prelude, cross-dressing; then, often, arousal and orgasm – 'monosexuality' (ibid., pp. 155–157). He suggested cross-dressing might be a way to escape from rigid gender roles usually assigned in Western capitalist society. It is a political as well as a sexual gesture. This was true for Robert, as it counterbalanced being a powerful lawyer, as well as being his dead sister. Now he'd not be 'a disappointment' to mother. It could also be an envious attack on them both, through caricature.

Freud examined sexuality in terms of object choice and activity. An unresponsive mother is substituted with a transitional object which, if sexualised, becomes a fetish – a *coniunctio* with an artistically created thing. This is concrete/ operational thinking. Clothing stands for a whole object, a mother. It may be a conditioned response: if your first orgasm comes when wearing your mum's bra, this is a strongly reinforcing experience. But why is a boy wearing his mum's bra in the first place? Is he playing at being her, or is he *being* her?

In 'Transitional objects and transitional phenomena', object relations theorist Donald Winnicott says 'the fetish can be described in terms of a persistence of a specific object or type of object dating from infantile experience in the transitional field, linked with the delusion of a maternal phallus' (1953). Like Trickster, here is a mother whose penis is detachable. In transference, this feels like 'not knowing where to put it'. There is a penis loose in the room, but whose? Kleinian analysts might symbolise this part object as 'the breast/penis' (an androgynic concept): both can be taken in, sucked and give out. Both can be signifiers of power, particularly the power to say 'no'. It is like reaching the Rosarium picture, 'the naked truth' but never getting into the bath or having intercourse. Whilst valuing psychoanalytic theory, which Robert probably understood better than I, I felt I needed a more symbolic way to theorise his dilemma. I looked first to Jung, then to mythology.

It is rather the incapacity to live which robs mankind of his possibilities. This world is empty to him alone who does not understand how to direct his libido toward objects, and to render them alive and beautiful for himself, for beauty does not indeed lie in things, but in the feeling that we gift to them. That which compels us to create a substitute for ourselves is not the external lack of objects, but our incapacity to lovingly include a thing inside of ourselves.

(Jung, 1919, p. 107)

In *The psychology of the unconscious* Jung described the ritual creation of fire. The fire stick penetrates the wooden fire block. Cross-dressing involves grasping the fire stick (ibid., p. 103). He goes on to talk about masturbation as theft, stealing possibilities of intimacy. Theft is part of the Oedipus story, as the lamed shepherd boy stole the kingdom of Thebes, which was rightfully his. In having sex mostly with himself, under his frock, Robert hid an undifferentiated and lonely child, lost in fantasy. In re-reading the Oedipus myth, I discovered a wise transvestite.

Tiresias was a prophet from Thebes, a clairvoyant blinded by the gods for revealing their secrets. On Mount Cyllene he met a pair of mating snakes, sacred to Hera, and killed them. Hera was furious and punished Tiresias by turning him into a woman. Tiresias interfered with a sacred marriage, and the mother-goddess took his gender – castrated him. After seven years, he again found mating snakes. He made sure to leave them alone, and was allowed to become a man again. In Sophocles' play, Oedipus asks Tiresias to find the killer of Laius, his predecessor. At first, Tiresias refuses, but eventually he reveals Oedipus himself (unwittingly) committed the crime, killing his father and marrying his mother. Outraged, Oedipus threw Tiresias out. Later, realising the truth, he blinded himself and went into exile.

This myth links two ways of theorising transvestism. Psychoanalysts look to an Oedipal model: mother (Hera, the mother goddess) is unobtainable, so she is enacted. The fetishistic object is a 'penis' analogue, mother's breast/penis which can be kept safe against castration, and banish castration anxiety. For analytical psychologists, a fetish object has a magical meaning; it is symbolic rather than signifying. Tiresias came back to himself when he could bear to watch a *coniunctio* (witness a primal scene). Freud and Jung agreed that in para-sexual behaviour there is sexualisation of anger and rage at a denying object – a withholding and/or abusive parent. For Robert, intimacy with mother was castrating. 'Being a girl' is an identification with the persecutor.

Robert Stoller, a Californian psychoanalyst, suggests three elements are involved in gender identity: hormonal influences, sex assigned at birth and psychological imprinting. He described 'perversion' (a term he was unhappy with) as an erotic form of hatred. He found threats to gender identity disrupted a child's sense of self, creating unconscious aggression and wishes for revenge (1966). Attachment is followed by undoing; frustration can't be tolerated, as transitional objects, the first symbols, cannot form. Before a child can form transitional objects, Stoller assumes, like Winnicott, they believe their own wishes magically create the desired object – a loving mother. Transitional objects symbolise good qualities, persist when the real mother is not there, 'are' her. Transvestites seem to act as if they themselves are the desired object: 'playing at being mummy' becomes *being* mummy.

Normally, as children, we eventually gain from the experience of frustration, developing a capacity to be with 'not knowing', to be, for a little while, out of control, not caring what is 'right', or 'what mummy wants', simply playing. Mother is a secure internal object. This is not possible if mother is absent, hostile, over-anxious or dead (Green, 1983, p. 142). Robert's concretisation of his need for a mother (and the feminine) could not resolve until he could bear the experience of lack – of loss, of frustration. Until then, his actions tended to 'eat themselves', that which was created was simultaneously destroyed.

The uroboric phase

Stoller's theorising of fetishism closely resembles what the analytical psychologist Erich Neumann described as 'the uroboric phase' of infant development. Alchemical metaphor and psychoanalytic theory here map the same territory: the first, a cultural guidebook; the second, a developmental atlas. Both are valid. Neumann was one of Jung's most gifted students: earning his PhD at 22. He suggests a mother holds the Self for her infant, receiving its projective identifications. This perspective explores our development of consciousness in a society and culture, rather than only as 'listen with mother'.

The uroboros is the serpent which eats its own tail. This symbolises the consciousness of early infancy. In Norse mythology, the Midgard Serpent surrounding the world is one of the children of Loki (the Trickster god) who was thrown out of Asgard. The uroboros is 'man and woman, begetting and conceiving, devouring and giving birth, active and passive, above and below, all at once' (Neumann, 1954, p. 10). It constantly re-creates itself, in a cycle that begins anew as it ends. Alchemists used uroboros to symbolise the circular nature of their work: for example, in distillation, the distillate is distilled again and again to concentrate it. The teleological aim of a repetition compulsion is to find the gold of the Self.

The uroboric phase, like the serpent, originates from being 'thrown out of Heaven'. We eat our own tails when mother is frustrating. This self-consuming rage, this animosity, inflates till it girdles the world. Without rage, we fear we'll end. With it come grandiose and omnipotent feelings, solipsism and self-reference. We say, as toddlers do, 'look what you made me do, you naughty mummy', even when mummy is in another room. There is a lack of conscious differentiation – if mummy has a feeling then *it must be* because of me. Freud called this childhood egocentrism, and primary narcissism. We are the centre and the container of the world.

'Uroboric' is short-hand for such states of mind persisting in adults. Coining a term, as we coined 'dishwashering', does not 'prove' they are remnants of real childhood experiences, recapitulations of actual traumas or misperceptions in the transference. The uroboric experience is real, imaginary and symbolic – all at the same time. A cross-dressing enactment expresses an emotional truth about frustration, rather than a forensic truth. It is a stuck, timeless and repetitive state, a closed system at the core of a core complex (Glasser, 1986). Repetition compulsion is uroboric – our life eats itself as we obsess, ruminate, intellectualise or get lost in addictive behaviour. Change comes about if the 'frustration' (real, imagined, or both) becomes a symbol, a synthesis, in which warring opposites tell us about how we continue to frustrate ourselves.

Thor, the red-headed hammer-wielding Norse thunder God, Loki's sworn enemy, defeated the uroboros in the last battle of Ragnarok. The world was flooded, but a new green one rose from the depths. The uroboric stage gives way to the heroic: braving our first day at school, taking the risk of making friends, beginning to make our way in our world, out of mother's world. Yet if the 'hero quest' for a boy is to be a girl, how is this 'being a hero'? He has to eat his own tail, have intercourse only with himself, exist in a closed system. The uroboric phase resolves as the negative – the experience of lack, of frustration – becomes heroically accepted. Then we can tolerate the existence of an other, an opposite, outside and independent.

Androgyne or hermaphrodite?

'The hermaphrodite is born from two mountains, of Mercury (Hermes) and Venus (Aphrodite). Like his father's caduceus, it is a double thing (rebis) that unites its two opposites, "the he and the she and the is of it".' The quote is from alchemist Michael Maier's work *Atalanta Fugiens* (Roob, 1997, p. 457). A hermaphrodite is 'a primordial unity in which male and female are unconsciously conjoined' (Samuels *et al.*, 1986, p. 65); it can unite only with itself. The androgyne, by contrast, unites the two, consciously conjoined, both separate and together. The alchemical idea behind the image is that Adam fell from celestial androgynity into the death-sleep of materiality. In the fall, this androgynous spirit split into male and female bodies. God followed Adam down into 'unreality' by creating Eve, the life-giving Anima who brings the possibility of redemption – *erosima*, where 'Eros' energy joins with Anima (see Goss, 2010, p. 47, and Chapter 14). Gnosticism turned medieval anti-feminism on its head. Women were created to redeem man, not to cause the fall. As this was heresy, alchemists were careful how they said it, hence their use of allegorical language.

'Hermaphrodite' refers to an undifferentiated sexual state, similar to Freud's idea of polymorphous perversity. Jung thought the image of the hermaphrodite did not represent the ideal and goal of the art of alchemy. The end point, he held, is symbolised by the androgyne: both male and female are present, as a unity, conjoined but not merged. That is, 'both have both' – boys have inner girls and boys, girl have inner boys and girls.

Transvestism might look like androgyny, but, for Robert, it was experienced as hermaphroditism – *coniunctio* with an other was impossible. The activity involves masturbation, is uroboric and anti-coital, and solves the Oedipal problem. If I stayed 'male' in his view, I was forcing him to be female: if I was 'female', I was taunting him. The hermaphrodite symbolises an 'either/or' way of thinking; the androgyne, a 'both/and': the first is thesis and antithesis; the second, synthesis.

How the Rosarium was used

The sexualism of the hermaphrodite symbol completely overpowered consciousness and gave rise to an attitude of mind which is just as unsavoury as the old hybrid symbolism. The task that defeated the alchemists presented itself anew: how is the profound cleavage in man and the world to be understood, how are we to respond to it, and if possible, abolish it?

(CW 16, para. 534)

The Rosarium pictures gave me a reflective space. It was not that, over eight years, the stages unfolded chronologically – several might be present in a single session. Robert might offer a story, like the King offering the Queen a flower. We might 'get naked' and share feelings about his story: be angry at a tale of injustice. We might 'immerse in the bath', exploring sensations around anger, but then hatred got in the way of going further. I began to experience 'perversion as an erotic form of hatred'.

Robert 'bubbled up' with rage, like Mercury's fountain. Emotions splashed into frequent rows with colleagues, and me. He'd overwhelm me with minute details, feel he was 'being done to', like an angry teenager. He'd get road rage, fume over 'bad service' in shops, storm out if an interpretation was 'a bit off . . .', or near the mark. I could never be as good as his previous analyst. Calling this narcissistic rage did not help, 'I know that already! I thought you Jungians had something special . . . !' I was never good enough, just as he was never good enough for his mother, not being a girl. An underlying problem could be that I was 'better' than his female analyst – I had a real penis – but this meant I was more potent than him, and had to be enviously attacked. He needed desperately to learn how to use his father's 'tool'. Because he fears he never could, his father's carpentry tools were enshrined, then given away to the charity shop.

The second picture is the King and Queen meeting fully clothed, offering each other flowers. This is about grand projections, King and Queen being idealised images for father and mother, me and his female analyst. The combination, he hoped, could produce 'the perfect transference'. He'd hold out a flower, a funny or lewd story, then pull it away, eating his own tale. It was confusing, not knowing if I was being flirted with as a boy or a girl, both or neither. Instead of being a 'both/and' I felt like a 'neither/nor'.

Immersion in the bath consisted of storytelling, using his experiences as if dreams or fairytales. In sessions, we'd play together. This might involve my telling him a myth, like the story of Trickster, or of Tiresias, the blind seer. We began to find symbols: the clothes hangers all having 'Roberta' written on them and the shrine to her on the mantelpiece became images of lack. He went to visit his sister's grave, to let her death become real.

The *coniunctio*, the union, took a long time to reach, probably due to my failure to imagine the 'turn on' in dressing up. Only years into the analysis when he spoke with joy of his first love with another boy did I begin to feel Eros. As Andrew Samuels said (1985), it is useful when there are problems in the erotic transference to imagine what sexual act you might share: not by enacting, but by free associating. As Robert told me this story, I could imagine being the other boy, about 11, going home with my friend and playing sexually, maybe coming together. Is this a *coniunctio* . . . are there opposites? I wondered if I'd mind, if I'd done this, that my friend liked to put on his mother's underwear, and realised I'd not care, because of the fun of doing something loving, forbidden and exciting.

This fantasy contained hope. Maybe he could take in something of mine, if we stayed playful. At first, after discussing this, his rageful acting out increased: a car accident seemed synchronistic, as if the world was saying 'stop!' Driving into the back of a scaffolding truck on the way to a session suggested to him we were 'putting up scaffolding' together; as he joked, 'sharing an erection'. He thought about developmental delay – he still felt in the same way an 11-year-old. For this to change would feel like death, the next picture. Robert had a serious illness, requiring surgery. As any Doctor might, I visited him in hospital. His near-death experience let him see the 11-year-old boy he had been was both a part of himself and 'no more'. Mourning began, grieving an unlived life. My being seen by him as a 'whole object' able to show genuine concern, and as a 'medical man' (not a boy) began to let him see both 'Robert' and 'Rachel' were two parts of one person, his Animus and Anima.

The next picture is the ascent of the soul. As an analyst, all you do is watch. Robert decided to retire, began discovering his family history, learnt his father was a firewatcher on St. Paul's cathedral during the war and started to see that 'the old man' was a hero. He found photos of his carefree young parents, touring on a motorcycle, which they took turns to drive. His 'primal scene fantasy' changed; there could have been joy in his conception. Perhaps he'd been wanted more than he imagined? 'Purification' might be no longer using prostitutes, though he would still dress up 'for old times sake'. 'I'll go and see my mates, put on a frock, share a pint and a roll-up, play darts and talk about football, just like any other group of guys down the pub.' This felt like a 'return of the soul'. Robert became more creative and found new uses for his legal skills. He had a set of personae, including 'Rachel' and, most importantly, a lonely 11-year-old who wanted his mother so much.

Conclusion

Jung said, 'to give any description of the transference phenomenon is a very difficult and delicate task, and I did not know how to set about it except by drawing upon the symbolism of the alchemical opus' (CW 16, para. 538). The Rosarium pictures helped me to symbolise a transferential difficulty. I imagined that *coniunctio* meant a '*coniunctio oppositorum*', a meeting of Animus and Anima: as if one gender has to be concretely in one person, and the opposite in the other. Being able to imagine 'coming together', to feel Eros with my patient as boy to boy, suggested Robert's gender fluidity had been and could be a bridge to another, rather than uroboric. The Rosarium pictures are symbolic, not concretisations. Using them helped me out of concretising the form a transferential *coniunctio* could take.

Acknowledgements

My thanks to Robert, who read and commented on this paper, written with his informed consent. Special thanks to Catherine Bygott, Dr Angie Fee, Rabbi David Freeman, Dr Carola Mathers, Chris Robertson, Keith Silvester and Dr John Stevens for help with earlier drafts.

References

Corbett, Lionel (1997) 'Seduction psychotherapy and the alchemical glutinum mundi'. In *Fire in the stone: the alchemy of desire* ed. by Stanton Marlan, Wilmette, Illinois: Chiron Press, pp. 125–160.

Glasser, Mervyn (1986) 'Identification and its vissicitudes as observed in the perversions' *Int. J. Psycho-Anal.* 67: 9–17.

Gordon, Rosemary (1993) *Bridges: metaphor for psychic processes* London: Karnak.

Green, Andre (1983) 'The dead mother'. In *On private madness* London: The Hogarth Press and The Institute of Psychoanalysis, pp. 142–173.

Goss P. (2010) *Men, women and relationships – a post Jungian approach: gender electrics and magic beans* London: Routledge.

Hirschfeld, M. (1910/1991) (trans. M. A. Lombardi-Nash) *Transvestites: the erotic drive to cross dress* Buffalo, NY: Prometheus Books.

Jung, C. G. (1953–1977) except where indicated, references are by volume and paragraph number to the *Collected Works of C. G. Jung*, 20 vol. (eds Herbert Read, Michael Fordham and Gerhard Adler; trans. R. F. C. Hull). London and Princeton, NJ: Routledge and Princeton University Press.

—— (1919) (trans. Beatrice Hinkel) *The psychology of the unconscious* London: Routledge and Kegan Paul.

—— (1998) (ed. Claire Douglas) *Visions: notes of the seminar given in 1930–34* (2 vols) London: Routledge.

Malan, David (1979) *Individual psychotherapy and the science of psychodynamics* London: Butterworth.

Mathers, D. (2001) *An introduction to meaning and purpose in analytical psychology* London: Routledge.

Neumann, Erich, (1954) *The origins and history of consciousness* Oxford: Routledge and Kegan Paul.

Plato (1966) (trans. Harold North Fowler; intro. by W. R. M. Lamb.) *Plato in twelve volumes* Cambridge, MA: Harvard University Press.

Radin, Paul (1972) *The trickster* New York: Schocken Books.

Roob, Alexander (1997) *Alchemy and mysticism* New York: Taschen.

Samuels, A. (1985) 'Symbolic dimensions of Eros in transference – counter transference: some clinical uses of Jung's alchemical metaphor' *Int. Rev. of Psychoanalysis* 12: 199–214.

—— Shorter, Bani and Plaut, Fred (1986) *A critical dictionary of Jungian Analysis* London: Routledge.

Solomon, Hester (1994) 'The transcendent function and Hegel's dialectical vision' *Journal of Analytical Psychology* 39,1: 77–100.

Stoller, R. J. (1966) 'The mother's contribution to infantile transvestic behaviour' *Int. J. Psycho-Anal.* 47: 384–395.

—— (1975) *Perversion: the erotic form of hatred* New York: Pantheon.

Tucker, Duncan (writer and director) (2005) *Transamerica* Los Angeles: Belladonna Productions.

Winnicott, D. W. (1953) 'Transitional objects and transitional phenomena—a study of the first not-me possession' *Int. J. Psycho-Anal.* 34: 89–97.

Part II

THE SYMBOLIC ATTITUDE

TRANSUBSTANTIATION

The lion eats the sun
and welcomes night,
descending like a velvet veil
as, gracefully,
she takes the sceptre
from his golden paw
to rule the darkness with.
Then Venus rises
where the sun has set,
goddess of love,
bright shining star
in our heaven.
As evening blue
is turning into black,
and diamonds are lit
like candles in the dark,
first one by one,
then everywhere:
bejewelled firmament—
there is a comet
lighting up,
and streaking
across an ever deepening black,
hurled there—by whom?—
for you to make a wish,
and to know
that we are not
alone.

Gottfried Maria Heuer
London, Good Friday, at the 12th hour,
2 April 2010

4

THE QUEEN AND THE SERVANT

Carola Mathers

Introduction

This chapter presents an analytic engagement illustrating the alchemical processes of *meditatio*, *imaginatio* and *amplificatio*. Images of the emergent self in dreams and fantasies weaved through transference – counter transference dynamics, both concrete (embodied) and abstract (reflected upon); my title reflects this duality. The fantasy of the queen (analyst) and servant (analysand) appeared first in a session, as an intra psychic event in the analysand and an intersubjective event between us. It transformed in dreams and further fantasies, appearing as an object in the final session. The queen–servant image functioned as a hologram showing different aspects and transformations of the emerging self in the relationship between us and within himself: a defensive strategy, a part–object relationship, the twosome enlarging into a threesome, the mother–child configuration.

The alchemical *opus* symbolises the process of analysis: the uncovering of the self through the work of *meditatio* and *imaginatio*. Jung writes:

> The word *meditatio* is used when a man has an inner dialogue with someone unseen. It may be with God, . . . , or with himself, or with his good angel.
>
> (CW 12, para. 390)

> The *imaginatio* is . . . the real and literal power to create images . . . (it) is the active evocation of (inner) images, an authentic feat of thought or ideation, which does not . . . just play with its objects, but tries to grasp the inner facts and portray them in images true to their nature.
>
> (Ibid., para. 219)

Jung shows us the dual nature of the *imaginatio* and its object, the symbol:

> The *imaginatio* . . . is in truth a key that opens the door to the secret of the *opus* . . . The place or the medium of realisation is neither mind nor matter, but that intermediate realm of subtle reality which can be adequately only expressed by the symbol. The symbol is neither abstract

65

nor concrete, neither rational nor irrational, neither real nor unreal. It is always both . . .

(Ibid., para. 400)

The forming self transforms the inner world of the analysand by means of imagery and through the living relationship with the analyst. *Amplificatio* brings the meanings of the images and the transference–counter transference to conscious awareness.

The clinical journey

My patient, John, a middle-aged professional, sought analysis for help with relationships. Whereas he found attending sessions difficult, I sensed a deep unconscious commitment to his process of self-discovery. He had a remarkable gift for responding to and engaging with dream symbols using free association and active imagination in a creative union. He spontaneously used events in his life and from the setting and container of analysis to amplify what was becoming conscious. The regression in the container or '*vas*' was in the service of progress, though sometimes we were both concerned he might get stuck there; as if in a uroboric unborn condition.

Early in the analysis there were two sessions containing spontaneous active imagination. On travelling to the first session, he was afraid something might go wrong. He felt I was on a faraway mountain and that he was making a sacred pilgrimage to me. He took care not to break his neck on the way. I suggested he feared I might kill him, the fear being projected onto his journey. He said it was fine for me to kill him, and proceeded to imagine I was driving a stake through his heart. He had a wonderful feeling of me concentrating all my attention on him, knowing every cell in his body. By knowing him so completely and paying such deep attention I was loving him. When I'd killed him he would be with me always, inside me, part of me. He wouldn't have to do anything, not have to work, just be there, completely accepted. The session nearly over, he wondered what to do with the body; he imagined a boy who crawled onto my lap, then a baby I was nursing. He became the father coming to collect his little boy. Talking about the fantasy later, he was drawn to the death experience, the wish to be permanently and passively inside me, as in a womb. I was interested in the birth of the baby, a rebirth into the world. This was premature, as there was much work to be done before the baby, as self, could be born. This fantasy showed John's regressive wishes and their link to death. It expressed his death wish, but he was also a vampire, with unconscious sadistic wishes to feed off me, sucking my blood.

The next session he dreamed Gordon Brown, the British Chancellor, gave him a pike. It was small, black and flat, like a fossil. He was full of feelings about the pike: he is king of the water and grows very large; malevolent, calculating, interested in you for what he can get out of you – a politician. The eye of the pike looks at you in a calculating way; powerful, self-serving, hard. John identified with

66

the pike, trying to second guess me. At the same time he wanted to get inside me, to be safe, relieved of the burden of living. The pike became a frequent figure in his imagination, representing a part of him which kept him above people, contemptuous. Sometimes he saw it as his persona, other times it resembled his father, who could be a bully but who also rescued him from bullies. The pike was the part of him wanting to leave the analysis, saying nothing had changed: exploring feelings was useless, hindering him. In the real world he could not afford to feel soft and vulnerable. Though the pike's way of being was outdated, like a fossil, it persisted throughout the analysis.

A few weeks later, in the session before a holiday break, he brought a dream: he met a woman in a shop near my house. They discussed the difficulty of making a home. He thought the dream asked: could he make a home here? No, because it's my room with my things in it. The only reason the room wasn't attacking him was my presence. The things in the room felt alive. Over the break, the room and I would be glad he was gone. I reminded him of his vulnerable and dependent feelings, recollecting the baby: the room's hostility could be his wish to attack me for going away. He said he wasn't aware of feeling hostile, but he should pay me proper respect. A ritual would make him safe; there's a procedure to be followed, as in a court. You don't just say 'Hi, Queen', you follow the procedure. He imagines arranging the room, tidying it up, making me as comfortable as possible. Then he sits on the floor and listens to my words of wisdom. He makes me so very comfortable I won't move until he gets back, I'll still be sitting in the chair. It'll be safe for him to leave then. As he was speaking, I felt disembodied, like the impotent white queen in Alice in Wonderland.

He continued imagining he was arranging the room. We reflected on how he had the power – I was queen, but he was in control. I said there was no relating. He agreed: he sits at my feet while I speak my words of wisdom but he doesn't have to listen, they go over his head. I said in this way he doesn't have to feel vulnerable or needy. Yes, the servant's role gives him power. He suddenly wondered what would happen if I asked him to do something he disagreed with, such as moving a picture. He thought he would refuse. I said, 'Now we know who's really in charge!' Again I had a strong embodied counter transference: I experienced myself as if on a high throne, watching him bustling around the room.

John's queen–servant fantasy, just before a holiday, illustrates his experience of the negative mother archetype, the room, in her engulfing, enveloping and intrusive aspect. To counteract this, he allows me as queen to appear in control, but makes sure he, as servant, holds the power. He controls me so I won't move from the chair until he returns: he need not feel I have left him. Although he sits at my feet, he pays no attention to what he scornfully calls my words of wisdom. I cannot reach him, there is no danger of intimacy or mutuality, nor anger or regret I'm going away: ritual replaces relating. A further twist is his hint that as masochistic partner he will never be left, because I, as sadistic partner, need to continue using my power over him, a power he has made illusory. Here we see the continuous and confusing to-ing and fro-ing of power and control; now I have it, now he does. John used masochistic power to control, elevating the other as outwardly powerful, sometimes godlike, as in the imagined pilgrimage to me, then subverting this projected power. But John felt acutely what he lacked; his scornful pike's voice was useless, since he felt empty and lonely. Despite the pike, he was allowing himself to experience these feelings. The *imaginatio* connected him both to his omnipotent masochism and his true aloneness, showing me the depth of feeling in his experience of separation.

The mother complex (maternal uroboros) appeared as the wish to be left alone, regressed to a baby state. Before sessions he sometimes dozed in his car outside my house, as if inside me. He fantasised about possible futures in work or relationships without taking action to achieve these. He remembered occasions when his mother tried to help him move away from her emotionally; he avoided them with tricksterish manoeuvres. A recurring defence was deathly nostalgia. He spoke nostalgically in the session about past sessions, eliminating the present as he did so. This made me impotent, like the fantasy queen.

Reflecting on the pike, I feared it would make mincemeat of the baby, bite its soft bottom. The pike told John he's the one to look after him; he's been doing it faithfully all these years without recognition. But the pike wanted my attention – like the elder brother of the prodigal son, who was with father all these years, not being a wastrel. John felt relieved and grateful when I acknowledged the pike, which he experienced as an icy grip on his heart turning him away from me. Slowly, positive aspects of the pike emerged. John was in a new relationship; although he was afraid the pike would hurt his girlfriend, the pike could also be strong for her. 'He's got some heart feeling. His coldness somehow creates a reflecting space where she can be.'

The first hint of the self was the baby, the second a feeling he described: 'I feel all square, I can't explain it – my heart feels square, calm'. It sounded like a mandala, four-sided. He retreated from this numinous feeling: I'd become too important. He imagined going off on his own to eat something stolen from me, cutting off the relationship. Movement towards the self was too dangerous. John oscillated between eliminating me by distancing talk, and feeling a voracious need for attention. The unmet need grew huge like a cavern, sucking me in and blowing me about. He imagined taking me inside him, to fill the huge space: he'd eaten me, it was a good solution. Now he didn't even have to come to sessions anymore. Then, he was remorseful, feeling like Bluebeard, as if he'd attacked me sexually, keeping me in a cellar to murder me.

The *amplificatio* began with his cavernous need, and anger that I wasn't filling it, and ended with him murdering me: a reversal of the earlier fantasy in which I killed him. He felt disgust at his triumph, and lonely. But the self always brought him back into relationship, through his feelings of emptiness and loneliness. He was courageous enough to listen to his unconscious and not run away.

In struggling with me and his new partner he noticed his fascination for, and disgust with, women. He felt small in relation to women's genitals: they were large, arrogant and demanding. He couldn't give them anything, nor could he go away, so he ended up standing with head down, turned aside. There was neither possibility of relating nor of escape.

Next day, in reminding him he was late, I became the indifferent powerful genitals, as if I'd taken away his 'bits'. Castration felt easier: 'we don't have to worry about all that erotic tension here'. As a eunuch, the women would include him, he'd know their secrets, be in their circle: accepted, attended to and eventually indispensable. Then he started feeling empty and depressed. I suggested he was beginning to want his genitals back. 'Yes, they may be small and useless, but they're mine and without them I'm not whole, I'm not me'. He noticed a difference relating to me without them; there was no competition, no sexual spark. He was glad to have them back and to know he was a man, not a boy. This was a reworking of the queen–servant fantasy. At the point of being in control, as indispensable eunuch, the awareness of the lack of relating hit him as in the first fantasy: he felt empty and depressed. Now he wished to relinquish sadomasochistic defensive power and relate to me as himself, acknowledging his deficiencies within the feeling of being whole.

A few weeks later he dreamed he was in a castle. Everyone had duties: he had to clean the toilets, and fight to defend the place. Horsemen were attacking with arrows; he had an arrow and defended successfully. This surprised him; in real life he would have been afraid. Then he went inside, up the stairs. On the stair was a man who looked soft, with green fluid seeping from him, clear bright green like new grass, viscous. The man had a disease of copper, causing the fluid to seep out.

John was contemplating moving in with his girlfriend. He dreamed of a Spanish girl, whom he ignored until his girlfriend pointed her out. The Spanish girl offered to teach him about love. Afterwards, he felt cold and lonely, though not empty. I suggested this was the pike, but he said not entirely, there was no energy, no meanness or hostility now. This was the first emergence of an anima figure in his dreams, and it needed another woman to highlight her. He was resistant to this anima and I had to keep reminding him.

The first alive *coniunctio* appeared in a dream of a fighting couple: John was in a garage which had repaired his car. A couple, male and female, were boxing energetically in their lunch break, treating each other as equals rather than engaging in a manipulative exchange. He was black, she was blonde. They were mechanics wearing overalls; she in a skirt of blue overall material. She was feisty, a good fighter. In *amplificatio*, John preferred to stay with his passive identity (the dream ego whose car was repaired) rather than be the heroic fighter, as in the castle dream. After this, he dreamed that a disreputable man wanted to pierce his face; John declined and the man didn't press him. The man had black hair like his father; his white shirt was dirty and bloodstained. Amplifying, the man changed into a numinous figure, a shaman, who gave him an initiation: John knelt before him, the man changed his face. To John this meant changing himself, inwardly and outwardly. With a changed face he would relate better to women, love and care for them rather than showing off to be admired. After this session he felt energetic, able to do things he'd been putting off for weeks.

69

He then dreamed of an eagle and robin in his garden. Instead of attacking the robin, the eagle just observed it. He associated the robin to himself, the eagle to the pike; the eagle as a more developed form of the pike. It is not defensive or hostile, though it is harsh, unafraid and destructive. As a creature of the air, it has a larger view than the water-bound pike. John would like to be fearless like the eagle, but feared the eagle would tear into and kill the robin – the softer, smaller, tamer part of himself. The transformation of the pike into the eagle followed the transformation of his face, suggesting deep as well as surface change.

In *amplificatio* he talked to the Spanish girl: he is shy at first, but she says she knows him well, she's always been there. When feeling love and tenderness he no longer wanted to dominate. He appreciated the analysis because with me he could feel his feelings, but he thought he should end since he had what he came for: a new relationship. He was moving between the opposites; the next session he felt down, the opposites had come apart, contact led to destructive withdrawal.

A crucial dream came next. He's in a large cathedral. It has a famous pavement, unassuming in looks: round, marbly, pale cream, grey and maroon. It's not in the centre, not underneath the dome, the sun does not shine on it. He suddenly realises the pavement's function: it interprets or gives meaning to what the huge cathedral space does. The space transforms people but they don't know it, or they don't know the meaning, until they look at the pavement. The cathedral has no meaning without the pavement, the catalyst. He goes outside where a friend is being brash and insensitive.

I was immediately struck by the awe-filled and numinous quality of the cathedral and pavement, which John didn't seem to notice, being more concerned with the friend outside. He acknowledged the magical and mystical aspect to the dream but felt uncomfortable. The atmosphere in the cathedral reminded him of how it sometimes was in the consulting room. Consciously, he could be brash and insensitive about analysis, but a part of him was fully engaged in the transformative process and in finding meaning. This part needed my help to be heard; he was impatient with me for 'dragging' him back into the cathedral while outside with his friend. The following sessions were full of resistance. The pike returned, greedy, withholding, wanting to impress.

He felt he froze up during the next break, though managed to unfreeze in the following session. Nevertheless the sadomasochistic defence was operating: he felt he had been humiliated here, yet had persevered, despite embarrassment. He wanted calm and peace, and linked this to his deathly nostalgia, where nothing can happen, where he withdraws from relating: all is under control. His nostalgia kills me and the lively part of him which the pike sees as crazy. The opposites again: life versus death, relationship versus dominance–submission, analysis versus nostalgia, progression versus regression. He realised by talking that he changed the experience of the session from one where we related to each other in a living silence, to one where he was alone in a fantasy about a powerful therapist queen, worker of spells. He could take her away, look at her occasionally, dispensing with the real alive me.

He dreamed of a homosexual man whom, as in the shaman dream, he initially rejected. The man appeared in a dustbin, naked and covered with sores. *Amplificatio* led to this tramp-like figure transforming into a numinous one. The naked man became an important internal figure whom John consulted when he didn't know what he was feeling; a recapitulation of the Spanish girl whose task was teaching him about love. The naked man seemed to represent his sensation function: he knows things and communicates them through his body, being vulnerable but not weak. John on the other hand felt guilty about his body, his sensuality and desires.

A key dream occurred during the break: a famous actress lives in a grand house in Mayfair; photographs of her adorn the walls. She's beautiful, like Marilyn Monroe. She doesn't go outside, just admires her photos all day long. Each photo was given by an admirer. Her husband comes to visit, he's been outside, it's a sunny day. He's devoted to her, brings her a leaflet about astrology, hoping it will help her go out. She tells the servant, a small sharp woman, to throw it away. The servant puts the leaflet in the fire but then mistress wants it back. She talks to mistress, distracting her, as if she knows mistress's wishes better than mistress does.

This dream indicated a regression to queen–servant relating during the break, when the relationship with me weakened. The fantasy has been internalised: the internal servant controls the internal actress queen who is beautiful but powerless. This sadomasochistic internal couple blocks change. The husband is a new third presence, bringing a possibility of change (the leaflet). The actress may also represent the baby in John who wants to be admired (not loved): to have everything done for him, the price being to remain stuck inside the house–womb, without growth: a restrictive rather than transformative container. The servant may represent the pike, envious and resentful, which hates coming to analysis. The husband is kind but passive, allowing the actress to stay stuck in nostalgia. The actress resembles a teenage part of him which contrived to stay at home with mother.

The following dream, after the break, continued the theme of queen–goddess. In the dream I have boxes of Vesta curry. I say I can't use them, I haven't got the mechanism. We think about the Roman Vesta, goddess of hearth and home. His are with his mother; he says he doesn't want me as his mother. I say, I don't have the equipment to deal with the Vesta curry: I'm not a goddess, not magical. After a long silence he says it's very important I said that: I'm not magical or a goddess, therefore I have to be formal, that protects me. Not being magical I am here, open, vulnerable and attentive. That's a form of love.

He looked up Vesta, Hestia in Greek. She was the first child of Chronos, the creator god, who swallowed her. She is said to have relinquished her place on Olympus for Dionysus. John's glad I'm not his mother anymore but feels sudden panic: 'maybe you need to be a mother, it's hard for you not to be'. I wonder if he projected his need onto his mother in a similar way. If I'm not mother, he has to be adult; this feels scary. I wonder if I've given up my place to the Dionysus in him, the sexual adult capable of enjoying life passionately. There was some regression after this exploration, and a wish to leave. He consulted the naked man, who didn't want to leave yet, but in six months' time. John had difficulty keeping that sensing, embodied part in mind. The pike opposes the naked man, though he is not aggressive or scornful anymore, he has become attached to me.

John dreamed about our impending separation. He's high on a mountain cliff, with a female colleague. A plane comes towards them, like a bird, with feathers, attacking. It's dangerous, flying close, then turns into an eagle. He holds the eagle's legs and it carries him off the mountain top. He expects to be dropped or have a harsh landing but the ground isn't far away and the eagle lands him gently. We talk about the eagle separating us. At first he is attacked by the separation but then he is given a soft landing. He expects to be dropped, but isn't. I'm reminded of the earlier eagle and robin dream, where we thought the eagle was a new form of the pike. The eagle is progressive aggression, the pike regressive. John felt a new sense of me inside him, like his other inner figures. He hated the analytic boundaries but knew they allowed him to explore and express his feelings in safety. Knowledge is gained by sacrifice of friendship. Thinking of the fighting couple helped him: we were struggling as equals, without need for a winner.

Near the end of analysis he dreamed of the novelist Doris Lessing presiding over a heap of corn. She speaks a Celtic-sounding word which means 'the corn's consciousness of itself'. To him, Lessing was strong, maternal, creative, the 'ideal woman'; like a goddess in the dream. I felt excited by this dream, which showed the fruits of our work. The great mother Demeter was giving him consciousness of himself, self-knowledge. She reminded me of the Tarot Empress who represents fertility and abundance. Later, John remembered the Celtic word means 'Holy Island'. We played with the idea of Holy and Whole: the corn's consciousness of itself as a whole entity. Then I felt inert and sleepy; he said he felt inert, heavy, as if dead. The life-giving symbol was followed by a deadly one. I thought of the Tarot Emperor, the stiff authoritarian ruler in his dry desert. I had a sudden ringing in my ears and such sleepiness. I suggested John might want me to share in his deadness. This helped him, he was grateful. The rest of the day I felt heavy, exhausted, my arms like lead: an embodied senex Emperor.

Next session, he wanted to hurt me, spoil my satisfaction in 'tying up the ends and sending me out cured'. I say 'I feel heavy and can't think'. He is appalled, and paralysed by fear he's hurt me. I say, 'I feel better now we're talking about it'. This doesn't help him. He realises he does this to people; they walk away and don't want to know him. He is abashed to experience his shadow, his destructive relating; previously, he knew about it but hadn't experienced it.

In the final session he gave me a Japanese print card with a woman and a small man, perhaps a child, on her lap. He remembered he had been a baby, and an imperious servant. He spoke about the archetypal great mother that I had been for him; the man on her lap looked smug and self-satisfied. He worried this was a regressive card; but maybe it wasn't. I spoke about the feminine in him which he still feared could overwhelm him.

The alchemical journey

The analysis developed along archetypal lines: dreams used the ageless symbolism of alchemy. Some of the dreams and fantasies were so powerful, I felt bowled over and uncertain: were John and I in a *folie a deux*, a collusive erotic linkage which could go terribly wrong; were we going to be stuck forever in a place of hellish fusion? During the analysis I was aware of powerful alchemical symbols in the imagery, though my theoretical reflections were mainly in the area of ego, self and individuation. Writing this chapter has given me the opportunity to explore the alchemical images in more detail. The alchemical journey was facilitated, or guided, by the symbols of John's dreams and fantasies. The goal was the Philosopher's stone, or the soul. Jung recognised the essential importance of images in this work: he wrote, in the *Red Book*, 'The wealth of the soul consists of images'; 'Dreams are the guiding words of the soul' (Jung, 2009, pp. 232, 233).

I found in the Fisher King (Rex Marinus) story an illuminating amplification of John's imagery. In *Artis Auriferae* it is told by Arisleus, and called the '*Visio Arislei*'. It is also part of the Rosarium Philosophorum text (see Chapter 3). Its theme is transformation and rebirth.

The Fisher King is ailing, his land is sick and sterile. He seeks counsel with the philosophers. John, like the king, realised his life was sterile: his relationships were not bearing fruit, he was stagnating. His unconscious propelled him to seek the help of the 'philosopher' or analyst. The remedy is for the king to mate his children, Beya and Gabricus. Beya, the sister, is depicted as the white one; Gabricus, the brother, is red, or sulphur. White represents alchemical silver, red represents gold. In some versions Beya is Gabricus' mother; both are carriers of the anima. The mating results in Gabricus' death, as Beya swallows him:

> Then Beya mounted upon Gabricus and enclosed him in her womb, so that nothing at all could be seen of him any more. *And she embraced Gabricus with so much love that she absorbed him completely into her own nature*, and divided him into indivisible parts.
>
> (CW 12, para. 439, my italics)

The similarity with John's death fantasy is striking. He experienced me as paying the greatest possible attention to him as I killed him, knowing every cell of his body: an act of love in which I took him inside me. Gabricus' death seems disastrous, but, as in the death fantasy, he is reborn 'bald as a baby'. The time inside Beya is a night sea journey: the hero's transformative sojourn inside another's belly, like Jonah inside the whale. Jung links it to the Immersion in the Bath of the Rosarium (CW 16, para. 455). The beginning of the alchemical work, like analysis, is fraught with danger: the division into 'indivisible parts' feels like disintegration. Jung says: 'Right at the beginning you meet the "dragon" . . . or . . . the "blackness", the *nigredo*, and this encounter produces suffering . . . The mystery of the *coniunctio* . . . aims precisely at the synthesis of the opposites, the

73

assimilation of the blackness' (quoted in McGuire and Hull, 1952/1977, pp. 228–229).

At the beginning of the *opus* the initial separated state leads to a union of opposites (*coniunctio oppositorum*), followed by the death of the product of the union and corresponding *nigredo*. The process of dying and blackening is part of the *mortificatio*. The *coniunctio* in the Fisher King tale led to the death of the son, who is subsumed by his sister–mother. Many patients worry about being subsumed by their analyst, but John lived it in fantasy in the session. I was shaken by it, as the alchemists were by their operations. They knew their psyches were intimately bound up with the work; their mental states were crucial to the work and they approached it 'with a free and empty mind . . . the mind . . . must be in harmony with the work . . . one must keep the eyes of the mind and the soul well open' (CW 12, para. 381).

John was astonished by his strong physical feelings in sessions; these more than anything helped him trust the analysis without 'head knowledge'; they helped him let go of the pike-like need for control. The pike represented resistance to the stirrings of life, the night sea journey, the *coniunctio oppositorum*. As King of the water (Fisher King), he is a fossil, an outdated king. King and pike are aspects of the *prima materia*. The Texan Jungian analyst, Stanton Marlan, refers to the toad, along with king and dragon, as an image of the *prima materia*. It 'represents the outcome of unrestrained, unstructured life . . . it drowns in its own greed and hunger . . . it dies, turns black, putrefies, and is filled with poison' (Marlan, 2005, pp. 19–20). This connects it to lead.

King and pike know something is amiss, yet change feels painful and frightening, requiring a relationship with another, relinquishing solitary power. The pike knows he is 'empty and lonely', but battles against John's deepening relationship with me. The pike as fossilised persona was embodied lead. This was my countertransferential experience when the pike dominated the session: I felt heavy as lead. Jungian analyst Marie-Louise von Franz says lead, as a poison, refers to the projection of unconscious destructive factors (1980, p. 22). She quotes Greek alchemist Olympiodorus: 'Lead is so possessed by devils . . . that those who want to learn about it fall into madness on account of their unconsciousness' (ibid., p. 82). When John projected his unconscious destructiveness, I 'fell into madness', unable to think.

After Gabricus' death, the king imprisons Beya and Arisleus the Philosopher with Gabricus' corpse in the underworld at the bottom of the sea, where they languish in an intense heat. Heat represents the intensifying of analytic work; patient or analyst may feel they are imprisoned together in a kind of hell. The queen–servant fantasy corresponds to this part of the story. It arose before a holiday break, a break from the fires of analysis. In the queen–servant fantasy we are a couple existing eternally in the consulting room, with him in control. This was a fantasy of power over me, hidden behind the servant mask. Such power would not excite envious attacks or challenges; it would not even be obvious, unless I wanted to change anything, or leave the room. It was a deathly *coniunctio*, showing me the strength of this archetypal sadomasochistic way of relating in John's psyche. I did not understand how the death and queen–servant fantasies connected, until I learned Beya was called the white woman and Gabricus the red servant (CW 13, para. 124). This paralleled my counter transference experience as the impotent Alice in Wonderland (white) queen.

Gabricus was reborn as hero in the form of the fighter in the castle. The Fisher King reappeared as the 'soft' man leaking green fluid: a disease of copper. At the time I was rather concretely wondering about actual diseases, but later I discovered alchemical copper is linked to Venus. This relates to the second queen–servant fantasy (in which John is castrated), and the disease of the Fisher King: a disease of love. The green fluid refers to spring, renewal, virility: the Green Man is a mythological figure relating to fertility and rebirth. The *imaginatio* of the dream tells us healing is on the way. Jung writes about the state of imperfect transformation as one of both inner torment and hidden happiness. He likens this to a

> hidden springtime, when the green seed sprouts from the barren earth, holding out the promise of future harvests. It is the alchemical *benedicta viriditas*, the blessed greenness, signifying on the one hand the "leprosy of the metals" (verdigris), but on the other the secret immanence of the divine life in all things.
>
> (CW 14, para. 623)

The dream contains parallels with Jung's text: the verdigris (copper, oxidised on a roof, is green), the seed looking ahead to the corn dream, and the secret treasure of life welling up from John's unconscious.

The hero had to clean the toilets: the shit or shadow was engaged with, not hidden and denied. Meanwhile, the psyche urged John to learn about relating and love through the anima, the Spanish girl. The 'treasure' first appeared in the image of the fighting couple, where dark and light dance together as equals. I pictured them as a yin-yang wheel of energy spinning in joyous motion (see Chapter 2, page 31). I see the fighting couple representing the self, soul or *lapis*, which continued through the analysis as treasure, or transformative symbol.

The Fisher King–pike would not release John just yet: his self image resolutely remained that of the passive, ineffectual man. As if to underline the developments of the analysis, he dreamed of the cathedral. To me this dream was a great treasure, but John wanted to side-step its numinous power.

Returning to the Fisher King, Arisleus, imprisoned with his companions, dreams of his master Pythagoras and asks for help. Jung tells us Pythagoras takes the place of God, completing the work of regenerating the sick kingdom (CW 12, para. 450). Similarly, the face-piercing shaman, from being despised, gave John a spiritual initiation, healing his sickness, the disease of copper, or love. His sick soul was fertilised and regenerated. This fructification is symbolised as a precious tree, satisfying all hunger (CW 12, para. 449); an anonymous author connected it to wheat (corn): 'look with the eyes of the mind at this little tree of the grain of wheat . . . that you may be able to plant the tree of the philosophers' (CW 12, para. 357). For John, the corn connected with Demeter symbolised the fructification of his dried-up psyche (the fossilised pike), and the resulting self-awareness (the corn's consciousness of itself), which was ever-nourishing.

The individuation journey

The alchemical journey and individuation are one and the same. In the section 'alchemical journey' I explored the metaphors and symbols of transformation as they arose in this analysis. In the section 'individuation journey' I describe the mediation of archetypal energies within the transference–counter transference. John's initial psychic state was uroboric unconsciousness, described by Jungian analyst Erich Neumann as the safety of being embedded in the Great Mother, not having to do anything (the latter a favourite phrase of John's):

> Uroboric incest is a form of entry into the mother, of union with her . . . it is . . . a desire to be dissolved and absorbed; passively one lets oneself be taken, sinks into the pleroma, melts away in the ocean of pleasure . . . always over uroboric incest there stand the insignia of death, signifying final dissolution in union with the Mother . . . Many forms of nostalgia and longing signify . . . a return to uroboric incest and self-dissolution.
>
> (Neumann, 1989, p. 13)

Sometimes uroboric incest took the form of John's absorbing me into him, as in the Bluebeard fantasy: if I was constantly with him, he had no need for a relationship with the outside world. The pike represented uroboric oneness within the mother, disturbed by the relationship with me. Release and healing came about through a relationship with the unconscious, mediated through the transference. In the death fantasy a central aspect of John's psychology was brought to consciousness – the mother complex and the seed of its transformation. John's response to the fantasy, wanting to remain inside me, was regressive, though he ended the fantasy by reclaiming his infant, the seed of his rebirth as an adult. The hint of the vampire (driving a stake through his heart) revealed his unconscious wish to damage and suck the life out of me, which could not yet be faced.

The queen–servant fantasy was stimulated by my absence. Despite himself, John engaged deeply. He unconsciously knew relationship, with me and with himself, was necessary to overcome the stagnation of emptiness and loneliness, the disease of love. He felt attacked by my withdrawal. Responding with power and control protected him from feeling abandoned, but this could be wielded only in the servant disguise. It replaced relating, eliminating the third born from the two. The queen–servant fantasy demonstrated a static, unchanging and sterile twosome, reminiscent of the Fisher King's sickness. Eventually, John recognised and experienced the emptiness of power and control. The *imaginatio* connected him to his omnipotent masochism and simultaneously showed him his true aloneness.

A glimpse of the 'treasure hard to attain', the self, appeared after the queen–servant fantasy as a feeling of 'squareness'. This reminded me of a mandala, and of Neumann's comment that the mandala is the uroboros in individuating form (1989, p. 36). Jung refers to the squaring of the circle as creating an inner readiness to accept the self, in whatever form it may appear (CW 13, para. 115). This squaring represented an inner space, or vessel, opening up in John. But the treasure was still too dangerous to approach: he retreated into nostalgia.

John reversed the regret of murdering and attacking me sexually in the Bluebeard fantasy into a fear of my sexuality as archetypally powerful. He was now a castrated servant in a reworked queen–servant fantasy, defended against accepting responsibility for feelings and fantasy action. In this fantasy he saw himself being swallowed up by the women even though the servant–eunuch position gave him power and access to feminine secrets; for once not wanting to be swallowed up, he rejected uroboric incest, reclaimed his genitals and dared to be an adult with erotic feelings. As eunuch he was indispensable and powerful because he was impotent: in a development of the sadomasochistic defence he is emasculated. Then an *enantiodromia* occurred, a movement into the opposite: by living his castration in fantasy, the life force stirred, the defence weakened, he started thinking of himself as a man, albeit one whose genitals were 'small and useless'.

In the maternal sphere, John lived in a world of sadomasochistic and power complexes. At first these appeared between us; as the work proceeded, they were internalised and appeared in fantasies and dreams, such as the castration fantasy and the actress–servant–husband dream. There, a third position appeared, offering the possibility of opening out the fixed, closed two-person opposition. Once John regained his masculinity, his maleness regenerated, symbolised in the castle dream where he successfully fought off the enemy and found the man leaking green fluid. The fighter hero met the wounded man. He could not identify with the hero, the sadomasochistic defence still operated: he expected if powerful he would be sadistic and damaging. This showed in his shock when I said I was feeling heavy and inert. Instead, he was destructive as the pike, in a passive, cold way, towards himself and others.

The enlivening spirit of love and increased interest in relating to women, his girlfriend and his analyst, showed in the dream of the fighting couple. He often referred to this dream, aware of its importance. It was the first clear image of the self, a dynamic *coniunctio* of equal partners, in contrast to the static incestuousness of the death fantasy. With movement into the world of the masculine, he was given his true face by the face-piercing shaman. He recognised the transformation consciously; unconsciously, too, in the image of the eagle, the pike's successor. The king of the water's mean, hidden, manipulative and cold power, and limited vision, gave way to the expansiveness of the king of the air.

The shaman and naked man both appeared as repellent and disgusting figures: the shadow of power and love. Using *imaginatio* and *meditatio*, with my encouragement, John found their deeper meaning. Both pointed to love and relationship:

his new face meant equal relating rather than sadomasochistic manipulation; new awareness of his sensuality and the awakening sensation function came with the naked man.

The cathedral dream illustrates Jung's description of the self archetype as both the centre and totality of the psyche. The self is the goal of the individuation process: the treasure or *lapis*. Jung compares the *lapis* to Christ (CW 12, para. 453); Jungian analyst Warren Colman says 'Jung's work on the self is at the heart of his investigations into the religious function of the psyche and the . . . ways . . . this has manifested in the historical consciousness of the West' (Colman, 2006, p. 153). Colman formulates the self as 'the self-organisation of the totality of psychic functioning' (ibid., p. 170). This formulation includes self as totality and self as centre and emphasises self as the structure of the psyche which is in continuous process of becoming.

The cathedral represents the self as totality. The pavement represents the centre of the individual. The centre gives meaning to the transformations of the whole: the whole cannot be understood without the centre. In the dream, the pavement is *off-centre*. I think this refers to the de-centring of the ego brought about by individuation: the ego is no longer the centre of the personality (in the dream the sun does not shine on the pavement). Jung speaks about the transformative process of analysis in which the unconscious is gradually assimilated:

> The centre of the personality no longer coincides with ego, but with a point midway between the conscious and the unconscious. This would be the point of new equilibrium, a new centering of the total personality, a *virtual centre* which, on account of its focal position between the conscious and the unconscious, ensures for the personality a new and more solid foundation.
>
> (CW 7, para. 365, my italics)

The dream shows us the 'centre' is indeed 'virtual': the eccentric pavement highlights the unexpected position of the new centre. Characteristically, John's ego recoiled from the cathedral's numinous atmosphere. In likening it to the atmosphere in the consulting room, he unconsciously rejected the creative union of our psyches, the mature as opposed to the incestuous *coniunctio*. Equally characteristically, he allowed himself to be 'dragged back' to explore the images creatively.

When we looked at his thank you card together in the final session, we remembered the movements from the externalised to the internalised sadomasochistic world, and thence to conscious knowing and experiencing. The defence was weakened by the benefits he experienced in relationships. Vulnerable feelings and love without sadomasochistic power were possible, and in being felt, led to equal relating and learning, as in the fighting couple image. The image of the queen–goddess changed from an archetypal projection onto the analyst, to an internal object. The internalisation was incomplete at the end of the analysis, as shown in the card in which the woman is larger than the man who sits on her lap. John was aware of this and it is likely his individuation process continued after our meetings ended.

Conclusions

This analysis demonstrates in symbolic form the transformation of the *prima materia* of the Fisher King–pike. The domineering conscious mind was changed by the processes of *mortificatio*: dying, killing, blackening. This movement took place through consciousness and unconsciousness coming into relationship by means of *imaginatio* and *amplificatio*. The way out of stagnation occurred through the death fantasy and the stages of the queen–servant imagery, through which a sadomasochistic defence (pike-like relating) was gradually changed into an experience of equal relating, as in the fighting couple. The queen–servant imagery was an immensely valuable lesson to me: it has helped me reach a better under-standing of this form of relating. The dream and fantasy images showed the psyche at its work of individuation.

Characteristically, these images were often ahead of conscious movement, as if the self was not troubled by the defences. The *lapis*, kernel or fruit of the work was consciousness, imaged as the corn's consciousness of itself.

References

Colman, W. (2006) 'The Self', in Papadopoulos, R. *The Handbook of Jungian Psychology* London: Routledge, pp. 153–174.

Jung, C. G. (1953–1977) except where indicated, references are by volume and paragraph number to the *Collected Works of C. G. Jung*, 20 vol. (eds Herbert Read, Michael Fordham and Gerhard Adler; trans. R. F. C. Hull). London and Princeton, NJ: Routledge and Princeton University Press.

—— (2009) *The Red Book* New York, London: W. W. Norton & Company.

McGuire, W. and R. F. C. Hull (eds) (1952/1977) *Speaking: Interviews and Encounters* Princeton, NJ: Princeton University Press.

Marlan, S. (2005) *The Black Sun* Texas: A & M University Press.

Neumann, E. (1989) *The Origins and History of Consciousness* London: Karnac.

von Franz, M. L. (1980) *Alchemy* Toronto: Inner City Books.

5

THAT MOMENT IN
THE ROSE GARDEN

Antonia Boll

Mythological thinking evolves alongside subtle changes in collective attitudes and these are reflected in the stories we choose to watch and tell and read. In this chapter, I describe some of the parallels between the imagery of fairytales and alchemy and show how Jungians have used stories to illustrate particular psychological themes. I comment on the commercialisation of traditional stories by film makers like Walt Disney and note emerging themes in contemporary films, video games and children's literature. I also celebrate that moment in therapy when there is a numinous meeting, when the mutual understanding between therapist and client seems to lie beyond the limitations of time. In alchemy this meeting is called the *coniunctio*, the inner or sacred marriage.

Fairytales and alchemy emerge from a common source, the ever-flowing stream of the imagination or collective unconscious. Images of the young man, setting off on his adventures, or the adept throwing his materials into the alchemical vessel represent the start of an inner journey which underpins the unfolding of human life. Jung saw this journey reflected in the archetypal structure of fairytales and drew parallels between the practice of psychotherapy and the procedures of alchemy. The essence of the personality (the true gold, or authentic self) is gradually revealed through the insight and understanding which emerges from the intimate interactions of the therapeutic relationship.

Myth, fairytale and alchemy are all products of the human imagination. I think of them as appearing on overlapping maps of the same territory. Myths tell the story of a tribe or a people while the narrative of the fairytale explores more personal situations. Similarly, the work of alchemy moves in a cycle representing inner states of being. Myth illustrates a soul's journey. Dale Mathers writes: 'Myths are cultural tools which help us understand suffering and use it creatively' (2001, p. 180). Joseph Campbell, the American mythological scholar, describes in *The Hero with a Thousand Faces* (1949) how the hero travels beyond the boundaries of the known world and performs great deeds. He is helped by supernatural forces, like the sun and the moon, and thwarted by dangerous creatures, evil witches and powerful monsters. The hero matures through overcoming these obstacles, returning with essential gifts for his people. Campbell's book inadvertently inspired many films including *ET* (Spielberg, 1982) and *Star Wars*

(Lucas, 1977), and gave rise to a textbook for modern screen play writers (Vogler, 2007). Campbell's further exploration of world mythology charts the transformation of myth through time, noting the subtle changes of emphasis springing from a particular culture or region, as I will illustrate next using versions of the creation myth.

Creation myths: Sky Father versus Earth Mother

The English Jungian scholar Susan Rowland (2012, p. 50) notes that *two* creation myths dominate the structuring of Western modernity, not one. The Bible tells of a Sky Father who creates the world and then moves away, emphasising the importance of separation (Logos). By contrast, stories celebrating the creative power of the divine feminine stress the value of connectedness (Eros). Modern consciousness suffers from an imbalance between these traditions. While not referring explicitly to the clash of creation myths, Jung frequently laments the ill-effects of this repression.

In their comprehensive study of the mother goddess, the English Jungian analysts Anne Baring and Jules Cashford (1991) show how the primordial image of the divine feminine, once worshipped right across the Mediterranean region, was suppressed by later patriarchal religions and forced underground. The theme of the sacred marriage, potentially re-uniting these competing archetypes, is secretly referenced in such stories of awakening as *The Sleeping Beauty* (Geronimi, Clark, Luske & Reitherman, 1959) and *Cinderella* (Geronimi, Jackson & Luske, 1950). The mystical theme of the soul's transformation 'from weeping soot-blackened drudge into radiant bride' (ibid., p. 655) can be traced like a golden thread through mythology and the Wisdom literature going back 5,000 years. The alchemist of transformation in the shape of the fairy godmother is Wisdom herself. She is the psychopomp enabling her divine daughter to be recognised.

Alchemy: the poetry of science

'Jung aimed to re-balance the relationship between the father god of separation and the mother goddess of entanglement, as complementary to each other' (Rowland, 2012, p. 52). This theme runs as a leitmotif through fairytale and alchemy. Alchemists kept their experiments deliberately obscure. Like all original thinkers living under totalitarian regimes, they were suspected and misunderstood by the ruling authority of the time (the church) which could impose serious punishments and death. 'Alchemists could never be straightforward Christians. Daringly, they saw the sacred *within* nature and matter, not above it' (ibid., p. 48). Alchemists were both observers and participants in their experiments. Simply dismissing alchemy as a product of the pre-scientific age ignores its far-reaching cultural influence. Jung thought the relationship between therapist and client was paramount: both people should be fully engaged, immersing themselves in the heat of the client's material. 'For two personalities to meet is like mixing two different chemical substances: if there is any combination at all, both are transformed' (CW 16, para. 163).

The imagery of alchemy is closer to art and poetry than the classifications of a medical dictionary. In *The Wounded Researcher*, Californian Jungian analyst Robert Romanyshyn invites us to imagine the alchemist in reverie, dreaming 'with eyes wide shut' before the fire: 'he sees a salamander roasting in the flames, or a green lion devouring the sun' (2007, p. 142). Such reveries are explored, by association and amplification, as one might play with dream images.

Fairytales: the dreams of a culture

Fairytales are not novels with developed characters. Marie-Louise von Franz, a classics scholar within Jung's original circle, pioneered their interpretation, inviting us to explore every detail as if the story were a dream. She tells us that each story encapsulates a particular problem and they all circle the theme of the self. The Brothers Grimm began collecting fairytales at a time of growing dissatisfaction with official Christian teaching. Their work was inspired by an emotional impulse to contact a vital, earthy and instinctual wisdom. By their very nature, fairytales reflect this movement towards wholeness, this search for mystical connection to each other and to the divine. The trials and tests of the fairytale are equivalents of the refining processes in alchemy. Innocence is tested in the encounter with evil. The personality has to find resources to deal with each emerging challenge.

Fairytales and alchemy are subversive. They support the underground current of Eros or relatedness, recognising the importance of mutual respect in relationship and dealings with the natural world – what Carl Rogers called the 'I-Thou' factor in relating. The Genesis creation story, with its masculine emphasis on Logos and separation, validated man's dominance over nature, a model of behaviour which led to the injustices of colonialism and disastrous exploitations of natural resources. Fairytales, with their emphasis on the importance of feeling and relatedness, courage and integrity, remind us of what has been lost in the dominant cultural discourse and point out alternative, more feminine, solutions. In alchemy, fairytale themes like the Search for the Beloved and the Treasure Hard to Obtain culminate in the *coniunctio* or sacred marriage, bringing together masculine and feminine within us. This moment of blissful connection with the transpersonal may be described as a peak experience.

Those who complain that happy endings in fairytales are factually untrue are too concrete in trying to fix a time-limit on something essentially timeless. The inner marriage or connection with the transpersonal occurs 'at the still point of the turning world' (Eliot, 1974, p. 191). Recollection of such experiences can be fixed in time, while the actual moment remains timeless. Jung described visions of the sacred marriage, when he was hovering between life and death:

> It is impossible to convey the beauty and intensity of emotion during those visions. I shy away from the word "eternal", but I can describe the

experience only as the ecstasy of a non-temporal state, in which present, past and future are one.

(Jung, 1963, p. 275)

Fairytales generally begin in a lop-sided way. A king and his three sons, or a merchant with three daughters, are living in a situation without partners. It is time for the young people to seek love and fulfilment. Their elders facilitate this, preparing to hand responsibility and ruler-ship to a suitable heir. People facing an important transition can feel stuck, knowing things must change but dreading the consequences. When they tell their story in therapy, it is like throwing raw materials from their life into the alchemist's vessel. No-one can predict the outcome.

The clinical value of myth is finding new meaning in a person's story, essential when faced with horror stories of abuse and neglect, which led to building a false self, a stiff persona, (or) a compliant external identity used for survival.

(Mathers, 2001, p. 200)

Characters in fairytales have to be open to the unexpected and ready to trust the unknown. They need flexibility and a willingness to listen to instinct and common-sense, but there are many pitfalls particularly when established prejudice is given precedence over the 'right' transpersonal route. Nature is often represented by a helpful animal or a creature of earth; a dwarf, an elf or a friendly giant. The voice of the spirit or inner wisdom is frequently represented by a wise old person (CW 9i, paras 384–488). During a period of intense inner work, Jung developed the method of active imagination. This involved personifying figures from his dreams and fantasies, painting and writing about them, and engaging in imaginary dia-logues. A record of his own inner journey appears in *The Red Book* (Shamdasani, 2009). In *Memories, Dreams, Reflections*, Jung says the flood of imagery which burst forth from the unconscious often threatened to overwhelm him, yet this rich material formed the basis of all his later work (Jung, 1963, pp. 165–191). As he came to understand alchemical symbolism, he saw 'that the unconscious is a process, and that the psyche is transformed or developed by the relationship of the ego to the contents of the unconscious' (ibid., p. 200). This realisation led him to the central concept of his psychology – the process of individuation (see Chapter 15).

Jung felt compelled to engage in this experiment on himself; a 'voluntary confrontation with the unconscious' (ibid., p. 172). It was an isolating experi-ence. Fairytales begin at a similar place of disorientation when current socially acceptable solutions no longer work, as imaged in the figure of the old king. In a typical fairytale, the society he rules needs new energy but is resistant to change. The king represents old attitudes and behaviours which cause stagnation. Typically, at the start, there is no sign of a viable new ruler. We find ourselves identifying with the youngest child, often seen as a fool, who challenges the status quo. In our own journey of individuation, we can feel like the outsider, the fool, the person who is not taken seriously. The fool talks to animals and birds, shares his meal with a stranger. People mock him but he stays true to his instincts and feelings. His brothers are narrow-minded and ruthless, representing the inflexibility of the established order. They think nothing of killing him and taking credit for everything he wins through his courage and endurance. They even try to steal and marry his bride. She is loyal and helps him out, as do the wild creatures he has befriended. The true bride acts like the inner partner, or anima, the inner integrity of an awkward external figure.

Such stories emphasise the importance of humility and patience and warn against sentimentalising the enemy. Trust must be given with discrimination. This is why it is usually the third or youngest child who becomes the new ruler. The bold-faced sun of our ego is eclipsed by a more important factor. The fool has the courage to stand out against the crowd. These stories are allegories reflecting the obstacles that confront the individual in staying true to his life's calling. James Hillman in *The Soul's Code* (1997) called this sense of connection to one's inner integrity the personal *daimon*. He likened this inner core to the tiny acorn which will one day become a mighty oak tree. As an example, he tells how the four-year-old Yehudi Menuhin flew into a rage when presented with a toy violin. The youngster already knew he must start practising on the real instrument which would bring him world renown as a violinist.

Alchemical parallels

I will now show three parallels between the transformational themes in fairytales and alchemy – *calcinatio*, *solutio* and *nigredo*, and illustrate with some clinical material.

Calcinatio: *transformation through fire*

Images of heating and burning are central to the work of alchemy. As we reflect on our inner images, we heat our material in the flask, burning away the dross through this accelerated attention. In contrast to the uncompromising challenge of the fool, we find many young girls in fairytales who are not so much awkward, as abnormally kind and forgiving. Their generosity is seen as stupid by their vain and greedy sisters. Writing about the Russian story of *Vasalisa* and her encounter with the Baba Yaga (the great witch of traditional Russian fairytales), the South American Jungian storyteller Clarissa Pinkola Estés (1992, pp. 74–114) shows how the too-good child learns to stand up to continual devaluation by her horrible step-family and her own internal critic. She must absorb some of the ruthless strength of the witch, and recognise the value of this shadow aspect in herself, before she can overcome their evil influence. The witch's gift of fire is carried in a lighted skull which actually burns the step-family to cinders.

Solutio: *the feminine and incubation*

Many fairytales involve a journey over sea or land in search of a missing treasure. The emphasis is on the active quest of the male hero. In contrast is a group of tales where the focus is on hiding, adopting a disguise, lying low and biding your time until outer circumstances become more favourable. A greedy father in *The Handless Maiden* (Grimm Brothers, 1984, p. 145) causes his daughter's hands to be severed. She wanders the wide world, through many further adventures, before this trauma is healed. Pinkola Estés explores a similar situation in the story of *Sealskin* (1992, pp. 256–297) where a seal-woman is persuaded to marry a lonely fisherman and live on dry land away from her natural home in the ocean. She pines away in this waterless environment. The author equates this situation with those feelings of suffocation and loss of identity when a person gets completely mired in domesticity and cannot see a way out. I understand these tales as describing the alchemical process of *solutio*, which is like the operation of a butter churn, or the varied programmes of a washing machine. The heroines are spun around, dissolving and coagulating. The long years of wandering in desert or forest represent a psychic process, a necessary period of reflection where one can find meaning in the suffering and allow the experience to strengthen the personality. This hard-won maturity is symbolised by reunion with the beloved. 'From the outside it looks like complete stagnation, but in reality it is a time of initiation and incubation when a deep inner split is cured' (von Franz, 1976, pp. 70–94).

Clinical example: Eleanor's story

This career-girl turned mother, caught in a sterile family situation, had repetitive dreams about starting at a new office where she could not find her desk, her papers, or anyone to show her what to do. Once the whole staff team had to switch off the lights and lie on the floor because the *Men in Black* (Sonnenfeld, 1997) were passing by. In her personal life, Eleanor felt trapped and unsupported. Her placatory compliance left her feeling impotent yet any attempt to break out felt like an act of betrayal towards her family. In other dreams, the pretty little house of her bachelor days had been re-modelled in brash modern style and the wilderness area with its rushing stream at the end of her garden had been concreted over. During therapy, we recognised the stagnation in her current life and linked this to the sense of suffocation experienced by the woman in the *Sealskin* story, symbolising a loss of connection to her authentic self. Later dreams showed Eleanor a graceful new house 'on many levels' where abundance reigned. Following these hints, she is beginning to reclaim the playful and spontaneous side of herself which has lain dormant for some while.

Nigredo: *being spellbound*

Fairytales often begin with one figure already caught in a spell. Developmentally, being spellbound is like being caught in a stuck place (depression, indecision, emotional paralysis) with no exit. As in Eleanor's story, breaking out of this stuck place can feel like an act of betrayal, with a choice between betraying others or betraying oneself. In *Hansel & Gretel*, for instance, (Grimm Brothers, 1984, p. 66) there is a necessary loss of innocence. The children are too trusting in the early scenes and return to the original dangerous place, failing to recognise the destructive intentions of their stepmother. Gretel has to absorb some of the witch's cunning and malevolence before she becomes powerful enough to destroy her.

Sometimes the hero is spellbound or keeps falling asleep and it is his partner (the princess or anima) who performs all the magic. Jung writes about a young man who dreamt that his fiancée walked out onto thin ice, which immediately began to crack (CW 7, para. 341). Rather than rush to the rescue, the dreamer remained a passive observer, showing he was still afraid to take on adult responsibility. He was caught in the womb of unconsciousness, represented by the archaic figure of the dragon. Like St George, he must do battle with this symbol of his unconscious inertia and separate himself from the entanglements of his mother complex.

Beyond ego: the animal bridegroom

A self-less action often breaks the spell and brings about the necessary transformation. Belle's compassionate kiss in the eighteenth-century French story *Beauty and the Beast* (De Beaumont, 1756) frees the Beast from his enchantment and shows that Belle is ready to drop her oedipal attachment to her father. Bruno Bettleheim, the Viennese-born psychoanalyst, says this story could reassure youngsters that their crude fantasies about the monstrous nature of sexuality may be exaggerated (1982, p. 303). The Beast is an inherently decent character, and the relationship grows out of loving companionship, whereas *Bluebeard*, the villain in *Fitcher's Bird* (see Stein & Corbett, 1991), is an altogether destructive figure.

Marina Warner, the English mythographer, whose series of radio talks (2012) celebrated the bi-centenary of the Grimms' first published collection in 1812, puts fairytales in their historical context in *The Beast and the Blonde* (1995). She finds origins of the monster story in Apuleius's novel *Amor and Psyche* (*Love and the Soul*), though the suspected monster in that story turned out to be the swooningly beautiful Eros, the god of love (ibid., p. 273). Psyche's sisters had been married off to brutal older men and all three feared Eros was a horrible snake. Von Franz (1970) gives a fascinating commentary on the tale, treating it like the analysis of a second-century Roman man with a negative mother complex.

Women, throughout history, have been compelled into loveless marriages in exchange for financial security, so the growth of true love really is a matter of good fortune. Similarly, the evil stepmothers who cast a long shadow in fairytales were usually widows who re-married out of stark necessity. Survival looms larger than love under such straitened circumstances. We also know the Grimms bowdlerised some stories, giving stepmothers the evil parts so the image of the real mother could remain idealised. Later writers have seen that it takes relative maturity, as in Melanie Klein's 'Depressive Position' (in Segal, 1979, pp. 78–111), for an infant to recognise the co-existence in the same person of the terrible witch-like raging mother and the generous all-forgiving mother, who enfolds them in her loving embrace.

Warner says the Disney film animation *Beauty and the Beast* (Trousdale & Wise 1991) was a terrific box-office success but risked dramatic collapse when the Beast changed into the prince: 'no child, in my experience, preferred the sparkling candy-coloured human who emerged from the enchanted monster; the Beast had won them' (ibid., p. 313). Cocteau's classic film *La belle et la bête* (1946) emphasises the darker, more sinister side of the story while a wonderful recent film *Beastly* (Barnz & Finn, 2011) gives an accurate contemporary version.

Disney studios launched the first of many fairytale productions in 1937 with *Snow White*, directed by David Hand. In these animated cartoons the music is exceptional, the settings are magnificent and the films continue to charm and delight. Shadow is largely missing, though Cruella de Vil is a spine-chilling witch in *101 Dalmatians* (Geronimi, Luske & Reitherman, 1961) and I shall never forget my little sister hiding under the cinema seat when the whale appeared in *Pinocchio* (Sharpsteen & Luske, 1940). That was my first experience of the fearsome night-sea journey, though I had no name to give it then.

With its cheerful, foot-tapping songs and powerful characters, *The Jungle Book* (Reitherman, 1967) has introduced Kipling's classic story (1894) to generations of children. In *Cinderella* (Geronimi, Jackson & Luske, 1950), the wholesome figure of the fairy godmother, with her jolly ditty: 'Bibbity, bobbity, boo' is actually an echo of the ancient figure of Wisdom, who enables her divine daughter to be recognised. 'The soul awakens to the kiss of the prince, who, as the solar bridegroom . . . personifies the divine life principle' (Baring & Cashford, 1991, p. 657). Yet both these rags-to-riches stories miss something important. Mowgli's and Cinderella's struggle to achieve real-life goals is made to seem too easy and deprives children of a chance to identify with a 'real' hero/heroine. The bravery, courage and integrity is taken out of Mowgli, turning the wolf boy, the wild child, into a figure of fun, while Cinderella's struggle to emerge from servitude gets caricatured as a mean family squabble. Here, 'Disneyfication' demeans real-life struggles and deprives children of a chance to identify with appropriate role-models.

Sex-role stereotyping for children

When they were very young, my grandsons loved parading in the silver shoes and glamorous ball-gowns their sisters had been given but soon discovered it was not thought macho to explore other realities in this way. The feathered head-dress of the Indian Brave or the skull and crossbones of the Pirate did not carry the same appeal as the glamorous finery their sisters wore. My friend Stephanie Richardson, English lecturer at Alton College, UK, told me:

Boys have to enter fantasy in a different way. They get the weapons, like the light sabres from *Star Wars* (Lucas, 1977), representing power and exploration in the outer world. It's basic phallic stuff. Age five, they go into dinosaurs. Boy readers go for dragon sci-fi fantasies where the boy hero becomes the leader. Boys who don't read can get Play Station three, with tapes of interactive fantasy adventures. You can choose to be Luke Skywalker and conquer the world!

Irvin D. Yalom, Professor of Psychiatry at Stanford University Medical School, writes: 'Many adolescents today may respond to death anxiety by becoming masters and dispensers of death in their second life in violent video games' (2008, p. 4). Fantasy console-games compete and draw strongly on written adventure stories. Both genres stay popular when their themes reflect archetypal patterns of heroic life.

Pantomime also continues to celebrate the fairytale, though the tone is cruder, with plenty of innuendo and sexualised jokes. The principal boy, a girl in tights, becomes a harmless hermaphrodite for the masses. His/her role is polarised with the dark feminine, the vulgar bawdy pantomime dame, played for ridicule and laughs by a man. Pantomime is myth plus irony. There have been ironic, tongue-in-cheek fairytale films like the *Shrek* series (Adamson 2001–2010) which cleverly mock Hollywood dramas. These films also promote large, ugly, good-hearted characters, whose unusual appearance challenges the current worship of celebrities which implies only handsome people have value in our society. Shrek, the young ogre, has to find the Princess Fiona to get the evil Lord Farquaad to give him back his stolen swamp. Shrek is helped by Donkey, a foolish trickster figure.

The trickster: spinning straw into gold

Greed for money and status is a common fairytale theme. Some alchemists claimed they could turn lead into gold, other fairytale fathers made ludicrous claims about their daughter's cleverness. Millers are often tricksters, turning wheat into flour and thence into material gold, but the Devil outsmarts them, luring the gullible into making stupid bargains without considering the consequences. Donkey in *Shrek* is just such a trickster, and Lord Farquaad is a greedy and stupid bully. For children, there is a sense of gleeful irony, almost relief, in the recognition that evil and injustice do exist and have to be reckoned with. For instance, the miller in *The Handless Maiden* (Grimm Brothers, 1984, p. 145) is seduced by promises of huge wealth and doesn't anticipate the Devil's trap. Another miller, in *Rumplestiltskin* (ibid., p. 247) is caught by a similar devilish impulse, to the consternation of his daughter. There are analogies here with alchemy. Turning base metal into gold is no more possible than spinning straw into gold, unless you have magic powers, but the raw material of the personality can change and the trickster element (Mercurius) is part of that transformation.

Rumplestiltskin is an interesting example of where a destructive intention (stealing the new child) is foiled by a collective effort of will. This is probably because it began as a racist story, perpetuating the mediaeval blood libel that Jews stole and ate babies, so they gang up on ugly Rumplestiltskin because he's a Jew. Myths carry people's folk beliefs, including their hostile prejudices. Because their themes are archetypal, these tales lend themselves to propaganda and were so used with evil intent under the Nazi regime.

Another trickster is the witch mother in *Rapunzel* (ibid., p. 77) who wants to protect her daughter from the world but in doing so, completely cuts her off from life. The witch's trick, of using Rapunzel's hair for a ladder, becomes the exit route into the world of everyday. Writing about *Rapunzel*, the New York Jungian analyst Donald Kalsched (1996, pp. 141–165) uses the story to demonstrate his theory of the self-care system. He links the witch to the predatory and persecutory aspect of the self which keeps the individual imprisoned in a realm of fantasy and enchantment. The prince is the emissary from the ordinary world. Just as, in therapy, the map is not the journey, so here, there are more struggles to endure before these opposites can be truly reconciled. *Tangled* (Fogelman, Grimm & Grimm, 2010) is a delightfully comical Disney take on the original where the hero is an incompetent youth, aided by two tricksterish villains. Rapunzel herself is a feisty heroine who gives as good as she gets.

Death and dismemberment

The destructive inner predator transmutes into the murderer in the story of *Fitcher's Bird*, better known as *Bluebeard*. An evil wizard entraps a young woman and lures her back to his castle. When he goes away on business, he hands her a bunch of keys but forbids her to enter a particular room. So of course she immediately unlocks that door! Death and dismemberment are the wizard's gruesome punishment for this disobedience. Writing about the negative animus and shadow in this tale in *Psyche's Stories* (Stein & Corbett, 1991, pp. 121–139), Swiss Jungian analyst Kathrin Asper suggests a woman's level of self-criticism can make her feel literally dismembered. The experience of guilt and shame about one's essential nature (including something as banal as being overweight in a society which only values skinny women) evoke these feelings continually. Such internalised dislike also attracts vicious attacks from others, notably bosses, partners, husbands and children. Indeed, the gruesome leitmotif of this tale is the chopping and cutting up of the feminine. Asper comments that 'the (negative) animus is extraordinarily creative in mounting new attacks' (ibid., p. 134). In *Fitcher's Bird*, only the youngest sister (the third attempt) is strong enough to destroy the wizard, who tricked the girls by preying on their innocence and gullibility. Outwitting such a predator involves harnessing one's own shadow levels of suspicion and vindictiveness. Asper says re-assembling the (mutilated) sisters is equivalent to handing back responsibility to the perpetrator and refusing to be scapegoated any longer (ibid., p. 135).

This is a bleak period in therapy when early abuse and the guilt of the perpetrators are recognised in all their horror. Alchemy offers the picture of a dismembered body, with neatly severed limbs, in the beautifully painted sequence of *Splendor Solis*, an early Renaissance alchemical manuscript, preserved in the British Library, and reproduced with a scholarly commentary by the San Francisco Jungian analysts Joseph Henderson and Dyane Sherwood (2003, p. 93). The 'murderer', a wild-looking man with a big sword, who bears an uncanny resemblance to the dead man, holds up the golden head which will be preserved until renewal is complete. The authors recount the dream of a man struggling to come to terms with the cruelty of his childhood experience, who dreamt he had to move corpses which are clogging up the town river, while the townsfolk pretend there is nothing wrong. He is helped by a strong 'father' figure, a vigorous new element of his personality with the potential for renewal. The bodies are buried in earth 'where their decomposition might provide food for new growth rather than contamination' (ibid., pp. 86–87).

Recognising shadow

The need for renewal is often represented in alchemy and fairytale by the figure of the old king (outworn persona) who has to die to make way for the prince (new adaptive behaviour). When a fairytale is 'Disneyfied' the messiness of the suffering and death required for transformation is minimised as if reality has to be sweetened to make it palatable, like the *Mary Poppins* song 'a spoonful of sugar makes the medicine go down' (Stevenson, 1964). Presenting children with a sanitised version of myths means they don't get properly scared so they can't use the story to confront their inner terrors and fears. In a nice twist, Princess Fiona in *Shrek* (op. cit.) has a guilty secret – she turns into an ogre at night. Unexpectedly, when the hero kisses her, she retains her ogre form and so they can marry.

In an older variant on this theme, an awkward wager commits Gawain, one of the Knights of the Round Table, to marrying an ugly hag, Lady Ragnall. In the bedroom, he discovers she's really a beautiful woman but magically compelled to conceal this in public. She asks him to choose where her beauty should be displayed. Gawain knows women long for sovereignty over their own lives so he hands the choice back to her: definitely the correct decision! While some women were venerated and put on a pedestal in medieval times, their power was also seen as seductive and dangerous. This led to much fear and loathing. Booker Prize-winning English author Hilary Mantel gives vivid descriptions of such gruesome punishments in her account of life at the court of Henry the Eighth in *Wolf Hall* (2009, p. 338) where witch-burnings and executions were still enjoyed as public spectacles. Not all of that prejudice has disappeared but we no longer take witch-burnings for granted.

Taking up the theme of the witch, Vermont-based Jungian analyst Polly Young-Eisendrath uses the story of *Lady Ragnall* to illustrate her work with couples in *Hags and Heroes* (1984). She quotes research on sex-role stereotyping which found women and feminine attributes were considered inferior and childlike while men and traditional masculine attributes, such as rationality, were considered superior and adult (ibid., pp. 25–26). She says this skewed set of values, accepted in our patriarchal culture for millennia, wounds us all in our relationships with the opposite gender: 'The tendency for women to denigrate themselves can be understood as social pressure to conform to a negative self-concept' (ibid., p. 26). And yet, experiences of denigration are so often part of a hero's journey.

Wandering in the Waste Land

For the Knight Parsifal, sleeping in his armour, alone and miserable in the forest, a new direction opens up when he hears his wife's voice in a dream. 'How did you find the Grail in the first place?' she asks. He replies: 'I let go the horse's reins.' Just dropping his ego-fixation on the goal enables him to find his next important teacher, the hermit Trevisant, cousin of the Grail King. Parsifal knows he has blundered so badly through ignorance and pride and blurts out his story. The hermit doesn't deny the gravity of Parsifal's mistakes but shows him a way forward, leading to reunion with his beloved wife and re-connection, through compassion and humility, with the Holy Grail. In Lindsay Clarke's powerful re-telling of the Grail Romance (2001) the women articulate the pointlessness of the knightly obsession with fighting and lament the futility of war. A pertinent alchemical image for this meeting of the masculine and feminine energies shows the lion swallowing the sun.

The proud ego, with its over-literal, rational attitude is submerged in the waters of the unconscious. Its daylight rationality is exposed to the mysterious moon-like qualities of feeling and intuition.

Figure 5.1 The green lion eats the sun
Source: CW 12, p. 232, fig. 169.

Opening to the sixth sense

The barren landscape of the Waste Land *nigredo* horribly reflects the experience of many when struggling with writer's block. In the alchemical teaching story, *The spirit in the bottle*, a lost boy finds a bottle under an oak tree. When he lets the spirit out, it threatens to kill him so he has to trick it back into captivity (see Chapters 13 and 14). Seamus Heaney, the Nobel prize-winning Irish poet, tells of his struggle to start writing again when the family had to move house to a more convenient place for schools and jobs. Shortly after moving, he dreamt:

> I opened the doorway to the attic and down the stairwell there came this immense flood of crystal clear water full of green roses, washing over me but not in any way panicking or threatening to drown me. A downpour that seemed to me to bode well.
>
> (Heaney & O'Driscoll, 2009, p. 231)

This attic was to be Heaney's new study. The previous house had been a bolt-hole, a place of stillness, where he could be open and empty, *open to the sixth sense*, as he calls it. Rather than pursuing a university teaching career, Heaney accepted work in a school because he knew this would bring in regular money while giving him the energy and space he needed for writing poetry. Remembering the earlier family house, he says:

> I was in absolutely the right place for writing. Every time I lifted the latch on the door into our little scullery, the sound and slack fall of it passed through me like gratitude. Or certitude. Theseus had his thread, I had my latch and it opened for me. Or rather, it opened *me*.
>
> (Ibid., p. 227)

The death of the heroic ideal: an emergent myth of our time

In 1913, during his own midlife crisis, Jung dreamt he had shot the great German hero, Siegfried, in company with an unknown brown-skinned man. With grief and remorse, he saw he had to sacrifice his own unconscious idealism, 'for there are higher things than the ego's will' (Jung, 1963, p. 174). He understood that psyche is transformed by its relationship to the contents of the unconscious. His years of disorientation (1913–1917) 'corresponded to the process of alchemical trans-formation' (ibid., p. 200).

With this dream, Jung realised the heroic myth of the conquest of nature which dominated Western cultures for centuries had outlived its usefulness. He didn't know about global warming or the accelerated rate of species extinctions but he intuited the industrialised nations' sense of mastery over nature (this includes the indigenous peoples of the earth) threatens the survival of the planet and all its life forms. The Santa Fe Jungian analyst Jerome Bernstein (2010, p. 16) sees us heading for 'species suicide' if we continue to deny the threat. His view is cautiously optimistic. He sees germs of an emergent myth in the film *Avatar* (Cameron, 2009). Here the greed and arrogance of a dominant race, aptly named the 'Sky People', threatens to destroy the exotic jungle-dwelling tribes of Pandora, a planet hiding a precious mineral, 'unobtanium' which the predators believe they have a right to seize. The hero betrays his own side in defence of ecological survival. Bernstein invites us to look at the film as a dream emerging from the collective unconscious.

> For all its shortcomings, *Avatar* portrays an emergent 21st century myth reflecting a shift in the nature of consciousness . . . from a dissociated ego cleft from Nature in the Garden of Eden, to one based on communion with all of life.
>
> (Bernstein, 2012, p. 1)

Susan Rowland (2012, pp. 132–150) also observes a new attitude emerging from the collective imagination through the portals of children's literature. In *The Secret Garden* (Hodgson Burnett, 1993), healing comes to crippled Peter and pasty-faced Mary through their work in reviving the old garden behind the wall. Colonial attitudes are dying (Mary is the sole survivor of her Anglo-Indian family's death by cholera). The psychopomp, or initiator of change, is the shaman-like figure of the local boy Dickon who combines a Pan-like energy with a sturdy Yorkshire homeliness. Turning her attention to *The Lion, the Witch and the Wardrobe* (Lewis, 1969), Rowland suggests both books celebrate a new kind of relationship with nature, where humans co-operate, rather than seeing it as a place to colonise or an obstacle to be overcome. In Narnia, mastery *over* nature is replaced with rulership *within* nature. There are obvious analogies with the Christian story, yet Aslan is different. He is wild and he is playful. The overlay of guilt and shame which has come down to us from our religious past is not included in Narnia's mystical vocabulary.

Conclusion

The spirit of the fountain never dies.
It is called the mysterious feminine.
The entrance to the mysterious feminine
Is the root of all heaven and earth.
Frail, frail it is, hardly existing.
But touch it; it will never run dry.

(Lao Tzu, verse 7 in Whitmont, 1983, p. 148)

'How does psychology translate the wildness of soul without taming it or breaking its spirit?' asks Romanyshyn (2007, pp. 309–310) in his discussion of 'how to square the language of explanation with the dream-energised language of being'. I have shown how some of the archetypal themes which underpin our lives are represented in fairytales and alchemy. They emphasise what is missing in our current cultural consciousness and suggest how a harmonious balance could be restored. They also present us with graphic metaphors for the power of the inner persecutor; for the experience of pain and loss; and the loneliness that comes from pursuing a path that seems at odds with the generality. These stories can be used creatively in the therapeutic setting and the individual's search for meaning. Or they can be made over, bowdlerised or 'Disneyfied' to make material gold.

Respect for the numinous value of a balanced relationship between the archetypes of sun and moon, king and queen, masculine and feminine, and human with nature, comes down to us in echoes of what was once held in reverence by our ancestors. In *The Jungle Book*, Mowgli makes a hero's journey from a wolf boy to a young man who can re-join human society. In *Cinderella*, the mystical theme of the soul's transformation is traced through the Wisdom literature going back to antiquity. This tradition has been cherished and passed down, often under the threat of persecution, and woven into the products of our modern imagination via the agency of traditional fairytales, children's literature, films, TV and video games.

This is a recognition that universal themes continue to affect our behaviour and cause tension in our lives when values are skewed in a one-sided way. In his collection of dreams addressing the crisis of nuclear and then ecological disaster, San Francisco author Michael Ortiz Hill (1994, p. 130) demonstrates the fertility of the human imagination as it attempts to make meaning of apocalypse. One dreamer sees herself as a survivor from a nuclear blast. She binds up the feet of the little children who are so hurt and wounded and carries them to a greener, safer place. She tells them stories, always stories, to prepare them for the future. She knows she is dying and must give them vital tools to begin the world anew.

Story-telling will continue until the end of time. It comes from the eternal fountain of the imagination: 'touch it, it will never run dry' (Lao Tzu, in Whitmont, 1983, p. 148). Psyche continually makes meaning out of disaster, preparing to begin again. With his lectures on the transformation of myth through time, Joseph Campbell showed how the human imagination endlessly renews itself, responding to change in ever new and inventive ways. The enduring attraction of stories reflects their importance to the human experience. Bettelheim (1975, p. 45) says: 'the answers given by myths are indefinite, for the fairytale is suggestive; their messages may imply solutions, but they never spell them out.' And so the storytelling continues, for psyche makes meaning of our lives through the medium of imagination.

Acknowledgements

This chapter is dedicated to friends, family, colleagues and students who helped me through numerous conversations to formulate and clarify my thinking. Special thanks to my family for their loyalty and support and to the clients who have been my companions in the search for understanding and healing. Where I have mentioned clinical material, identities are disguised. Thanks also to the mentors who set me on my path and to the students and teaching teams at AJA, Re.Vision, in Sweden and the Ukraine, who continue to engage with me in psyche's creative dance.

References

Adamson, A. (2001) *Shrek* Hollywood: Dream Works.

Baring, A. & Cashford, J. (1991) *The Myth of the Goddess* London: Viking.

Barnz, D. & Flinn, R. (2011) *Beastly* New York: CBS and Stovefront films.

Bernstein, J.S. (2010) *Borderland Consciousness* Guild of Pastoral Psychology, Harrow: Abacus Print.

—— (2012) *Borderland Consciousness* London: CAP/AJA/GPP lecture flier.

Bettelheim, B. (1982) *The Uses of Enchantment* London: Penguin.

Cameron, J. (2009) *Avatar* Hollywood: 20th Century Fox.

Campbell, J. (1949) *The Hero with a Thousand Faces* Princeton, NJ: Princeton University Press.

Clarke, L. (2001) *Parzival and the Stone from Heaven* London: Harper Collins.

Cocteau, J. (1946) *La belle at le bête* Paris: Discina Co.

De Beaumont, J-M.L (1756) *La belle at la bête* (in Warner, M. (1995) *The Beast and the Blonde* London: Vintage, p. 292).

Eliot, T.S. (1974) *Collected Poems 1909–1962* London: Faber.

Fogelman, D., Grimm, J. & Grimm, W. (2010) *Tangled* Hollywood: Walt Disney.

Geronimi, C., Jackson, W. & Luske, H. (1950) *Cinderella* Hollywood: Walt Disney.

Geronimi, C., Luske, H. & Reitherman, W. (1961) *101 Dalmatians* Hollywood: Walt Disney.

Geronimi, C., Clark, L., Larson, E. & Reitherman, W. (1959) *Sleeping Beauty* Hollywood: Walt Disney.

Grimm Brothers (1984) *The Complete Illustrated Stories* London: Chancellor Press.

Hand, D. (1937) *Snow White* Hollywood: Walt Disney.

Heaney, S. & O'Driscoll, D. (eds) (2009) *Stepping Stones* London: Faber.

Henderson, J.L. & Sherwood, D.N. (2003) *Transformation of the Psyche* Hove: Brunner-Routledge.

Hillman, J. (1997) *The Soul's Code* New York: Bantam Books.

Hodgson Burnett, F. (1993) *The Secret Garden* London: Wordsworth Editions.

Jung, C.G. (1953–1977) except where indicated, references are by volume and paragraph number to the *Collected Works of C.G. Jung*, 20 vol. (eds Herbert Read, Michael Fordham and Gerhard Adler; trans. R.F.C. Hull). London and Princeton, NJ: Routledge and Princeton University Press.

—— (1963) *Memories, Dreams, Reflections* London: Collins and Routledge & Kegan Paul.

Kalsched, D. (1996) *The Inner World of Trauma* London: Routledge.

Kipling, R. (1894) *The Jungle Book* London: Macmillan.

Lao Tzu (1962) (trans. John C.H. Wu) *Tao te Ching* New York: St John's University Press.

Lewis, C.S. (1969) *The Lion, the Witch and the Wardrobe* London: Penguin.

Lucas, G. (1977) *Star Wars* Hollywood: Lucas film, 20th Century Fox.

Mantel, H. (2009) *Wolf Hall* London: Harper Collins.

Mathers, D. (2001) *An Introduction to Meaning and Purpose in Analytical Psychology* Hove: Brunner-Routledge.

Ortiz Hill, M. (1994) *Dreaming the End of the World* Dallas: Spring Publications.

Pinkola Estés, C. (1992) *Women Who Run With the Wolves* London: Rider.

Reitherman, W. (1967) *The Jungle Book* Hollywood: Walt Disney.

Romanyshyn, R. (2007) *The Wounded Researcher* New Orleans: Spring Journal Books.

Rowland, S. (2012) *The Eco-critical Psyche* New York: Routledge.

Segal, J. (1979) *Klein* Glasgow: Collins Fontana.

Shamdasani, S. (ed.) (2009) *The Red Book* New York: W.W. Norton.

Sharpstein, B. & Luske, H. (1940) *Pinocchio* Hollywood: Walt Disney.

Sonnenfeld, B. (1997) *Men in Black* Hollywood: Columbia Pictures.

Speilberg, S. (1982) *E.T.* Hollywood: Universal Pictures.

Stein, M. (ed.) with Corbett, L. (1991) *Psyche's Stories* Wilmette, IL: Chiron Publications.

Stevenson, R. (1964) *Mary Poppins* Hollywood: Walt Disney.

Trousdale, G. & Wise, K. (1991) *Beauty and the Beast* Hollywood: Walt Disney.

Vogler, C. (2007) *The Writers Journey* Studio City, CA: Michael Wiese Productions.

von Franz, M.-L. (1970) *Apuleius' Golden Ass* Zurich: Spring Publications.

—— (1976) *The Feminine in Fairytales* New York: Spring Publications.

Warner, M. (1995) *The Beast and the Blonde* London: Vintage.

—— (2012) *Grimm Thoughts* London BBC Radio 4.

Whitmont, E.C. (1983) *Return of the Goddess* London: Routledge & Kegan Paul.

Yalom, Irvin D. (2008) *Staring at the Sun* London: Penguin.

Young-Eisendrath, P. (1984) *Hags and Heroes* Toronto: Inner City Books.

6

A POINT IN TIME

The Horoscope as a Living Mandala

Karin Syrett

> As we all know, science began with the stars, and mankind dis-
> covered in them the dominants of the unconscious, the 'gods', as
> well as the curious psychological qualities of the 'zodiac'; a
> complete projected theory of human character. Astrology is a
> primordial experience similar to Alchemy.
>
> (CW 12, para. 346)

Introduction

In the twenty-first century, the great ancient arts of alchemy and astrology have
been relegated to fruitless attempts to turn lead into gold, with cheap sun sign
columns in magazines and newspapers. Alchemy and astrology tend to be regarded
as 'non scientific' and therefore not valid as they contradict the dominant cultural
discourse of scientific materialism. In the same way, it may appear that the efficacy
of analysis and psychotherapy are difficult to objectively judge. Certainly attempts
to scientifically measure are challenged when experiences are so subjective.

Jung, with his search for wholeness, teleological forward thinking and quest for
individuation was fascinated by both alchemy and astrology. He believed the
search for meaning is one of the human psyche's deepest and most urgent needs,
and saw correlations between the therapeutic process, the alchemists' attempts to
turn base metal into a pure substance and the birth-chart as a map of the psyche.
He recognised the horoscope as providing a way to penetrate the persona, the face
we present to others or to ourselves. The horoscope reflects all of this, contains all
parts of human experience and behaviour, and as such is a mandala, the symbol of
wholeness.

The horoscope, very much a living mandala, is made up of a circle representing
eternity containing the cross of matter. The visual image of the horoscope shows
the quaternity of elements (fire, earth, air and water), the four seasons (spring,
summer, autumn and winter) and the four directions (east, west, north and south).
It is a symbolic map of the position of the planets in the heavens at the time of

birth. For astrologers it represents the picture of an individual's potential psychological and spiritual make-up. It 'lives' because the picture changes from the static positions of the planets at birth into different patterns made by their transits and progressions over a lifetime, discussed in greater detail later in the chapter. Jung used to draw up some of his patients' birth charts in an attempt to further his understanding of their personalities, 'Since an astrological constellation makes diagnosis possible, it also indicates the therapy' (CW 15, para. 29).

Astrological and mythological symbolism

I attempt to show ways in which the symbolism of the ancient arts of alchemy and astrology can be used as a model of thinking in the analyst's consulting room. Think of astrology as seeing, alchemy as doing and analysis as understanding. While many people know what their 'sun signs' are (Aries, Taurus and so on), they may not necessarily understand that what this actually means is that the sun was passing through a particular sign of zodiac at the time of their birth.

In order to 'cast a horoscope', the time, date and place of an individual's birth is used to create a picture of the heavens capturing the positions of the planets at that moment. The ten planets (Sun, Moon, Mercury, Venus, Mars, Jupiter, Saturn, Uranus, Neptune and Pluto) are in constant motion through the zodiacal constellations making symbolic patterns with each other called aspects. Astrologers decipher these planetary placements to give information about an individual's psyche: their potential strengths and weakness. Certain characteristics and particular archetypal images can be interpreted by looking at the natal horoscope. The planets themselves symbolise archetypes, and indeed are named after the gods and goddesses of Greek mythology. Myths, which can be thought of as an early form of psychology, explain mysteries, ranging from why the seasons change, to why humans are a complicated mixture of animal and divine.

One version of a Greek myth about Prometheus charmingly reveals the reason behind humankind's complex and contradictory nature. Prometheus the Titan created all animals and human creatures out of red earth and his own tears. He loved mankind and angered Zeus by stealing divine fire to give his little men an advantage over the animals. Once a gift has been given it cannot be changed, so Zeus resolved to punish man and make mankind's existence a misery by creating woman. He ordered Hephaestus, god of the forge, to create a woman in the likeness of the beautiful goddesses. He then instructed all the Olympians to give her something of their nature: Ares, god of war, gave her a wicked temper, while Demeter, the earth mother, gave her a womb. Aphrodite gave her sensuality and vanity; Artemis gave her modesty; Athene gave her wisdom; Hermes gave her cunning and curiosity while Zeus breathed life into her. This beautiful but contradictory creature called Pandora was sent to earth to marry Prometheus' brother, Epimetheus. She brought with her a chest which she was warned not to open but of course because she was curious she disobeyed the warning and all the spites that trouble man to this day escaped: old age, illness, madness and pain, infecting mankind forever. Only hope remained behind without which mankind would probably not have survived (Garfield & Blishen, 1970, pp. 77–79).

This myth explains symbolically how man acquired his conflicting and contradictory nature: rage, love, kindness, cunning and curiosity are all qualities acquired from the divine which, through Pandora's children, mingled and mixed with the earthy nature of the men made from clay. Astrologically, the seven heavenly bodies, named after Roman gods and goddess, were thought to embody their characteristics, as they describe different aspects of human nature: the Sun represents the heart of the individual, the Moon reflects the soul, Mercury/Hermes the mind, Venus/Aphrodite the capacity for attraction and love, Mars/Ares the desire and passion, Jupiter/Zeus stands for expansion and generosity of spirit, while Saturn/Cronus shows the place of fear, of limitation and inhibition. The more distant planets, Uranus, Neptune and Pluto, indicate shifts in the wider world. Their relationship to the personal planets also influences how much an individual relates to the collective currents. Uranus is the planet of radical change, rebellion, liberation and independence. Its discovery in 1781 coincided with first the American and later the French revolution. Neptune's discovery in 1846 coincided with a rise in spiritualism and the discovery of anaesthetics and hypnotism. Pluto is linked with the underworld of death and rebirth. Its discovery in 1930 coincided with the rise of fascism in Europe which led to the Second World War. The three outer planets move very slowly so their synchronistic effect on the collective lasts many years. 'For astrology is the last remnant, now applied to the stars, of that fateful assemblage of gods, whose luminosity can still be felt despite the critical procedures of our scientific age' (CW 18, para. 1182).

In a horoscope, the positions of the planets in zodiac signs, and the patterns between them at the time of birth, create a map of the inner world of the individual born under that particular influence. Many modern astrologers, for example, Liz Greene, Melanie Reinhart, Robert Hand and the late Howard Sasportas, concentrated on interpreting the horoscope from a psychological and spiritual perspective, one facilitating the discovery of meaning.

Liz Greene, an astrologer and a Jungian analyst, studied the ways Jung's psychological typology and astrology compliment one another, and how Jung's four functions of consciousness connect with the four elements in astrology: intuition–fire, sensation–earth, feeling–water, thinking–air. She writes:

> the apparently extraordinary fact that people do tend to fall into certain groupings of temperament has long been a preoccupation of medicine, philosophy, and the arts. Before that, it was the preoccupation of astrology, which offers what is perhaps our earliest description of typology. Jung's four function types fit hand-in-glove with astrology's ancient division of the four elements. It is not a case of one being explained away by, or derived from, the other; rather, each is a distinct way of describing the empiric observation of the same phenomenon.
>
> (Greene, 1977, p. 53)

The horoscope can reveal unconscious complexes and typology, helping the analyst gain insight into the inner world of the analysand. Subtle issues can be identified which might not otherwise have come to light. The analyst does not need to be explicit about using the chart or making direct interpretations from it, but knowledge of it, and knowledge about symbolic thinking, can be very useful. The 'objective reality' of astrology matters far less than its ability to increase understanding of 'subjective reality' and to develop a capacity for symbol formation. The point is, whatever scientific materialism might say, astrology really does improve our ability to form and use symbols – which is why I use it.

The birth chart does not make a person; what matters is what the person makes of their birth chart over their lifetime. Engaging consciously with one's horoscope can offer more of an opportunity to become the person one is meant to be – a psychic integration with the cosmic energies, which Jung calls 'individuation', thus achieving higher levels of awareness. 'Astrology led the conscious mind back again and again to the knowledge of Heimarmene, that is, the dependence of character and destiny on certain moments in time' (CW 12, para. 392).

Heimarmene is the goddess who personifies fate and destiny in Greek mythology. She presides over the orderly succession of cause and effect, or rather, the fate of the universe as a whole, not the destiny of an individual. One could say destiny leads the willing while fate drags the unwilling who wish to stay unconscious.

Transits and progressions in astrology

The life force is teleological – a term Jung used to mean the ultimate purpose of the psyche is to lead to a meaningful life. While the natal horoscope can hint towards the process of individuation, transits and progressions of the planets indicate the possible timing of growth through external events or internal pressures. The natal chart reveals the position of planets at the time of birth but of course the planets continue to move. New positions form aspects to the natal planets offering opportunities for growth and change. This transformation does not just happen once, but is continuous. Transits and progressions indicate trends rather than events; if there are connections to the birth chart, these indicate certain qualities are ready to be integrated symbolically. Sometimes these trends can be experienced in projection onto outer events and relationships: they are enacted. In ancient times, and for more concrete astrologers, transits became a predictive tool. 'The psychological rule says that when an inner situation is not made conscious, it happens outside as fate' (CW 9, para. 126).

Transits can be seen as measuring dynamic time. Dale Mathers says 'ego (chronos) time is linear, serial, particular, and *now*: something happens out there, something happens in here. Self (kairos) time is cyclical, parallel, wave and *eternal*' (2001, p. 143). The planet Saturn is associated to chronological time, giving a feeling of time as limited, showing the boundaries of ageing and pushing the individual towards maturity, often through a crisis. When an astrologer has referred people to me, most of the time Saturn was active in their birth chart synchronistically (see clinical examples below). Progressions are another type of calculation indicating change, and are seen in the developmental, internal growth patterns, depending on which planet is activated.

Transits and progressions can give a sense of order in the face of chaos. We ask ourselves: 'Why now? What do we have to learn from it? What is the meaning?' Looking at a horoscope, the astrologer can interpret the movements of the planets through the natal chart as opportunities to integrate neglected aspects of the personality, at the time when an individual is ready. Transits and progressions are only probabilities and do not predict the future, but do allow educated or intuitive guesses. Looking is not the same as seeing; the person has to find meaning for him- or herself in the information. Here is an example of the way transits and synchronicity work together.

Harry, a single man aged 28, came to see me while under a particularly significant Saturn transit. In mythology Saturn/Cronus devoured his children at birth, as he feared being overthrown by them. Saturn in astrology represents restriction and inhibition, and opposes growth. His seven-year cycle gives an opportunity for change from unaware to aware. Harry had an unacknowledged drinking problem and developed a way of constantly moving town and city to try to escape from his self. One house move brought him to a flat above an Alcoholics Anonymous centre but as soon as he realised he quickly moved out. He did not want to meet all those 'drunks' and continued to deny his own alcoholism. It took seven years, the time it takes Saturn to make its quarter cycle, before he was ready to accept his problem and join Alcoholics Anonymous. When reflecting on his geographical moves in his analysis, he admitted that previously he'd had an inkling of its meaning but was not then ready to listen to the message from his unconscious.

Saturn's possible effect is to teach life's great lessons. He is described by Liz Greene as the 'bringer of light in darkness'. She says 'human beings do not earn free will except through self-discovery, and they do not attempt self-discovery until things become so painful that they have no choice' (1976, p. 11). The shadow brings substance. There is no light without a shadow. The brighter the light the darker the shadow, and as we have seen in many leading figures, misuse of power undoes us. James Hillman takes Plato's concept of soul as fate or destiny. 'The soul of each of us is given a unique daimon before we are born, and it has selected an image or pattern that we live on earth' (1997, p. 8).

Synchronicity

Synchronicity plays a major part in astrology. Taken from his memorial address in 1930, Jung says, 'In so far as there are any really correct astrological diagnoses, they are not due to the effects of the constellations but to our hypothetical time qualities.' We perceive time passing as sequential or in a continual line while astrology shows time passing in a cyclical planetary motion. Synchronicities are chance occurrences or coincidences that are not connected, but have a great subjective impact on the individual. Events become meaningful and often change our perception so a new attitude can appear. Its numinosity bypasses the rational mind and connects to archetypal experiences.

In '*Synchronicity: an Acausal Connecting Principle*' (CW 8), Jung conducted an experiment to see what kinds of astrological configurations married people had, by comparing their horoscopes. He found there were a significant number of Sun/Moon, Sun/Sun, Moon/Moon, ascendant/descendant connections either in conjunction, opposition or other close aspects in their birth charts. His astrological research on marriage partners was not validated quantitatively and has been criticised for being too subjective. His experiment could be seen as qualitative. There was a meaningful attraction, neither good nor bad, with an opportunity to integrate projective shadow aspects and/or bring out the best potentials of the individual. In his essay 'Marriage as a Psychological Relationship' Jung explains these attractions in depth (CW 8, para. 872 ff.). I noticed when comparing Jung's chart to his wife Emma's, her Moon in Leo is in the same sign as his Sun, suggesting she reflected his need to be special and shine in the world.

I wondered if Jung saw the deep connection he had with Freud astrologically, as Jung's Moon in Taurus is conjunct Freud's Sun in Taurus, suggesting he could relate to Freud's nature instinctively. Their close meaningful relationship changed the way the world viewed depth psychology; both were transformed by their connection. Freud has a strong Taurus/Scorpio theme in his chart, which seems to aptly reflect his theories of oral gratification (Taurus–earth–sensation) and Oedipal complexes and fixations (Scorpio–water–feeling). Jung, on the other hand, has five planets in Leo (fire–intuition), with Aquarius rising (air–thinking) and terms like *individuation*, the *collective unconscious* and even *archetype* seem to reflect this configuration. Although their relationship was transformational it was also fraught with tension. This is seen in the number of squares – the aspect of tension – between the fixed earth and water signs in Freud's chart and the fixed fire and air signs in Jung's chart.

It is interesting to note the transits at the time Freud and Jung split. In February 1912, Uranus began to transit Aquarius opposing Jung's planets in Leo while squaring Freud's planets in Taurus. That same year Saturn transited Freud's planets in Taurus while squaring Jung's planets in Leo. Saturn represents tradition and structure while Uranus represents sudden, unpredictable changes of direction. In myth, the sky god Ouranus pushed his children, including Cronos/Saturn, into Tartarus because they displeased him. Eventually Cronos rebelled and castrated his father, and started a new Golden Age, just as Jung split from Freud, resulting in a new order.

The horoscope forms a mandala divided into segments. Each represents different life experiences symbolically, and shows the planets within the circle of eternity. In Jung's case, his Sun in Leo gives him the charisma to influence others, and attract admiration. Leo is the sign of the lion, which leads his pride of females, a role Jung played as many women fell for both his charm and intellect. He could be authoritarian and stubborn, a characteristic of the fixed fire sign Leo, especially

Sigmund Freud

Natal Chart
Tuesday, May 6, 1856
6:30:00 PM CZOT
Príbor, Czech Republic
Tropical Placidus True Node

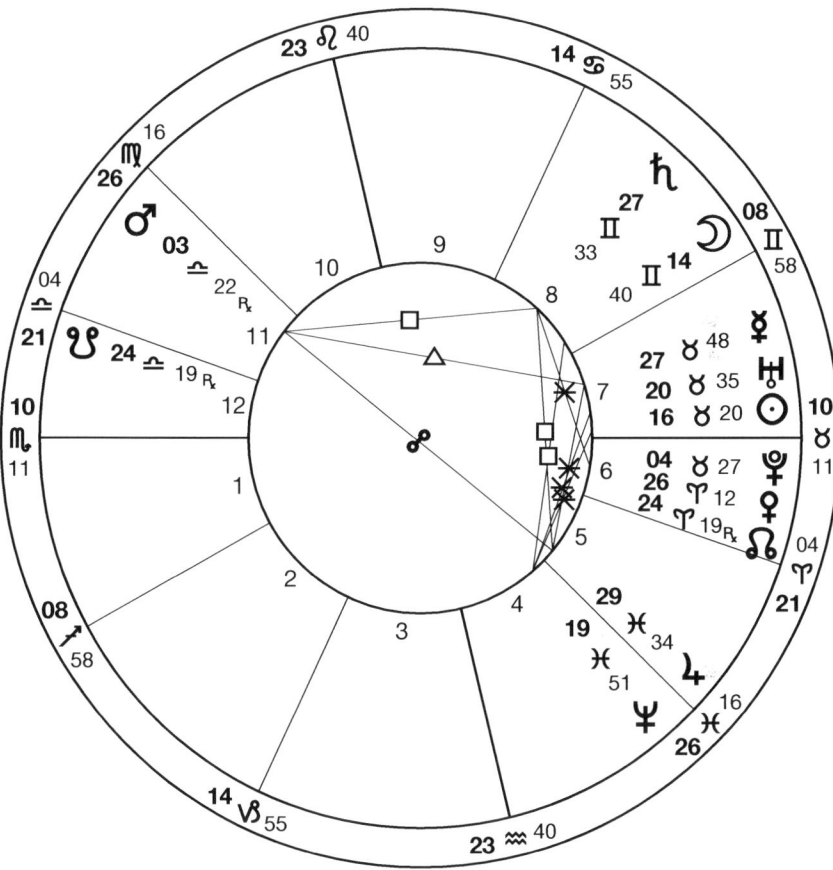

Figure 6.1 Freud's birth chart

Source: Karin Syrett

when his talents were not recognised, as in his split with Freud. Jung's need to understand and explore the unconscious arose from dreams and spiritual experiences which he experienced from early life onwards. An astrologer would see this tendency in his chart by looking at the aspects: Neptune square Sun, and Sun/Pluto conjunct Moon, all planets with underworld connections. Jung's ascendant in Aquarius, the sign of mankind, made him want to share his discoveries with

103

Carl Jung

Natal Chart
Monday, July 26, 1875
7:32:00 PM SZOT
Kesswil, Switzerland
Tropical Placidus True Node

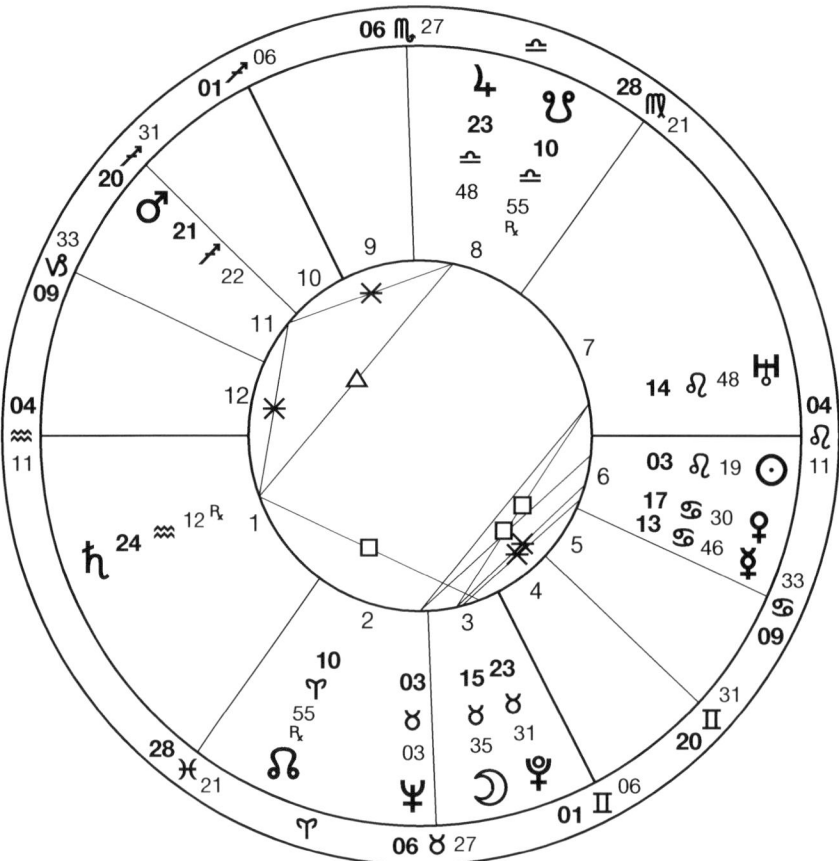

Figure 6.2 Jung's birth chart

Source: Karin Syrett

the rest of humanity. Saturn's position in Aquarius shows his scientific side, through which he explored subjects methodically. His love for travel is represented by the planet Mars in Sagittarius. This placement is thought of as indicating a passionate philosopher seeking to find the truth.

Jung was a complex person who wanted to understand his multi-faceted nature and find healing within himself. The publication of *The Red Book Liber Novus* (2009) showed how he struggled with his unconscious through a dialogue using active imagination and art. One of his first mandalas was an image he drew of his horoscope, which appears in the 'Black Book' (1916) 'Systema Munditotius' and referred to in *Liber Novus* (2009, p. 363).

Alchemical symbolism

The alchemical process required action to achieve transformation. Combining opposites by heating, dissolving, mixing and separating resulted in all the substances being changed. Spiritual alchemy works by experimenting with new ways to think and feel, bringing feelings to consciousness so they can be re-evaluated and integrated at a higher level: refining base emotions into spiritual gold. The natal chart is an inherent pattern activated through transits and progressions. In synchronicities, life experiences act like mirror images between inner and outer. This is known as the unity of the *unus mundus*, meaning 'one world'. Jung used the term in relation to archetypes and synchronicity, suggesting 'meaningful coincidence' was made possible because the observer and connected event ultimately stem from the same source. Alchemists' theories of the *unus mundus* suggested 'what is above is like what is below, to perpetrate the miracles of one thing', taken from the Emerald Tablet of Hermes Trismegistus. Alchemists saw the earth as microcosms (below), which reflected macrocosms (above), the realms of the gods. The study of alchemy can promote a relationship between the 'higher' and 'lower' parts of ourselves: bringing about regeneration and an integration of body, soul, mind and spirit in a holistic personality as we increase our functional ability with symbols.

Alchemy and analysis offer tools for self-transformation throughout life. Both arts believe the human soul tries to incarnate into matter, and matter can incorporate soul. Analysis can speed up the process of development. I find individuals tend to seek analysis when they suffer from what could be called divine discontent, common during a midlife crisis. Astrology can indicate what may need to be worked on, either spiritually or creatively.

Renaissance alchemists, including Marcilio Ficino, Solomon Trismosin and Paracelsus were also astrologers. They perceived the law of nature through observation of the stars and believed that it was the alchemist's role to help speed nature up to enable her to reach her potential more rapidly. Paracelsus said: 'What nature is slow to perfect, the alchemist can help her to perfect' (Dooling, 1978). Alchemists used astrology to ascertain the best time to initiate the 'Great Work'. Likewise, it is advisable for an analyst to wait for the right time to give an interpretation. I have sometimes found an interpretation did not mean anything to the analysand at the time it was given yet six months later the insight re-emerged, seemingly spontaneously, from them. Some astrologers might say this can occur during a retrograde period of a planet – when the movement of the planet as seen from the earth appears to go backwards and then progress forward. We may need to repeat the 'circumulatio', the going round and round, perhaps even in a spiral, to be sure we have fully understood its meaning.

An understanding of alchemy and depth psychology can help us not to act out or repress complexes, but to endure and understand them. This resembles the heating process in alchemy in which the alchemists cook the substance and sometimes become cooked themselves in return, over and over until the shadow is purified, and from the blackening something new starts to emerge. Transpersonal psychologist Barbara Somers (2004, pp. 35–36) explains that the stages of *solutio/*water; coagulate/earth and sublimation/air overlap in the process of transmutation. The opus, or work, consists of three parts: insight, endurance and action. Moral integrity is the main ingredient furthering this process. In my clinical example, Harry initially lacked sufficient moral integrity to confront his alcoholism, even though he was living above Alcoholics Anonymous meeting rooms. Through a lengthy process of analysis he eventually achieved enough personal insight and integrity to acknowledge his initial refusal to accept the message his unconscious offered. He could atone with his self.

Another example is Helga: a middle-aged, attractive, single woman, working in a high-powered job in the city, who wanted to marry and have a child but never seemed to attract the right partner. When found at a scheduled check-up to have deposits of micro-calcification in her breast duct she saw literally how her nurturing side was blocked. This discovery coincided with major transits in the health areas of her birth chart; Saturn was then in a difficult connection to Pluto. Synchronistically, she brought me an article from an astrological website which said she needed to watch her health. This was a time to take a look at herself, rather than ignore meaning. Her physical experience mirrored her psychic state; her illness became a symbol.

Shared symbolism in astrology and alchemy

In her book *Relating*, Liz Greene refers to Renaissance philosophy that posited four basic temperaments based on the theory of the 'humours': melancholic (earthy), phlegmatic (watery), sanguine (airy) and choleric (fiery). The poet and priest George Herbert, in one of his lighter moods, wrote in 1640: 'The Choleric drinks, the Melancholic eats, the Phlegmatic sleeps. What the Sanguine does is left to the imagination, but as he is "ethereal" or airy, we may assume that he probably philosophises' (Greene, 1977, p. 52). It is interesting to see the shared symbolism and imagery between alchemy and astrology. Some alchemical stages correspond to astrological elements, the four humours and Jung's psychological types:

Alchemy/Element/Type/Humour

- Calcinatio/Fire/Intuition/Choleric
- Solutio/Water/Feeling/Phlegmatic
- Coagulatio/Earth/Sensation/Melancholic
- Sublimatio/Air/Thinking/Sanguine

Mythology/Astrology/Metal

- Apollo/Sun/Gold
- Luna/Moon/Silver
- Hermes/Mercury/Mercury
- Aphrodite/Venus/Copper
- Ares/Mars/Iron
- Zeus/Jupiter/Tin
- Cronus/Saturn/Lead

167. A royal art conjured up in the darkness of closed eyelids and governed by nature's earth-returning, or regressive, instincts.

Figure 6.3 Artis auriferum

Source: Fabricius (1994), p. 199, fig. 167. Foto Deutsches Museum

The alchemical plate (Figure 6.3) shows the combination of the zodiac, the planetary gods, the alchemical stages and the four elements, which are all necessary to the Great Work.

Analysis as understanding

Analysis requires understanding, as it is a process that can give meaning to life. The three arts complement each other in the search for self-knowledge, but looking at or studying astrology and alchemy is not the same as seeing their meaning symbolically. Analysis is about developing our capacity to symbolise. Like an alchemist, an analyst has to be very patient as most of the material their analysands bring is repetitive. Jung calls this the 'perambulation about the Self' (CW 12, para. 170.) This is necessary to refine the base material, at which point the nigredo may be reached. If the alchemy and the analysis can weather the storm of the nigredo, the stage of transformation can be achieved. The Jungian analyst Michael Fordham's concept of the primal self is much like the undifferentiated self as the *prima materia*. He says:

> Jung's material shows many features of infantile states and his interpretation of the quaternio as representing the *prima materia* in which elements of the self are not integrated is one of them: it represents deintegration of the self resulting in identity of subject and object such as we find in infancy as well as in alchemy. It is the splitting processes on which Jung lays emphasis and shows that they lead on to states of integration. My own experience of full analysis depends on reaching, through representations, the initial state of wholeness – the primary self – from which maturation can proceed.
>
> (Henderson & Sherwood, 2003, p. 144)

This process is worked in the analysis through transference and counter transference. Regressive and progressive cycles are part of the self-regulating psyche as the fragmented parts of the self strive to be integrated. The undivided whole first needs to be divided then reconnected to the whole with conscious understanding. The symbolic concept in alchemy is of the first undifferentiated *coniunctio*, which separates to be followed by second *coniunctio* of Sol and Luna, the mystical marriage of male and female (see Chapter 2). This process is seen as the repetition of purification, where one goes through many cycles of transformation to achieve individuation. Life cycles are natural occurrences of loss and gain, making space for something new, as reflected in nature through the season changes. Astrology can indicate the timing of these cyclic movements through transits and progression.

Case history of a dream analysis

I will show how some of the symbolic language shared between the ancient arts of astrology and alchemy applied in the consulting room. In my clinical work I prefer to use the term 'analysand' instead of 'patient', because the term 'patient' implies for me a medical model suggesting illness, rather than a person suffering from a 'Meaning Disorder' (Mathers, 2001, pp. 6–7). The analyst's consulting room can be likened to the alchemist's *vas* or *alembic*, a sealed container or *temenos* – in Greek, this means a sacred place around a temple. In this safe place analysands may explore their dreams, nightmares, thoughts and feelings, however horrifying. Dream images often correspond to alchemical images, as follows:

Connie, an attractive, young-looking-old dancer in her thirties was in an unhappy marriage. An astrologer referred her. She had never had any psychotherapy, initially had little insight and was surprised the astrologer was able, from her horoscope, to identify a childhood pattern of feeling unloved and abandoned by her mother, a theme repeated in her marriage. She symbolically married her mother as her husband shared the same birthday (not year) and was seen as having many of her mother's negative traits of indifference and selfishness.

Her midlife crisis was reflected in her birth chart by Saturn's transits, as well as a difficult Pluto and Sun connection. Pluto is the planet of death and evolution. When something has outlived its usefulness and it is time for it to die, Pluto transits can alert us to this. Combined with her natal Sun, Pluto in Connie's chart seemed to be saying it was the right time for her to pay attention to her inner self, and give up trying to please her husband/mother in order to keep their love. She craved the care and affection she never had from her mother; her childhood was filled with rejection, repeated in her failing marriage.

'The greater the area of unconsciousness, the less is marriage a matter of free choice, as is shown subjectively in the fatal compulsion one feels so acutely when in love' (CW 17, para. 327). If someone lives too much from one part of the self, then the unconscious constellates the opposite. Jung calls this 'enantiotromia' (running round in a circle). It seemed to Connie she was too introverted and her husband too extroverted. His emphasis was on thinking, hers on feeling. What attracted at first repelled later; a new balance needed to be found.

Connie and her husband seemed unable to integrate this opposition. Her husband's Sun opposed her Sun, as did her mother's. His Moon was in the same sign as her Sun, which could have been positively reflected. However, he projected this 'lunar' emotional quality into her, as he perceived emotionality as weakness and vulnerability. The alchemical/astrological ingredients could have been ripe for transformation. I found myself asking what was her husband living out for her and she for him? While the pull of opposites could have been an opportunity to strive for integration on both sides, her husband refused to acknowledge any of his problems, and demanded she change to please him. 'For two personalities to meet is like mixing two chemical substances, if there is any combination at all, both are transformed' (CW 16, para. 163).

In alchemy, the first conjunction is an undifferentiated internal Sol and Luna psychic component while the second conjunction is where Sol and Luna unite in a chymical marriage of spirit and soul, uniting male and female aspects in the psychic *heiros gamos* (sacred marriage). Connie and her husband were unable to achieve this, so they split up. This collision of different temperaments was a catalyst leading to Connie's journey of self-examination. Her astrologer had penetrated the surface of her persona and view of herself as always being a victim. Seeing herself as 'unfortunate' prevented her from developing her innate potential. In fact, rather than being weak and ineffectual, she was actually a creative, intelligent individual in search of meaning and fulfilment.

Initially, in spite of the difficulties, Connie did not want to give up hope that her marriage might be resurrected until she brought a dream that a building was on fire with her husband inside. She awoke most upset. Next day when she drove past the Registry Office where they married, she saw fire engines putting out a fire there. She was astonished but immediately saw the message, and told me she could no longer ignore the dream's meaning. While dream and event had no relationship to each other, there was, as Jung describes, 'an a-causal connecting principle'. Its intense emotional effect on Connie finally changed her perceptions. She started to believe she could let go of her marriage and using the motif of fire, both in her dream and reality, she could work on her inner rage and anger.

Connie started to make real progress; she took back projections and began to acknowledge her own part in the marital interaction. In analysis she became argumentative, especially as we started to work on her passive-aggressive controlling side. Although she denied her shadowy behaviour at first, eventually she was able to integrate this into her personality, finding more assertive and less aggressive ways to meet her needs.

She was intuitive and brought many dreams with alchemical imagery. She dreamed she was pulling a tame baby dragon on a lead. The full force of her aggression was not yet accessible hence the dragon, a potentially dangerous, fiery creature, was seen as tame. Later she was able to contact her anger, metaphorically spitting fire at me and the world, rather than being resentful, or worse, turning it inwards and plaguing herself with imaginary illnesses and using food for comfort. She also suffered a phobic fear of enclosed spaces. An example was when she went see the film *Alien* (Scott, 1979) where a monster grows inside an astronaut, finally gnawing out of his stomach with large teeth. After this she was so frightened she could not sleep for weeks, sitting up in bed with the lights on. This became another symbol for repressed rage, and she began to understand her fear of her own destructiveness. As she owned this rage she could sleep again and her claustrophobia subsided (see Chapter 13 for an account of a similar fear of enclosure).

Another alchemical symbol is the hermaphrodite, who has masculine and feminine in one body (see Chapter 3). Connie dreamed she saw a man walking towards her, an orthodox Jew, naked apart from his shoes with a hat over his long locks. He had large breasts and a limp penis, as if the feminine and masculine were still undifferentiated. Her association was of mixed-up spirituality; she nurtured others with the large breasts but could not assert herself and stand up for her beliefs, as symbolised by the limp penis.

She dreamed of floating in the sea and seeing an old castle in the sky. It had four towers and looked secure. She could not tell what was real, her floating or the castle in the air. I interpreted the dream as a mandala – a symbol of the wholeness expressed in astrology and alchemy as the four functions of air, water, earth and fire, with the castle foundation giving a structure. We looked at the possibility she could be building castles in the air, by romanticising. I think both interpretations applied.

Connie dreamed she was being driven in a white car. The driver wore white leather and a winged helmet covering his face. She asked where he was taking her. When he would not answer, she grew frightened and asked him to stop to let her out. He did so but first removed his helmet so she could see that instead of a face, it was a skull. When he opened the door to let her out, he turned into a handsome man. Connie did not know what to make of this, except she did not want to be symbolically driven by a man again, as it would be the death of her psychologically. A week later she had a serious car accident yet escaped only with a bruise. This time she associated the man in the dream to Hermes/Mercury who wanted to take her to the underworld. She refused the journey.

Mercury in astrology, alchemy and mythology is the divine messenger carrying information from the gods to man. Hermes is also a psychopomp, a guide of souls to the underworld. In alchemy, he is the catalyst for the work to begin and a binding force, the archetypal trickster and healer. This was a powerful alchemical dream. It changed the way she perceived her passivity. She became determined to be in the driving seat from then on. The synchronicity around this dream and the accident show a larger pattern is at work, an *a priori* knowledge of the numinous, which allows a different awareness to arise and connect us to the spiritual. Such synchronicities frequently occur in times of crisis or change, as a message from the unconscious may have been ignored, or projected. 'Thus the first knowledge of psychic law and order was found in the stars, and was later extended by projection into unknown matter' (CW 13, para. 285).

The misuse of these arts

Astrology, alchemy and analysis all have a shadow side. It is common for analysts to be admired by their analysands. Some fall into the trap of identifying with this 'magical' projection. Both astrologer and analyst must be aware of the possibility of their client/analysand unconsciously projecting onto them power beyond their capability, of being seen as an all-powerful soothsayer. This is called a 'mana transference' or idealisation. Astrologers are especially likely to have an all-powerful, all-seeing magician projected onto them. Anyone working as astrologer or analyst should be aware of this, and remain rigorous about their 'internal hygiene'. It is for this reason analysts need analysis and regular supervision. Astrologers may be less psychologically aware and more susceptible to falling into their shadow.

Philosophers and psychologists have long puzzled over the complexity of personality and individuality, and typing people is a way to bring some order to the immense and bewildering variety of human beings. Health professionals and some lay people tend to use these labels as a diagnosis rather than viewing typology as a holistic approach to understand the personality. Star signs truly ought not be used as deterministic or as an over-simplified form of categorising.

Another possible misuse of astrology is blaming the stars for one's character traits, rather than working on shadow elements to develop potentials. The horoscope is a map not a person, but it can indicate the journey of life, through transits and progression. Astrology deals with possibilities and probabilities, not inevitabilities. The integrity of both astrologer and analyst comes through a spiritual attitude towards the work shared by alchemists. All are Sacred Arts. Individuation is a process to develop the true self, from unawareness to awareness, wholeness rather than dividedness: this does not mean perfection can actually be achieved.

Conclusion

I see astrology (seeing), alchemy (doing) and analysis (understanding) as art forms in which intuition, imagination and reflection are enacting the process of individuation and the search for meaning in life. Individuation is not linear but a circumambulation of the self; a spiral journey towards wholeness where the head and heart work together; a life-long process of integrating the opposite, bringing split-off parts into more holistic personality. The ability to reflect on one's thoughts and feelings, to be conscious and aware of one's actions, can bring resolution to conflicting inner dynamics: *solve et coagula* – analysis and synthesis. Astrology can help reveal the rhythms of life. Spiritual alchemy deals with the purification of base emotions, thoughts and actions, bringing them into clearer ways of existence; therefore, in analysis the relationship with the psychoanalyst can transcend the original chaos. Nathan Schwartz-Salant says:

> the main reasons to study Jung's research into alchemical symbolism are: the relative independence of its alchemical imagery from cultural bias; the historical and psychotherapeutic vantage-points that alchemy provides; the way in which alchemy offers elaboration and augmentation of Jung's thought.
>
> (1995, p. 19)

I have given a brief overview of the shared symbolism between astrology and alchemy and shown some ways this can apply in the analytical consulting room. As Jung wrote in a letter to the Hindu astrologer, B. V. Raman, (6 September 1947):

> Since you want to know my opinion about astrology, I can tell you that I've been interested in this particular activity of the human mind since

more than 30 years. As I am a psychologist, I am chiefly interested in the particular light the horoscope sheds on certain complications in the character. In cases of difficult psychological diagnosis I usually get a horoscope in order to have a further point of view from an entirely different angle. I must say that I very often found that the astrological data elucidated certain points which I otherwise would have been unable to understand.

(Jung, 1973, p. 475)

References

Dooling, D. M. (1978) *Parabola, Myth and the Quest for Meaning, Inner Alchemy, Vol.111*, New York: Society for the Study of Myth & Tradition.

Fabricius, J. (1994) *Alchemy, The Medieval Alchemists and their Royal Art*, London: Diamond Books.

Garfield, L. & Blishen, E. (1970) *The God Beneath the Sea* London: Victor Gollancz.

Greene, L. (1976) *Saturn, A New Look at an Old Devil* New York: Samuel Weiser Inc.

—— (1977) *Relating* London: Coventure.

Henderson, J. & Sherwood, D. (2003) *Transformation of the Psyche. The Symbolic Alchemy of the Splendour Solis* London: Brunner-Routledge.

Hillman, J. (1997) *The Soul's Code* New York: Warner Books, published by arrangement with Random House.

Jung, C. G. (1953–1973) *Collected Works*, eds M. Fordham, G. Adler and W. McGuire, 20 vols. London: Routledge & Kegan Paul.

—— (1930) *In Memory of Richard Wilhelm*, memorial address delivered in Munich, 10 May 1930. Wilhelm's *The Secret of the Golden Flower* was published in 1931. Jung's memorial address was not included amongst Jung's Foreword and Commentary until the 5th Edition in 1957.

—— (1973) *Letters 1: 1906–1950* selected and edited by Gerhard Adler in collaboration with Aniela Jaffe, trans. R. F. C. Hull, London: Routledge & Kegan Paul.

—— (2009) *The Red Book Liber Novus* edited and introduced by Sonu Shamdasani, New York: Norton.

Mathers, D. (2001) *An Introduction to Meaning and Purpose in Analytical Psychology* London: Routledge.

Schwartz-Salant, N. (1995) *Jung on Alchemy* New York: Routledge.

Scott, R. (1979) *Alien* Hollywood: 20th Century Fox.

Somers, B. (2004) *The Fire of Alchemy. A Transpersonal Viewpoint* London: Archive.

7

LEARNING TO MOVE

Imagination and the Living Body

Richard Wainwright

Giving priority to the body

There has probably never been a time when the body has been more valorised, scrutinised, textualised, theorised and psychologised than now. Perhaps we can think about these often bewildering devotions to the body as driven by an ambition to extend explicit knowledge of bodily process and as an expression of the body's implicit knowing, informed by a longing to recover our *body selves* as sources of feeling knowledge. In other words, these devotions can be re-cognised as expressions of an aspiration to repair what we sense has been broken. We give priority to the body in being open to our bodies' ways with knowing.

In Jung's reframings of the split between mind and body, soul and world, the psyche is conceived as an intermediate body mediating with and implicitly participating in the life of the physical and spiritual realms whilst being identical with neither. This conception of psyche and psychic reality is foundational to his recognition of the reality of imagination to the alchemist as forerunner and implicit paradigm for the psychic labour and crafting we now recognise in the work of the modern psychotherapist. 'The concept of *imaginatio* is perhaps the most important key to the understanding of the *opus*' (CW 12, para. 396). The alchemical forge and laboratory is both the imaginal and concrete predecessor of the modern consulting room, otherwise known as the temenos – the containing space for the individuation of the therapeutic opus. In the alchemical frame imagination is the primary datum informing the 'Coniunctio' mind/matter.

In this chapter I give three clinical vignettes where the analyst and patient are working together in scenes disclosing different degrees of deficit in the lives of the patients. Afflicted with fissures in their capacities to imagine, they find different ways of communicating what it is like to suffer the absence of an on-going experience of not being imagined. These vignettes are held against evocations of work in a 'theatre laboratory' to provide informing commentaries, rather than interpretations, concerning how the total situation in the clinical scene might be re-imagined. The theatre laboratory provides an imaginal world located behind the scenes of the clinical work. It allows for reflection on the three scenes from psychotherapy as re-castings of clinical experience informed by dramaturgical awareness in response to experiences in the laboratory. This allows for the overlap and interpenetration of different voices, for multi-vocality allows for 'a dialogic web of inter-animating presences human, textual and non-human', as Susan Rowland has it with Jung's conception of alchemy in mind (Rowland, 2005, p. 117).

Rite de passage

When a person arrives in therapy they take the risk of entering into a different relationship from whatever it is they've been used to. They are also taking the risk of entering into a different relationship with themselves, being moved by a self that might be seeking to renegotiate the contract of a stuck situation, seeking a different way of being in the world. However welcome the prospect might be, it is likely there will be a degree of foreboding and apprehension. They are entering a liminal space, betwixt and between where they've come from and where they might be going. (The person who has entered a therapeutic training is similarly placed.) Their position can be imagined as something like this:

> The *me* that I was may not be me any longer and the *me* that I want to be and can only imagine, I am not yet. Being situated between the *me* that I might be leaving behind and the *me* that I'm waiting to embrace I don't quite recognise who I am.

Laboratory 1

The theatre laboratory is where dancers and actors, training as therapists, are engaged in movement improvisations, summoning forth and encountering the un-foreseen. It is not a place of judgement or exposure, but of exploration and discovery. It isn't therapy, but a use of theatre for personal research. By that I don't mean it is confined to the private. On the contrary, this work is rooted in being by inter-being with others where Active Imagination and the imagination of action are as involved with each other as mind and matter. It's a place for encountering the limiting repertoires of those habits that like us and do not take lightly to being unlearned. A theatre laboratory devoted to the work of exploring and re-presenting autobiographical material provides opportunities for alterna-tive sightings and re-castings of those habits and the limiting forms they have assumed. Taking time to cultivate extended repertoires of self-disclosure is indispensable to training.

What do we hope for in a therapeutic training? Faced with this question a person often feels pulled into concerns with skill or personal development. In the theatre laboratory I'm speaking about those questions are respected, but people who come here come perhaps for something else. It's difficult to define. If you seek mastery through skill and technique you're unlikely to get an experience of the creative process. In dance, in drama, in art of any kind and particularly in analysis we learn to be creative by finding interesting ways of losing.

The laboratory has revealed itself to be a place where the fallen, the excluded, the feared and the despised have a chance to be reclaimed, recuperated, or recycled. It is a place where improvisation has provoked and called forth the unforeseen. It's where people come together to move with each other to explore, to seek and often find strange messengers with whom to converse, or collaborate. They usually begin at home, so not too strange to begin with. Come and meet the family. Later things warm up, as in the alchemical Fermentatio, which needs the safety of a particular kind of vessel.

In alchemy, the Fermentatio images the unsettling process of a soul's incarnation to animate an apparently lifeless body. The lifeless body is not literally a dead body. It's a body identified with habits of compliance, with devices for remaining attached to 'homespun', or encased in defensive amour. This is a version of the body as an object of inscription by family and the collective. Its status as a *creative body* is 'waiting to be found', awakened in its longing to become a *breathing* subject. The awakening anticipates the re-union of body and soul in the process of individuation.

> It's the second session of our first day's work. We are learning how to be with each other. Everyone begins lying on the ground. Breathing is enough to begin with. Bodies need time to settle to submit to the unforced pulse of inspiration, time for the habits that preoccupy to dissolve. From stillness minimal movements extend into rolling and the pleasures of infolding and unfolding. Already a sense of rhythm is born from the body's awareness of whatever is other: the floor, the walls, the sources of light, other bodies, extending in space to the others of others. Simple rolling provides the dynamus needed for rising on to knees and descending to the ground. The open vision of exploration moves us to the point of divining where things might go from here. When we are in the zone of body's intuition we need sensation to bring home what's been divined. The way down to the ground is the way we go to come up. In the rhythms and cadences of falling and rising we are moved into standing, into walking, opening potentially into running. Through exploration we discover intention and at that point of our awareness you could say we've moved, or been moved from exploration to seeking.

Winnicott recognised the creative value of aggression in emotional development in terms of movement, for instance: 'the environment is constantly discovered and re-discovered because of motility' (1984, p. 211). In the language of neuropsychology the seeking system is understood as an 'emotional operating system'. It is factored into the central nervous system and it relates us to our remotest ancestors. It's about:

- locating resources, foraging, searching
- persistent forward locomotion, sniffing, motor arousal
- curiosity, investigation, anticipation
- spontaneously active associative networks (fantasy)
- also known as a motivational system because it drives and energises. It's the neural correlate of vision

(Panksepp, 1998, pp. 144–163)

Choreographic possibilities emerge from physical involvement, extending the range of relationship between moving bodies, moving in relation to the space they inhabit. Behaviour becomes more complex as it becomes more social. Playful apparitions from an in-between world crawl, sit back on haunches, run on all fours, explore new territories, encounter objects and obstacles which engage, or move them into spontaneous exchanges, while seeking and foraging like Satyrs or Sileni who bridge the animal and the human, being both and neither. This is borderland work where imaginations of the body, seeking form in play, disclose extended repertoires of affinity.

Both theatre and therapy can help us to explore, seek, discover and *behold* how we can feel familiar and strange at the same time.

Explorers are playing and being played by strangers that leap into being, seeking to be characters. Others emerge from hiding in the corner, sometimes insinuating themselves rather than revealing who they are. One person in their life may play many parts, but one body houses many more parts than are played in a life. The work has been focussed on where the troupe of emerging characters may take each person individually, rather than lapsing into the refuge of caricature. Characters emerging from physical imagination seem to have a life of their own: 'It's like I've never met this crazy woman, but I've known her forever'; 'He reminds me of my Dad, though he's not remotely like him in appearance. I guess it's how I feel him.'

We reflect on the categories of *me* and *not me* and how they allow only for sameness and difference. To say you've always known someone you've never met is to be graced with mythological imagination, which conceives of events that never happened, but are always true. Our bodies implicate us in myth as myth implicates our bodies. We get trapped in pathology when the circuit breaks down. When we recognise in personified images of our feeling connections to people we know, or think we know, (in spite of the evidence that image and person bear no literal resemblance), we might feel as if we're dreaming.

Active Imagination is akin to 'dream work'. Both engage with the plays of appearances between objects and their images; both are concerned with not confusing *likeness* with either *sameness* or *difference*. Metaphor and symbol are born from the same stream as erotic love, each is predicated upon likeness, as Jung recognised in his use of the Rosarium to evoke and re-vision the transference. The fragility of personal identity is acknowledged when we recognise how implicated we appear to be in so many 'other' identities that are neither *me* nor *not me*. In improvisation, collaboration allows us to second sight the borderlands of experience where we feel implicated in the play of *me, not me* and *not not me*.

Encounters with the unforeseen evoke unexpected memories of childhood. In the process of reflection there are several recognitions that it was not just in the detail of recollection that a connection to childhood was restored. It was more in the sense of a frame of mind, or a way of imagining. You can only feel like a child when you are not a child. The child remembered is a version of *me* in the past, a version of me and *not me* in the present and a connection to *not not me*, located in the present informed by both the past and the prospect of a future. The remembered child is both *me* and *not me*, whilst being identical with neither.

Ariane Mnouchkine, the director of Theatre du Soleil, captures the importance of this dimension in theatre: 'I think there is something in the actor's work which compels him or her, not to *fall back into childhood*, but to enter childhood' (Williams, 1999, p. 171). In play and in theatre, to 'enter' childhood rather than regress into it invites openness to emotion in the service of an embodied action. The director Peter Brook sees this state of openness as a discovery of 'innocence', shining through and illuminating experience. Discovered innocence de-ranges the dispositions of our habitual behaviours. Habits that block loosen and drop away when accustomed hierarchies lose their controlling grip. One is free to play when nobody is on guard, because *everyone* is disarmed (Brook, 1993). In a state of play you are free not to lie.

When we are moved by interest in whoever peoples our stage, our inter-actions may leave us dis-composed in a state of *inter/esse* – inter-being. We might be more disposed to ask not 'How are you?' but 'Who's here?' In this territory our idea of personal identity and person/ality can be understood as spaces, or scenes. When respect for scene moves us from acting to inter-acting, we are released from the trap of literalism. Imaginal bodies in the theatre and body's imagination in the *temenos* (therapeutic space) are haunting allusions to each other and to the ever-changing subject who attends and moves both, but cannot be possessed by either. In a state of play, which is also known as possession, we are open to visitations, inhabitations and raptures that invite collaboration.

Perhaps Peter Brook (1993) had something like this in mind in giving a new twist to the meaning of 'brain washing' as a solvent to the agitations of the insistent mind, that keep us in thrall to limited repertoire. 'When the mind's free the body's delicate' (Shakespeare, *King Lear*: Act 3, scene 4). In conditions of trust we are free to move and inter-act with others – free to imagine the others of others with whom to be convivial. The word is made flesh.

Analytic scenes: the anatomy lesson

The body's delicacy renders it vulnerable to calamitous inscriptions from intrusive or unresponsive environments, locking it into the carapace of a 'tremulous private body' (Barker, 1984), pre-disposed to the law of prescription and likely to be subjugated to a travestied version of the word.

Today I am particularly aware of his hands. His arms seem to extend forever on each side of his body, loosely draped in charcoal grey. His way with clothes accentuates my sense of his body's desperate need for flesh. His relentless gaze remains fixed 'at home in no house and no country'. I accept his nobody stare in small doses, keeping my eyes open to the space beyond his head and the wall behind him where the glass framing two radiant images of ancient Etruscans dancing, reflects trees in the garden beyond the window behind me. The prints were brought home years ago from the now resealed burial chambers in Tarquinia.

Here in the cave of his gaze I am barely aware of breathing. The lightest or the slightest movement towards life is a risk beyond calculation. His voice arrives. He would like to discuss his 'case' further. From his reading it's clear he's 'psychotic'. He reels off his symptoms, memorised to perfection from DSM4. I've become accustomed to this moment in the session when it's assumed the consultant psychiatrists will don white coats and confer, while the patient in the room is left to recline in his own absence. I comment on the scene, aware of his desperation to take up residence in me and how enraging it is to be thwarted by the reality of our separateness. His head lifts, turning slightly to one side. Yes that's what's happening, but it's not what I sense. It's as if he were standing outside himself, manipulating his body.

I'm reminded again of Rembrandt's painting *The Anatomy Lesson* where the anatomy text at the feet of the cadaver is the object of the spectator's gaze rather than the corpse laid out before them. It is flesh made word, or body rendered into a text by an act of legitimated violence, revealed and concealed by the conventions of another kind of performance art in a late renaissance version of a theatre laboratory (Barker, 1984, pp. 71–112). The painting foreshadows the mind-set of the modern diagnostic manual in which the psychic body and its interior are objectified and abstracted. The imagined scene recapitulates the 'absolute' division between 'the Cartesian subject, and corporeal object, between an *I* that thinks, and an *it* in which *we* reside' (Sawday, 1995, p. 29). This catastrophic division between mind and body, subject and object, is the antagonist of the alchemical *coniunctio*. It is inherent in the project of attempting to depend on the mind as a minding object to the exclusion of other objects for the patient who is committed to self-sufficiency as a cure for dependency and, by extension, the possibility of play (see Corrigan and Gordon, 1995).

I am moved to speak: 'It's as though you are saying you are not a person but a category, which is a way of telling me (*reporting* was how I experienced his comment) how frozen you feel.' When he speaks it's as if he's speaking a second language when he hasn't got a first, rendering the possibility of meeting in a conversation almost unthinkable. I remarked in our first session over two years ago how it felt to me as though his way forward would be in finding his own speech and his own voice, perhaps sensing that it would take a very long time to make a move in this direction.

Today, trying not to repeat myself, I'm on the point of saying: 'I think you're reminding me of how desperately you want to feel alive and all of a piece in your body with a life of your own.' I recognise with mild embarrassment I'm not quite myself. I'm warding off danger, signalled by the prompt of an irritation, inviting him, as he has let me know, to add my defensive observation to his repertoire of imitations. It is a question of keeping faith with what it might be possible to do *'towards bringing the patient from a state of not being able to play into state of being able to play'* (Winnicott, 1985 p. 44). I invite my patient to paint whatever comes to mind on the sheet of paper I'm laying on the floor. He sets about it with a relish, thick daubs of black and marine blue which he will score with wide open ragged eyes, laced with red, staring out from the dark.

We'll be here for a long time.

Analytic scenes 2

She arrives with her usual cargo of written material in a plastic bag marked Safeway. Last week she asked if she could bring some of her toys, dolls and teddies. She said she would like me to meet the family who meant most to her. We have talked about them for months. She likes to keep her characters, her tendencies to exist, off stage. I have huge doubts as to whether I am a person at all. I am used to being addressed as if I were a thing, an object, a toy, at best a voyeur – anybody but somebody.

A hint of hysteria: (in the laboratory)

One of the women wraps herself around a huge ball entrusting herself to be moved by its momentum. The act of allowing herself to be taken off balance while speaking brings new richness to her voice, a hint of hysteria. Here the principle of conversion giving priority to the body is a virtue. As each person explores and finds their way of rolling with the ball, they experience how their names sound and feel in new and unexpected voices. Dislocations of the voice elicit recognition of having more than one voice presented through a favourite persona and having more than one name. Nicknames and diminutives are disclosed and shared in an atmosphere of growing trust. Each name and diminutive has a story, which is a connection to a world of stories of families, friends and other important people who arrive as imagined guests. Play encourages disclosure and disclosure breeds conviviality.

Playful use of a simple proposal to speak while moving on a ball goes right to the heart of the principle of de-integration/re-integration from our beginning. Individuation begins *in utero*.

Analytic scenes 2 (continued)

Her proposal might be the messenger of an aspiration to exist. I anticipated she would need to be extravagant, perhaps as many as six or seven dolls, perhaps as many as a Safeway bag could contain. She arrived at the next session with two bags bulging with her imaginal life, which I knew she knew was real. She disposed families of teddies and dolls throughout the room, handing me her favourite. Having instructed me how to hold her favourite, she introduced me to the company one by one, gifting each with a story, a history and an evaluation.

After she'd finished the guided tour she sat down, picked up her latest acquisition and tore it to pieces, screaming abuse as she threw the pieces around the room. In this scene of spectacular dismemberment, the lacerating intensity of her voice, enacting a state of deranged possession, made the deepest impression. The imagination of a baby was being shredded, summoning the mythic image of the baby Dionysos chillingly dismembered by Titans, directed by Hera in a moment of jealous possession.

As infants we need maternal handling and reverie to contain the terror of de-integrating from the undifferentiated enclosure of a primal self. The body's experience of being handled by another and contained in relationship is crucial to the psyche's capacity for self-regulation.

She carried on screaming. Still holding the favourite teddy, I looked at the clock. She stopped: 'Don't tell me to go.' She picked up the pieces and collected the teddies together. 'It wasn't meant to be like that.' Sensing her comment as a possible way into a place between what happened and what might have happened I replied: 'I'm not so sure, perhaps it needed to be like that.'

In the laboratory vignette, the process of de-integration was constellated in the moment that breathing inspired trust in the ball as an embodied medium of communication, leading to trust in its supportive viability.

The laboratory 2 (continued)

Echoes of the Hysteria festivals of the ancient world where men and women reversed roles and personae (and with Carnival in our own world) were welcomed as creative provocations, reminding us of our bodies' open repertoire and our susceptibility to cultural inscription. Everyone agreed to an artistic proposal to return to the ball with their narratives and only speak when they were able to speak so that their voices were not over-controlled by their moving bodies. In this way narratives were released into new territories of meaning, as each moving speaker was able to wait for opportunities to speak in short phrases. Not being able to speak continuously allows the narrative to be broken down, allowing us to realise what we say in the spaces between phrases and sentences. It sensitises the moving speakers to the vitality of the moving object, which is also a subject. The witnesses become aware of being moved into experiences of *in between listening*, as body and text inform each other rather than being confused, or divorced.

Not being able to speak without considering an object that eludes the speaker's control cultivates a respect for the kind of space a hesitation offers. Hesitation can be re-valued as a way of keeping faith with the unforeseen arriving unannounced. The loosening of the ego/author's grip invites the unintended to break in, providing opportunities for mover and moved in a state of 'free listening' (Phillips, 2002,

p. 31), to be touched, led astray and discomposed by realising what we say and what we hear simultaneously.

Analytic scenes 2 (continued)

Today, she unpacks her bag, lifting out a familiar wad of notes. I ask if she would like to be here without her text. She puts down the papers beside her and rehearses being still. The duration of a short pause is enough for her to disclose from the stifled shudder of her retreating body that being alone with another is unbearable. She picks up her text to disclose the meaning of last week. The performance, as she has it, pre-empting what I 'must think', confirms what she's not known all her life; she's a 'hysteric'. I am recruited as the audience of authorities, all too present in their absence. Breaking things up can be thought about from the perspective of the laboratory as subverting the parental author's intention. Here in the analytic space she assumes her enactment will lead to the diagnostic manual and the body as object.

Fordham translated Jung's core idea of individuation into infancy. His translation and the developmental model which came from it owed a great deal to his other translations of Klein, Winnicott and other contributors to the 'Object Relations' tradition into a Jungian idiom. Moving between the analytic scene and infancy, he presents a version of an infant, adaptable from the beginning, needing the containing presence, voice and preoccupation of a mother. Meeting these needs she combines embodiment with relatedness by taking the baby's emotions into herself and handing back something manageable, or useable (Fordham, 1985, pp. 50–63).

Laboratory 2 (continued)

We agreed to devote time to the imagination of the voice. The phrase 'having a voice' is a way of formulating an aspiration. Having a voice means having more than one voice, one tone, one style. The idea of extended repertoire can also be welcomed as a way of thinking about participation in other kinds of bodies – family, community, profession and opening to the world. 'It's made me see how much of me gets missed out most of the time'; 'You become aware of parts of yourself you didn't know, or maybe just didn't want to know'. There is nothing miraculous or revelatory about either response. What matters is their ordinariness. A therapy devoted to an extended repertoire may find a place for unheard and unheeded voices. Our depressions and grievances might owe more to an unlived life than the life we protest we've actually led. Both weave in and out of each other like conscious and unconscious. Our bodies are the hosts and guests of both.

The sense of de-integration/re-integration in the laboratory refers us to the unfolding nature of the psyche, of emergence and movement towards the potential of integration and renewal, both personal and professional. Here in a supportive environment it is possible to recognise the pull of limiting securities, to rehearse new moves, take up new possibilities, discriminate what can be used, re-cycled, or buried. Like the alchemical *separatio* differentiating spirit and matter, the psychic process de-integration/re-integration configures and reconfigures the moving co-ordinates of individuation.

Analytic scene (commentary)

The patient's presentation of her dolls and teddies grimly theatricalised the dilemma of a person who from infancy had not been met with a 'containing presence', nor achieved 'unit status' in Winnicott's language. She was intelligent and professionally able, yet every attempt she made to move out from the precarious security of her internal nursery exposed her to the terror of crossing a ravine on an unfinished bridge. Learning to move involves trust that the bridge will support us. The alternative, as she knew, is to remain stuck in rage and terror.

Development is based on movement which Fordham termed de-integration/re-integration. Parts of the 'primary self' are matched by a mother mediating the infant's encounter with the environment. Mother and infant is a relational field. Mother's embodied responsiveness facilitates the infant's sense of self and with it the psyche's capacity for self-regulation. From the beginning, relationship is based on the inseparability of body and mind: 'Relationship damage is functionally equivalent to embodiment damage' (Totton, 1998, p. 150). In Fordham's language this is equivalent to dis-integration, which follows if de-integrative experiences are not contained. The imagination of the baby in a state of dismemberment evokes archetypal territory: the image of the baby Dionysos, dismembered by the Titans, amplifies the dissociative quality invoked when relationships are damaged through radical impingement, or absence of attunement.

When de-integrative experiences are not contained, the dance of de-integration/re-integration breaks down. The alchemical project, a metaphor for the labour of devotion to the making, the unmaking and the remaking of the body in psyche and psyche in the body, is a devotion to the living body which is always in the making and the unmaking. The inspiration of creative risk will have a better chance with us and we with it when we are able to distinguish loss from catastrophe.

She stayed long enough to imagine some of the bridges she could cross to be a player in the world.

The living body

'In reality, there is nothing but a living body. That is the fact; and psyche is as much a living body as body is living psyche: it is just the same' (Jung, 1988, Vol. 1, p. 396).

Jung couldn't have made it clearer. The living body has psychic properties and is a moving interaction between our body selves and the objects of the world. We experience these movements through kinaesthetic sensations, essential to our constitution and extension in space. The living process of the body knowing itself and the world through movement is foundational to our human being. The relation I/Thou is created and discovered through our relations with the moving world, which is there from the beginning. This is close to the descriptions and concepts of neuroscience and analytic psychotherapies, which evoke the rhythms of inter-subjectivity and co-ordination in early infancy in terms of movement: gesture, breathing, eye contact, sound and affect attunement. 'I' comes into being through spontaneous acts of attention and intention, matched by core regulatory emotions. Mother and baby learn from each other through their plays of anticipation and expectation in cycles of arousal and resolution. Their plays are literally the origin of daily movement and interaction which are foundational to dance through a process of elaboration. Kinaesthetic awareness and self-awareness are born before speech in the plays of face and voice, the rhythmic cycles of accepting and rejecting contact. Our early plays and moves constellate the basis of consciousness and knowledge.

These ways of thinking are of particular interest to movement-aware therapists as ways we access somatic counter transference. How we feel in our bodies in relation to another, or others, is informed by what is present in between us. The in between space is the living source of our capacity to symbolise. This area was referred to by Winnicott as transitional space. For Jung it was the site of the transcendent function which bridges conscious and unconscious, whilst being identical with neither (CW 8, paras 131–193). It is where Henri Corbin, the French philosopher, theologian and scholar of Islamic mysticism, has located the presence of a *Mundus Imaginalis* – an imaginal world, which is quite different from the imaginary world of the purely subjective. This concept of an imaginal world was indispensable to Archetypal Psychology as developed by James Hillman and occupies an important place in Jungian discussions of embodied counter transference (Samuels, 1989, pp. 161–172).

Analytic scenes 3

Moving with the patient – an embodied counter transference.

In Dance Movement Therapy, a movement proposal is a response to what is present; it is not an interpretation in a direct sense. Its imaginal scope, or meaning, can only be realised through an experience of inter-being, bearing in mind that embodiment is a word for the inter-weave of body and imagination.

For the second time she has time off because of a fall. On the first occasion she tore ligaments in her ankle. Nine months later she has a broken wrist. 'Something is wrong' she tells me on the phone, connecting her fall with 'always trying to be nice' when she's 'angry'. She returns angry to tell me she is giving up her job. It's *that* which has caused her so much grief. She 'can't stand it anymore' and 'will leave immediately, without notice.' We sit in the silence, both aware of the hurt in her imperious rage. An obvious interpretation presents itself: 'Is there a chance that you feel I've let you down and that it's therapy that's caused you so much grief?' Fortunately I hesitate long enough to make a space for the voice I heard on the phone 'something is wrong'. We continue to sit in the silence. Her hands are folded across her stomach.

Laboratory 3

In the laboratory a woman is rehearsing an autobiographical fragment. A girl is trying to live up to her parents' expectations in a refined and pastiche, ballet style. She is suffering the agony of being a body that's always going up. Hardly able to breathe, she suddenly runs from the scene she's in towards a wall. She jumps, hitting it with both feet and falls to the ground. Standing up she returns to her starting position to repeat these moves remorselessly. Each time she gets further up the wall, to fall again and again like a stone. Each time she stands she returns to where she came from. She could be a refugee from the Pina Bausch Tanztheater Wuppertal in the early 1970s. Bausch's choreographics were famous for their uncompromising use of repetition to realise the structure of stuck situations, the rules governing the roles informing 'the inhumanity of men and women toward each other and the callous indifference of the world that surrounds them' (Ross, 1999).

The situations in the consulting room and the laboratory are haunting allusions both to each other and to the *Nigredo* phase of alchemy. The *Nigredo* is a metaphor for an experience of light extinguished; a descent into total darkness where the habits and devices of the past, which were once the matter of survival, break down and decompose. The Putrifactio (see Chapter 1) is both a process and a habitation for the rotting of the ego's accustomed cradling in a persona, a preferred version of self, an assumed identity composed of habits, as familiar as our skin, which resists the threat of becoming compost. We are in the domain of Saturn (Roman), or Chronos (Greek) where illusion cannot enter. Chronos is the archetypal waiter, generator and diviner of boredom, the divinity of chronic repetition. This is the metaphorical territory of despair, the dissolution of hope, the death of the resourceful mind, but a potential opening to sources beyond the mind's control. As in the laboratory, the way down is the way we go to come up.

Analytic scenes 3 (continued)

She's sitting on the couch but I experience her as standing by the door. I feel alarmed. She's jumping into open space with nobody to catch her, or is it that she's being thrown? The sense of falling forever leaps up from what I experience as a rush of vertigo. I feel a huge gap in the middle of my body and a momentary brush with the prospect of nausea gathering in free fall.

As in the laboratory, the therapist has a live encounter with how our bodies implicate us in myth and myth implicates us in our bodies. A mythic image, not consciously apprehended, but experienced concretely in my body, summons a feeling for receiving, containing and crafting. The therapist's body as the organ of the counter transference registers the experience of compensating for the patient's temporary state of disassociation. The reflective function containing the experience is moved to re-locate it in association with the mythic image of the Greek god Hephaistos, thrown out of Olympus at birth by his mother (for being ugly) to fall to earth. The mythic image registers the shocking conjunction of violence and terror. Hephaistos was destined to be a worker and fashioner of metals as smith, craftsman and jeweller to the gods, perhaps the misshapen personification of the wounded healer and alchemist.

I ask if she can swim. She says she can't, but why do I ask? I invite her to imagine what it would be like to enter a swimming pool at the shallow end. Calming down, she's visibly amused at the prospect. She unfolds her hands and takes off her shoes. We enter the pool side by side very slowly. I attend to the importance of breathing and the sensing of pulse. She's 'not used to being aware' of her breathing. We move slowly: nothing too deep to begin with. She's beginning to enjoy the sensation of kicking water everywhere. We move deeper and she's still kicking as she would in the shallows even though the (imagined) water is up to our waists. I comment that water is quite dense and heavy. Why not enjoy its resistance and feel its support? She begins to move with the water, enjoying the sensation of leaning into it which allows her to be slow. Exploration is a matter of negotiation and re-negotiation.

There is time for reflection after disengaging from the imaginal pool. She remembers being very difficult as a child. Her mother was 'never quite sure', she said, how to 'handle' her. She recalls the stories she's brought many times of her father's ridicule for her 'ungainliness'. Towards the end of the session, sitting *en face*, she says: 'I think we're dancing.' She mused on the experience of being supported in the dance and the feeling of water. 'We were moving in time with a heartbeat. I've always been afraid of water. Perhaps I'll learn to swim and lie on my back and feel the sound of the sea all around me.'

Our work takes us into linking sensations, images and words. In the next few weeks she links her fear of water and difficulties with co-ordination with feeling ashamed and humiliated at home, at school and particularly at work where she is learning to move from a fixed position. She has recognised it would be better to negotiate a redundancy deal rather than trying to save face by a petulant walkout, or fallout, as I experienced it. I find myself becoming more and more aware of the interface between the functions of dramaturge and analyst following the routes to roots of the transference where distinctions between leader and follower are always shifting.

In the theatre the dramaturge reports to the director on what they saw. Assisting in the process of weaving, unweaving and reweaving the dramatic score, the interweave of action, text, 'the floor, the walls, the sources of light, bodies, extending in space to the *others* of others', they are free to be alert to what the author represses and what the actor, in a moment of inspiration, reveals through what they appear to avoid. Dramaturgical alertness in the consulting room assists with registering who or what is absent, as well as present, in what is remembered and forgotten. It prompts the configuration of therapist/patient to re-imagine a stuck situation, which can't be forgotten, as a defence against remembering what has been forgotten.

Laboratory 3 (continued)

The stuck position rehearsed here in the laboratory is one of not being able to move out of the force field of an internalised ideal and demand, signifying a desperate need to move from an old body to a body still waiting to be found. In role this woman is unconcerned about the physical risks she is taking. She is a skilled, determined and daring performer who is alert to the creative value of aggression in emotional development and clearly in touch with how the environment is 'discovered and rediscovered' through movement.

Her performance explores aspirant relationships outside of home and family. There is a clear distinction between self and others. *Me* and *not me* are separated by the devices of time, place, age and gender. The persecuting others are located in another time, another place and of a different generation. They are clearly *not me*. The dramaturgy is mainly linear with action tending to be subordinate to narrative, but the piece is informed by an impassioned aspiration to find a way out of the repeated mis-en-scène of the past by re-entering it as a resource.

Preparations for a second autobiographical performance six months later involve working with leader-follower principles. Three women exchange the roles of leader and follower, enabling each to have multiple experiences of assuming each other's movement idiom in their own bodies. They are rehearsing moving from one to the other. The movement from improvisation to rehearsal re-defines the process of collaboration allowing us to second sight 'the borderlands of experience where we feel implicated in the play of *me, not me* and *not not me*.'

In the performance we witness an epic struggle between three moving bodies. Though the same performer begins as a clearly delineated protagonist, her two antagonists challenge that status, providing the dynamic for a battle between all three. Power moves from one to the other; alliances form and re-form over and over again. This is a shadow land where integrity is off limits. Playing itself out, it concludes in total exhaustion, but not the death of the actors, who have become more like personified forces than people. All three figures are versions of *me*; their statuses, but not their actions, are interchangeable. Nothing is disowned. The staging has moved from its previous proscenium arrangement with its projection screen effect and face-on presentation. The action moves in and out of the audience who are allowed to see all sides of the actors' bodies – to see them from different positions, whilst at the same time removing from the audience the conceit of being able to see everything. The movement from initial research, discovery and disclosure has involved the struggle we have just witnessed in this performance. It evokes the sense of an authentic self whose status is immanent and in the making – and whose evolution in the life of an individual is the real subject of autobiography.

Leaders and followers

One of the ways we learn something of the other in dance is in leader-follower structures. We cannot literally become the other, but we can adopt their way of moving and sense what it feels like to move in ways we could not arrive at without attending to the moving other. We move from imitation to identification (empathy) and incorporation in which the *not me* is transformed and re-presented as a potential extension of our repertoire. This involves the complementary process of locating and embodying the likeness of the other in our body selves. If we are open to the other, we are moved to recognise that we do not belong to ourselves alone.

A therapeutic endeavour, open to moving and being moved, will devote close attention to body states and the relational fields between bodies, whether or not they are literally moving. Our bodies are moving even when they appear to be still, because our bodies are the sites and vessels of emotion. Emotion and the motion in emotion are experienced in the body, which is why the body is the organ, or instrument of the counter transference.

The psychoanalytic concept of projective/introjective identification describes and theorises the experience of psychic inter-penetration. It is foundational to our capacity for empathy. This state of identification, in which 'one unconsciously subjugates oneself in order to free oneself from oneself', as the psychoanalyst Thomas Ogden has it, needs to be mediated by an act of imagination (Ogden, 1994, p. 103). As in the practice of Active Imagination, we need to be able to move from inside an experience to being outside it: to move simultaneously between subjective and objective or, to use a theatrical metaphor, between being the actor or mover involved in a dramatic plot or score to being the witness. Another psychoanalyst, Christopher Bollas, addresses this complex mode of psychic functioning in distinguishing projective identification from perceptive identification:

> If projective identification gets inside the other, perceptive identification stands outside to perceive the other. The term "identification" means quite different things for each concept. In projective identification it means identifying with the object, in perceptive identification it means perceiving the identity of the object. Both forms of knowing need to work in tandem with one another in a creative oscillation between appreciating the integrity of the object and perceiving its identity, and then projecting parts of the self into the object, a form of imagination.
>
> (Bollas, 2007, p. 68)

The analyst working with this 'creative oscillation' in whatever analytic idiom models it for the so-called patient. The living body is a moving inter-action between self and other.

The new anatomy class and the living body

The neuroscientist/analyst Allan Schore, speaking in the neuropsychological idiom of the new Anatomy Class, suggests that 'projective identification is an affect regulating strategy that is used in right-brain-to-right-brain communications, a pre-verbal bodily based dialogue between right lateralised limbic systems . . .' (Schore, 2003, p. 70). It follows from this that 'right lateralised operations . . . allow for the adaptive capacity of empathic cognition and the perception of the emotional states of mind of other human beings' (ibid., p. 71). Not surprisingly, given how deeply embedded in our being it is, 'unconscious processing of affective information is extremely rapid, the dynamic operations of these processes cannot be consciously perceived' (ibid.).

In a more evocative description of the right hemisphere's domain, the Harvard neuroscientist Jill Bolt Taylor tells us:

> It's all about *right here, right now*. Our right hemisphere . . . thinks in pictures, it learns kinesthetically through the movement of our bodies. Information, in the form of energy, streams in simultaneously through all of our sensory systems and then it explodes into this enormous collage of what this present moment smells like and tastes like, what it feels like and what it sounds like.
>
> (cited in Tweedy, 2012, p. 7)

The capacities for empathy and kinaesthetic awareness are aligned in the same area of the brain which is disseminated throughout the body. In other words, imagination is factored into our body selves, which is precisely what Jung intuited in referring to the primary datum informing the 'Coniunctio' mind/matter: 'The concept of *imaginatio* is perhaps the most important key to the understanding of the *opus*' (CW 12, para. 396).

The alchemical imagination complements the modern need to re-align the imaginative and the analytic, the evocative and informative or, as William Blake had it: *The Marriage of Heaven and Hell*, where 'Body is a portion of Soul discerned by the five Sense . . .' (Blake, 1975, p. xvi). Any creative process of exploration and discovery in which the senses are 'the active antennae of the soul' (Porter, 2003, p. 443) requires a condition of availability to what is other for something received to be incarnated. The body in a state of receptivity is not inclined to demonstrate, but rather, it *allows something to be – and to be seen.*

Having experiences of being movers, actors and witnesses in any number of styles and modalities gives us foundations for being available, open and flexible to the unforeseen demands of time, fate and image. The characters and images that appear don't just come out of private space, but are constellated by a play of bodies, exploring, seeking and finding. A state of discovered innocence, to echo Blake and Brook in particular, is both open and active. Being open to the unforeseen, it opens us to the dynamic of self and other, the common ground of our human disposition for symbolic communication. Self and other, like *I* and *thou*, are disseminated throughout the body as a living organism. Like the Philosopher's Stone of Alchemy (*the stone that is no stone*), 'neither mind nor matter . . . neither real nor unreal', it is always in the making and the unmaking, being 'neither abstract nor concrete. It is always both . . .' (CW 12, para. 400).

References

Barker, F. (1984*)* *The Tremulous Private Body.* London and New York: Methuen.
Blake, W. (1975) *The Marriage of Heaven and Hell.* Oxford: Oxford University Press.
Bollas, C. (2007) *The Freudian Moment.* London: Karnac.
Brook, P. (1993) Personal notes taken from a lecture given by Brook, 19 October 1993, under the auspices of the Institute of Psychoanalysis.
Corrigan, E. and Gordon, P. (eds) (1995) *The Mind Object.* London: Karnac.
Fordham, M. (1985) *Exploration into the Self.* London and New York: Karnac.
Jung, C.G. (1953–1973) *Collected Works*, eds Sir H. Read, M. Fordham, G. Adler and W. Maguire, 20 vols. London: Routledge, Kegan Paul.
—— (1988) (ed. Jarret, J.) *Neitsche's Zarathustra: Notes of the Seminar Given 1934–39*, 2 vols. Princeton, NJ: Princeton University Press.
Ogden, T. (1994) *Subjects of Analysis.* London: Karnac
Panksepp, J. (1998) *Affective Neuroscience.* Oxford and New York: Oxford University Press.
Phillips, A. (2002) *Equals.* London: Faber.
Porter, R. (2003) *Flesh in the Age of Reason.* London: Allen Lane.
Ross, J. (1999) *Difficult Dances: The Choreographies of Pina Bausch.* Stanford, CA: Stanford Presidential Lectures in the Humanities and Arts, Stanford University.
Rowland, S. (2005) *Jung as a Writer.* London: Routledge.
Samuels, A. (1989) *The Plural Psyche.* London: Routledge.
Sawday, J. (1995) *The Body Emblazoned.* London and New York: Routledge.
Schore, A. (2003) *Affect Regulation.* New York and London: W. W. Norton and Co.
Totton, N. (1998) *The Water in the Glass.* London: Rebus Press.
Tweedy, R. (2012) *The God of the Left Hemisphere.* London: Karnac.
Williams, D. (1999) *Collaborative Theatre.* London and New York: Routledge.
Winnicott, D. (1984) *Through Paediatrics to Psychoanalysis.* London: Karnac.
—— (1985) *Playing and Reality.* London: Penguin Books.

Part III

THE SPIRIT AND THE
NATURAL WORLD

HERMES

Into harbour they sailed
telescoped together
playing the well-brought-up,
friendship bound.

They found Hermes, the messenger,
the connecter of dreams,
master of treachery.

The sea visitors, capable of love,
but unprovided for,
practiced old arts
in an alien land.

Fascinated with boundlessness
Hermes played his games,
bounced in and out of their lives.

His harsh note hung in the ear.
Sobered by his tempering music
they went navigating beyond day
into unknown frontiers.

Given to the received,
king of no country,
Hermes laughed.

Adele Davide

8

THE NATURE OF BURN-OUT AND THE BURN-OUT OF NATURE

The Sloth and the Chickadee

Gottfried M. Heuer

Preface

Only Robinson Crusoe
  got everything done by Friday.
           (Anon., n.d.)

Let us begin with the sloth, bestowed with the name of one of the Seven Deadly Sins, that 'is a highly intriguing creature . . . It sleeps or rests an average twenty hours a day . . . How does it survive, you might ask. Precisely by being slow . . . The . . . sloth lives a peaceful . . . life in perfect harmony with its environment' (Martel, 2003, pp. 3–4). And now, from the jungles of South America, where the sloth lives, to our habitat, or 'Welcome to the Age of Exhaustion' (Hall, 2009):

> Work-related stress is soaring . . . Technology was supposed to create a leisure society. Yet the British are experiencing unprecedented job intensification . . . as a cult of efficiency drives ever more exacting targets. The phenomenon has been masked by a type of management which promises much but delivers one of the most exploitative and manipulative work cultures developed since the Industrial Revolution.
>
> (Bunting, 2004a, back cover)

This was written in 2004 by journalist Madeleine Bunting about what she called 'the overwork culture', where a health (!) magazine suggests, 'Be a lean, mean, fat-burning machine!' (Bean, 2004), where a popstar defiantly states, 'better to burn out than to fade away' (Young in Sandall, 2005, p. 26) and leisure clothes advertise with, 'Die of exhaustion not boredom' (Minx, 2006), another with, 'Impatience is a virtue' (Samsung, 2009). The front page of the German *Stern* announced, 'Work is the new Sex' (Barth, 2011). The current economic climate is unlikely to have improved the situation. The question is: *are we part of the problem or part of the solution?*

Introduction

Self-love, my liege, is not so vile a sin
as self-neglecting.

William Shakespeare, *Henry VIII*, III. ii. 444

The problem is not just a recent one. Would Shakespeare have said this if it had not been a noticeable issue? Two hundred years later, Goethe, combining speed, *velocitas*, with Lucifer, inveighed against the 'velociferic' age (in Schnabel, 2012, p. 177). From the nineteenth century we have Edgar Allan Poe's tale, chillingly titled, 'The Man That Was Used Up' (Hoffman, 1985, pp. 193–195). Later in the nineteenth century, with time and motion studies speeding up industrial production, a labour leader spoke of 'the organization of exhaustion' (in Solnit, 2003, p. 212). In 1878, Nietzsche prophesied, 'From lack of rest, our civilisation is ending in a new barbarism' (in Schnabel, 2012, p. 177). A hundred years ago Jack London, writing manically until he apparently committed suicide at the age of 42, referred to himself as the 'Work-Beast' (in Sansom, 2010), saying, 'I would rather be ashes than dust, a spark burnt out in a brilliant blaze' (in Newcomer, 2009, p. vii). And from the mid-twentieth century there is Graham Greene's novel, 'A Burnt-out Case' (2001).

A patient of mine who had suffered burn-out in her high-strung career, dreams:

> Being chased by two women, I get on a motorbike, but they throw grenades after me – or make the bike explode under me. I get burnt, my face is burnt. Poirot appears, wraps a sheet around me, but I cannot breathe. I have to poke a hole into the sheet.

Immediately, she associates, 'It's burn-out!'

In recent years, hardly a week has passed by without articles in the popular press about overwork, stress and their dire physical, emotional, political and further effects. 'Sloth' for example, asks A. A. Gill, 'Is it a sin or a virtue? We have all the time in the world to decide' (2004). A host of books have been published on the subject: *Speed. A Society on Drugs* (Dany, 2008), *Faster. The Acceleration of Just About Everything* (Gleick, 1999). The journalist Ulrich Schnabel speaks of 'the acceleration society' (2012, p. 16). By contrast, there is also, *In Praise of Slow. How a Worldwide Movement is Challenging the Cult of Speed* (Honoré, 2004), *How to be Idle* (Hodgkinson, 2004), *Meditations for Men/Women Who Do Too Much* (Lazear, 1993; Wilson Schaef, 1990). One of the earliest of these texts against overwork is actually 'The Right to Laziness', written in 1883 by Paul Lafargue, Karl Marx's son-in-law. None of these, though, has been written by a psychoanalyst.

The term 'Burnout Syndrome' was first used in 1974 by the New York psychoanalyst Herbert Freudenberger from his observations of care-workers. Cleric Stephen Wright explains, 'burnout tends predominantly to affect professional carers of all sorts who may be bringing their natural heart-centredness into their jobs. In doing so they seem to get into patterns of over-giving while under-receiving' (2010, p. 5). Significantly, I have only found a single text in the analytic field on the subject, published well over 25 years ago by the American psychoanalyst Arnold Cooper (1986). Might we interpret this as an indication of resistance? What if we followed Andrew Samuels' suggestion of taking the public 'as our social critic – perhaps even . . . analyst' (1996, p. 295) and assume this touches a sore point the profession needs to protect? Why this reluctance, especially, it seems, from analysts/therapists to look at an endemic addictiveness to self-abusive overwork which leads to burn-out, and is, ultimately, a question of life or death? With all these implications – personal, social, political, ecological, ethical and spiritual – this is a multi-faceted issue which requires an interdisciplinary approach.

I divide my chapter into five parts. My argument is not linear, but rather follows a circular orbit which is the way I believe the alchemical process portrayed in the alchemical *Rosarium* woodcuts, used by Jung in 'The Psychology of the Transference' (CW 16) needs to be understood: with neither specific beginning nor end, always returning to the beginning in the cyclical arc of waxing and waning, death and rebirth.

Beginning with 'Analysis', I introduce the problem as one of self-neglect which can be understood as ultimately suicidal. Here I give a brief outline of the aetiology of the pathology, before indicating the direction in which healing may lie. Next, in 'Alchemy', I trace the origins of a holistic world view which enables us to see the unity in the complexities of the different facets. I present this in referring to ancient teachings of Chinese alchemists which later were reflected in the *unus mundus* concept of first Egyptian and Arabic, then European alchemical traditions. In 'Eco-psychology', I link these ideas to recent and current ecological concerns, drawing parallels between one of the most important European alchemist-healers of the past, Paracelsus, and, moving to recent modern times, Wilhelm Reich – both of them hotly debated (and derided) to this day. I am particularly concerned with the later period of Reich's work which continues to be doubted as the work of a 'crackpot' (Hillman, 2006, p. 29). Echoing Jung's take on Paracelsus (CW 13), and almost presenting 'Reich as a Spiritual Phenomenon', I want to show how, with his holistic perspective, Reich can not only be seen as continuing the alchemical traditions, but should also be respected as the first eco-psychologist. His ideas can be linked to both the ancient Taoist and alchemical teachings as well as to modern quantum theory. Already in 1968, R. D. Laing wrote about Reich, 'Even his later work on bio-physics cannot be so glibly confined to cranksville as it was ten years ago' (in Boadella, 1973, p. 8). In 'Radical hope', I tease out the spiritual implications of these ideas, towards a re-sacralisation of analysis and radical (eco-) politics, which is how the healing arts started. I end with 'Healing grace': possible solutions of the present dilemma of individual, collective and global burn-out in linking 'radical hope' (Lear, 2006) with the numinous.

Analysis

Essentially, one might say, the cure is effected by love.
(Sigmund Freud, 1906, in Freud/Jung, 1974, p. 12)

Those who initiated the clinical work, right from the start, inflicted their own pathology on it by setting the standard for overwork in analysis: Freud 'worked nine to eleven hours a day with his patients and then, at eleven at night, settled down at his desk to write' (Clark, 1982, p. 145). 'At present I am devoting ten hours a day to psychotherapy', Freud wrote to Jung in 1906 (Freud/Jung, 1974, p. 12). And Jung is known to have said, 'Patients eat me' and 'I have far more work now than I can do' (in Bair, 2004, p. 376). Some 20 years ago I read Christopher Bollas' 'The *Shadow* of the Object: Psychoanalysis of the *Unthought* Known' (1987, my italics). Right at the start, he writes, 'When I practise psychoanalysis, seeing ten people a day five days a week . . .' (1987, p. 10). From where I'm looking today, I would call this not only self-abusive but abusive of other(s), his patients, too. These two always go together: abuse of self mirrors abuse of others. The culture of overwork is deeply rooted in our psyche. From a Jungian perspective, we may understand this as a being stuck in the negative pole of the archetype of the wounded healer: rather than being aware of their wound – 'Physician heal thyself!' (Luke 4:23) – many analysts seem to masochistically idealise it. And this – as 'actions speak louder than words!' – is being transmitted to our patients.

Thus, like a virus, something truly deadly may pass from analyst to patient. It is the analyst's task to pick that up and stop that process. Cooper states unequivocally that, 'it is clear that the analyst has an obligation to know a good deal about what frightens him . . . what brings out his sadness' (1986, p. 578) – might we add, 'what brings out his or her depression?' 'In gloomy moments', Cooper continues, 'it has sometimes seemed to me that the life course of too many analysts begins with an excess of curative zeal and proceeds in the latter part of their careers toward excessive therapeutic nihilism' (ibid., p. 577). He links this with cumulative burn-out: increasingly, burn-out is being understood as a euphemism for depression (Dettmer *et al.*, 2011, p. 116). We may well understand Freud's growing pessimism as well as Jung's bitterness towards the end of his life in this way. Today we think in terms of a work/life imbalance. Some 30 years ago, German psychoanalyst Wolfgang Schmidbauer spoke of the

> "Helpers' Syndrome" as the incapacity that has grown to become part of the character structure, to express – and, I would add, even to become aware of – one's own feelings and needs, combined with the seemingly omnipotent, impregnable façade in the area of social services.
>
> (1982, p. 12)

Schmidbauer gives a chilling example in the form of a nightmare in which a care-worker traces a whimpering sound to a garden shed where he discovers a skeletal child, half dead from thirst, covered with dirt and cobwebs, wedged in between old junk (ibid., p. 15). Is it this that too many analysts 'need to hide out of sight', as it were? Is the subject of self-neglect not being touched because it is 'too close to the bone', 'touches a raw nerve'? Often it seems that men tend to be easier cut off from their feelings, their needy selves, as the ratrace in the 'Overwork Culture' (Bunting, 2004b) seems to encourage characteristics which may traditionally be regarded as masculine: the manic defense of hunting for more, more and more, ever higher achievements in order not to have to bother with the near-corpse in the shed of the unconscious. Recently, the *Financial Times* asked, 'Charming, materialistic, aggressive, self-centred, Machiavellian, thrill-seeking alpha males with little respect for rules who eat stress for breakfast – sound like a banker you know? If so, think again: it is a summary of the traits of psychopaths' (Mackintosh, 2011). The spiritual teacher Eckart Tolle comments:

> The unchecked striving for more, for endless growth, is a dysfunction and a disease. It is the same dysfunction that a cancerous cell manifests, whose only goal is to multiply itself, unaware that it is bringing about its own destruction by destroying the organism of which it is a part.
>
> (2005, p. 37)

Given these exaggerated and bellicose 'masculine' values of capitalism and Social Darwinism, is it a mere coincidence that it should have been be a *woman* analyst, Sabina Spielrein, who recommended long holidays? In 1929 she writes, 'psychoanalysis exhausts . . . It follows that the . . . psychoanalyst requires an extended holiday, probably longer than . . . a 2 ½ months summer break' (1987, p. 343). My friend and colleague Martin Stone quotes Gerhard Adler: 'I need long holidays in order to be able to work with my patients, and I need to work with my patients in order to pay for my long holidays' (2010).

So, what is this deadly virus we need to be careful not to pass on to patients? One way of understanding the 'hereditary illness' may lie in the sphere of relating – both within as well as outside of ourselves, the self/other issue Otto Gross initially introduced to the analytic discourse. Irrespective of whether or not we believe, as Melanie Klein did, that 'the primitive' – i.e. inborn – 'love impulse has an aggressive aim' (in Winnicott, 1987, p. 22) (personally I *don't*), it does make sense that with the Winnicottian 'good enough' mothering, as he put it, 'ruthlessness gives way to ruth, unconcern to concern' (ibid., pp. 22–23). We might speak of the birth of love from love received, and assume this applies to both self and other. Lack of this, as Winnicott chillingly puts it, results in the feelings of 'going to pieces', of 'falling forever' and of 'having no relationship to the body' (ibid., p. 58). These are issues of life and death: 'to be, or not to be' (Shakespeare: *Hamlet*, III.i.56) in the profoundest sense of the word. A way to protect against such 'unthinkable and archaic anxieties' (ibid., p. 61) and to survive them as best as possible, is to develop what Winnicott calls a false self that uses power to relate to both self and other.

This, in a way, is identifying with the depriver/aggressor in an emotional maneouvre which, again, Gross was the first to describe. In his terms, the 'will to relating' gets replaced by the 'will to power' (Gross, 1919; Heuer, G., 2001, pp. 662–663). We come to favour 'unconcern' – being cool! – over concern, power over love. Winnicott speaks here of a 'manic defense', the attribute merely hinting at the panic of despair that fuels such action. More vividly, psychoanalyst Sue Grand calls it 'the bestial gesture of survival' (in Benjamin, 2009, p. 55); the action taken to escape catastrophe and inflict suffering rather than bear it oneself. Indeed, this violence, as Eckhart Tolle states, 'is weakness disguised as strength' (1999, p. 36). Yet, that outward-directed violence takes an even greater toll where it is mirrored intra-psychically by a relentless self-destruction. The Brazilian writer Euclides da Cunha speaks of 'a man working to enslave himself' (in Gann, 2009, p. 75).

Again, we might consider how this hostile attitude towards the other favours characteristics traditionally seen as masculine – hardness, coolness, agression and doing – over those traditionally seen as feminine – softness, feelings, receptivity and being. This finds its expression not only in the gender wars but also in a masculine-oriented warlike attitude against all that is regarded as feminine: that is not just woman, but also body – as in matter, derived from *mater*, mother – as well as 'mother' nature, the totality of the global and cosmic environment. Cleric Peter Millar writes, 'Hand in hand with the subordination of women has gone the neglect of the earth and an abuse of the human body' (2007, p. 23).

Consider Lenin, speaking in 1920:

> Nothing is lovelier than the *Appassionata*! I could listen to it all day! . . . But I can't listen to music! It gets on my nerves! It arouses a yearning in me to babble about nothing, to caress people . . . But nowadays if you stroke anybody's head, he'll bite off your hand! Now you have to hit them on the head, hit them on the head mercilessly . . . though in principle we oppose all violence!
>
> (In Makavejev, 1972, pp. 135–136)

Psychologist Isabella Heuser understands 'burnout predominantly as a male term . . . It's no coincidence that it's been invented by a man.' The term contains the message that at least they did make an effort. 'That may well be something men might just about be able to admit to when they are taken ill with depression' (Dettmer *et al.*, 2011, p. 116). This seems to be clearly expressed in *Beautiful Burnout*, Bryony Lavery's play about 'the explosively visceral world of boxing: the soul sapping three minute bursts where men become gods and gods become men' (Anon., 2012).

Wilhelm Reich saw the inner conflict portrayed here as also a collective, political and global one of the alive against the dead(-ened). This is how he understood the Christian parable of 'The Murder of Christ' (1972). He called the resulting pathology 'Emotional Plague' (1972). The prevailing negativity can thus be understood as a manic defense, driven by the despair to not stop and *be*, as that might entail becoming aware of those unbearable 'archaic anxieties' (Winnicott, 1987, p. 61). Understandably, such awareness needs to be suppressed, *de*pressed, and this blanks out positive vision. This inner depression then being projected onto the outside world – 'the end is nigh' – creates a fear industry caught in the vicious circle of an ever increasing fatal dialectic with an addictive craving for misery, suffering and catastrophe. In sum, as *The Guardian* recently put it, 'An insatiable appetite for evil' (Dugdale, 2011, p. 1) – just watch the news tonight.

Alchemy

> You are the macrocosm.
> (Rumi, 1999, p. 4)

This holistic Reichian perspective can be seen as located in the alchemical tradition. Uncertain whether this originated in China or Egypt (Holmyard, 1957, p. 23), what we call alchemy in the West is a holistic world view in the profoundest sense: not only is there no separation between science and religion, man, woman and God, there is also none between the inanimate, the animate and the spiritual world. This has been called the '*unus mundus*', one world, linked, all-pervaded by and consisting of different forms of energy, at times called Mercurius, the messenger between the gods and earth, expressed in the maxim, 'as above, so below' and Tao, in the East, 'That which produces and composes the universe . . . the undivided oneness or ultimate nothingness' (Ni, 2008, p. 12). In the last century, science, in developing quantum physics, has created a rapprochment to these concepts, prompting their revaluation.

One of the most important European alchemists and healers was Paracelsus (1493?–1541). One biographer speaks of his 'tender medicine, the profoundest basis of which was love' (Meier, 2004, p. 11) and writes, 'Unique in his total work . . . is his perspective that embraces medicine, cosmology, psychopathology, magical aspects and political critique' (ibid., p. 12). Paracelsus already admonished that 'the good doctor . . . should not practise self-abuse' (in Ball, 2007, p. 209). Yet, just some years earlier, a contemporary had observed Paracelsus, 'sleeps but little, with boots and spurs and fully dressed, he throws himself into bed for three hours or so, then writes again' (ibid., p. 260). Interestingly, this self-neglect is mirrored by one of his patients, the renowned Erasmus of Rotterdam (1465/66–1536), who wrote after a consultation:

> At present I have no time for a cure, indeed I have no time either to be sick or die, for I am engaged in exacting studies. However, if you know something that might give me relief, please let me know it.
>
> (Ibid., p. 195)

Some ten years later, a year before he died, aged 70, Erasmus regretted, 'I have lived a long life, counting the years; but were I to calculate the time wrestling with fever, the stone and gout, I have not lived long' (ibid., p. 195).

Eco-psychology

The only myth that is going to be worth thinking about
in the immediate future is one that is talking about the planet
and everything on it.

(Joseph Campbell, 1986, in Opus Archives, 2009)

In the brief history of psychoanalysis during the past 125 years, Freud's initial
focus on a one-person-psychology shifted with Otto Gross (1877–1920) to a
relational perspective. Gross also radicalised Freud's tentative links between the
individual neurosis and that of the collective: he taught and lived an active
engagement in revolutionary politics: 'The psychology of the unconscious is the
philosophy of the revolution' (Gross, 2009, p. 78). Jung developed these ideas
further towards an intersubjective approach in the clinical setting and paralleled
this by postulating – as Gross had before him – a corresponding dialectical
relationship between the human and the divine. Based on his study of alchemy as
well as Eastern philosophies, Jung also assumed an unconscious interconnected-
ness between human beings independent of time and culture, the collective
unconscious.

What remains excluded from their '*unus mundus* perspective'? All three, Freud,
Gross and Jung were medical doctors, yet they did not really concern themselves
with the bodies of their patients, although Freud initially included practices similar
to later body psychotherapeutic techniques, Gross saw that 'each psychical process
is at the same time a physiological one' (Gross, 1907, p. 7), and Jung developed a
concept of a psychoid subtle body, an in-between state between matter and psyche.
Excluded were matter, earth and the cosmos, the world at large.

The man who filled this gap was Wilhelm Reich (1897–1957). Initially a pupil
of Freud's, he incorporated working directly with the body into his psychoanalytic
practice. This was based on his discovery (as far as the Western scientific discourse
is concerned) that repressed emotions are stored in the body in the form of
muscular tensions. If these became chronic, Reich spoke of a muscular or character
armour. With him, more or less all current forms of body psychotherapy originated. Reich continued and expanded Gross' work on the links between psychoanalysis and radical politics. This cost him the membership of the International
Psychoanalytic Association in 1934 at a time when this organisation wanted to
come to an agreement with the Nazis who had been voted into power in Germany.
Persecuted and exiled, his research, first in Scandinavia, later in the USA, led
Reich to the manifestations of psychic energy first in the human body, then in
matter and he came to later discover it in the surrounding atmosphere and in the
cosmos. His name for what the ancient Chinese had called 'chi', and what the
alchemists had named 'Mercurius', was 'Orgone Energy'.

The American writer and psychotherapist Paul Goodman seems to have been
the first to call Wilhelm Reich an alchemist, and compare him to Paracelsus (1969,
p. 13). The logo Reich devised for his work can be seen as a modern version of the

Figure 8.1 Reich's sigil
Source: Gottfried M. Heuer

staff of Mercurius, with the life energy flowing forth from a starting point, dividing into opposing forces in order to reunite – and create another beginning.

Reich's understanding of the links between neurotic self-abuse and the neuroses enacted in society and politics, which he saw mirrored in the way we treat the environment, make him also the very first eco-psychologist. Already in 1973 his biographer David Boadella wrote, 'his studies led ultimately to the planetary issues of human ecology, where the problem of pollution became a primary concern' (1973, p. 7). Reich subsequently developed methods of weather modification and control, thus, in effect, becoming the first eco-psychotherapist. He devised ways to collect and concentrate 'orgone energy' to supplement emotional healing on an energetic level, and drew parallels between the emotional/muscular armouring of people – which he understood as an inner 'emotional desert' (in Greenfield, 1974, p. 171) – and the alarming spreading of deserts as well as atmospheric pollution, a 'planetary emergency' (ibid., p. 137). In 1952, Reich devised a weather control apparatus, and experimented successfully with it both in the northeastern USA as well as in the Arizona desert, concentrating on 'rain-making' (ibid., p. 291) as a form of 'atmospheric medicine' (ibid., p. 186). Einstein 'confirmed some of his findings and said it would be a bombshell to physics if Reich's findings were true' (ibid., p. 7).

Yet with the all-encompassing range of his work which included also spiritual dimensions, Reich was so far ahead of his time that he became a despised outsider, whose later work was supposedly that of a 'madman', and hence not to be taken seriously – in spite of the fact that some of Reich's weather control experiments were successfully repeated in the early 1960s by Charles Kelley (1922–2005), a nationally renowned meteorologist (1961), and in the 1990s by James DeMeo in California, Israel and the South-East African Sahel Desert (1992; n.d.; Bechmann, 1997). Heiko Lassek, M.D., has successfully been treating cancer patients in Berlin for many years with 'orgone energy' (Bartuska, 2004; Lassek, 2006). Speaking of cancer, it has recently been found that 'stress furthers the growth of cancer-cells', in that heightened adrenaline weakens the immune system and thus stops it from destroying degenerating cells (Anon., 2007).

'Radical hope'

God is our hope and strength:
a very present help in trouble.
Therefore we will not fear,
though the earth be moved
and though the hills be carried
into the midst of the sea.

Psalm 46

Self-love, let us return to where we started from, 'love thy neighbour as thyself' (Lev. XIX: 18). With quantum theory, science appears to come full circle, confirming much of what the ancient Eastern and Western alchemical traditions have described for millennia, that all and everything is interlinked in an ocean of energy, implying a world soul or *anima mundi*.

The Talmud states, 'We do not see things as they are. We see them as we are' (in Plimer, 2009, p. 15). Following Nietzsche's 'Man can stretch himself as he may with his knowledge . . .; in the last analysis, he gives nothing but his own biography' (1906, I, No. 513) for Jung, 'every psychological theory should be criticized in the first instance as a subjective confession' (CW 10, para. 1025). When I survey the doom-laden field of eco-psychology from this perspective, I understand the apocalyptic predictions for a future which cannot possibly be other than catastrophic, and there is nothing we can do about that anymore, as an all-pervading depression projected outward. Just as Jung – even with the hindsight of some 40 years – failed to see his own 'subjective confession', as it were, in his dream of late 1913, where he saw all Europe flooded by blood (1963, p. 199): rather than understanding the symbolism 'in the first instance' as reflecting the emotional catastrophe of his breakup with Freud, Jung 'persuaded himself that . . . the dreams were "a true precognition of war,"' – a possibility I do not mean to exclude – 'and tried not to worry about them in a personal sense' (Bair, 2004, p. 243).

Correspondingly, when, very shortly before his death, Jung wrote that our 'immediate communication with nature is gone forever' (CW 18, para. 585; cf. Bernstein, 2010, p. 16), this, I believe, is better understood in connection with his aforementioned resigned bitterness towards the end of his life. Somewhat provocatively, Eckhart Tolle writes, linking the intrapsychic realm with the collective as well as the ecosphere, in

> resisting what *is* , . . . you are creating unhappiness, conflict between the inner and outer. Your unhappiness is polluting not only your inner being and those around you but also the collective human psyche of which you are an inseparable part. The pollution of the planet is only an outward reflection of an inner psychic pollution.
>
> (1999, p. 65).

Negativity is . . . a psychic pollutant, and there is a deep link between the poisoning and destruction of nature and the vast negativity that has accumulated in the collective human psyche. . . . Your perception of the world is a reflection of your state of consciousness. . . . our collective reality is largely a symbolic expression of fear and of the heavy layers of negativity that have accumulated in the human psyche.

(Ibid., pp. 157, 164–166)

Winnicott, in 'Fear of Breakdown' (1989, pp. 87–95) describes the psychic mechanism used to survive trauma, by definition the onslaught of overwhelming feelings: they get split off. But they do not vanish. The repressed returns to haunt us in the form of terrors, anxieties of *future* catastrophes. Winnicott understands these as the traumas of a past we have already survived – at the cost of current depressions. These hauntings do have a purpose other than making our lives a misery, as the feelings that were too much to cope with in the past demand to be dealt with. But passing them on like the proverbial hot potato by projecting – literally throwing them out – or passing them on to patients, is no way to do that. Conservationist does not at all need to mean conservatory, yet, in this sense, the vast majority of eco-psychologists work hand in hand with politicians and the media in what has aptly been called 'the fear industry'. Catastrophist views abound. The editors of a recent collection of 'Psychological Responses to Ecological Crisis' (Rust & Totton, 2012) head their introduction with a quote from George Orwell, 'The actual outlook is very dark, and any serious thought should start out from that fact' (p. xv). This dialectically corresponds to an apparently growing addictive craving for misery. Some 150 years ago Charles Baudelaire commented,

Every newspaper from the first to the last line is a web of horrors. And this disgusting aperitif every civilised European takes for his daily breakfast. I do not understand how a clean hand can touch a newssheet without getting cramps of nausea.

(1925, p. 356)

Therefore, nutritionist Andrew Weil actually recommends 'news fasts', abstaining from news for periods of time because, 'Most news reports increase anxiety . . . Many people are addicted to reading newspapers and news magazines, and to listening to news programs on radio and television . . . News addiction is a major roadblock to learning to relax' (1998, p. 117). Weil underpins his recommendation by what is now known about the directly measurable weakening effect distressing news and images have on our immune system (ibid., pp. 92–93, 134, 138, 200–201, 256).

See-saw-like, the 'imminent terror' changes from one extreme to the other: since being scared in the mid-1970s by the 'news' of a new ice age was imminent, the emphasis has shifted to a ubiquitous end-of-the-world-scenario by global warming. In 2012, we may well be on the cusp of yet another change as the popular press announces 'Ice age is put on ice' (Leaver, 2012, pp. 12–13), as if the immediate onset of another ice age had been foremost on our minds. Professor of Earth Sciences Ian Plimer writes:

> Climate changes are cyclical and random. . . . To argue that we humans can differentiate between human-induced climate changes and natural climate changes is naïve. . . . The slogan "Stop climate change" is a very public advertisement of absolute total ignorance as it is not cognisant of history, archaeology, geology, astronomy, ocean sciences, atmospheric sciences and life sciences.
>
> (2009, pp. 11–12).

Plimer concludes by saying:

> The greatest global threat . . . is from policy responses to perceived global warming and the demonising of dissent. . . . There are calls for trials and imprisonment for those scientists who, on scientific evidence, do not agree that human emissions have changed climate. Such scientists are called deniers and are compared to Holocaust deniers.
>
> (Ibid., p. 435)

Recently, James Lovelock, who formulated the Gaia theory of Earth as a self-regulating, single organism, said in an interview, 'I am allowed to change my mind' (Hickman/Lovelock, 2012). He 'predicted in 2006 that by this century's end "billions of us will die and the few breeding pairs of people that survive will be in the Arctic where the climate remains tolerable"' (ibid., p. 35). He now admitted that he had been mistaken in 'claiming to know with such certainty what will happen with the climate' (ibid.). He also expressed criticism of the cultish aspects of the green movement, saying 'if there's a cause of some sort, a religion starts forming around it. It just so happens that the green religion is now taking over from the Christian religion . . . it's got all the terms that religions use' (ibid., p 36).

Let us turn here to the myth of Pandora (see Chapter 6, pp. 98 ff.). She is assumed by some to be a denigrated nature-goddess. One way to translate her name is 'the All-Giver' (Panofsky & Panofsky, 1991, p. 4). The evil ways we usually associate with her are seen as the result of patriarchal defamations. In early versions of the myth she does not have a box but a huge storage jar. Apparently, the aforementioned Erasmus, in his referring to the myth, changed the storage jar to a small box (ibid., pp. 14 ff.), a make-up case, thus pushing the story towards that of an alluring *femme fatale* carrying a box which contains all the evils of the world. But there is something else: the myth tells us that at the very bottom of this box, once all the evils have been released, there is hope. In view of what I have said so far, might we, from an analytical perspective, understand the mythical Pandora in one aspect as an anima/soul, holding for us all that which we have found impossibly overwhelming to deal with? Might the myth also be suggesting a solution to our dilemma in the direction of setting free the traumas of the past – poisonously self-destructive only as long as they are being internally re-/depressed? And might that put us in touch with hope, hope that has thus far been buried?

There are two kinds of hope: one that grows out of what Freud calls a 'turning away from reality' (in Lear, 2006, p. 116), turning a blind eye. Clearly, this cannot be the kind of hope the myth speaks of: a hope that is found 'at the very bottom', after all the evils have been faced. Rather, it is a hope that squarely does face reality, including all its shadow sides and evils. This is the second kind of hope which the American philosopher and psychoanalyst Jonathan Lear calls '*Radical Hope*' (2006). In the context of his alchemical studies, Jung said, 'the shadow can contain up to eighty percent pure gold', its essence is 'pure gold' (in Tuby, 1984, p. 13). This perspective leads us back to the original Pandora as a nature goddess with a large storage jar. We may understand it as a cornucopia full of life, life energy, in its multiple forms, as Jungian Gail Thomas beautifully describes in *Healing Pandora: The Restoration of Hope and Abundance* (2009).

And this, finally, brings me to the chickadee, a small, titmouse-like bird of North America. In his book, *Radical Hope: Ethics in the Face of Cultural Devastation* (2006), Lear develops the concept with the help of the biography of the Native American Crow Chief Alaxchiiaahush or Plenty Coups (referring to the number of times he had touched enemy warriors in battle, called 'counting coups' (1846/7–1932)). His lifetime nearly spans the century when the Native Americans faced cultural devastation and total annihilation: 'not only the loss of their entire way of life . . . but the concepts that made life meaningful beyond mere survival. . . . The young future chief was called to dream on behalf of the tribe when he was nine years old' (Eyres, 2009). He dreamed of the annihilation of the different Native American people and their way of life in seeing all the trees of a forest being blown down by a mighty storm, except for one: the tree that housed the chickadee, 'the most insignificant of all forest creatures. But the chickadee made up for in mental strength what he lacked in physical power: the chickadee was a great listener, willing to learn from others' (ibid.). The interpretation given by the tribe's elders was 'that the Crow-people should learn from the wisdom of the chickadee; not succumb to despair or go down fighting in a blaze of glory' (ibid.), as some neighbouring tribes did. The path Plenty Coups chose, based on his childhood dream, was with an immense courage to find an alternative to the tribe's warrior tradition and to arrange themselves with the overwhelming might of the whites. Fully facing their cultural devastation, his radical hope 'wagers a visceral trust that there is enough goodness in the world for things to turn out . . . alright' (ibid.), even if there is nothing rationally knowable on which to base such trust.

In ecological terms, Plenty Coups' listening to the chickadee unmistakably speaks not only of the necessity of 'an immediate communication with nature', as Jung expressed it, but also, in contrast to him and most current eco-psychologists, of a continuing potential to do so. To be clear, the communication I mean is, as

Jerome Bernstein puts it, 'not a regressive return to a state once lived but is developmentally progressed in evolutionary terms' (2010, p. 21).

Healing grace

From a depth-psychological perspective, we might understand the mighty storm in Plenty Coups' dream as a force of archetypal dimensions. A regressive – and neurotic – response might well be a capitulation to this destructive force. Consideration of the Winnicottian manic response to 'the feeling of falling forever' referred to earlier, takes me to a strong component of addiction in the individually self-destructive patterns of this our 'Age of Exhaustion' (Hall, 2009). Already in 1883, Paul Lafargue begins his above-mentioned pamphlet by speaking about 'a strange addiction . . . that, in modern society results in misery for both the individual and the masses, . . . the frantic work-addiction that leads to . . . exhaustion'. For a while now, the term 'workaholism' has been in use for this addiction – again, a theme predominantly taken up today by journalists: 'This pressure – I can't live without it' (Munday, 2009); 'The rise of the activity junkie' (Hutton, 2004); 'Might as well face it: you're addicted to stress' (Leve, 2004). Yet, the issue is literally a deadly serious one. Jungian analyst David Schoen defines addiction:

> The addictive substance, activity or behaviour must ultimately take over complete and total control of the individual, psychologically. . . . And the second part of this definition is crucial: the addiction takes over control in an inherently destructive and ultimately life-threatening way. It is not an addiction unless it is a death sentence . . . of the mind, the body, and of the spirit. It is death sentence to the addict's career, community, marriage, family and friends. It is not an addiction unless it has the lethal capacity and potential, the power to kill the individual.
>
> (2009, pp. 3–4)

If we consider addictions are attempts to protect from unbearable pain, then the pain at the root of the addiction to overwork and burn-out might well be understood as that of never having felt good enough, never having experienced our mother's delight in our being who we are. 'No, I've never had that!' a patient recently exclaimed with shocking spontaneity in response to my having mentioned this affirming delight. So, the burning question becomes, 'Will I Ever Be Good Enough?' as psychologist Karyl McBride asks in her book (2009). From this perspective, we can understand workaholism as being very similar to that 'desperate gesture of survival' (Grand in Benjamin, 2009, p. 55), or, as my colleague Catriona Howatson puts it, 'clawing myself out of a black hole' (2009).

Jung understood addiction as ultimately a striving for the numinous by famously seeing the spiritual dimension in the alcoholic's craving for spirit. This later led to the basis of Alcoholics Anonymous (Schoen, 2009, pp. 9–29).

Correspondingly, Stephen Wright, yet without referring directly to Jung, regards burn-out as 'a spiritual crisis on the way home' (2010), and speaks of a:

> subjective turn . . . where we seek inner understanding and meaning, exploration of the self. . . . Burnout is a desperate cry of the very essence of who we are/the higher self/the soul to break free. . . . It is the struggle to be in the world in which we find and give love and compassion.
>
> (pp. 4, 7)

For me, individual and collective healing meet in the turning point of the 'subjective turn', invoking the spiritual dimension that we may call grace. Psychotherapist Gerald May writes:

> Understanding will not deliver us from addiction, but it will, I hope, help us appreciate grace. Grace is the most powerful force in the universe. It can transcend repression, addiction and every other internal or external power that seeks to oppress the freedom of the human heart. Grace is where our hope lies.
>
> (1988, pp. 4–5)

The heading of this section 'healing grace' refers to the work of Jungian analyst Birgit Heuer who extensively argues for both the return of the Divine and the healing function of grace in the clinical hour (Heuer, B., 2003, 2004, 2008; see Chapter 9). It is to her credit to have allowed the spiritual dimension to descend from its lofty theoretical heights and to ground it in actual clinical practice (Heuer, B., 2010).

I see grace as the essence of the radical hope Lear speaks of. It is the *temenos* where the concerns of ancient indigenous and Western healing arts alchemically melt together with contemporary psychoanalysis and therapy: this is the direction where healing lies – just as Jung wrote in 1945, 'my work is not concerned with the treatment of neuroses but rather with the approach to the numinous . . . that . . . is the real therapy' (1973, p. 377).

From this perspective, that longing can only be fulfiled when we can say, 'God loves me as I am. I love myself as I am' or, in the words of a poem I wrote about this very experience under the dome of the *Frauenkirche* Church of our Lady, Dresden, where, in a different incarnation, Pandora, as the archetypal goddess, gets reinstated as the 'All-Giver':

> I hold this dome
> inside me now,
> so, when in need,
> I can sit underneath
> this waterfall of grace
> that never ever ends,
> remembering

. . .

that *any* wound
can heal,
be healed,
and, really,
that the dome of heaven
in our Lady's blue,
is always sheltering me
as I
live right inside
Her sweet, angelic breast
in the land of milk
and honey –
paradise regained!
        (Heuer, G., 2010, p. 140)

Conclusion

Don't just do something – sit there!
        (T. Nath Hanh, in Schnabel, 2012, p. 129)

Beginning with a sociological take on our current Western 'overwork culture', I considered the extent to which we, in our field of psychoanalysis/therapy are part of this problem and whether we might be capable of becoming part of its solution. I give these concerns both an historical as well as a holistic dimension by tracing them back to the *unus mundus* perspective of the alchemists past and present, using Paracelsus and Wilhelm Reich respectively as examples. I gathered these thoughts together in order to arrive, with the help of the Greek myth of Pandora, and the dream of a nineteenth-century Native American at the concept of 'Radical Hope: ethics in the face of cultural devastation' towards healing on individual, collective, planetary and cosmic levels: in clear distinction to mere optimism, we can have a profoundly spiritual trust in an unknowable future. Let us hope – dare I say, pray? – that we, too, can listen to the chickadee – and also learn from the sloth.

According to Wilhelm Reich, 'embracing lovers radiate a bluish light, orgone illumination, the same sort of light the astronauts saw in outer space', and he called on us to 'reactivate the natural vibrations within ourselves and society. Let the currents stream sweetly through . . . our muscles! Feel free to tremble and cry!' (in Makavejev, 1972, pp. 32–33).

Acknowledgements

Different versions of this text have been published in *Zeitschrift für Körper-psychotherapie*, 16: 53/54, Vienna, 2010, 41–56; *Psychotherapy and Politics International*, 8:1, 2011, 29–42; and *Montreal 2010. Facing Multiplicity: Psyche,*

Nature, Culture. Proceedings of the XVIIIth Congress of the International Association for Analytical Psychology, P. Bennett, ed., Einsiedeln: Daimon, 149–158 (CD); and presented at the 2nd International Conference of the International Association for Jungian Studies, 'Psyche, Power and Society', in Cardiff, 11 July 2009; The Cambridge Jungian Circle, Cambridge, 19 February 2010; The Association of Jungian Analysts, London, 8 June 2010; the XVIIIth Congress of the International Association for Analytical Psychology, 'Facing Multiplicity: Psyche, Nature, Culture', Montreal, 22–27 August 2010; and the C.G. Jung Public Lectures, Bristol, 12 February 2011.

References

Anon. (2007) 'Stress fördert Krebszellen' *Geo,* 7, 187.

Anon. (2012) www.nationaltheatrescotland.com/content/default.asp?page=home_Beautiful Burnout (Accessed 30 September 2012).

Anon. (n.d.) Greeting card. London: Cath Tate Cards.

Bair, D. (2004) *Jung* London: Little, Brown.

Ball, P. (2007) *The Devil's Doctor* London: Arrow.

Barth, R. (2011) 'Arbeit ist der neue Sex' *Stern,* 51, 1, 36–44.

Bartuska, C. (2004) 'Heiko Lassek über Wilhelm Reich' *Zeitschrift für Körperpsychotherapie* 11, 38, 4–21.

Baudelaire, C. (1925) 'Mein entblösstes Herz' *Kritische und Nachgelassene Schriften* München: Müller, 343–363.

Bean, A. (2004) 'Be a lean, mean fat-burning machine' *Top-Santé,* February, 99–102.

Bechmann, A. (1997) *Über Wilhelm Reichs OROP Wüste* Frankfurt: Zweitausendeins.

Benjamin, J. (2009) 'Mutual acknowledgement?' In G. Heuer, ed., *Sacral Revolutions* London: Routledge, 51–58.

Bernstein, J. (2010) *Borderland Consciousness* London: Guild of Pastoral Psychology.

Boadella, D. (1973) *Wilhelm Reich* London: Vision.

Bollas, C. (1987) *The Shadow of the Object: Psychoanalysis of the Unthought Known* London: Free Association.

Bunting, M. (2004a) *White Slaves* London: HarperCollins.

—— (2004b) 'Sweet smiles, hard labour' *Guardian Weekend,* 12 June, 17–22.

Clark, R.W. (1982) *Freud* London: Granada.

Cooper, A. (1986) The 'Burnout Syndrome'. *Psychoanalytic Quarterly,* LV, 576–598.

Dany, H.-C. (2008) *Speed: A Society on Drugs* Hamburg: Nautilus.

DeMeo, J. (1992) *OROP Israel 1991–92.* El Cerrito: Manuscript.

—— (n.d.). *Green Sea Eritrea* Manuscript.

Dettmer, M., S. Shafi & J. Tietz (2011) 'Ausgebrannt' *Der Spiegel,* 4, 1, 114–122.

Dugdale, J. (2011) 'Library chart 2010' *Guardian,* 19 February, *Review,* 1, 19.

Eyres, H. (2009) 'When hope is all you have' *Financial Times,* 28 February/1 March, 22.

Freud, S./C. G. Jung (1974) *The Freud/Jung Letters* London: Hogarth, Routledge and Kegan Paul.

Gann, D. (2009) *The Lost City of Z* London: Simon and Schuster.

Gill, A. A. (2004) 'Sloth' *Sunday Times, Style,* 28 November, 102.

Gleick, J. (1999) *Faster. The Acceleration of Just About Everything* London: Abacus.

Goodman, P. (1969) 'Introduction'. In I.Ollendorff, *Wilhelm Reich* New York: Avon, 11–15.

Grand, S. (2002) *The Reproduction of Evil* Hillsdale, NJ: Analytic Press.

Greene, G. (2001) *A Burnt-out Case* New York: Vintage.

Greenfied, J. (1974) *Wilhelm Reich VS. The U.S.A* New York: Norton.

Gross, O. (1907) *Das Freudsche Ideogenitätsmoment und seine Bedeutung im manisch-depressiven Irresein Kraepelins* Leipzig: Vogel.

—— (1919) 'Zur funktionellen Geistesbildung des Revolutionärs' *Räte-Zeitung*, 1, 52.

—— (2009) 'On overcoming the cultural crisis 1913' Appendix to G. Heuer, The sacral revolution, *International Journal of Jungian Studies*, 1, 1, 77–80.

Hall, A. (2009) 'Welcome to the Age of Exhaustion' *Observer Magazine,* 12 July, 1, 20–26.

Heuer, B. (2003) 'Clinical paradigm as analytic third. Reflections on a century of analysis and an emergent paradigm for the millennium'. In E. Christopher and H. McFarland Solomon (eds), *Contemporary Jungian Clinical Practice.* London: Karnac, 329–339.

—— (2004) 'Buddha in the depressive position. On the healing paradigm'. In L. Cowan (ed.), *Barcelona 04. Proceedings of the 16th. International IAAP Congress.* Einsiedeln: Daimon, 328–336.

—— (2008) 'Discourse of illness or discourse of health'. In L. Huskinson (ed.), *Dreaming the Myth Onward* London: Routledge, 181–190.

—— (2010) 'The experience of the numinous in the consulting-room'. In M. Stein (ed.), *Jungian Psychoanalysis.* Chicago: Open Court, 234–242.

Heuer, G. (2001) 'Jung's twin brother: Otto Gross and Carl Gustav Jung' *Journal of Analytical Psychology*, 46, 4, 655–688.

—— (2010) Dresden, in 'Die Heiligkeit der Liebe' oder: 'Beziehung als Drittes, als Religion', in W. Felber, A. Götz von Olenhusen, G. Heuer, B. Nitzschke, eds. *Psychoanalyse und Expressionismus. 7. Internationaler Otto Gross Kongress, Dresden.* Marburg: LiteraturWissenschaft.de, 109–153.

Hickman, L./Lovelock, J. (2012) 'I'm allowed to change my mind' *Guardian*, 16 June, 35–37.

Hillman, J. (2006) 'The azure vault'. In L. Cowan (ed.), *Barcelona 04. Proceedings of the 16th International IAAP Congress* Einsiedeln: Daimon, 25–39.

Hodgkinson, T. (2004) *How to be Idle* London: Hamilton.

Hoffman, D. (1985) *Poe* New York: Vintage.

Holmyard, E. J. (1957) *Alchemy* Harmondsworth: Penguin.

Honoré, C. (2004) *In Praise of Slow. How a Worldwide Movement is Challenging the Cult of Speed* London: Orion.

Howatson, C. (2009) Personal Communication. 8 June.

Hutton, D. (2004) 'The rise of the activity junkie' *You Magazine*, 28 November, 98–100.

Jung, C. G. (1942–1977) except where indicated, references are by volume and paragraph number to the *Collected Works of C. G. Jung*, 20 vols. London and Princeton, NJ: Routledge and Princeton University Press.

—— (1963) *Memories, Dreams, Reflections* London: Collins.

—— (1973) *Letters. Vol. 1 1906–1950* London: Routledge and Kegan Paul.

Kelley, C. (1961) *A New Method of Weather Control* Ojaj: Radix Institute.

Lafargue, P. (1883) Das Recht auf Faulheit. www.sopos.org/aufsaetze/3b0bf233eb8e3/1.phtml (Accessed 31 July 2012).

Lassek, H. (2006) 'Erfahrung mit der Behandlung schwerstkranker Menschen' *Zeitschrift für Körperpsychotherapie*, 12, 43, 5–11.

Lazear, J. (1993) *Meditations for Men Who Do Too Much* London: Thorsons.

Lear, J. (2006) *Radical Hope: Ethics in the Face of Cultural Devastation* Cambridge, MA, London: Harvard University.

Leaver, H. (2012) 'Ice age is put on ice' *Metro,* 25 January, 12–13.

Leve, A. (2004) 'Might as well face it: you're addicted to stress' *Elle*, September, 377–380.

McBride, K. (2009) *Will I Ever Be Good Enough?* New York: Free Press.

Mackintosh, J. (2011) Hitchcock's 'The Bankers'. *Financial Times, Wealth,* Summer, 8.

Makavejev, D. (1972) *WR: Mysteries of the Organism* New York: Avon.

Martel, Y. (2003) *Life of Pi* London: Canongate.

May, G. (1988) *Addiction and Grace* New York: Harper Collins.

Meier, P. (2004) *Paracelsus* Zürich: Amman.

Millar, P. (2007) *Iona* Norwich: Canterbury Press.

Minx (2006) *Woman* 26 June, 43.

Munday, M. (2009) 'This pressure – I can't live without it' *Sunday Times Magazine*, 5 April, 12–18.

Newcomer, T. (2009) *The Call of the World* New York: iUniverse.

Ni, H.-C. (2008) *Tao* Los Angeles: Wellness Press.

Nietzsche, F. (1906) *Menschliches, Allzumenschliches* Leipzig: Naumann.

Opus Archives (2009) *Announcing the New Mythos Research Grant* Santa Barbara: Pacifica.

Panofsky, D. & Panofsky, E. (1991) *Pandora's Box* Princeton, NJ: Princeton University Press.

Plimer, I. (2009) *Heaven and Earth. Global Warming: The Missing Science* London: Quartet.

Reich, W. (1972) *The Murder of Christ* New York: Farrar, Straus & Giroux.

Rumi (1999) *The Teachings of Rumi* Boston, MA: Shambhala.

Rust, M.-J. & N. Totton (eds) (2012) *Vital Signs* London: Karnac.

Samsung (2009) 'Impatience is a Virtue' *GQ*, August, 53.

Samuels, A. (1996) 'From sexual misconduct to social justice' *Psychoanalytic Dialogues*, 6, 3, 295–321.

Sandall, R. (2005) 'Rebel without a pause' *Sunday Times Magazine,* 30 October, 26–30.

Sansom, I. (2010) 'The price of candy' *Guardian Review*, 31 July, 7.

Schmidbauer, W. (1982) *Die hilflosen Helfer* Reinbek: Rowohlt.

Schnabel, U. (2012) *Muße.* Munich: Pantheon.

Schoen, D. E. (2009) *The War of the Gods in Addiction* New Orleans: Spring.

Solnit, R. (2007) *River of Shadows* New York: Viking.

Spielrein, S. (1987) Zum Vortrag von Dr. Skal'kovskij. *Sämtliche Schriften.* Freiburg: Kore, 335–344.

Stone, M. (2010) *Gerhard Adler* Eulogy, given at The Association of Jungian Analysts, London, 2 February. Manuscript.

Thomas, G. (2009) *Healing Pandora: The Restoration of Hope and Abundance* Benson: Goldenstone.

Tolle, E. (1999) *The Power of Now* Novato: New World.

—— (2005) *A New Earth* London: Michael Joseph.

Tuby, M. (1984) *The Shadow* London: Guild of Pastoral Psychology.

Weil, A. (1998) *Natural Health, Natural Medicine* Boston, MA: Houghton Mifflin.

Wilson Schaef, A. (1990) *Meditations for Women Who Do Too Much* San Francisco, CA: Harper & Row.

Winnicott, D. W. (1987) *The Maturational Processes and the Facilitating Environment* London: Hogarth and The Institute of Psychoanalysis.

—— (1989) 'The fear of breakdown' *Psycho-Analytic Explorations* London: Karnac, 87–95.

Wright, S. G. (2010) *Burnout* Redmire: Sacred Space.

9

EMBODIED BEING AS ALCHEMY
A Post-Postmodern Approach

Birgit Heuer

Introduction

In this chapter, alchemy is approached from a conceptual point of view which highlights its capacity to contain paradox and accommodate opposites, such as spirit and matter or immanence and transcendence. Rather than reifying paradox by envisaging the world through pairs of opposites, paradox is presented in a complex manner, emphasising a synthesising and linking faculty. Metaphorically speaking, this might be expressed as a loving, wavelike embrace of all things. As the chapter unfolds, it will become clear that synthesis via loving embrace alters the Hegelian dynamics which, arguably, underpin much of Jung's thought (Solomon, 2007). The human ability to experience being can be seen to have a similar connective effect. It links our everyday ordinary awareness to the deeper strata of inner and/or transpersonal reality. In this sense, being might be called an alchemical state. In addition, the body shall be conceived through the capacity to be which is seen as an important aspect of ego-development, and reference is made to Winnicott's developmental theory. It is pointed out that, whilst theories of human development are concerned with being-based processes, these are usually not mentioned in clinical accounts and therefore not a valued ingredient in the analytic clinical hour.

The alchemical function of being-based processes is worked out through connecting them with two different, yet related, areas where contemporary scientific research and philosophical thought emerge most prominently. I shall argue that quantum theory revolves around paradox in a particular, complex manner and trace ways in which this relates both to alchemy and the experience of embodied being. Post-postmodern thought similarly reaches beyond binary reason and embodied being then relates to a post-postmodern, quantum-rational approach. The alchemical project of *mysterium coniunctionis* – the mysterious marriage of opposites – is seen from a perspective of contemporary science and philosophy and reintroduced into the clinical hour from a fresh, body-oriented point of view. Some emphasis is given to depicting the complexities of quantum dynamics and its conceptual links with alchemy, mysticism and being. This facilitates an approach to knowing and thought, which might be described as thinking-in-being and yet be referred to as rational and logical. In moving beyond – yet not doing away with – postmodern analytical and critical faculties, a contribution to the project of post-postmodernism is made. Post-postmodernism emerges as a manner of envisioning that involves a 'squaring of the circle' and enables richer, fuller, more flavoursome ways of apprehending reality.

In addition, a metaphoric reading of quantum theory implies what might be called the emergence of the Divine as a fulcrum of the notion of reality. Most schools of meditation rely on the experience of being as a route to the Divine, whilst the Bible tells us that 'in my flesh shall I see God' (Job 19:26). Embodied being equally fosters an opening toward the direct experience of the Divine. Elsewhere (Heuer, 2008; 2010), I have suggested a conceptual link between hope, positive change and the Divine. Here, I shall explore the experience of embodied being as the living stage upon which such transformations unfold. From a Jungian perspective, this is a version of the alchemical opus, for alchemy, conceptually, extends from paradox to metamorphosis.

In sum, this chapter touches upon three different discursive fields, namely divergent readings of the bodily dimension and its clinical implications, a quantum discourse ranging from viewpoints originating within physics to its reception by other disciplines, and a discourse on emerging forms of rationality as part of post-postmodern philosophy. Each of these will be briefly flagged up in order to give context to my explorations.

Embodied being

The approach to the body advanced here is specifically through what I refer to as *embodied being*, for speaking of 'the body' suggests an object in the mind, while *body as being* evokes something that can be experienced. The bodily dimension features in Jung (CW 9i, para. 291) and it has subsequently been taken up by Jungian authors. To date, analytic reception of this vital aspect of human experience has come either through body-movement therapies, or understanding the body as expressing archetypal imagery or via symbolic readings of bodily symptoms. Conversely, I am concerned with the actual experience of embodied being and bringing being-based values to the analytic clinic. Whilst it is helpful and valuable to think about the body in symbolic or archetypal ways (Conger, 1988, 1994; Mindell, 1982, 1985; Schwartz-Salant & Stein, 1986), or to express it in terms of spontaneous movement (Bloom, 2006; Chodorow, 1991; Woodman, 2001; Wyman-McGinty, 1998), clinically speaking, patients may need strengthening their actual capacity to be. Embodied being can be conceived as a capacity acquired in infancy and here Winnicott's developmental theory provides an intricate map. Other developmental approaches tend not to feature being as an accomplishment in its own right, reducing it to an implicit aspect of mind. In addition to exploring it developmentally, I envisage embodied being as an experience that can be evoked. This section addresses both aspects, theoretical and experiential, starting with the latter.

Embodied being and its analytic reception

In approaching the body through the dimension of being, it is useful to offer a working definition of embodied being. This dimension, first and foremost, belongs to experience and defining it seems akin to catching a butterfly. As a quality of experience, being needs to be evoked rather than defined. To this end, I would like to invite the reader to imagine the state we enter just before falling asleep. When things are going well, we become more and more relaxed, perhaps more aware of our body, aware of some of its tensions too, aware of thoughts and feelings left over from the day, before letting go and drifting off into sleep. We are relaxing and slowly relinquishing focused thought, yet still aware. This is an example of a being-based state where we are linking with our being. Something similar happens in meditation, with awareness and being coming together not as awareness *of* but awareness *in* being. Breath and breathing yield another example. Every breath potentially links the whole of our being in a spontaneous way as it flows into the following breath. Each cycle of breath has an active and a passive phase and a null-point that occurs after the out breath and before the next in breath. We may cut ourselves off from being by breathing shallowly, or physically suppress one or the other part of the cycle. On the other hand, when we gently connect with our breathing, it usually deepens and opens up our being-experience.

As a vital dimension of human experience, embodied being tends to be overlooked in the analytic clinic, for most clinical accounts do not mention it. Conversely, some humanistic approaches such as Neo-Reichian body therapy (Boyesen, 1995) pay close attention to both body-impulses and spontaneous, involuntary movement. These tend to inspire the focus of a session, which then arises out of the patient's being-experience. The values informing the analytical clinical hour at present are to do with relating – inwardly and outwardly – and making meaning. In analysis, details of experience on a being-level are usually not valued in themselves and clinical accounts consider being-experience mostly with regard to meaning. As others have noted (Plaut, 1993; Schafer, 1976), clinical accounts tell us *what* is said rather than *how* it is said (tone of voice, body-expression), or how an interpretation is received by the patient's being. Analysis is then concerned with generating narrative, geared toward meaning, and based on transference/counter transference experience. In positively including the dimension of being, this chapter seeks to enable the perception of patients' states of being and their need for embodied experience. Making meaning is then complemented by linking with one's being and deeply experiencing 'what is'.

Developmental theory

In order to make the notion of embodied being more substantial to the reader, this section gives a brief outline of how the capacity to be might be acquired in infancy. Winnicott's developmental theory is exceptional in that it features being in its own right, rather than as an aspect of the developing mind. As the main purpose of the summary sketched here is to illustrate and enrich my theme, Winnicott's ideas on being will not be discussed in any depths, other than taking him to conceive being as both innate/primary capacity and developmental achievement. He describes three stages of development: Integration, personalisation and object-relating (Winnicott, 1987, p. 60). Integration can be understood as the baby's developing experience of continuity from one minute to the next and of coming together bodily which Winnicott relates to the holding provided by the mother, that is the mother's attuned responses to her baby. Integration represents a huge achievement on a being-level and leads to a capacity for a non-fragmented experience within one's body/being. The integration aspect of being is then about the capacity to feel oneself to be embodied, without undue anxiety, in a continuous way.

Winnicott's second stage, personalisation, denotes the baby's experience of itself as a separate unit with the skin as limiting membrane and develops in relation to the mother's handling of her growing baby, that is her responsive attunement to its bodily needs. The ability to experience oneself as separate and held together by one's skin on a being-level is another great achievement. The focus here is not on the symbolic act but on a state of unity-in-being and the ability to relax into one's being with pleasure rather than fear.

Winnicott's third stage, object-relating, is closely interwoven with the mother's object-presenting. Importantly, he conceives object-relating as linked to the infant's creation of reality and as leading to a capacity for sharing interpersonal reality. As object-relating involves the two stages already mentioned, one must conclude that, for Winnicott, relating and reality are being-based. Being then bridges creativity and reality and becomes the *sine qua non* for both. Winnicott's developmental theory thus puts being on the analytic map, although this does not automatically mean it is valued and attended to in the clinical hour.

Quantum logic, post-postmodernity and alchemy

The reader might well ask what quantum theory or logic has to do with the experience of being. Here I shall suggest a vital connection, traced through approaches to logic, such as quantum logic, which can be shown to evoke being or even include it. Although needing to be expressed in fairly abstract language, on a deeper level this section is also meant poetically. Moreover, where the capacity to contain opposites is seen as the heart of alchemy, exploring the connection of logic and being becomes an alchemical task. The emerging philosophy of post-postmodernism questions accepted notions of binary rationality – where yes and no are exclusive positions that allow no overlap – seeking to be more inclusive and holistic, yet non-regressive. Jung's notion of an *unus mundus* – a unity via pre-connectedness of all things (see Chapter 6) – can easily be critiqued as regressively pre-modern in conceptually not being sufficiently distinct from fundamentalist pre-unity where difference is intrinsically feared and attacked. In my view, Jung's *unus mundus* becomes more complex, yet clearer when approached through *henadism* rather than holism. As I shall explain in more detail below, *henadism* is a concept of *a priori* unity that relates to quantum logic and, crucially, includes differentiation. It is conceived via paradox and yet is rationally intelligible. Post-postmodern thinker Epstein (1997) has put forward the notion of trans-rationality which this chapter augments by elaborating specific links between quantum logic, alchemy and mysticism.

Generally speaking, binary logic informs language and science, no matter whether its methodology is empirical or hermeneutic. Binary logic depends on an exclusive yes/no distinction with a *tertium non datur* – third possibilities are not allowed. However, contemporary quantum science, based in empirical quantum mechanics and the mathematical formulae that govern it, has arrived at forms of logic able to express complexity and paradox without becoming either nonsensical or completely random. This evokes the principles of alchemy as well as its language and imagery. Importantly, though, it does not involve regression to pre-modern forms of unity which rest on a complete and utter identity of all things. Goernitz and Goernitz (2006), a quantum scientist and a psychoanalyst respectively, suggest the term *henadism*, rather than the more ubiquitous holism, to express a complex idea of unity which includes forms of differentiation. To clarify such concepts, it is helpful to begin with a brief remark about quantum theory and its reception by analysis to date.

When approaching quantum theory as a non-physicist, it is important to be able to distinguish between different levels of explanation. If this step is omitted, it engenders confusion between the empirical facts of quantum theory and their various levels of interpretation. To date, I have not come across an analytic reception of quantum theory that has not limited its own scope in this regard. Rosenblum and Kuttner (2007), two quantum physicists who have introduced seminars for non-physicists at the University of California, Santa Cruz, suggest that – once the quantum-mechanical facts are properly understood – workers from other disciplines are entitled to comment on what the authors term the 'quantum enigma' (ibid., p. 5). However, considerable understanding is necessary to comprehend quantum mechanics, as this, arguably, involves irreducible paradox in something that finds its practical application in our everyday world, from microchips and lasers to MRI scans. Whilst quantum mechanical applications account for nearly 40 per cent of Western economies, its theory, historically and currently, is a highly discursive field. I shall argue that approaching quantum theory itself in binary ways limits its complexity for the perceived gain of making clear statements about its implications. Conversely, I shall suggest that alchemical-mystical-henadic forms of post-postmodern reasoning are better suited to the nature of quantum dynamics.

Quantum principles and explanatory levels

Quantum theory has never been disproved and is currently accepted by physicists as the best theory explaining the physical world. The standard model of quantum theory is generally upheld by physicists and, in this sense, has been referred to as quantum orthodoxy. Whilst not objecting to the empirical fact expressed in the standard model, Rosenblum and Kuttner argue that it fails to account for the complex implications of quantum mechanics. My suggestion is to introduce a hierarchy of explanatory levels of quantum theory to clarify and ease discussion. Whilst needing to be differentiated for clarity, quantum theory also implies that its explanatory layers are intricately and irrevocably linked. Thus the explanatory pyramid presented here distinguishes between empirical fact and meaning in a manner that is eventually superceded by the implications of quantum mechanics. I am using the term 'fact' for the purpose of differentiation in full awareness that this notion changes in quantum theory. An ordinary fact presupposes a Newtonian world in which things are physically and logically entirely separable. As this aspect radically changes in quantum theory, what constitutes a fact needs to be rethought.

The pyramid's foundational layer (level one) is made up of the quantum mechanical findings as experimentally proven and expressed in the standard model of quantum physics. Closely linked to this – and because of their logical equivalence at the same explanatory level (one) – are the abstract mathematical formulae expressing quantum mechanics. The so-called *Copenhagen interpretation* is often associated with the standard model and implicitly taken to be part of the foundational layer. This interpretation, usually attributed to Nils Bohr, differentiates between the world of small particles and the ordinary world of classical physics. It states, 'whenever any property of a microscopic object affects a macroscopic object, that property is *observed* and becomes a physical reality. No property of a microscopic object exists until it is produced by observation' (Rosenblum & Kuttner, 2007, p. 103). Conversely, Rosenblum and Kuttner argue, atoms consist of micro-particles, and therefore quantum physics must apply to the world of the large as well as the small. They stress the interpretation's practical implications which allow physicists to get on with the important business of calculating whilst relegating quantum mechanic's paradoxical features to the microscopic world. As Barad (2007, pp. 68, 251) points out, many different physicists contributed to this version of the Copenhagen interpretation, and it is attributed to Bohr erroneously for it short-circuits the complexity of his philosophical thought.

Importantly, in terms of explanatory hierarchy, any reading of the Copenhagen interpretation needs to be situated at a separate level, level two. As an interpretation of quantum mechanics, it is not reducible to them nor does it necessarily follow. There is a further explanatory layer, level three, at which concepts such as the *zero-point-field* (McTaggart, 2003) are located, the idea that quantum behaviour originates in a particular field of influence. The term *zero-point-field* was introduced by scientists from other disciplines but is not used by the majority

160

of physicists and thus must be grouped as a para-scientific concept. The next explanatory level, level four, contains ideas about the nature of reality as well as human experience which relate to quantum theory. In not being reducible to experimental facts or mathematics, these are metaphorical translations, important from a perspective of *weltanschauung* and philosophy. Here a host of discoursive facets arises and their place in the pyramid of explanatory levels needs to be clearly indicated to lend them validity.

The explanatory pyramid also relates to the philosophical question of realism and its relation to physics. According to Davis (2006, p. 12), most physicists are realists in the sense that they believe the standard model (levels one and two) to be identical with physical reality. Discussing the philosophical implications in more detail, Barad (2007, p. 318) outlines a scale ranging from entity realism – the version mentioned in Davis – to theory realism. Theory realism means a toned-down belief in the implicit identity of physics and physical reality, whilst still believing in the reality of level one phenomena. Such weak realism is necessary for explanatory levels three – para-scientific concepts – and four – metaphorical translations – where the relation with empiricism is preserved, yet elastic.

Most analytical receptions of quantum theory make use of the Copenhagen interpretation – explanatory level two – and its distinction between the world of small particles and the ordinary world. Here the quantum world has no intrinsic, ontological – being – status and is only made real in relation to empirical measurement. Reading this as a level one explanation, analytic reception translated the Copenhagen interpretation into a relation between unconscious and consciousness (Mindell, 2000; Morgan, 2000; Schwartz, 2009), giving the unconscious quantum status whilst seeing conscious processes as Newtonian. In my view, this approach overemphasises binarity – conscious as distinct from unconscious – and misses the deeper complexities and implications of quantum theory.

Quantum enigma

To open up such complexities, it is useful to give a brief description of the 'quantum enigma' (Rosenblum & Kuttner, 2007), the paradox revealed by quantum mechanics. The difficulty with saying anything definitive about this is that ordinary language implies binarity and reduces the impact of paradox. To preserve paradox in ordinary language, one might need to say that a contradiction is true in both its aspects, yet more true in one. The following description is thus expressed as factual – in terms of explanatory level one – yet should also be read as fluid and open-ended.

Quantum systems, whilst containing unlimited potential particles, operate as a unified wave. When an observer asks the system a specific question regarding its properties and prepares for measurement of this, the quantum system will answer the question in the positive within certain intrinsic parameters. However, this generally leads to answers which, in binary logic, both contradict and exclude each other. These logically exclusive positions/answers can be experimentally generated over and over again. Although not occurring simultaneously, this nevertheless asserts a paradox. In addition, quantum theory is regarded, in principle, as extending to the whole of the physical world including human beings, as the macro-world is made up of atoms and thus micro-particles. The Copenhagen interpretation addresses both contradictions by creating a dichotomy between micro- and macro-levels via measurement and by viewing paradox as a feature of the quantum world's potentiality only. This allows the physicist to put aside the 'quantum enigma' for practical purposes as is necessary to proceed with practical applications. As mentioned earlier, this chapter approaches alchemy as the principle that both allows for, and holds, paradox and thus conceptually corresponds to quantum theory. In terms of explanatory level four, alchemy could be regarded as a metaphoric expression of quantum dynamics. However, an even closer relation is possible as quantum information theory addresses experimental paradox by providing a different kind of logic which is able to accommodate contradiction.

Quantum logic

For the purpose of everyday reality as well as empirical science, we use binary logic which originated with Aristotle. McNeill and Freiberger (1993, p. 53) have termed this 'cookie-cutter' logic, for the outlines of logical entities are sharply delineated – as if effected by a cookie-cutter – with no overlap allowed. Quantum logic is different and, in terms of explanatory layers, situated at level two, consistent with empirical facts and their mathematical expression. The basic measurement in quantum-information theory is called a quantum bit. An ordinary non-quantum bit is the basic unit of information which can only be in two states, namely on or off. A quantum-bit, however, can be in both states at once, or any combination of the two. It possesses a very large amplitude which equals the circumference of the entire cosmos (Goernitz & Goernitz, 2006, p. 736). This means the quantum-dimension basically operates as a unit, as one, or *hen* in Greek. In other words, it is fundamentally *henadic* or unitarian. Yet, as quantum computers can process a near infinite amount of information in a very short time, they can quickly arrive at a very small detail. The crucial feature is that any small detail arises out of unity and there is no separation to begin with. In addition, the sum is always greater or smaller than its constituent parts and there are no exclusions, whereas cookie-cutter logic depends on exclusions. Quantum logic, then, is paradoxical, unitarian and inclusive. For anything taken to be the case in quantum logic, 66 per cent have to be taken to mean 100 (ibid., p. 772). Even after this step, which would fully exclude its opposite in conventional reason, there is always 33 per cent of fluidity left. Facts conceived through quantum logic are thus overflowing with exuberant possibility and, recalling Wordsworth, are trailing clouds of 33 percent of quantum glory. Any statement, then, also entails a veiled inquiry into this cloud of abundant potentiality. This leads to an extraordinary amount of inherent openness and fluidity of argument and a softer attitude suggests itself, as the idiom of exclusivity seems under-equipped for such extravagance. When scientific reason requires poetic language, change is clearly afoot and a post-postmodern vista arises. This, however, does not lead to relativism, rather, it means further possibilities are always inherent and cannot be successfully eliminated. The circle is being squared, as things can be said relatively distinctly whilst also being conceived of as fundamentally fluid. When approached this way, the alchemical opus, conceptually, emerges slightly less reliant on polar opposites, gaining wavelike wings and emphasising its transformative capacity.

Forms of knowing: mysticism, alchemy and post-postmodernism

Henadism implies an identity of subject and object which includes their separability, recalling the mystical manner of apprehending the Divine. Ferrer (2000) argues mysticism, rather than being about exalted experience, is actually a method of apprehending reality and thus a mode of knowing based on a specific form of reason. Such mystical rationality is strikingly similar – complex, paradox, unitarian – to the logic of quantum information theory. It is best described as a knowing *in* as well as a knowing *of*, or perhaps a knowing *of* through knowing *in*. In Jungian terms, all four functions – thinking, feeling, sensation and intuition – are utilised simultaneously. This can also be seen as an alchemical state, expressing something like *knowing in being*. It is likely that Jung, had he had quantum information theory rather than quantum mechanics available to him, would have found it easier to reconcile his scientific-empirical and metaphysical views.

Envisaged as a form of rationality, alchemical-mystical knowing has a strong resonatory aspect – knowledge *in* that is non-binary and reminiscent of coherent quantum-waves – which simultaneously includes knowledge *of* – reminiscent of quantum measurement and involving binarity. The Copenhagen interpretation mentioned above requires strict delineation of quantum states and their measurement. This rests on stringent binarity and as such, in my view, is insufficient for accommodating quantum complexity. Conversely, the model of knowing advanced here, involves access – via henadic identity – to the *quiddity* or ontological so-ness of the object, and simultaneously rests on a measure of separation from it, with either aspect potentially being more the case than the other, at any one time.

Whilst the reader might find it unusual, yet perhaps surprisingly uncomplicated, to envisage this, it seems an apt rendering of quantum complexity as well as being highly compatible with alchemy. It also links to a discourse on the manner of rationality acceptable to science that ranges from the logical positivism of the Vienna Circle at the beginning of the previous century (Dreher, 2000) to the contemporary concept of *trans-rationality* put forward by post-postmodernists such as Epstein (1997). Post-postmodernism set out as an aesthetic critique

(Turner, 1965), involving ethics (Gans, 1993) and developed trans-rationality as an alternative to the perceived reductionism and negativism of analytical, postmodern thought. This debate is advanced by supplying a model of knowing that involves a complex, non-binary relation of unity and separation, linking quantum logic with mysticism, alchemy and embodied being. It is important to reiterate that this model does not simply replace binarity with its antithesis, unity or complete identity, thereby creating a fresh pair of opposites, rather, it reaches beyond binarity, yet remains inclusive of it. This leads to positives, in that things can be known in their quiddity, their essential so-ness, whilst also possessing outlines and boundaries which enable their discussion. There are many philosophical connections that could and should be explored here, chiefly among them Heidegger's ontology and Polanyi's approach to knowing, however, these are beyond the scope of this chapter.

Embodied being and the Divine

Returning to the chapter's clinical theme, embodied being, the similarities between the world of quantum logic and embodied being are now emerging: Both involve henadic unity and states of flux combined with differentiation, both imply *knowing in being*, and, whilst *knowing of* might recede temporarily, it is not suspended. This can be experienced immediately by closing one's eyes and taking a couple of deep breaths. The world of differentiation ebbs, as the world of flow and interconnection arises, yet both states coincide and one is slightly more the case than the other. I am not alone in suggesting being might be a state that fosters awareness of/in quantum coherence (Goernitz & Goernitz, 2006). Physicists with experience of meditation, such as Goswami (1995), Mansfield (2008) and Russell (2002), make a similar point, although their focus reaches beyond the experience of being or meditation. Instead, these physicists elaborate the links between the quantum dimension and the Divine. In my pyramid of explanatory levels, these are metaphoric readings, situated at level four.

Russell, a Buddhist and physicist, reviews Einstein's work and argues, even at the speed of light, that reality is utterly altered and begins to resemble states of mind usually to be found in deep meditation and mystical experience (Russell, 2002). Russell also notes that spiritual language constantly invokes light and wonders whether the same spiritual light might pervade both quantum physics and spiritual practice:

> Physical light has no mass and is not part of the material world. The same is true of consciousness; it is immaterial. Physical light seems to be fundamental to the universe. The light of consciousness is likewise fundamental; without it there would be no experience. Do physical reality and the reality of mind share the same common ground – a ground whose essence is light?
>
> (Ibid., p. 70)

Russell presents us with a Buddhist inquiry into the Divine as universal, non-substantial light/consciousness. Interestingly, there is a level-one explanatory equivalent, arising from the empirical research into so-called *biophotons*, in the 1960s, by the German bio-physicist Popp (McTaggart, 2003). Popp researched photon emission and reception in living cells – first in small organisms and later in humans – at quantum level and irrespective of photo-synthesis. Mostly conducted in complete darkness, Popp's research shows the existence of very low voltage light in living organism being both emitted and received, as well as exchanged with other living beings. Popp theorised that this light orchestrates bio-chemical processes – via coherent quantum-wave synchronised information – in living beings. Rather than using such research reductively as proof that human beings are essentially creatures of light – and whilst not disputing this – I suggest a metaphorical reading which emphasises that qualities, hitherto ascribed to the Divine, are being seen to emerge irrevocably linked with empirical research in the human sphere.

Mansfield and Goswami also propose Buddhist readings of quantum complexity. Goswami (1995) advocates the idea that consciousness collapses the quantum-wave and therefore must be conceived as the ultimate reality, whereas Mansfield (2008) argues a more stringently Bohrist view of a fundamental non-reality. To my mind, the importance of these approaches lies in their metaphysical, transpersonal impetus and they represent serious level four contributions. However, they also address quantum paradox in quite determinate ways, which reduces quantum complexity akin to a measurement and therefore yields 'not enough' of an answer. Whilst Goswami has been criticised as idealist, and Mansfield as contaminating science with Buddhist beliefs, in my view both determine ultimate reality rather too strongly, even though Mansfield argues ultimately nothing is real. Henadism and quantum logic, as outlined above, stress a conceptual emphasis on adding and linking or, in poetic language, on loving embrace. From this point of view, questions enquiring into the 'how' of a situation are conceptually useful in embracing quiddity, essential so-ness, whereas 'why'-questions tend to reduce quiddity, whilst both approaches are needed. This has profound implications regarding the use and purpose of analytical clinical language, for orienting the latter slightly more towards 'how' opens up the so-ness of an experience, inviting and stressing embodied being.

Clinical use of language has been reflected upon previously (Schafer, 1976; Plaut, 1993) and, more recently, radically re-thought by The Boston Change Process Study Group for Clinical Change. The Boston Change Process Study Group (2010) proposes a paradigm, in the sense of exemplar, for re-orienting the clinical hour towards more being-based processes and values. This effort could be strengthened by locating it within the discourse on thought and rationality outlined and developed in this chapter.

It is important to note that metaphysical readings of quantum theory, as offered by the authors mentioned earlier, retain close links with quantum mechanics in that its enigmatic complexity invites metaphysical inquiry. Implicit is a co-joining of philosophical value spheres that are traditionally strictly segregated. Not only can *qualia* of experience be argued to emerge with quantum complexity but also what might be termed a metaphorical emergence of the Divine from within empirical science. This, of course, is an alchemical image for a contemporary phenomenon. There is a further way in which Divine qualities can be seen to emerge with quantum science – from a level four point of view – concerning the rationality of mysticism. Mystical experience, particularly of the via positiva – the mystical path oriented towards love rather than sacrifice (Klein, 2003, p. 231) – involves being-based, *knowledge in-of* the loving Divine. There are numerous physical, level one, equivalents to this, such as the properties of so-called super-conductors which involve perpetual motion without energy input and the overwhelming tendency of seemingly chaotic systems towards synchronising and order (Gribbin, 2005). By level-four analogy, such examples invite metaphysical metaphors such as the mystical Divine, expressing perpetual love or generosity without cause, offering profound attention to the smallest details of daily life whilst also proposing eternity – lovingly immanent as well as transcendent.

The Divine arguably represents the excluded in the Freudian analytic tradition (Blass, 2006). Whilst metaphysical concerns can be said to be a fundamental feature in Jung's writing, they seem equally excluded in the Jungian clinical tradition in that the living reality of the Divine is not usually an acknowledged ingredient of mainstream clinical work, writing or teaching, although this is beginning to change. I recently presented a paper on the experience of the numinous in the consulting-room (Heuer, 2010) which gives details of the prayerful states of mind I enter as part of my ordinary analytical work, and describes how I maintain my consulting-room as a holy space. The moving response from some of my colleagues was: 'You are putting into words that which has been forbidden'.

In the light of the link between the quantum dimension and the Divine, a direct experience of the Divine opens up through our embodied being (perhaps akin to the quantum cosmological wave of all possibilities, without collapsing the wave). This can take many forms, from relaxation and deepening of experience to *knowing in being*. In contemplative traditions, being is part of the pathway toward the Divine, although quantum logic would suggest that whilst we are traveling we are already arrived. Deep prayer is also being-based. Openness to being-experience allows the Divine to be real, here and now, allows eternity and reality to flow together (Heuer, 2003). Being deepens all experience as there is a letting go, a sinking back, a relinquishing of control without losing all structure. It is this little bit of letting go which furnishes an opening for the Divine to flood in. The Divine is always waiting passionately and timelessly for this moment and will seize the smallest opportunity. In the clinic therefore, consciously valuing being-experience, and making space for it, emphasises a transformative aspect and creates a purposeful space for the healing Divine to unfold.

It is important, however, to be inclusive of past achievements, for adding and embracing is pivotal to a quantum logical, post-postmodern approach. Thus, in physics, classical laws still apply for classical purposes whilst in analysis an awareness of the negative and what is wrong retains purpose and value. This can be approached in the spirit of clinical generosity (Symington, 2008), where analytic inquiry is mainly motivated by concern for ways in which the patient might hurt him- or herself. The classical Jungian analytic imperative, that the shadow must be made conscious and that this, in itself, is therapeutic, recedes whilst some of its essence is retained. Such shifts in therapeutic outlook involve a discourse about clinical *a priori*, such as how the patient is conceptualised or implicit models of clinical change. I have traced this previously (Heuer, 2008) and proposed a re-reading of the analytic patient from a mystical, post-postmodern perspective (Heuer, 2010). Being-based experience, accompanied by clinical language appropriate to it – more oriented towards 'how' than 'why' – serves to augment and balance classical analytic stances. This chapter, then, offers embodied being as developmentally theorised and clinically realised, as an opening towards the Divine, a profoundly alchemical state, mystical and quantum rational, and as a tool for clinical change and healing.

Conclusion

I would like to end with a somewhat bold sketch of post-postmodern philosophy which may equally be read as contemporary alchemy. Whereas quantum logic suggests that statements about the nature of reality should be both kept fluid and decisive, quantum mechanics also points toward a fastening of previously sharply segregated spheres such as physics and metaphysics or empiricism and intentionality. Importantly, such synthesis retains the inherent integrity of its ingredients, whilst providing more than their sum. In particular, matter, information and meaning can be seen to come together in such a way that, metaphorically speaking, the dynamics of symmetry-breaking (Cambray, 2009, p. 58) gently recede, whilst the dynamics of loving embrace gain momentum. The principle of synchronicity – Jung's acausal connectedness of matter and meaning – rather than being a special case, then appears irreducibly linked to the emerging structure of reality, for matter, information and meaning can neither be successfully separated nor are they reducible to either sphere. Theoretical physicist Barad conceives this as onto-episto-mattering (Barad, 2007). In her model, neither sphere has primacy as they co-create each other and their separation becomes a functional rather than a fundamental matter. My approach concurs with the importance she gives to moving beyond binarity. However, validating the use of metaphor – explanatory level four – allows a reading of reality where matter, information and meaning emerge suffused with the energy of loving embrace whilst a generous measure of separateness from it, and thus love's opposite, is retained. Metaphorically speaking, quantum logic suggests love to be the stronger principle that, in an exuberant, flowing way, is unable to stop itself from embracing friend and foe.

In this chapter, I have explored the theme of embodied being as an alchemical process. Having sketched its developmental origins, I suggest that being become a more valued ingredient in the clinical hour. In addition, embodied being has been linked with alchemy, mysticism and the quantum dimension in terms of a common form of rationality, a *knowing-in-being*. Some emphasis has been given to the complexities of quantum mechanics and the logic of quantum information theory. In this context, I have explored a non-reductive linking of previously segregated value spheres, involving a metaphoric emergence of the Divine from within quantum science. Representing a specific contribution to the philosophy of post-postmodernism, here the notion of reality – conceived as constantly evolving – changes to reveal softer sensibilities inspired by loving embrace, and positives, from goodness to the Divine, become a dynamic feature of reality, whilst binarity and opposition are retained, yet recede. I would like to leave the reader with a similar metamorphosis of the ancient Grail question, in which the old, trans-formative words 'what ails you?', still echoing, are superceded by 'what heals you?. 'What heals you' emerges as a fulcrum of the clinical hour as the Divine unfolds in the depths of embodied being.

References

Barad, K. (2007) *Meeting the Universe Halfway* Durham USA: Duke University Press.

Blass, R. (2006) 'Beyond illusion: psychoanalysis and the question of religious truth' *International Journal of Psycho-Analysis*, 85: 615–634.

Bloom, K. (2006) *The Embodied Self: Movement and Psychoanalysis* London: Karnac.

The Boston Change Process Study Group (2010) *Change in Psychotherapy: A Unified Paradigm* New York: Norton.

Boyesen, G. (1995) *Von der Lust am Heilen* Muenchen: Koesel.

Cambray, J. (2009) *Synchronicity* College Station: Texas A&M University Press.

Chodorow, J. (1991) *Dance Therapy and Depth Psychology: The Moving Imagination* London: Routledge.

Conger, J.P. (1988) *Jung and Reich: The Body as Shadow* Berkeley CA: North Atlantic Books.

—— (1994) *The Body in Recovery. Somatic Psychotherapy and the Self* Berkeley, CA: North Atlantic Books.

Davis, P. (2006) *The Goldilocks Enigma: Why is the Universe Just Right For Life?* London: Allen Lane.

Dreher, A.U. (2000) *Foundations for Conceptual Research in Psychoanalysis* London: Karnak.

Epstein, M. (1997) 'The place of postmodernism in postmodernity' In *Russian Postmodernism: New Perspectives on Late Soviet and Post-Soviet Culture* http://www. focusing.org/apm_papers/epstein.html (Accessed December 2009).

Ferrer, J.N. (2000) 'Transpersonal knowing: a participatory approach to transpersonal phenomena' In T. Hart, P.L. Nelson & K. Puhakka (eds), *Transpersonal Knowing: Exploring the Horizons of Consciousness* Albany, NY: State University of New York Press.

Gans, E. (1993) *Originary Thinking: Elements of Generative Anthropology* Stanford, CA: Stanford University Press.

Goernitz, Th. & Goernitz, B. (2006) 'Das Unbewusste aus Sicht einer Quanten-Psycho-Physic. Ein theoretischer Entwurf' In M. Buchholz and G. Goedde (eds), *Das Unbewusste in Aktuellen Diskursen* Giessen: Psychosozial-Verlag.

Goswami, A. (1995) *The Self-Aware Universe* New York: Tarcher/Putnam.

Gribbin, J. (2005) *Deep Simplicity* London: Penguin.

Heuer, B. (2003) 'Clinical paradigm as analytic third' In E. Christopher and H. Solomon (eds), *Contemporary Jungian Clinical Practice* London: Karnac.

—— (2008) 'Discourse of illness or discourse of health' In L. Huskinson (ed.), *Dreaming the Myth Onward* London: Routledge.

—— (2010) 'The experience of the numinous in the consulting-room' In M. Stein (ed.) *Jungian Psychoanalysis* Chicago and LaSalle, IL: Open Court.

Jung, C.G. (1949) *The Psychology of the Child Archetype*. CW 9, i, Princeton, NJ: Princeton University Press, 1968.

Klein, J. (2003) *Jacob's Ladder* London: Karnac.

Mansfield, V. (2008) *Tibetan Buddhism and Modern Physics* West Conshohocken, PA: Templeton Foundation Press.

McNeill, D. & Freiberger, P. (1993) *Fuzzy Logic* New York: Simon & Schuster.

McTaggart, L. (2003) *The Field. The Quest for the Secret Force of the Universe* London: Harper Collins.

Mindell, A. (1982). *Dreambody. The Body's Role in Revealing the Self* Santa Monica, CA: Sigo Press.

—— (1985) *Working with the Dreaming Body* Boston, London, Melbourne and Henley: Routledge & Kegan Paul.

—— (2000) *Quantum Mind. The Edge Between Physics and Psychology* Portland, OR: LaoTse Press.

Morgan, H. (2000) 'The new physics through a Jungian perspective' In E. Christopher & H. Solomon (eds) *Jungian Thought in the Modern World* London: Free Association Books.

Plaut, F. (1993) *Analysis Analysed: When the Map Becomes the Territory* London: Routledge.

Rosenblum, B. & Kuttner, F. (2007) *Quantum Enigma. The Spooky Interaction of Mind and Matter* London: Duckworth.

Russell, P. (2002) *From Science to God* Novato, CA: New World Library.

Schafer, R. (1976) *A New Language for Psychoanalysis* New Haven and London: Yale University Press.

Solomon, H. (2007) *The Self in Transformation* London: Karnac.

Schwartz, C. (2009) 'Quantum physics and the dream' *Harvest*, 1: 84–102.

Schwartz-Salant, N. & Stein, M. (eds) (1986) *The Body in Analysis* Wilmette, IL: Chiron Publications.

Symington, N. (2008) *The Spirit of Sanity* London: Karnac.

Turner, T. (1965) *City as Landscape. A Post-Post-modern View of Design and Planning* London: Taylor & Francis.

Winnicott, D.W. (1987) 'Ego integration in child development' In *The Maturational Process and the Facilitating Environment* London: The Hogarth Press.

Woodman, M. (2001) *Coming Home to Myself* Newburyport: Conan Press.

Wyman-McGinty, W. (1998) 'The body in analysis: authentic movement and witnessing in analytic practice' *Journal of Analytical Psychology*, 43: 239–260.

10

AURUM VULGI

Alchemy in Analysis, a Critique of a Simulated Phenomenon

Michael Whan

> it is much more difficult to find a reliable criterion for determining
> what true soul phenomena are, in contra-distinction to simulated
> ones . . . using Jung's terminology we can say that we need here a
> highly developed, differentiated *feeling function* . . .
>
> (Giegerich, 2012, p. 206)

This critique is not aimed at individuals – even where particular authors are referred to. It focuses on what Jung long ago identified as psychology's own neurotic way of thinking: 'Psychotherapy today . . . Still has a vast amount to unlearn and relearn . . . but first it must cease thinking neurotically and see the psychic process in true perspective' (CW 10, para. 369). More recently, the contemporary German analytical psychologist Wolfgang Giegerich has taken this critique forward – following in the spirit of Jung (CW 6, p. xv) – to develop a notion of a 'critical psychology' in his thought-provoking and seminal works, especially *On the Neurosis of Psychology or the Third of the Two*: 'So psychology itself must be its own *first* patient' (2005, p. 58).

In their search for the philosopher's stone, alchemists made a critical distinction between what they called the *aurum nostrum* and the *aurum vulgi*; between gold in the alchemical, philosophical sense and the (literal) gold of ordinary people. Likewise they differentiated between the *opus magnum* and the *opus parvum*, the 'great work' and the 'lesser work'. To clarify these distinctions in Jung's psychological thinking and practice, I will begin by examining some lines from *Mysterium Coniunctionis* (CW 14), which indicate the difference between the ordinary, all-too-human, empirical individual personality and the psyche; understood in its original meaning as *soul.*

The notion of the soul is Jung's most fundamental psychological thought; underpinning his entire psychology is this insightful recognition of psychology as *the logos of the soul.* For, he observes: 'Psychology . . . is neither biology nor physiology nor any other science than just the knowledge of the soul' (CW 9i, para. 63; translation modified by Giegerich, 2012, p. 22). Elsewhere, he writes: 'we can perhaps summon up the courage to consider the possibility of . . . a "psychology *with* soul," that is, a psychology based on the hypothesis of an autonomous mind' (CW 8, para. 661; translation modified by Giegerich, 2012, p. 6).This difference based on the notion of the soul gets lost in much Jungian thought and practice, including when alchemical metaphors are 'applied' to the work.

Despite his great insight into the soulful nature of psychology, this confusion is also found at times in Jung's writings. Nevertheless, he offers us important recognitions in which he holds to this foundational difference, well brought out in a passage on the meaning of the alchemical process known as the *nigredo*. Jung observes the alchemist beset by a 'melancholy': 'it cast the shadow of its melancholy over his own soul . . .' and then makes this critical point: 'In the blackness of a despair which was not his own, and of which he was merely the witness . . .' (CW 14, para. 493). The key difference is between the alchemist's personal despair as an empirical individual and his witness of 'a despair which was not his own'.

The difference is not purely between the soul and an actual individual personality, but pertains to the empirical personality at the level of abstract concept. The notion of the positive-factual individual as the real reference of the alchemical discourse has to be dialectically surpassed, logically overcome: that is, the logic of the notion of empirical subjectivity, its conceptual self-definition, has to be subjected to the wounding negations of psychological thinking.

For the 'melancholy' Jung refers to is not of an actual individual – Jung says 'he was merely the witness' – it describes the soul's self-movement in the *nigredo* stage of the alchemical *opus*, expressed as a mood. From the perspective of the soul's mercurial logic, the alchemical melancholy reflects the work of *negation* in the soul's dialectical movement, expressed emotionally. Confusing the analysis of an individual with the *opus magnum* obliterates the differentiation between the mercurial logic of psychology as the *logos* of the soul (*opus magnum*) and the psychology of the actual analysand and their personal (modern) subjectivity (*opus parvum*) (Giegerich, 1998, p. 138).

Identifying modern subjectivity with the alchemical metaphor fails to recognize the historical and (psycho-) logical differences which alchemy exemplified. Some modern alchemically orientated approaches want this both ways: to assert both mythological and alchemical meanings – possible in medieval alchemy, but not in post-modern psychology. Ignorant of historical consciousness, analytic practice which draws upon alchemy often blends alchemical images and mythic ones. Mercurius, for instance, becomes equated with the god Hermes, as if likeness signifies identity. Such an approach treats the time of alchemy and our radically different time of post-modern subjectivity as if no historical transformation had occurred; as if we could unproblematically drop back into both the historical alchemical world and, indeed, the ancient mythic world. This fails to perceive alchemy as different from the mythic mode of being-in-the-world. As Giegerich astutely observes:

> in the stage of mythology man was *surrounded on all sides* . . . by mythological reality. The alchemist by contrast . . . has put *the whole stage of* mythological, imaginal consciousness *into the small retort before* Him that he is able to observe . . . He has sublated it and himself risen above this stage to a new stage of consciousness.
>
> (1998, p. 138; my italics)

Hence, as Jung states, the alchemist witnessed the despair as not his own. For the alchemist it lay before, in front of, consciousness; not enclosing him, as in the mythic mode of being. Despair was enclosed in the alchemical retort, allowing witness; a prelude to the modern concept of observation, or intentionality of consciousness (consciousness *of*), different to mythic being-in-the-world. The alchemical retort was a concrete means through which witness of the soul's mercurial logic could occur, though in imaginal form. The alchemist was no longer enclosed within a mythic world: the imaginal, mythical reality was interiorized within the alchemical vessel, as it is today in the vessel of psychology. It is sublated – a term derived from the German *aufheben*. ('Sublation' is the English rendering of this difficult to translate German term, *aufheben*. It has three senses: (1) to raise, to hold, lift up; (2) to annul, abolish, destroy, cancel, suspend; (3) to keep, save, preserve.)

Hegel draws on the second and third senses simultaneously in the same act of reflection, in which something is removed from its immediacy of meaning or being, that is cancelled out – at that immediate level – but taken up dialectically, its initial meaning to be included and preserved, in a higher, more complex concept. It is preserved and changed through the interplay of its self-contradiction. The difference between the usual Jungian sense of uniting the opposites, as in Jung's Transcendent Function, is that the opposites in dialectical thought are not simply external opposites, simple differences, but opposites internally different to themselves, opposites of themselves. As I mention elsewhere in this chapter, in alchemy there is intimation of this in the notion of 'the stone that is no stone', hence, the 'spirit in the stone' or 'the philosopher's stone' (see Inwood, 2003, p. 283; Brinkmann, 2010, pp. 123–125).

Conflation of alchemy with the mythical in the analytic context is a neurotic flight from historical awareness, essentially a regression from meeting the truth of the historical moment, corresponding to what the Roumanian philosopher of religion Mircea Eliade called the 'terror of history': a denial of time, and human finitude. Alchemy, already differentiated from mythic consciousness, was a:

> *mixtum compositum* in which both the structure of modern consciousness as a reflecting, self-conscious and *logos*-bound consciousness and the inherited ancient imaginal form of the contents of an innocent *anima-*

bound consciousness come together . . . alchemy provides the *real* bridge upon which the soul could pass from its former status (mythologising) to its new, modern status of (psycho-) logic . . .

(Giegerich, 1998, pp. 138–139)

Confusing the great work with the lesser work, the mythic with the alchemical, collapses the bridge – which the soul had already crossed into modernity – to seek egoic refuge through a *simulated* alchemical imagery in an equally *simulated* all-encompassing mythic world, and thereby not to deal with that *as which* the soul exists today.

Giegerich has introduced and addressed this critical difference in his seminal works *The Soul's Logical Life* and *What Is Soul?* describing it, after Heidegger's notion of 'the ontological difference', as 'the psychological difference' (1998, p. 123; 2012, pp. 54–55). He notes that alchemy symbolically articulated the 'psychological difference', though of course never expressed such a notion in a psychologically explicit way: alchemists said *aurum nostrm non estaurem vulgi*, 'our gold is not the gold of the people' (Giegerich, 2012, p. 81). There are other alchemical sayings such as *Mercurius non vulgi* ('not the common mercury'), and descriptions of the philosopher's stone as 'the stone that is not a stone'. These sayings mark a *psychological* distinction and an 'encompassing both' of the imaginal and the logical, the imaginal substance (the alchemical lead, mercury, salt, gold), and the noetic or notional, but an as yet not fully distilled, dialectical concept in the image: mercurial logic (Giegerich, 1998, p. 124).

'Encompassing both' the imaginal and notional does *not* denote the 'both/and' of metaphor and figural speech, which preserves the sense of a 'natural likeness' and hence keeps consciousness stuck at a naturalistic level. It belongs to dialectical thought, to the soul's *logos*, the unity of identity and difference. The psychological difference which alchemy described as an *opus contra naturam*, the 'work against nature', is the soul's self-differentiation from its former naturalistic (mythic) consciousness.

Let me describe the alchemical notion of the 'stone that is not a stone' dialectically. At first (in the logical, not temporal sense) there is a positivistic statement referring to an actual, empirical thing, a 'stone'. Something is asserted to actually be. Next, this is cancelled out, negated. It is said to be 'not a stone'. Then follows a second absolute negation, it is '*neither* a stone *nor* not a stone'. The positivistic logic of being and non-being is overcome by a second absolute negation, which absolves the being/non-being duality. The statement positing an actual 'stone' is annulled, then preserved. The negation of the negation raises the thought to a higher notional level (is a sublation, see above). From this thinking, embedded in the alchemical imagination, was distilled the notion of the 'spirit in the stone'; a 'spirit' reducible to neither a literal nor imaginal stone. Alchemists called this the philosopher's stone.

Describing it in terms of philosophy clearly identifies it as a matter of thought. Giegerich puts this succinctly:

1. The stone is a stone. 2. The stone is not a stone. 3. Despite being not a stone, it is not anything else nor simply nothing at all, but nevertheless a stone. And only as this *in itself* (innerly) negated stone is it the *philosopher's stone*.

(2006a, p. 132)

This critical difference belongs to the distinction between alchemy as an historical manifestation of the soul's self-expression and self-relation and to that of the ordinary individual in his empirical being. It is a difference which has also to be thought of in relation to the abstract concept of the empirical individual, the conceptual notion of modern subjectivity. For it is this conceptual level which itself, in psychology, has to undergo and suffer the alchemical process, be subject to the alchemy of dialectical thought. It has to let itself become the *materia* to be worked upon, rather than be taken as if it were the *a priori* ground of psychology: as if any empirical patient in any consulting room were psychology's real subject-matter.

The concept of the empirical person in its self-definition, the logic of its self-relation, has to undergo the process of alchemical negation, the corrosive action of its mercurial logic. In terms of 'man', it is not the empirical subject which is the subject-matter of the alchemical *opus*, rather the "archetypal" Purusha, Anthropos, or Adam Kadmon, or, less imaginally speaking, the *concept* of man, the logic of man's self-definition, and mode of being-in-the-world.

(Giegerich, 2012, p. 311)

Jung's central theoretical insight is soul as both *subject* and *object* of psychology. Psychological thought is the soul's self-expression, a production of the soul: dialectically speaking, soul is a product of psychological thought – hence the notion of psychology as soul-making. Psychology is uroboric, like the proverbial mercurial serpent swallowing its own tail. As the *logos* of the soul, psychology exists as the soul's self-relation, self-expression and self-knowledge. We have no Archimedean point outside the soul from which to observe.

Two statements of Jung's demonstrate how, for him, uniquely, psychological thought was already and always *interior* to the soul itself. Psychology is the soul speaking from within itself. He said: 'We should never forget that in any psychological discussion we are not saying anything *about* the psyche, but that the psyche is always speaking about *itself*' (CW 9i, para. 438), and: 'every psychic process ... is essentially *theoria*, that is to say, it is a *presentation*; and its reconstruction – or "re-presentation" – is at best only a variant of the same presentation' (CW 17, para. 162). He articulates the uroboric logic of his psychology, which indicates why alchemical thinking was the essence of his *theoria*. Recognizing the uroboric logic at the heart of Jung's thinking demonstrates how any empirical patient could never truly serve as the subject of a psychology predicated on the dialectical thinking of alchemy.

Personalistic, positivistic approaches re-assert themselves in contemporary analytical psychology as often-heard objections to thinking, to intellect, to giving priority to Jung's *theoria*, conceiving it as a digression into abstraction ('being in the head') from 'real' matters such as 'the body', 'true emotion', 'soulful experience'. This fails to recognize theory's function as the soul's *logos*. Such objectors want to replace the speech of the soul with the personalistic voice of an actual individual, even when their rhetoric remains one of so-called soul-making. The objectors fail to recognize the difference between psychological and positivistic theories. Positivistic theories are indeed abstract, but in a different way. They have their referent *outside* themselves: chemistry deals with actual physical phenomena, theorizing it abstractly in formula. Psychology contains its referent *inside* itself, it is uroborically self-referring: the soul speaking from and to itself. Jung depicts this with his notion of the soul's interiority: 'Psychology is doomed to cancel itself out as a science and therein precisely it reaches its scientific goal. Every other science has so to speak an outside; not so psychology, whose object is the inside subject of all sciences' (CW 8, para. 429).

The word Jung's English translator, R. F. C. Hull employed in this passage, 'to cancel', loses its richer German meaning. In the original, Jung writes: '*Sie muß – sich als Wissenshaft selber aufheben.*' The word '*aufheben*', as mentioned, was used by the German philosopher, Hegel, to describe the dialectical movement of thought, in which an initial meaning is cancelled, redefined and taken up at higher level. Hence, Jung cancels out a positivistic notion of psychology's 'object' (the inner and outer at the level of an empirical person), and takes it to a higher, more complex and subtle level of meaning as an absolute interiority. Thus, as Jung put it, the 'inside' of psychology, which has no 'outside', dialectically contains its own 'outside' inside itself.

This 'inside', Jung claims, is also the 'inside' of 'all the sciences'. It is an *absolute interiority*. Further on, Jung depicts this interiority as an 'absolute subjectivity and universal truth' (CW 8, para. 439). This 'absolute subjectivity' cannot refer to an empirical subject, who cannot represent an absolute interiority. To claim this would be hubris, to confuse the *opus magnum* with the *opus parvum*, to posit a positive-factual individual as the 'absolute subjectivity'.

Alas, alchemy is often used in the Jungian world in a way which collapses 'the psychological difference'. Many are drawn to the spirit of his psychology through a romantic ('romantic' in an emotional, not philosophical or feeling sense, since they require deep philosophical thinking) transference to alchemical images. We hold transferential feelings towards theories no less than to a therapist or other significant figure. We fall 'in love' with the mystique of the images, led through the forest of symbols by a beguiling anima (*anima alba*, the whitened, innocent anima).

The appeal of alchemical imagery rests on many factors. Not least is Jung's own turn to alchemy, asserting its role as carrier of 'mystery' (the numinous), and as a proto-psychology, which both reinforce transferential identifications with Jung as 'mana-personality', analytical psychology's 'hero-father'. For him, alchemy was an historical antecedent to his own psychology. He took alchemy's *lumen naturae*, the 'light of nature', as a metaphor for the individuation of the empirical personality. In this questionable way of thinking, the alchemical *opus* provides an analogy for the individuation process in analysis. Personalistic feelings, thoughts, dreams and fantasies of the patient find supposedly symbolic equation in various alchemical images. The transformative alchemical *opus* of 'lead' into 'gold', its various stages such as *nigredo*, *albedo* and *rubedo*, its operations like *mortification*, *calcination* and notions such as the *coniunctio*, the conjunction of *Sol* and *Luna*, and the 'goal' of the philosopher's stone, are employed to give imaginal expression to the transformation of the empirical personality. Alchemical tropes are supposed to serve the narration of our innermost subjectivity: they turn the 'gold' of alchemy into the 'lead' of cliché.

Are alchemical images in the so-called 'clinical' context *truly* self-expressions of soul, or rather *simulations* (sincere, but inauthentic) applied in the service of an egoic hunger for transcendent or mystical meaning? One finds in Jung's own writings precedent for treating alchemical imagery as 'clinically' relevant to the empirical personality of the actual patient. Alchemy was, for him, not merely a 'matter of alembics and melting pots', there was essentially an 'alchymical' philosophy, the groping precursor of the most modern psychology. Its basic secret, for Jung, was 'the transcendent function, the transformation of personality through the blending and the fusion of the noble with the base components, of the differentiated with the inferior functions, of the conscious with the unconscious' (CW 7, para. 360).

Alchemical process is used as a meaningful narrative, aggrandizing otherwise all-too-human tribulations, experiences and subjectivities. Employed as genuine psychological descriptions of an actual person's process in analysis, alchemy becomes something external; a way of feeding the longings of what Hegel called the 'beautiful soul'. It no longer offers a true reflection of the soul at this historical moment, as a self-expression of the soul's *logos*. Rather, it expresses our egoic romantic, nostalgic wishes.

In his essay, 'Psychology of the Transference', Jung asserts in 'the case of alchemy it is quite evident that the unconscious content is of human origin . . . ' (CW 16, para. 383). He firmly places alchemical images as of 'human origin', as if they are projected straight from a patient's 'unconscious' psyche, from the immediacy of the patient's analytic experience, rather than belonging to the mediating function of the *logos* of psychological theorizing. In this essay, Jung equates the psychology of the transference with the *coniunctio*, the alchemical union of opposites. Referring to one of the Rosarium woodcuts, 'King and Queen' he writes that the psychology of this image 'Above all else . . . depicts a human encounter . . .' (CW 16, para. 419). Jung concludes that in the history of alchemy, the 'important part played . . . by the *hieros gamos* and the mystical marriage, and also by the *coniunctio*, corresponds to the central significance of the transference' both in psychotherapy and 'normal human relationships' (CW 16, para. 538). But is the *coniunctio* really the same as transference phenomena in psychotherapy and 'normal human relationships'? Doesn't this equation actually inflate transference with a transcendent meaning beyond its all-too-human aspects?

In alchemy the *coniunctio* expressed the soul's mercurial inner dialectical self-division and self-unity, the unity of identity and difference. In his psychology, Jung named this the syzygy (from the Greek for 'a married couple'), a unity formed from the identity and the difference between anima and animus. In *Memories, Dreams, Reflections*, he points to this critical difference, saying 'objective cognition' lies *behind* 'the attraction of the emotional relationship; it seems to be the central secret. Only through objective cognition is the real *coniunctio* possible' (1963, p. 297).

The immediacy of the emotional relationship is not the *coniunctio*, as an analytic approach employing alchemical imagery often supposes. The phrase 'objective cognition' directs us instead to *logos*, to mercurial logic, rather than to a romantic worship of emotionalism. 'Objective cognition' belongs with *relatedness*, as a matter of *feeling* in Jung's sense of the word. This is significantly different from emotion (Giegerich, 2012, pp. 206–207; CW 6, paras 595–643). For Jung, feeling is rational, designating value, significance, evaluation: a cognitive function – thoughtful, objective.

Jung seems to identify the alchemical *coniunctio* with transference phenomena; and then, conversely, point to it as what lies behind the transference, as 'objective cognition', a negation of the immediacy of the 'emotional relationship'. 'Objective cognition' describes mercurial logic. Transference involves the coming together of two individuals whose relationship is one of externality: each person exists apart from the other. At the human level of their individual personalities, they slowly relate in a manufactured, analytic 'union', like a couple working through difficulties in marital therapy.

Equating transference with an alchemical *coniunctio* is common among contemporary Jungian analysts. This is incorrect. Transference pairs together human subjectivities by projection and interpretation. The otherness of patient and therapist is a positive-factual one. Even where there is psychic confusion, the work is to realize externality, otherness. This is not the interior otherness of the *coniunctio*'s dialectical synthesis and separation, as Jung describes in the subtitle of *Mysterium Coniunctionis* as *An Inquiry into the Separation and Synthesis of Psychic Opposites* (CW 14). In this subtitle, the 'and' of the 'Separation and Synthesis' is dialectical, not temporal: not synthesis following separation, but both simultaneously, logically so. Transference is a relation of subjectivities, not of 'objective cognitions'. The *coniunctio* entails an absolute negation, which cancels out and at the same time takes up (sublates) transference at a human level to the perception of mercurial logic. It signifies the distillation of the absolute negative interiorization of the soul into itself. It denotes interiority as a psychological notion, not as what is going on in an emotional immediacy.

In his introduction to a collection of alchemical readings from the *Collected Works*, the New York analytical psychologist Nathan Schwartz-Salant interprets elements of the *coniunctio* in terms of gender difference. He reduces soul to social and political concerns. These may be an issue to actual men and women, but are not the concern of alchemical mercurial logic. Schwartz-Salant writes: 'Women will also suffer a *nigredo* after the *coniunctio*, but my experience is that they will often have a greater natural capacity than a man to stay with the resulting sense of loss and despair' (1995, p. 25). Here, Jung's great insight into the alchemical melancholy of the *nigredo* is lost: reduced to anthropological, humanistic factors. An all-too-human (genderized) despair is elevated to a metaphysical level – the alchemical *nigredo*. Elsewhere, Schwartz-Salant again reduces alchemical insights to positivistic notions of psychopathology, equating alchemy with 'those states of mind often called mad or psychotic . . . this madness is a central feature of the alchemical *prima materia*' (1998, p. 17).

Donald Kalsched, an analytical psychologist practising in upstate New York, in a paper entitled 'Hermes-Mercurius and the Self-Care System in Cases of Early Trauma' takes a similar approach: 'I will be setting forth the idea that Hermes-Mercurius what might be described as an archetypal self-care system which accounts for the fierce resistance to individuation that we find in patients who have suffered early trauma' (1997, p. 95). Why is a 'self-care system' archetypal? Why isn't it a psychic defence at the ordinary, human level? With his approach, Kalsched brings together two different logics: developmental thinking about trauma and mytho-poetic/alchemical rhetoric. The psychic problems of early childhood are confused with soul matters. This is not to dismiss the genuine personal suffering entailed in childhood trauma, nor the astute (psychoanalytic) insights Kalsched offers. Why wrap them in myth, fairy tale and alchemy, as if the language of the all-too-human wasn't enough?

The 'plight' of the soul is of a different order (Giegerich, 1998, p. 176). Developmental psychology cannot simply be juxtaposed alongside the mytho-poetic as both represent different logics. Bringing them together is a hermeneutic sleight of hand, exchanging mystification for genuine mystery. A further differ-ence arises from the principle of 'efficient causality' within developmental psychoanalysis: childhood factors are taken as causal for psychopathology, whereas soul is self-moving. Jung asserted the autonomy of soul; its causes are wholly within itself (Giegerich, 2012, pp. 31–32). As Plato declared, the soul is that which moves itself (*Phaidros*, 245 c 7). 'Hermes-Mercurius' (even if such a hybrid 'god' existed psychologically) could not be constellated by 'develop-mental' factors, nor be a product of trauma, nor part of a 'self-care system'. Why inflate egoic or supposed defences of the self (however necessary) with a divine pneuma? Leave the gods alone to rest in peace. Besides, there is a great difference between the Greek god, Hermes, and the alchemical spirit, Mercurius. They cannot be simply equated. To do so is a pure abstraction from their historical contexts, disguised as the personifying imagination.

Alchemy's truth was never the transformation of human personality. Writing in *Psychology and Alchemy*, Jung says as much:

> In a sense, the old alchemists were nearer to the central truth of the psyche
> . . . when they strove to deliver the fiery spirit from the chemical ele-

ments, and treated the mystery as though it lay in the dark and silent womb of nature.

(CW 12, para. 562)

Giegerich stresses this: 'the alchemist did not search for *his* self, but for the spirit Mercurius as the mystery deeply hidden in the real'. Alchemy was concerned with 'the inner truth or the inner nature of nature. It is a speculative kind of natural philosophy' (2006b, pp. 37–38).

But rather than recognize the alchemical meaning of the philosopher's stone for the 'old alchemists' as the truth of the 'nature of nature' (a truth now firmly in the grasp of natural science), contemporary Jungian analysis draws on a misappropriation of alchemy to bolster the empirical personality as a singular, last refuge of transcendent, symbolic significance. The empirical personality is flatteringly enthroned as the true reference, the 'real' secret (the 'truth') of the alchemical mystery. The soul's dialectic is abandoned for the grand narrative of a personality cult.

Cautioning against the use of alchemy in this egoic way, the Japanese Jungian analyst Toshio Kawai observes: 'If we should try to make alchemy a model of psychology, we would lose Jung's spirit. Rather alchemy was his psychology in itself' (Kawai, 1998, p. 232 in Tanaka, 2001, p. 11). Another Japanese Jungian analyst, Tanaka, critiques how alchemical imagery was used by Jung initially to 'interpret, or amplify, individual dreams, visions and the process of psychotherapy', a practice followed uncritically by many Jungians since. Drawing upon Jung's alchemical writings, such analysts turn alchemy into 'a frame of reference for psychology', into '*illustration*' (Tanaka, 2001, p. 11). Missing the distinction of Jung's psychology as a psychology with soul, alchemical images are 'applied' as a 'therapy of humans', whereas 'only when we can fully recognize that psychotherapy is therapy of the soul by the soul, can we patients and therapists first face each other as complete human' (ibid., p. 13).

The late James Hillman argued that using alchemical imagery does not guarantee therapy is soul-making: 'Any student of alchemy, any borrower of its tropes for one's own, art or practice, doing the work for one's nature, remains Promethean, a secular humanist, a gold digger'. The rhetoric of soul-making is insufficient, for 'soul-making of the individual or even of the collective still remains human'. The task of an alchemical psychology is 'to be focussed on "perfecting the substance" not the subject', else 'practitioners of therapy will find themselves chained to a rock of dogmatic person-centered humanism' (2010, p. 28). Hillman differentiates Jung's notion of a psychology *with* soul from the conception of psychology as focussed on the inner life of human subjectivity.

In *Mysterium Coniunctionis*, the section the 'Paradoxa' (CW 14, para. 93) brings this out strongly in identifying the alchemical way of thinking. Jung quotes from a letter of February 1567, in which the alchemist Richard White writing to Johannes Turrius, observes, 'Thus, if the soul would know herself, she must contemplate herself, and gaze into that place where the power of the soul, Wisdom,

179

dwells'. This corresponds to the principle in Jung's psychology of the soul as both 'subject' and 'object': the uroboric logic of alchemy's emblematic symbol, the mercurial serpent swallowing its tail.

Imagining that the referent of the alchemical *opus* is the empirical personality fails to recognize that alchemy gave Jung insight into the soul's mercurial dialectic. Confusing the mercurial *logos* with the empirical subject turns the soul's interiorizing self-reflection (the soul's self-gazing, self-relation) into external reflection. Alchemical imagery serves our interpretative efforts in order to stimulate our imagination through the unfamiliar, exotic, the esoteric (Giegerich, 1998, p. 166). Such positivized reflections act out theoretically on behalf of the ego-personality, reducing psychology's *logos* to the (empirical, psychoanalytic, developmental) cause-and-effect logic.

Jung understood a dream as being its own interpretation; he advises 'sticking to the image', and in working with a fantasy image: 'Above all, don't let anything from the outside, that does not belong, get into it, for the fantasy image "has everything it needs"' (CW 14, para. 749). In this definitive statement, Jung reminds us that psychological reflection, as alchemist Richard White recognized for alchemy, is the soul's self-reflection. Hillman puts this well:

> Mental events as images do not require and cannot acquire further validation by virtue of exteriority. The soul's life is not upheld by virtue of exteriority. But neither are mental events validated by virtue of my "having" a dream, "thinking" an idea or "feeling an experience".
>
> (2010, p. 189)

The fantasy image has its referent wholly within itself: just as psychology, in Jung's understanding, is the soul's inner dialogue with itself.

In the 'Epilogue' of *Psychology and Alchemy*, Jung draws attention to this collapse of difference between the empirical personality and soul. As I read him, he is essentially showing how the modern personality identifies itself as the central meaning of the alchemical *opus*. I contend that Jungian psychology likewise falls prey to this misrecognition. The 'Epilogue' charts the historical development of alchemy, describing how alchemical thought had 'reached its final summit, and with it the historical turning point, in Goethe's *Faust* . . . [which is] . . . steeped in alchemical forms of thought from beginning to end' (CW 12, para. 558). Faust exemplifies the way the modern subject has forcefully pushed itself centre-stage. Jung describes the 'essential Faustian drama' as that 'expressed in the scene between Paris and Helen' (ibid.). In this part of *Faust*, a 'play' is performed where Faust appears to conjure up by 'magic power' the phantasms of Paris and Helen. On the appearance of Helen, Faust exclaims:

> Have I still eyes? Has beauty's fountain-head
> Itself flooded my inmost mind? So blest
> Is my reward after that fearful quest!

How empty all the world was, closed and dead
To me until this priestly revelation
Founded it fast, a timeless, loved creation!

(Goethe, 1994, pp. 56–63)

Faust's cry is the longing for meaning and beauty in a world 'empty . . . closed and dead'. It is the search of the modern man for transcendence (psychologically, compelled by an infatuating anima figure) to quell the nihilism of his existence. Faust pledges himself to the Helen figure, his:

whole desire
Passion's quintessence, all the fire
The Idolatry, the madness of my heart.

(Ibid., p. 60)

The term 'idolatry' points to the inception of what in our times has become the culture of simulation: permeating also, I suggest, analytical psychology. As the 'play' closes, Paris is overwhelmed by Helen's beauty:

With sudden strength he lifts her – seems to bear
Her off, indeed –

Faust intervenes:

Rash fool! How does he dare?
Stop! Can't you hear me? I must intervene.

(Ibid., p. 62)

Gone is the soulful standpoint of which Jung spoke when he described the alchemist's witness of the *nigredo*. Faust, unrestrained, asserts, 'I'll rescue her, and she'll belong to me.' He seizes her, but 'her shape grows dim', there is an explosion, Faust falls to the ground and the spirits dissolve into mist.

This scene points towards the kind of romantic, aesthetic transferential attachment which may occur in analytical psychology to the mystery and beauty of alchemical symbols, serving iconically to connect us to the en-trancements of a 'return to Greece' (Paris and Helen), to side-step 'How empty all the world was', rather than face it. Behind this stands a beguiling anima complex, seducing psychological practice and thought into a programme of the 'rescue' of 'the beautiful soul'.

Contrary to these Faustian longings the medieval alchemist would, Jung suggests, have understood this scene in terms of 'the mysterious *coniunctio* of Sol and Luna in the retort' (CW 12, para. 558). He goes on to show how 'modern man, disguised in the figure of Faust', puts 'himself in the place of Paris or Sol, takes possession of Helen or Luna, [as] his own inner, feminine counterpart' (ibid.).

Jung's comments are as relevant to analytical psychology now as when written in 1944. If the *coniunctio* is typically interpreted as meaning the transference, the whole 'objective process of the union' is transformed into 'the subjective experience of the artifex': a 'transformation' is reduced to an imitation. (The 'artifex' is the alchemical name for the refiner; the one knowledgeable in ores and metals.)

Equating of the 'artifex' with the analyst and/or the analysand misrepresents the artifex's role, whose work, as Hillman stresses, was concerned with the 'substance', not the 'subject'. Jung suggests interpreting the *coniunctio* in terms of 'personal psychological experience' bringing it to consciousness (CW 12, para. 559). But, as is clear from his comments, this bringing into consciousness is an unconscious move: not a witnessing, but an identification with what is transformed. This risks inflation: 'Faust's sin was that he identified with the thing to be transformed and that had been transformed' (CW 12, para. 560). This is the Faustian bargain of modern-day analytical psychology, puffing up the empirical personality pneumatically with the 'natural philosophy' of alchemy (alchemy's 'puffers'). When we identify ourselves as the central figure in the alchemical *opus*, we ignore what Jung meant by the 'objective psyche'.

Interpreting alchemical images and thought in terms of our self-development is precisely to commit 'Faust's sin', valorizing the concrete personality of the individual as alchemy's *prima materia*. Alchemy's artifex was not in it for 'personal development'. Jung's naming analytical psychology as a psychology with soul means it needs to be understood as the soul's *logos* working on, in and through itself: the soul interiorizing itself into itself. Psychology, for Jung, arises because 'the psyche has attained its present complexity by a series of acts of introjection' (CW 9i, para. 54). The old alchemists were not mistaken, were not projecting their own psychic hinterland onto matter, when they 'ascribed their secret to matter'. Analytical psychology errs if it asserts it is 'we' who 'embody the secret in ourselves' (CW 12, para. 564), adorning and inflating our all-too-human inner life with the fetish of alchemical meaning.

References

Brinkmann, K. (2010) 'The Dialectic of the Inverted World and the Meaning of *Aufhebung*', in *The Dimensions of Hegel's Dialectic* ed. N. G. Limnatis, New York: Continuum International Publishing, pp. 123–139.

Christou, E. (1976) *The Logos of the Soul* Zurich: Spring Publications.

Giegerich, W. (2005) 'On The Neurosis of Psychology, or the Third of Two,' in *Spring 1977, An Annual of Archetypal Psychology and Jungian Thought*, Zurich: Spring Publications, pp. 153–174.

—— (1987–1988) 'Jungian Psychology: A Baseless Enterprise, Reflections on our Jungian Identity', in *Harvest 1987–88, Journal for Jungian Studies*, vol. 33, London: Analytical Psychology Club.

—— (1998) *The Soul's Logical Life. Towards a Rigorous Notion of Psychology* Frankfurt am Main: Peter Lang.

—— (2006a) (ed. by Downing, C.) 'Once More "The Stone Which Is Not A Stone": Further Reflections on "Not"', in *Disturbances In The Field*: *Essays in Honor of David L. Miller* New Orleans: Spring Journal Books, pp. 127–141.

—— (2006b) 'Closure and Setting Free or the Bottled Spirit of Alchemy and Psychology', in *Alchemy, Spring 74, A Journal of Archetype and Culture* New Orleans: Spring Journal, pp. 31–62.

—— (2012) *What Is Soul?* New Orleans: Spring Journal Books.

Goethe, J. W. (1994) (trans., with an introduction by D. Luke), *Faust: Part Two* Oxford: Oxford University Press.

Hillman, J. (2010) *Alchemical Psychology*, James Hillman Uniform Edition, Vol. 5, Putnam: Spring Publications.

Inwood, M. (2003) *A Hegel Dictionary* Oxford: Blackwell Publications.

Jung, C. G. (1953–1977), except where indicated, references are by volume and paragraph number to the *Collected Works of C. G. Jung*, 20 vols., eds Herbert Read, Michael Fordham and Gerhard Adler, trans. R. F. C. Hull. London and Princeton, NJ: Routledge and Princeton University Press.

—— (1963) *Memories, Dreams, Reflections* New York: Pantheon Books.

Kalsched, D. (1997) (ed. by Marlin, S.) 'Hemes/Mercurius and the Self-Care System in Cases of Early Trauma', in *The Alchemy of Desire* Wilmette: Chiron Publications, pp. 94–124.

Kawai, T. (1998) *Jung*, Tokyo, Kodan-Sha, quoted and referenced in Y. Tanaka (2001).

Schwartz-Salant, N. (1995) (ed.) *Jung on Alchemy* London: Routledge.

—— (1998) *The Mystery of Human Relationship*: *Alchemy and the Transformation of the Self* London: Routledge.

Tanaka, Y. (2001) 'Alchemical Images and Logic in Analytical Psychology', *Harvest, Journal for Jungian Studies*, vol. 47, no.1, London: Karnac Books for the C. G. Jung Analytical Psychology Club, London, pp. 7–30.

Part IV

CLINICAL APPLICATIONS

THE HOURS OF THE DAY

In the blood of the cup
fire and ice cauterise me.
burning to burning I am renamed,
reduced to powders, to liquidity.

The insoluble does not die.
I do not die.
I am the ashes of the flower,
the bird of the stone.

How could I ask of my dilemma:
throw away this stone.
It is my journey
and my foundation.

Adele Davide

11

ATONEMENT

Ruth Williams

Lords, I protest my soul is full of woe
That blood should sprinkle me to make me grow.
Come mourn with me for what I do lament,
And put on sullen black incontinent.
I'll make a voyage to the Holy Land
To wash this blood off from my guilty hand.
(King Henry on hearing of Richard II's murder.)
          (Act 5, Scene 6, *Richard II* by William Shakespeare)

On this earth, there is no return,
No great salvation.
Some may say they find it in wine,
Other (sic) in the turning of the tide,
But for those who do wrong
There is no rest.
          (Tracey Emin in *Strangeland*, 2005, p. 122)

'What makes alchemy so valuable for psychotherapy', Jungian Analyst Edward Edinger suggests, 'is that its images concretize the experiences of transformation that one undergoes in psychotherapy . . . Alchemy provides a kind of anatomy of individuation' (1994, p. 2). Individuation cannot happen without atonement on some level for gaining maturity inevitably involves wounding and reparation. My chapter focuses on the collective rather than the personal unconscious, as I explore the concept of 'atonement' through a psycho-spiritual lens. I apply different conceptual stances to explore atonement. This chapter is about alchemy within the political world – how the alchemical metaphor contributes to reconciliation.

Introduction

We all wound each other on a daily basis. Being imperfect is part of being human. This puts us all in touch with the concept of atonement, a process of growth and expansion, thought about here in terms of spiritual and alchemical transformation.

Atonement is studied in Biblical and Cabalistic texts, in art, literature and film. I think here of the passages quoted above, and particularly Ian McEwan's novel *Atonement* (2001, an Oscar-nominated film) in which a young girl witnesses a sexual scene she does not fully understand. This has devastating consequences to the characters she inadvertently betrays, thinking the man was hurting the woman, her sister. Roland Joffé's film *The Mission* (1986) in which the hero kills his brother in a jealous rage also deals with atonement. His journey to self-forgiveness takes the form of the Sisyphean task of dragging a load up and down a mountain until the hero cracks and the tears of pain and sorrow can finally be released. Only then can genuine atonement be achieved. I will conceptualise atonement in both analytic and alchemical terms using gestalt psychology to illustrate my meaning. It is an idea of central importance which warrants closer examination. I hope to show that Analytical Psychology uniquely elucidates its meaning; atonement requires a transpersonal perspective to fully capture its purpose.

Some elements in the cluster of ideas examined here were explored by British psychoanalyst Melanie Klein in a model looking back to infant anxiety. Klein, a pioneer of child analysis in Britain and of the British Object Relations School, believed the superego – a kind of ego ideal – operates in children as young as two. (The superego forms part of Sigmund Freud's tripartite model of the mind made up of ego, id and superego (Freud, 1962).) Klein argues that children go through various developmental stages which enable them to cope with internal conflict. The 'despotic' superego finally recedes, becoming more persuasive than commanding. This shift is seen as part of the early development of conscience (Klein, 1988, pp. 251–252). To atone is an act of conscience, a developmental achievement.

I will consider atonement in the context of world events to which it provides the philosophical backdrop, such as the Truth and Reconciliation Commission in post-apartheid South Africa. In Britain and elsewhere, atonement is explored in experiments with restorative justice in which criminals face their victims. I will look at a talk given by Cherie Booth (the professional name Cherie Blair uses in her work as a Human Rights Lawyer and High Court Judge) and an experiment reported in *The Observer* newspaper in 2004 in the UK. The Black Reparations movement (where the focus is on concrete financial restitution) seems to me to substitute a material answer to a spiritual question and fails to meet the abiding need for atonement. The Australian Government's generous apology to the Indigenous Peoples is an important example of atonement and how reparation might be made (see http://australia.gov.au/about-australia/our-country/our-people/apology-to-australias-indigenous-peoples). I begin with the Jewish festival of Yom Kippur, or Day of Atonement, which I discuss below. Although British psychotherapist Eduardo Pitchon's formulation is included to amplify the concept of atonement and give a frame of reference, my focus is on this concept as a secular – albeit spiritual – process corresponding with the alchemical 'opus'.

Definition of atonement/conscience

Atonement is an archetypal idea. An archetype is 'an irrepresentable, unconscious, pre-existent form that seems to be part of the inherited structure of the psyche and can therefore manifest itself spontaneously anywhere, at any time' (CW 10, para. 847). Repentance (being contrite and feeling regretful) is a necessary first step in the process of atonement and the establishment of penitence. Only when this has occurred can reconciliation (an attitude of concern for the victim) take place. The atonement then recognises the wound, creating scope for transformation. Repentance can be seen as a holding of opposites in Jungian terms. It requires facing what one has done, making it right, perhaps getting forgiveness. But what has been done can never not have been done. Jung discusses conscience in a wonderfully evocative dream about a man with 'dirty hands' (CW 10, para. 826). The man's dirty hands in the dream point to an unconscious attitude about a moral dilemma regarding a dodgy business deal. Jung deduced from the dream that the man's 'bad conscience' is missing and contrasts his own formulation with Freud's concept of the superego. He suggests that, because the dreamer did not recognise the dubious nature of the dilemma 'and therefore lacked any motive for repression' (ibid., para. 828), the idea of conscious repression could not apply. Atonement is a conscious humbling rather than a moral superego flagellation from 'on high'.

In this chapter I sidestep a discussion about any moral imperative to atone, to advance a psychological interpretation of atonement in Jungian terms. Andrew Samuels discusses morality in the context of Yom Kippur – the Day of Atonement in Judaism – in *The Plural Psyche* (1989, pp. 201–204) where he helpfully contrasts what he calls 'original morality' with 'moral imagination' in a way that enables one to discuss this subject without resorting to moral superiority or becoming judgemental about outcome. An apology does not necessarily equate to an atonement. An atonement is a genuine, profound expression or feeling of sorrow which requires deep self-examination and reflection. Nor does atonement necessarily involve an act of sacrifice, except perhaps self-abasement. Jung's exposition of sacrifice has only limited use for the present purposes (CW 11, paras 247–273). Atonement usually relates to expiation for a particular injury or injuries, as opposed to guilt which is, or can be, an endless experience able to transmute itself and re-attach to other injuries.

In the absence of atonement, *someone* becomes scapegoated and is left carrying the Shadow (Jung's term for 'the thing a person has no wish to be' (CW 16, para. 470). The Shadow falls within the *nigredo* stage in alchemy. The *nigredo* – or blackening – is a long, arduous process of grappling with the *prima materia* and is much more than exploration or confrontation of the Shadow. 'The scapegoater feels a relief in being lighter, without the burden of carrying what is unacceptable to his or her ego ideal, without shadow' (Brinton Perera, 1986, p. 9). *So the absence of the atonement is not a neutral act.*

There have been eras where atonement was common within cultures. For example, Marie Louise Von Franz informs us that in ancient China synchronicity

191

was routinely considered to aid understanding by, for instance, interpreting natural phenomena such as earthquakes as auguring well or ill. She tells us the emperor was responsible for harmony in nature and in society:

> If the emperor or his government deviated from Tao, heaven expressed its anger in the form of unusual phenomena. These were appropriately interpreted, and the ruler then had to atone for his past behaviour and change his ways.
>
> (1993, p. 192)

British psychotherapist Eduardo Pitchon (who worked with the Orthodox Jewish community) brings the spiritual nature of the concept of atonement into a secular setting when he reflects on Teshuvah (Hebrew for repentance) as an attitude or path of individuation:

> It could be argued that the whole of psychotherapy is a process of repentance. When a person makes the decision to come into therapy it is a transformative and profound decision. Though he might not know at the time, he has made a choice . . . to follow a path that leads ultimately to the goal of becoming a whole man or indeed a whole woman. In order to achieve this a person has to follow what in Kaballah is known as the path of the Zaddik; the path of honesty. . . . He becomes consistent, and he reaches deeper levels of himself which are a closer and more faithful reflection of who he really is. So a peaceful heart is the necessary herald of the coming of the Messiah and a necessary consequence of Tikkun Olam [healing the world], the reparation which leads to Atonement – AT ONE-MENT.
>
> (1997)

He emphasises the interpretation of the word 'at-one-ment' as implying a one-ness with God, consistent with my argument about the potential inherent in a genuine process of atoning. This accounts for the immanence, the numinous quality associated with the sense of completing a gestalt achieved in fully embracing atonement and experiencing the transcendent function at work, mediating opposites. In Jungian terms, the transcendent function 'facilitates a transition from one psychological attitude or condition to another' (Samuels *et al.*, 1986, p. 150).

James Hillman, pioneer of Archetypal Psychology, comes near to these ideas in *Betrayal* where he talks of trust and betrayal as two sides of the same coin; trust has within it the seed of betrayal, betrayal the seed of forgiveness. Betrayal he sees as the dark side of both trust and forgiveness 'giving them both meaning, making them both possible' (Hillman, 1964, pp. 25–26). He suggests perhaps betrayal is indeed 'the human gate to such higher religious experiences as forgiveness and reconciliation' (ibid.) and that forgiveness 'probably requires atonement' (ibid., p. 27). He cautions against this process being purely intra-psychic, adding that atonement is probably more effective when actually expressed to the other. I agree that the humbling required in making such an expression is a necessary part of the process which is why ability to atone is connected to one's ego strength.

If the site of the betrayal or 'sin' is one suffused with narcissistic wounding, shame or hubris inhibit the ability to atone. It therefore takes humility – on both the world stage, and in personal situations – to allow it to unfold. Atonement is often avoided by manic reparation, a neurotic/defensive wish for premature closure, possibly a Tricksterish device, to avoid tolerating the suffering involved in bearing the difficulties being described. (When Jung talks of the Trickster he is referring to the shape-shifting, Mercurial nature of that archetype conceived as both mythical god and inner psychic experience.)

Collective clinical examples

Having briefly outlined the concept of atonement, I will illustrate it referring to the Jewish Day of Atonement.

Yom Kippur

Yom Kippur – the Day of Atonement – is the most sacred and solemn day in the Jewish calendar, ten days after Jewish New Year. This ten-day period is known as The Days of Repentance or Days of Awe. Yom Kippur is marked by fasting, abstaining from work, sex, washing, wearing of perfume and leather shoes (much like the Christian period of Lent). Yom Kippur is spent in continuous prayer for forgiveness. To truly engage with such a process has a transformative effect, although, as with all religious dogma, it can simply be treated as a ritualistic act.

> In the Jewish tradition, we say that the "book of life" is open . . . till the end of Yom Kippur . . . In that book of life our fate for the next year gets written and then at the end of Yom Kippur it is sealed. In *Tikkun* [a spiritual progressive community], we've transformed that imagery into a deep spiritual truth: we are taking a ten day period to examine what changes are needed in our lives, and how seriously we will take the (full year) process of making those changes. By condensing the period of heightened attention to ten days, we are making sure that we have a time when these issues are totally "front burner" in our consciousness. If we haven't been able to make any progress in self-awareness and steps toward change in those ten days, then in a certain sense our fate is sealed: we will continue to receive the karmic consequences of being the way that we are at the current moment, and to the extent that we want that to change, this ten day period becomes a spiritual retreat and intensive short-term psychotherapy to work out what we need to be.
>
> (Lerner, 2006)

This represents a modern/progressive interpretation of the Jewish Day of Atonement. In ancient times, the High Priest conducted a sacrificial ceremony in the wilderness. Clothed in white linen he successively confessed his own sins and the sins of the people before sprinkling the blood of sacrifice. The priest then sent a goat (the 'scapegoat') off into the wilderness, where it was driven to its death, to symbolically carry away the sins of Israel. This idea was originally recorded in Leviticus (Chapter 16, verse 21). Yom Kippur is the Rabbinic substitute for the scapegoat ritual so that in Yom Kippur each person takes personal responsibility for their own deeds and gets personal forgiveness rather than relying on the collective cleansing inherent in the scapegoat ritual.

Jungian Analyst Sylvia Brinton Perera's etymological analysis in *The Scapegoat Complex* is enlightening: 'The Hebrew word for atonement, *kipper*, is related to *kippurim*, eliminatory procedures . . . A Babylonian rite on the fifth day of the ten-day New Year festival was called *kippuru* and involved purgation, purification, confession of sins and a human sacrifice' (1986, p. 11). In fact, Teshuvah (Hebrew for repentance) means 'to return' implying that in Yom Kippur the idea is one 'returns' to the person sinned against to atone. This might involve restitution. Three appeals for forgiveness may be made in this way and Jewish lore then deems that, if no forgiveness is forthcoming, it becomes the other person's sin that they are unwilling or unable to forgive.

The Truth and Reconciliation Commission

The Commission was set up by the Government of National Unity in South Africa in 1995 to help heal the traumatic effects of apartheid. It established a Reparation and Rehabilitation Committee to provide victim support to enable – via atonement – a process of restoring victims' dignity, to formulate policy proposals and recommendations on rehabilitation and healing of survivors, their families and communities. The envisaged overall function was to facilitate non-repetition, healing and healthy co-existence. There was also an Amnesty Committee. Being granted amnesty for an act meant the perpetrator was free from prosecution for that particular act (www.doj.gov.za/trc/). This was a necessary incentive to encourage people to endure the difficulties of entering into such a painful process of self-examination, and in the spirit of the Commission with its enlightened focus on the urgency of the spiritual transformation required.

Many people expected chaos when apartheid was overthrown. Establishing the Commission was an act of enormous dignity and maturity which left many in awe. The leadership of Nelson Mandela enabled this. I agree with Jungian analyst Lyn Cook when she describes him as 'that supreme exemplar of tolerance and reconciliation . . . who embodied the transcendent function in this process whose example constellated the archetype of wholeness' (2003, p. 1). As an individual Mandela was able to hold the warring opposites to facilitate the process of transformation. I would go further. Without him, history might have been quite different. Consciousness needs a person to incarnate the process; to catalyse change. Mandela's ability to transcend opposites – and resist the desire for revenge or retribution – enabled the transcendent function to constellate and the potential for a new era to manifest; though, as Samuels rightly argues, there is a danger in setting leader and led in opposition. This can inflate the leader in unhealthy ways and disempower the people (2010, p. 247).

Cook tells us about the South African philosophy of *ubuntu*, a Xhosa word. This emphasises the connection between the individual and the collective. It perhaps facilitated the balance of understanding and reparation rather than the path of vengeance and retaliation. The Commission Chair, Archbishop Desmond Tutu (of Xhosa descent), writes about the principles of restorative justice (discussed more fully below), which underlay the Commission, being rooted in *ubuntu*.

> It is the essence of being human; a person is a person through other persons. . . . The totally self-sufficient person is subhuman for none of us comes fully formed into the world. . . . For ubuntu, the greatest good is communal harmony. If one person is dehumanised then inexorably we are all diminished and dehumanised in our turn. A criminal offence causes a breach in relationship and the purpose of the penal process is to heal the breach, to restore good relationships and to redress the balance.
>
> (2004, pp. 4–5)

South African Jungian analyst Astrid Berg also refers to this idea in her chapter on *ubuntu* published in *The Cultural Complex* (Singer & Kimbles, 2004, pp. 239–250). The link between atonement and forgiveness is expressed well by Father Lapsley (one of the victims of violence quoted by Cook): 'Forgive I will be able to, but then the asking of forgiveness must take place within the framework of repentance' (ibid., p. 7). Repentance here is identical with atonement.

Restorative justice

In restorative justice the criminal faces his/her victim. This idea has been gathering momentum for only about a decade. I think it needs to find more acceptance, not only because it is a psychologically mature means of dealing with crime, but pragmatically it has the potential to solve the serious prison shortage and save money, making it politically expedient. In Texas a $600 million prison-expansion plan was shelved in 2007 in favour of a $241 million plan to expand community-based drug and alcohol treatment services, after researchers convinced legislators this would lower crime rates more than expanding the state's penal infrastructure (www.tikkun.org/tikkundaily/2010/07/22/could-oakland-become-a-restorative-justice-city/). The prison population has indeed declined.

The City of Hull in Yorkshire, England, is working towards becoming a restorative city. Their aim is for everyone who works with children and youth in Hull, an economically and socially deprived city, to employ restorative practices (www.restorativejustice.org/RJOB/will-hull-uk-become-a-restorative-city).

Fred W. M. McElrea (2012), a semi-retired District Court Judge in New Zealand writing in *Tikkun* magazine, tells us his country has run its entire youth justice system in a non-adversarial manner since 1989. This is the world's strongest example of how a national juvenile system can transition to something incorporating restorative justice. It inspired restorative approaches in New Zealand's adult system, resulting in less reliance on prisons and a far better deal for victims. Importantly, it supports indigenous ways of dealing with conflict and builds on the strengths of Maori people.

We have so much to learn from First Peoples, the name chosen by indigenous groups for themselves. From South Africa, we have the Xhosa notion of *ubuntu*. McElrea refers to the Maori influence in New Zealand. Jerome Bernstein, a Jungian analyst in Sante Fe, New Mexico, explains that amongst the Navajo:

> The cosmos, including us, has an order – to whatever degree we know it or sense it. Our work, from their perspective, is [to] restore balance in the face of imbalance *out of respect* for the (natural) order of things. That is what so many of their ceremonies are about.
>
> (Bernstein, 2010)

He continues how, from a Navajo perspective, 'all illness is a result from a wound to or from nature. That keeps us permanently connected to the cosmic order and working with psyche' (ibid.).

This shift towards restorative justice based on a spiritual ethos is coupled with a movement towards forgiveness epitomised by The Forgiveness Project, a UK-based charity running restorative justice programmes in prisons. It works at a local, national and international level to help build a future free of conflict and violence by healing the wounds of the past. By collecting and sharing people's stories, and delivering outreach programmes, The Forgiveness Project encourages and empowers people to explore the nature of forgiveness and alternatives to revenge.

Cherie Booth, talking on Radio 4 in a series entitled 'Lent Talks', related her experience of restorative justice. She interprets atonement using the Biblical story of Zacchaeus (a tax collector seen as a master of white collar crime). Jesus engineered a meeting between Zacchaeus and the people he has wronged, a model for restorative justice. The approach sees offending as a breach of relationships between each other and with the collective (Booth, 2007). She cites a moving example of the efficacy and transformative power of restorative justice in a young man who committed two burglaries. The situation was so transformed that the victims wanted to keep in touch with him. The young man agreed to write a letter to them to say how things were going for him and his new family. His victims wanted him to break the cycle he was caught up in from a young age (ibid.). In restorative justice, meetings only take place with the willing participation of the victim, who has the power to effectively confront a criminal with the reality of their actions. It is in face-to-face human contact that transformation takes place and atonement becomes possible.

The Observer newspaper journalist Mary Riddell tells us that 75 per cent of victims rising to almost 90 per cent say they are helped an immense amount by this process (2004). She was the first journalist allowed to sit in on such an experiment in Pentonville Prison, London, UK. The offender could see the common humanity between himself and the family he burgled, and recognised the harm he caused. This produced a dramatic shift in affect and a healing was achieved. 'When the crying stops and the shabby room is empty, it feels as if a seance has been ruptured' (ibid.). It was a numinous experience.

These examples (from personal and collective) contain the psychologically nuanced thinking which society badly needs. Organisations such as Psycho-therapists and Counsellors for Social Responsibility (PCSR) in the UK seek ways for the insights from the consulting room to be brought into the public domain. They aim to incorporate emotional and psychological perspectives into current debates on social, cultural, environmental and political issues. Andrew Samuels (one of the founders of PCSR) has been in the vanguard of such movements. In *Politics on the Couch* he says 'Those with a materialist outlook would assert that the psychological realm is utterly subordinate to the nitty-gritty economic forces that have inexorably constructed our world' (2001, p. 12). Restorative justice has, I believe, – with its emphasis on atonement – the potential to appease both 'gods'.

This is also a step on the way to an idea Samuels suggests, that politicians might be *allowed* to be 'good enough' (ibid., pp. 79–100); might be allowed to make mistakes – to atone – and be forgiven without having to go through ritual resignations. These achieve nothing useful as the resigner often becomes the scapegoat.

Theoretical formulation

Thinking about how atonement and forgiveness seem inextricably connected at a personal level leads me to consider the transformative effects these encounters have at a cultural level, elucidated by Joseph Henderson (1984) (analysand, student and colleague of Jung from the late 1920s), Thomas Singer and Samuel L. Kimbles (2004), all three Jungian analysts from San Francisco. The 'cultural complex' is seen as situated between the personal and archetypal realms of psyche (Singer & Kimbles, 2004, p. 20). Singer and Kimbles applied Jung's theory of complexes to the cultural level of the psyche and group (2004, p. 2) suggesting that, in the same way as personal complexes arise from the personal unconscious, cultural complexes arise from the cultural unconscious as it interacts with arche-typal and personal realms of the psyche (ibid., p. 4). The dynamic of atonement-forgiveness is not only a personal matter. The healing dynamics between atonement and forgiveness apply at the collective level. The consequences have ramifications on the cultural, the collective consciousness and the spiritual:

> So, when the psychotherapist has to struggle with difficult transference problems, he can at least take comfort in theses reflections. He is not just working for this particular patient . . . but for himself as well and his own

soul ... Small and invisible as this contribution may be, it is yet an *opus magnum*, for it is accomplished in a sphere but lately visited by the numen, where the whole weight of mankind's problems has settled. The ultimate questions of psychotherapy are not a private matter – they represent a supreme responsibility.

(CW 16, para. 449)

Metaphorically, the dynamic of atonement-forgiveness takes place both consciously and in the *unus mundus*, as explained below (and in Chapter 6). Jung links the *unus mundus* to the psychoid, a term he created to describe the embodied unconscious inaccessible to conscious awareness. This expands the field from a personal dispute between victim and perpetrator to a change on a collective level where the alchemical metaphor can equally apply – as in the union or marriage of opposites in the *Coniunctio*. Victim and perpetrator are joined by an act for which atonement is the necessary release. They are caught in an energetic field – or complex – in a *participation mystique* until the atonement breaks the spell. *Participation mystique* is a term Jung borrowed from anthropologist Claude Levy-Bruhl. It refers to the way people can become caught in a metaphorical fog, unable to tell what feelings/qualities belong to whom. The shift happens via the transcendent function – a key to understanding the natural healing function of the psyche – which 'arises from the union of conscious and unconscious contents' (CW 8, para. 131) creating a bridge allowing a change in conscious attitude.

The concept of *unus mundus* helps us to understand these phenomena because within the *unus mundus* there is no artificial split between mind/thought and body. This mystical/Gnostic notion refers to the unitary nature of the world not divided by the material/spiritual dichotomy; one can conceptualise the personal and spiritual as bound as they are already linked in that realm.

Alchemical formulation

Analytical Psychology can make a unique contribution to the phenomenology of transformation and expression of self. Psychological processes are not neat and therefore cannot be described neatly. In alchemical terms, the process could look like this:

Problem, or the act to be repented of (*prima materia*/chaos, or *massa confusa*) – beginning to identify issue (*separatio*) – leading to grappling with 'sin' (*nigredo*) – leading to atonement (*albedo* or the whitening) which is the beginning of synthesis (see Chapter 2). The sequence does not necessarily follow a strictly linear form. We go back and forth through different phases of the process before finding resolution. Edinger's diagram (1994, p.16) gives a sense of the fluid nature of the process and how the connections are multiple and complex.

In Figure 11.1, the *Calcinatio* at the centre is linked to fire which is usually seen as the beginning of the alchemical work. Metaphorically you could say fire is the catalyst. The lack of symmetry in this diagram captures the chaos inherent in

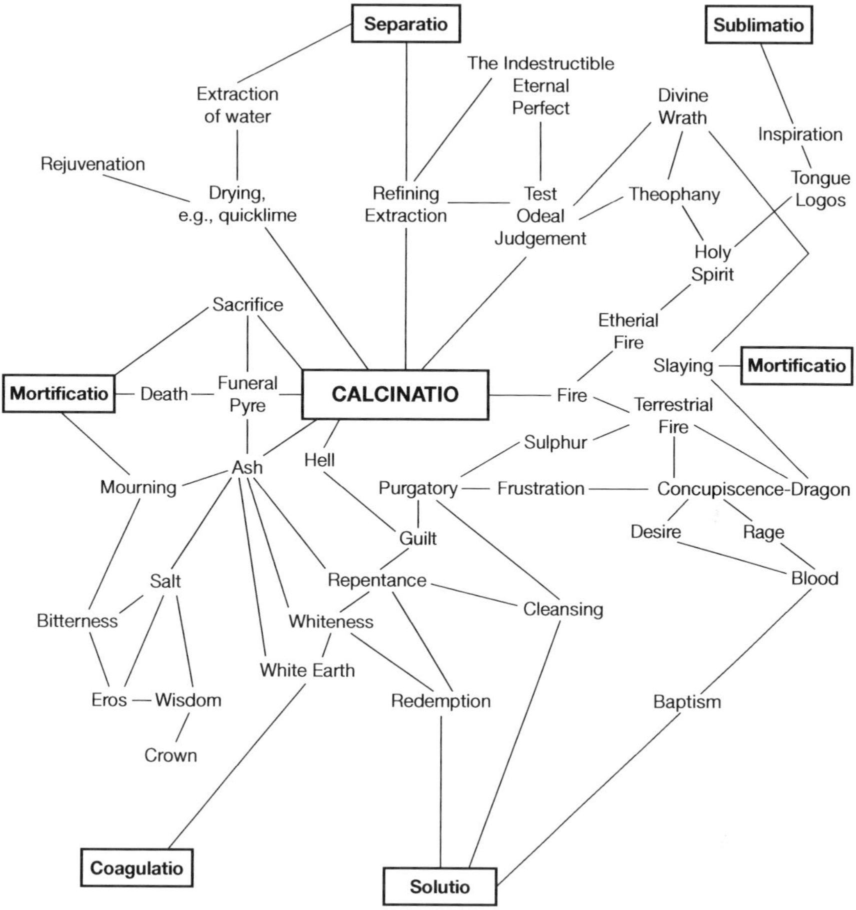

Figure 11.1 Calcinatio
Source: Edinger (1994), p. 16.

approaching unconscious material. The gestalt cycle of awareness is a useful way to understand this process. It is a cycle of awareness-excitement-contact and relates to macro and micro levels, as in Figure 11.2.

The area inside the wheel refers to experience as felt by the self from the inside; the area outside the wheel refers to the environment, or outside world. Each stage may be experienced in either or both ways In any given situation one might experience many small gestalts which might build into a more complete gestalt. The whole of life might be thought of as a gestalt. There is no completely accurate translation of the German word 'gestalt', which means roughly 'configuration' or whole/meaningful pattern. The cycle of awareness breaks down each step of the process. Sensation in gestalt (different to the Jungian 'sensation' function) refers

Gestalt Cycle of Awareness
The awareness – excitement – contact cycle

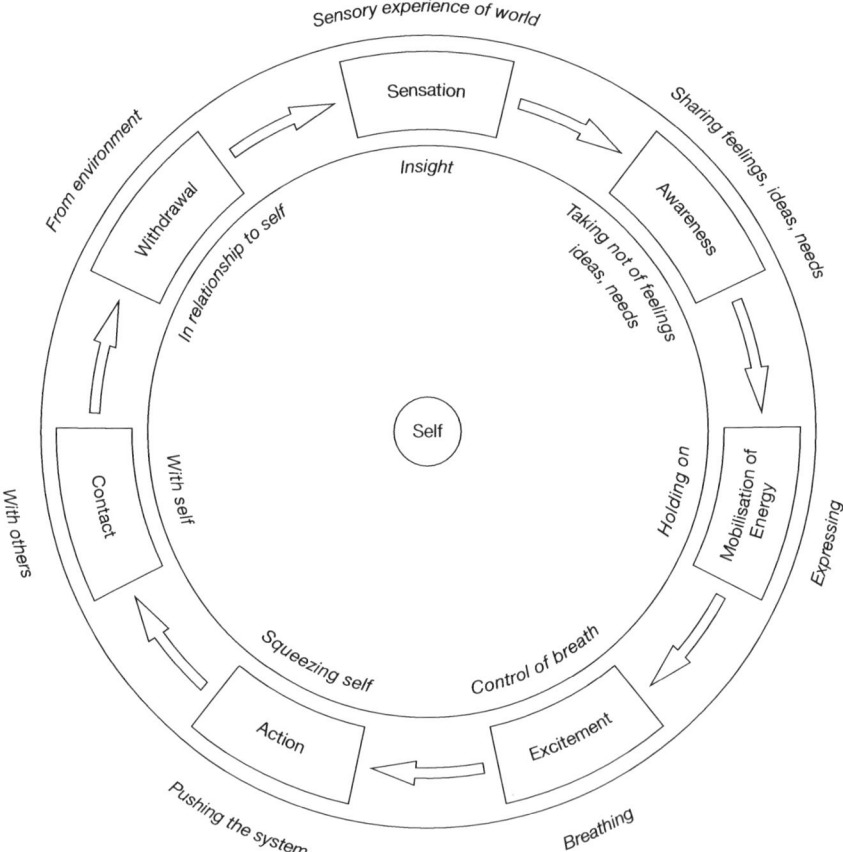

Figure 11.2 The gestalt cycle of awareness
Source: Ruth Williams

to the initial contact with the act or feeling. If I use atonement as an example, sensation would be the act itself or 'sin', followed by awareness of the action, words which might be discussed and felt, mobilising one's energy to decide how to act; excitement is closely connected to the mobilisation of energy and the shift into action. Contact might be the atonement itself followed by a release of energy and withdrawal when the catharsis is achieved in completing this cycle.

Linking this to the alchemical process, the sensation stage, or act to be repented of, would be seen as the *massa confusa* or *prima materia*. The growing awareness, mobilisation of energy, excitement and action might be part of the *nigredo* as one battles with the dilemmas involved in the problem, potentially internally and externally in the environment. This could be a long period involving terrible pain and suffering. If the atonement itself takes place at the contact stage, this would connect to the *albedo* or whitening in alchemy and the beginning of synthesis which frees up energy and allows withdrawal from the situation. Achieving this could be seen as the *rubedo*. I have simplified this process to try to articulate it clearly.

It is often necessary to go through and round issues many times from different angles to achieve the sought-for release from torment or guilt. The symbol of the spiral is helpful. It captures the way we go round and round an issue in a growth-ful way rather than the unhelpful image of going round and round in circles. Individuation as a process is never complete. A person is constantly individuating which requires devoted self-examination up and down the spiral or through the gestalten, panning the *prima materia* for gold dust.

The psychoid unconscious and the archetype of the *unus mundus*

Without atonement, there is no forgiveness. The two are a linked pair – a syzygy (meaning inextricably connected, from the Greek word for a married couple) – belonging to the realm of the *unus mundus*. Jung first suggested the idea of a psychoid unconscious, completely inaccessible to consciousness, in 1946. He went on to link this to the idea of the *unus mundus*, one world – everything is connected on a subtle level. This is at odds with scientific materialism, but not with quantum reality (see Chapter 9) and contrasts with 'psychic reality'. He calls the *unus mundus* a 'metaphysical speculation' providing the means to experience the unconscious indirectly via its manifestations (CW 14, para. 660) and 'the potential world outside time' (ibid., para. 718). The psychoid:

> has a tendency to behave as though it were not located in one person but were active in the whole environment. ... As soon as the dialogue between two people touches on something fundamental, essential, and numinous, and a certain rapport is felt, it gives rise to a phenomenon which Lévy-Bruhl fittingly called *participation mystique*. It is an uncon-scious identity in which two individual psychic spheres interpenetrate to such a degree that it is impossible to say what belongs to whom.
>
> (CW 10, paras 851–852)

Jung located the psychoid archetype 'beyond the psychic sphere, analogous to the position of the physiological instinct, which is immediately rooted in the stuff of the organism and, with its psychoid nature, forms the bridge to matter in general' (CW 8, para. 420). We could say it is where psyche and matter meet. Roderick Main of the Centre for Psychoanalytic Studies at the University of Essex encapsulates the complexity; he suggests the concepts 'of psyche and matter and space and time merge into a psycho physical space-time continuum '. . . where

Jung considered the archetypes themselves . . . ultimately to be located' (1997, p. 36). Main describes this dual nature as being 'at once psychic and physical yet neither because beyond both' (ibid., p. 36). Synchronicity and the psychoid are 'helping to bring about a rapprochement between psychology and physics' (ibid., p. 19).

Jung sees the psychoid as possessing parapsychological qualities. These he groups with synchronicity due to a close association with archetypal events. He saw archetypes as situated within the collective unconscious. Because of this melding of space and time, Jung inferred the collective unconscious has a spaceless and timeless quality (see Chapter 9). He then went further, speculating it was indeed probable that 'an archetypal situation will be accompanied by synchronistic phenomena' (CW 10, para. 849). His formulation of synchronicity (first made in 1928) has always been at a cutting edge to scientific understanding. In discussions with Albert Einstein and Wolfgang Pauli, Jung found the principle 'bore parallels to certain discoveries in relativity theory and quantum mechanics' (Tarnas, 2006, p. 50). Richard Tarnas is Professor of Philosophy and Depth Psychology in San Francisco. He says: 'the dramatic coincidence of meaning between an inner state and a simultaneous external event seemed to bring forth in the individual a healing movement toward psychological wholeness, mediated by the unexpected integration of inner and outer realities' (ibid., pp. 50–51). Synchronicity, which Jung referred to as an 'acausal connecting principle' (CW 8, paras 417–519), gives a sense of meaning to otherwise random events.

In 'A Psychological Commentary on the Tibetan Book of the Great Liberation', Jung contrasts Eastern and Western modes of thinking. Written before he formally theorised the psychoid unconscious, the linked nature of 'one mind', is emphasised:

> The statement "Nor is one's own mind separable from other minds" is another way of expressing the fact of "all contamination". Since all distinctions vanish in the unconscious condition, it is only logical that the distinction between separate minds should disappear too.
>
> (CW 11, para. 817)

I speculate that atonement and forgiveness are linked, like synchronicity and psychic phenomena, in the *unus mundus*.

Conclusion

Atonement can be thought about spiritually and alchemically. Acts of atonement and forgiveness are linked. The process involved is in part located in the psychoid unconscious. A failure to atone often produces a scapegoat. We are tied to each other through the collective unconscious and the psychoid so one person's failure to act has a significant impact on the ability of the other party to forgive. Such situations can be intransigent and seem incapable of change. Blame is then likely to arise. When the spark is lit in the meeting of atonement and forgiveness, the transcendent function constellates and deep intra-psychic shifts becomes possible. This is a *coniunctio* as powerful as that of Sol and Luna (see Chapter 2).

Atonement proves profoundly beneficial to the collective, as in the Truth and Reconciliation Commission and through restorative justice. Jungian theory helps us understand how and why atonement is so important. The idea is less common in secular society, though it often forms part of religious debate. I may not have put sufficient emphasis on the Shadow projections which are intrinsically con-nected with the scapegoat complex, inevitably involved when responsibility is *not* taken by the wounding party; but I have also looked at how this process of confronting the Shadow is formalised in the religious ritual of Yom Kippur.

The problem of atonement is described as having a defined scope (contrasted with guilt). Life being life, we move on to other situations inevitably involving further encounters with wounding acts. I do not wish to be seen to be describing a neat process for atonement that is fraught with all human emotions. Achieving atonement is never an easy task. What commonly passes for forgiveness is often denial or dissociation. Forgiveness, as Andrew Samuels reminds us, 'has much to do with suffering'. This applies to both parties.

> For the sinner to *feel* a sinner, he or she experiences suffering. At the same time, the one who is to forgive will also have to suffer – for there can hardly be any forgiveness where there is no price to pay.
>
> (Samuels, 1989, p. 203)

Acknowledgements

Jessica Woolliscroft for the original inspiration; Professor Roderick Main, my tutor at the Centre for Psychoanalytic Studies, University of Essex when I first wrote about atonement; Rabbi David Freeman for conversations and guidance on Yom Kippur; Professor David Tacey from whom I discovered the Australian Government's apology (IAJS Discussion List 18 November 2008); Jerome Bernstein for allowing me to quote from his letter to the IAJS Discussion List dated 16 September 2010; Professor Andrew Samuels for support throughout.

References

Bernstein, J. (2010) IAJS Discussion List, 16 September.

Booth, C. (2007) *Lent Talks* Radio 4 broadcast on Wednesday 14 March (transcript at www.bbc.co.uk/religion).

Brinton Perera, S. (1986) *The Scapegoat Complex: Toward a Mythology of Shadow and Guilt* Toronto: Inner City Books.

Cook, L. (2003) *Forgiveness and Reconciliation: Soul-Healing in South Africa* Guild of Pastoral Psychology pamphlet No. 281.

Edinger, E. (1994) *Anatomy of the Psyche: Alchemical Symbolism in Psychotherapy* Chicago and La Salle, Illinois: Open Court.

Emin, T. (2005) *Strangeland* Stirlingshire: Spectre.

Freud, S. (1962) 'The Ego and the Id' in Vol.19 of the *Standard Edition of The Complete Psychological Works of Sigmund Freud* London: Hogarth Press.

Henderson, J. (1984) *Cultural Attitudes in Psychological Perspective* Toronto: Inner City Books.

Hillman, J. (1964) *Betrayal* Lecture 128, London: Guild of Pastoral Psychology.

Joffé, R. (1986) *The Mission* Warner Bros. Pictures.

Jung, C. G. (1953–1977) *Collected Works of C.G. Jung,* (eds Sir Herbert Read, Michael Fordham, Gerhard Adler & William McGuire; trans. R. F. C. Hull), 20 Vols. Except where indicated, references are by volume and paragraph number. London: Routledge & Kegan Paul.

Klein, M. (1988) 'The Early Development of Conscience in the Child' in *Love, Guilt & Reparation and Other Works 1921–1945* London: Virago Press, pp. 248–257.

Lerner, Rabbi M. (2006) Personal communication.

Main, R. (1977) *Jung on Synchronicity and the Paranormal* Princeton, New Jersey: Princeton University Press.

McElrea, F. W. M. (2012) *Tikkun* published online 10 January 2012.

McEwan, I. (2001) *Atonement* New York: Anchor Books.

Pitchon, E. (1997) Teshuvah (Repentance). www.pitchon.com.ar/.

Riddell, M. (2004) 'Face to Face, A Victim Seeks Justice from her Burglar' in *The Observer*, 5 December 2004.

Samuels, A. (1989) *The Plural Psyche: Personality, Morality & The Father* London & New York: Routledge.

—— (2001) *Politics on the Couch: Citizenship and the Internal Life* London: Profile Books.

—— (2010) 'The Transcendent Function in Society' in *Journal of Analytical Psychology* Vol.55 (2), pp. 228–253.

——, Shorter, B. & Plaut, F. (1986) *A Critical Dictionary of Jungian Analysis* London: Routledge & Kegan Paul.

Shakespeare, W. (1999) 'Richard II' in *The Complete Works of William Shakespeare* (eds S. Wells and G. Taylor) New York: Oxford University Press.

Singer, T. & Kimbles, S. (2004) *The Cultural Complex: Contemporary Jungian Perspectives on Psyche and Society* London & New York: Routledge.

Tarnas, R. (2006) *Cosmos & Psyche: Intimations of a New World View* London & New York: Viking Penguin.

Tutu, D. (2004) *The Longford Lecture* 16 February 2004, London. www.prisonreformtrust.org.uk/pdf%20files/LngfordLectTutu.pdf.

Von Franz, M.-L. (1993) *Projection and Re-collection in Jungian Psychology: Reflections of the Soul* La Salle & London: Open Court.

12

SULPHUR RISES THROUGH THE BLACKENED BODY

Maryann Barone-Chapman

'Something is putrid in Peru!' was the saying in my high school biology class when an experiment was going wrong. One of us had overstepped the formula with a compound changing the stability of a preserved specimen. The stink was unmistakable inside the laboratory, far down the hall and into other classrooms: the smell of rotten eggs, the chemical sulphur rising out of a process of decomposition. In the alchemical phase of *putrefactio* (see Chapter 1), sulphur is the quickening toward decay necessary for psychic change. Alchemist Gerard Dorn (1602: CW 14, paras 654–700) referred to it as a symbolic death; the soul leaves the body, uniting in spirit in a *unio mentalis*. In the alchemy between analyst and analysand, the soul (CW 6, paras 797–811) seeks the body to forge a new link with spirit (Haule, 1984; CW 14, paras 654–700).

On display in this chapter is the process of finding the compound in order to re-find the body. Working with the blackened dung, the *prima materia* of one-sided ego consciousness, we find memories of emotional and physical trauma that reveal a gendered shame in both the male and female to do with denigration of the feminine. What's important to see is how the alchemical phases in themselves are not gender biased, though the ingredients inside the alchemist's vas, mercury and sulphur, were thought of as male and female respectively. Too often the principle of 'masculine' and 'feminine' is concretized, a false adaptation to compensate for psychic wounds to sexual identity aroused by conformity to cultural stereotypes. Amplification of the alchemical process, to extract the gold, elevated the opposites to the regal status of Sol King (conscious) and Luna Queen (unconscious). In every culture these motifs, intuitively drawn to signify psychic renewal, forecast how dominant factors in the psyche undergo processes of decomposition and clarification by fire, out of which emerges the 'new king' or new consciousness.

James Hillman (1989), Jungian analyst and archetypal psychologist, referred to *putrefactio* as the 'yellowing of the work', the phase after the black *nigredo* when no light reaches the conscious, and after the whitening phase of *albedo* when the first dawn of new insights begin their revelations (see Chapter 14). The 'yellowing' is the first tinge of fires to come in from the reddening stage of *rubedo*. I think of it in terms of the seafarer's adage, 'Red sky in morning, sailor's warning.' It is not just rot and decay but a tumultuous combustibility Jung referred to as the 'principle, which hinders perfection in all its works' (CW 14, para. 138).

Queer as folk

I propose there is a parallel between Jung's alchemical opus and Queer theory regarding psychic development in relationship to the syzygy (any linked pair of opposites in union or opposition: (CW 9ii, paras 41–45)). Both theories value emergence and fluidity as a process towards union, which is not definitively gendered. In alchemy the phases of *solutio* and *coagulatio* dissolve concretized qualities associated to 'male' and 'female'. From the alchemical text *Splendor Solis* (Trismosin, 1532–1535) we learn these two processes were spoken of in terms of 'Woman and Man, or Milk and Cream' (McLean, 1981, p. 16). Queer is the essence of a third, which defies definition of either gender, as in the Rosarium the baby as the third comes after lovemaking, but we do not know the sex of the child.

This new consciousness, found in a subtle field of emerging shifts in the spheres of social biology, economics and technology, brings disenchantment with a fundamentalist, stereotypic union of opposites. New understanding of the opposites is called for on behalf of 'integrating one's opposite' from a phase of *separatio* to a new *coniunctio*. Queer is the essence of a third that defies definition of either pole and makes these poles irreparably indefinable.

Queer began its linguistic life as a slur for non-normative sexual behaviour.

Moving into gay and lesbian caucuses, then feminist politics and academic institutions, in parallel to rising awareness of AIDS (Jagose, 1996), the trajectory turned on gender itself as an encasement in an 'oppressive system of classification – both heterosexuality and homosexuality . . . as artificial categories' (Young, 1992/1972, p. 29). The ways in which identity, in particular gender identity, is formed came under the purview of Judith Butler in *Gender Trouble* (1990/1999) and destabilized prior notions of subject formation through observation of the disparity between identity and performance. In Butler's analysis of linguistic processes the conditions precipitating emergence (Entstehung) of a subject and their identity could not be reduced to a historical moment as fact any more than fabrication (ibid., p. 15).

Queer is evasive. 'Just what "queer" signifies or includes or refers to is by no means easy to say' (Abelove, 1993, p. 20). Queer is 'a relation of resistance to whatever constitutes the normal' (Jagose, 1996, p. 99), the 'open mesh of . . . excesses of meaning where the constituent elements of anyone's gender, anyone's sexuality aren't made (or *can't* be made) to signify monolithically' (Sedgwick, 1993a, p. 8). Queer as a theoretical and *non-predictive-performative* condition may be emerging as a new signifier of normative behaviour. In this way Queer undermines notions of feminine, masculine and eclipses both the conflict and union of opposites, something Jagose describes as 'holding open a space whose potential can never be known in the present' (1996, p. 107).

Putrefaction can be seen as a difficulty to create or maintain *two-ness* in an analytic couple when the exacting principles of animus and the conceited needs of anima prevent making a symbolic baby. Sulphur cannot rise and dissolve (*solutio*) the barriers between conscious and unconscious, matter and spirit. The symbolic third appears from a union (*coniunctio*) of opposites when neither masculine nor feminine are installed with denigration. In very different ways both analysands were attempting to bring soul back into a body with 'black marks' against it.

Bob, who tried to be a tough boy and man, rejected his inner girl, yet played the part of a girl with male friends and business partner. Audrey was convinced she had to give up being a girl after reaching puberty as her sex was too much for her Afrikaans culture, leading to her having a breast reduction, later cutting her hair to run around with a tough gang of boys. In this chapter, two of my analysands allow readers to see into the alchemical phase of *putrefactio* when things in their outer world began to reflect the decay in their inner world. Trained to be mother's helper and housemaid, Bob, 35, suffered the abuses of his Irish parent's immigration, alcohol and adultery. Through a projective process, his dislike of women turned a female partner, with whom he felt desire, into a man. Bob's ailing compounds are described in the section 'A case of concretization'. Fuelled by the cultural ailments of apartheid, denial of her embodied feminine by her Afrikaans family, Audrey, 30, gave up female performative identity, thinking she needed to function as a man to be safe. Her turning point is described in 'A case of black and white'. I am grateful for their courage to let the sulphur rise.

Both Bob and Audrey suffered psychological abuse and physical violence regarding their gender. In gender disturbance, the characteristics of masculine and feminine between analyst and analysand can become fluid, reflecting a phase of *sublimatio* attempting to transform the two initial male and female ingredients in the alchemical vessel, turning hermaphrodite qualities into those integrated qualities of the androgyne. For these analysands, events in childhood blackened a secure enough body identity, resulting in the sulphuric stench of un-containable shame. Originating in the war between their respective parents, a bi-sexual identification to a hermaphroditic imago of mother was frozen at early infancy (Fabricius, 1994, p. 218, note 10) leaving imprints of the denigrated feminine to spill into analytic work.

Turning dung into gold represents the work of individuation, appearing as an intra-psychic marriage between masculine and feminine energies within people of either gender. Sometimes these energies are referred to as archetypes, anima for the feminine and animus for the masculine. I emphasize the gendering within the Medieval art and its acquisition within the Jungian framework to advance thinking on a union of opposites outside of gender performance. The American Jungian analyst Susan McKenzie (2006) found anima/animus linked to the paradigm of emergence:

Kate's story (case material) illustrates gender and sexuality residing in the borderlands of Western culture and resonates with postmodern queer theory that denies fixed identities and calls into question the assumed relationships between biological sex, gender and sexual desire. The term queer can also be used in a dynamic way to describe identity under construction, in the act of becoming. In this sense queer is not an identity but is, instead, a critique of fixed identities.

(2006, 51:2, p. 403)

Bob – a case of concretization

The psychoanalyst Marion Milner connected the ability to form symbols to early affective states, suggesting symbols required a 'relation to an external object of feeling' (1955, p. 86). Bob, a builder, had a difficult relationship to symbols; he took them concretely. For instance, he thought there should be a blueprint for how to talk to women. One of the first goals in Jungian clinical work is finding where the battle is, where the rubbing of two becomes one. Bob's un-containable shame, about what *is* and what *ought* to be masculine and feminine regularly spoiled the Eros between us. Bob had little access to judgement and discernment, or to the intuitive and symbolic. In the battle for relationship to the feminine, we needed to form two bridges, one to the anima and the other to the animus to make a connection between ego and Self (Ulanvov, 1992, p 26). Finding equal oppositions which crossed gender certainty in the inter-subjective field was a constant tension between, 'who will get to be the female today?' and, 'there can only be one male in the room at a time!' This made it difficult to create or maintain two-ness and come together to make the symbolic third (Benjamin, 2004).

Bob told me straight up in our first session, 'I want to get my head straight so I can move on and give the problems I've had some closure.' He asked for closing before he had barely opened. He continued, 'The way my brain works, I can't open up to women and I need to try and live again.' I became curious about his regard for women. But all he could suggest was that he found it hard to communicate with girlfriends, not women in general. He started to explain, 'It's hard for me to let them into my little . . .' but could not finish: he could open but he could not close. In the long silence that followed I felt the urge to chase after him, as I later learned many women had. Then he said, 'I want to be able to settle down. I feel like I'm stumbling around as a single guy just working too hard, going to pubs, and the rest.' In effect, Bob asked me to help him become a better man so he could find a wife and have a child. He felt as though it's what he *ought* to do.

The *ought*/*is* dilemma was set out in the work *A Treatise of Human Nature* by Scottish philosopher David Hume (1740/1888/2003). Hume examined the language of writers who made claims about what ought to be on the basis of what is (Temple, 2002–2012). From this Hume found a disparity between descriptive 'what is' statements and prescriptive 'what ought to be' statements, with the latter presenting as normative (ibid.). Hume's explorations of emotions and ethics behind language pertain to Bob (and Audrey) in their longings to move from *is* to *ought*, and *ought* to *is*. Often our work became a version of Hume's *Guillotine*

208

(Temple, op. cit.; Hudson, 1969); an attempt to differentiate *is* from *ought* and *ought* from *is*. As in Queer theory, language indicates aspects of existence. Hume's *Guillotine* and Queer theory are philosophical siblings wrestling with morality and performance. Through such a lens, Queer theory has the potential to separate performance identity of male and female from anima and animus, returning them to symbols of soul and spirit.

The dung in the vessel

Bob's family system was organized around running away. His mother left Ireland, at 17, to escape raising her 11 younger brothers and sisters. His father was caught out-of-collar from the priesthood with a woman in Dublin. De-frocked, he left for London. He and Bob's mother enjoyed carousing until she fell pregnant with his older sister. Bob followed a year later. His parents did not marry until the family pressured them ten years later, when his mother was pregnant again. Bob knew he wasn't happy being regularly beaten. It wasn't until he saw his mother shower the younger ones with love that he realized she was cruel. He learned that girls had more value than boys, recalling his mother and sister cuddling by the fire on cold mornings while he was pushed away. He described how each time a relationship ended, his difficult feelings were made worse by going back to live with his mother. Bob kept trying to please a mother who continued to make demands on him during his workday. This angered him, feeling he couldn't claim autonomy without her crying.

Memories of childhood were sparse, woven around fear, shame and retreat. His mother drafted him into house chores to fill in for his father who spent his time and money at the pub rather than come home to their loveless marriage. Bob wasn't allowed out to play with friends like his older sister, but kept at home for his mother to take out her disappointment on her son, her lackey (enacting a 'queen–servant' fantasy: see Chapter 4). Gaps between chores and school were spent in his room sleeping, with no constructive play or relating. From neglect, he thought of himself as a naughty boy seeking attention.

At 12, Bob started making his own money and easily developed friendships with other boys. Many continued into adulthood. As a group, they had a long history of truancy and being lost for days at a time. He suggested they explore the limits of their sexuality, tolerances and desires with each other, to make their own family, with their own rules, stretching the boundaries of childhood well into their mid-thirties; an extended adolescence. These were 'the guys' Bob turned to when he had no one else. Bob was out with them and could not be found when his father died.

Events at six and 18 to 24 months revealed the spoiling compound. Bob was surprised when he brought his first dream, about six months into analysis. He thought he never dreamed. Though only a fragment, it contained the very issue we would face over and over again – 'I am being chased by something or someone and about to be attacked'. Who or what is it Bob runs from? Many women came

209

to his mind yet he excluded me, perhaps to keep me safe. He ran away through drink, always thirsty for intimacy. Other affects developed in relationship to the feminine in female form. 'Women always have to be right', Bob sneered. He described what lay behind the sneer. Ongoing shame at being physically beaten by his mother, later chastened by his sister and a string of girlfriends led to keeping his feelings out of relationships with women. Time as a linear construction and time as an anniversary of past trauma played upon his mood and subsequent enactments. When he began to express concretized erotic feelings for me, wishing to make a symbolic baby, I closed down, feeling disoriented. He had aroused an unconscious withholding of metaphoric erotic mirroring, inducing my maternal preoccupation, the thing he both looked for and came to hate, in sexual relationships.

A woozy, sleepy feeling moved me ever closer to becoming an object in his internal world, which he might turn and meet, before he decided to run. Slowing him down enough to look at choice became a regular event to counter regular threats to leave. Later I realized his first dream spoke in past, present and future tenses: Bob has run from women; a relationship to the feminine is chasing him through our work; at some point he will run again. The history of his relationships with women showed a vicious cycle of seeking mothering, strength, comfort and sex then having to cheat. He said he got to a point, at six months, 18 to 24 months, into a relationship where he felt 'strangulated'.

Slowly I introduced him to his feeling states, asking, 'Where in your body can you feel when it's time to end a relationship?' There was something in his gut that stayed with him. In time his 'gut wrenching' feeling found its memory through to my body when Bob confessed he was not allowed to cry or show anger as a child. I struggled to mask a yawn, feeling a big weight pushed into me. I wanted to go to sleep. Suddenly his anger exploded, connecting to memories of his abusing mother. In fighting back a yawn, I mirrored a mother who was tired of mothering before she was 20 years old.

Bob's psychic pain could not be thought about between us and was pushed into the psychosomatic realm. He associated to one of a handful of early childhood memories of being rejected by his mother. One had to do with his projectile vomiting at six months. He told me the story his mother told him: 'She became fed up with me after months of this and when I was nine months old she handed me back to the hospital'. He gestured with both arms his handover, demonstrating his mother's disgust with him internalized forever more. Diagnosed with a twisted gut, perhaps an early somatization of emotional upheaval, surgery and hospitalization were his first separation. I understood a lack of love was communicated by a lack of physical holding. Turning girlfriends into his mother and hating them for it created the animus-led woman who could be a father to him. Bob successfully separated hate from love, having worked through separating love from sex, but success offered him little comfort. Bob expected me to be the mother he wanted (and hated). Any Eros I had was limited to caring about what happened to him.

As an external object of feeling I wanted to stay in the here and now. Patterns emerged making symbol formation collapse into me as in a stupor, challenging my linking and thinking. Bob wanted power over me. When he used indirect thinking (feeling) I went to direct thinking and vice versa (for more on 'two kinds of thinking' along gendered lines see CW 5, paras 4–46). I wondered if we unconsciously maintained opposition to make a chymical wedding. We could work together well when we were both using indirect thinking (feminine to feminine). However, what aroused his passion was when we were both in direct thinking (masculine to masculine). Afterward, he would want to take a nap or have a cigarette, as if he had enjoyed a sexual release. The attitudes and characteristics of masculine and feminine reflected a phase of *sublimatio* attempting to transform hermaphrodite qualities to those of the androgyne. In the shared-field experience of the analytic container, the evolution from *putrefactio* to *coagulatio* demonstrates how fluid the parts within the syzygy can be.

Once interpenetration began, Bob could start to think. Finding it exciting to connect thinking and feeling under my attentive gaze, he spoke of a 'high' feeling. However, from these lofty heights he felt my interpretations brought him down to earth, and he fiercely objected. My sleepy, woozy sensation became a signal that unconscious shame was present, mirroring an inability to be in the body. Intense moments of meeting between us would follow, culminating in his expressing gratitude and affection to me. In my mind, I likened Bob to a child who liked getting lost so he could be found. The woozy, sleepy stupor was part of Bob's desire to bring me into indirect thinking, a product of projecting his anima into me. As Bob told me, 'All you women seem to have an answer for everything . . . but', he continued, 'you're smart, really smart and I'm not used to that with a woman, and I'm sure not comfortable with it'. What affected me most was how his narrow experience of women inspired the projection of a smart anima. Bob was trying to install a good mother to release a spell.

He had also been hard at work trying to install a good father in the form of his business partner Tom. A 'pub man' like Bob's father, Tom gave Bob the opportunity of wealth, raising him up from the ashes of alcohol, adultery and abuse. Like his father, Tom was absent if not from the home, then from the business, leaving Bob to shoulder the responsibility. The complexity of Bob's problem was compounded by the considerable wealth he accumulated with Tom, which he displayed prominently. Coming from a similar family filled with greed, envy and betrayal, Tom not only provided the missing father – he was a dynamic replica of the mother who took great delight in telling Bob he wasn't doing enough. The confusion between these two imagos enacted the inner tension between *ought* and *is*.

Tearing down the house

No sooner had Bob become aware of his difficulty with both his mother and Tom, did they form an alliance to literally tear down his mother's house for re-development. Here was the making of a living symbol (Adler, 1961, p. 41), a result of an insurmountable conflict between opposites. Buying his mother's house brought his 'libido to flow back to its psychic source' (ibid.), to his mother. Whenever he discussed the difficulties within this triangular setup, another woozy, sleepy sensation spoiled my direct thinking, pushing me into indirect thinking. His mother's house provided a metaphorical matrix for the alchemical instruction.

> Therefore pull down the house, destroy the walls, extract the purest juice with the blood, and cook that thou mayest eat. Wherefore Analdus saith in the Book of Secrets: purify the stone, grind the door to powder, tear the bitch to pieces, choose the tender flesh, and thou wilt have the best thing. In the one thing are hidden all parts, in it all metals shine. Of these, two are the artificers, two the vessels, two the times, two the fruits, two the ends, and one the salvation.
>
> (CW 14, para. 179)

Pulling down the house is to pull down a conscious identification with the mother through the interaction of analysand and analyst, with attention to unconscious affects. Jung called this 'brooding over the slow fire' (ibid., para. 280) the alchemical stages of *decoctio*, *digestio*, *putrefactio* and *solutio*, which awaken the unconscious. 'Pulling down the house' is 'breaking down the barriers' (op. cit.) which separate the unconscious from consciousness.

At 24 months into our work, Bob's unconscious processes took his company into bankruptcy, a match to the second developmental point mentioned earlier for ending a relationship. We found a parallel to his being run over by a car and left unconscious for over 24 hours at two years of age. Unconsciously Bob had been run over, not by a car, as at the age of two, but by inflation and an inability to stand up to Tom on how the company was run. Tearing down his mother's house was a concrete enactment of a symbolic ritual – separation from his mother and father. Bob needed to take the emotional and physical deprivation he experienced in the house of his childhood, the *prima materia*, and turn it into gold, to release his unconscious from mother's animus and father's anima. I use the word 'tearing' to describe a difficult clinical situation where my capacity to think and analyze were received as sadistic attacks on his grand designs; a match to his parent's marriage. A match to a poorly installed anima and animus.

Twisted guts, projectile vomiting, being knocked down, often being beaten around the head paralleled what happened between us. Bob said he knew things would go horribly wrong with Tom, who he'd never trusted. Once the spoiling compound was matched to Bob's fate he began to face questions about his destiny. He started doing hard work in the real world and recognized how dependent he had become on other people to do his thinking for him. Staying with the affects around Tom gave Bob the courage to talk about his hatred for women, 'Seeing what I saw as a kid, I think I've got gender issues. I feel like I've taken on female roles because of the way things play out in relationships and this is connected I think to my feelings about women.' Bob was speaking about aspects of the feminine installed (in him) as inferior traits, resembling not an archetype, but a denigrated stereotype.

A bi-sexual perspective of anima and animus in equal position, not necessarily in balance, helped me understand how Bob had been running away from his inner woman. Though he projected denigration onto women, he was stuck in idealized homoerotic projective identification with Tom, as part of a Queer identity. The woozy, sleepy stupor invited me to hold a challenging union of opposites, using both direct and indirect thinking. Finally, the stupor came and went, just like Bob's feelings of wanting to be a woman came and went so he could become a man. Bob's concretization of a union of opposites to create a third involved making a legal marriage and having a baby. Like Dionysus, Bob worked on new rituals of the feminine only to find gender and gender performance was neither *ought* nor *is*. Sulphur and mercury had found *solutio*.

Audrey – a case of black and white

Queer, once considered an insult, has emerged as a linguistic sign of a fluid sexual identity in the making (Jagose, 1996, p. 1). It is both an affirmation of gender neutrality and resistance to such classification. Clinical work suggests there is more to Queer than body politics. Jungian psychoanalyst Andrew Samuels offers a way through the problem of gender difference as requiring an 'animated moderation' suggests – 'How to find a way of not being *too* gender certain or *too* gender confused – somewhere in the middle, just a little mixed up' (1986, p. 75) begins to connote an aspect of Queer's emergence, as a 'third' transcendent reality.

It would seem Audrey was fated to a Queer identity. Born into a white Afrikaans family with deep hatred of indigenous black people and women, Audrey never realized she identified with the denigrated aspects of her birthplace. Her feelings for black South Africans, though consciously empathetic, held her shadow.

Uncannily her unconscious brought her to untenable situations, which she could only see in terms of black and white. South Africa's transition out of the dark days of apartheid is an allegory of her cycling from *nigredo* to *albedo* and *rubedo* repeatedly until the sulphurous compound could be brought to consciousness.

Her body spoke through food allergies, intolerances, acne, herpes, blood, and genital irritations which appeared whenever her attention turned to gender identity. An opening had to be found where her essential personality could break the grip of hatred for the other as her mother (the Opus Solis). Her first sexualized experience happened at three with a 12-year-old male cousin touching her genitals. This resulted in Audrey being beaten by her maternal grandmother, who called her a 'slut'. The name stuck. Audrey used her intellect to make up for a body rejected by her family, culminating in breast reduction surgery at 15, at her parents' insistence. In her late teens she began, like the serpent Uroboros, to eat her own tail; cutting her hair like a boy, cutting off from girlfriends and running with a group of lads who welcomed her as a younger brother. With them, she could safely

Figure 12.1 The Exorcism
Artist: FLB

hang out and travel. No longer voluptuous, her family continued to call her a slut but no longer beat her.

At 25 Audrey was rejected by her male gang and had to find a way back to the world of women. When I met her she had just been beaten by her last boyfriend, and didn't know why. It became clear how she exasperated men and women alike, attempting to show her mind as superior. Her inner world was a black and white construction, little understood by others, let alone herself. She began to reflect on how she had learned early in childhood to outwit her mother and stay safe from her attacks. For Audrey, the battle between her sexual body and gender identity as an honorary boy created a fire-breathing chimera. To compensate she went to the other extreme of girlish pink-ribboned dresses and demure courtesies to be in relationships with women. At our first meeting she appeared as a society hostess welcoming me to my own consulting room.

Following in her mother's footsteps, Audrey attached herself to the dark pole of feminism, the devouring aspect of the mythological first Eve, Lilith. Sex, sexuality and gender norms were impossible with either gender. Her relationship with the masculine was as a warrior, competing to prove superiority. When she began to ride a scooter she looked like a 'biker boy'. It wasn't until dream images began a long season of fighting off male domination that Audrey could make contact with the sulphuric stench.

Dreaming of the devil within

I was in a car with other people; we were fleeing from bad people who tried to drive us off a cliff. Then we met a couple that had been hiding out for many years, fighting the bad people we were fleeing from. They took us in. We had much to learn from them. All of a sudden, the bad people, the male demons, caught up with us. The men on our side got killed. Just the wife and I are left. I feel huge guilt, like I brought this on them. In the chaos of fighting the male demons took us captive. Some men came along and pulled back the hands of the guy threatening me. I thought they were on my side – they told me to punch this bad guy. However, when I did, they let him loose and started laughing at me. They were all on the same side! This bad guy (dressed in jeans, T-shirt and cape) was very strong. He tried to throw me out the window but I pulled him with me. As we were falling we kept on fighting. I fell hard onto a garage roof, surprised I wasn't dead, but played dead so he would leave me alone. He said, "Stop playing dead or I will really kill you".

Audrey's dream shows an experience of the 'dark masculine', feeling 'de-railed' and pushed to the 'edge of a cliff' by men at home and work. Swiping at them had no good effect. The duplicitous nature of the male demons is an image for the problem of an externalized masculine trying to kill off the internalized feminine. Trapped in an encapsulation of fear and anxiety justified by the fast changing moods of a bi-polar mother, who often threatened, 'I will fuck you up', Audrey learned to continually approach the world with 'animus-ity'. She knows the masculine and feminine co-exist in her body, but cannot differentiate them well enough to feel trust in relationship with either (Samuels, 1988). She discovered, whilst amplifying this dream, that she believed having a baby would be too dangerous for her. It took much longer to discover it was what she longed for.

An Acquired Immune Deficiency Syndrome

Though no longer living in South Africa, Audrey feared contracting AIDS and began to verbalize this on a regular basis. She was in a monogamous, committed relationship and had protected sex, but refused to have either herself or her partner tested. Her fear of AIDS was not reality based, but she couldn't tell me this, for the subject made her choke through tearful gasps. I had to 'bump into it' in a session, just as her body bumped into things that hurt her. Her psyche kept bumping into hating the masculine way she behaves when her anxieties rose. In this fight with herself, confusion is displaced onto the other, through a fear of being known, clinically seen as resistance to interpretation.

Analytical interpretation is a way of arousing metaphorical interpenetration, allowing analyst and analysand to make a symbolic baby – something new, which can change the course of fate. Audrey's history of boyfriends cheating on her was a match to not allowing any of them to penetrate her in a way which brought on Eros. Her body spoke through severe bouts of acid reflux, acne, weight gain and nausea as she began bringing her inner man into relationship with the feminine. When she had to mediate between 'two macho men' at work competing for territory her body invoked all her symptoms at once. Audrey likened the image of two men fighting as a symbol for how it is inside her mind. She remembered how she made herself unattractive as a young teen by being 'macho'. She used the externalized problem of the two men as a reparative exercise, employing a soft, easy manner with them until they found the solution. When this succeeded, Audrey accessed an early memory of her body.

'Koekie' in Afrikaans means 'little cake', a cultural idiom for a woman's genitals. The memory of being two or three years old and having to sleep in her parents' bedroom because her asthma became acute was associated to hearing her mother ask her father to play with her 'little cake'. It wasn't long before Audrey wanted to copy her mother and asked her father to play with her 'koekie' too. It began playfully between her and her father until her mother shouted at them. Suddenly metaphorical erotic play, and all other play, stopped between father and daughter. Audrey only has the dim memory and photographs to recall her earliest years when as the first-born she was a delight to her father. Witnessing the actual primal scene prevents it from becoming a fantasy, which it has to be to form a symbolic image of the *coniunctio* (Samuels, 1989, p. 129). Her memory of these events linked to the anxiety and shame she felt about expressing herself with another. The frozen trauma was asking to separate out from an intolerable identification with an animus-ridden mother, who stood in for an absent father. The memory of her parents' bedroom is central to her fears she was/is not allowed to be female and enjoy erotic desire.

Social health studies coming out of South Africa are rich in noting how gender dynamics, intimate partner violence and dominant role norms influence not only the spread of HIV and AIDS, they stigmatize the female's sexuality and the child born from violence (O'Sullivan *et al.*, 2006; Campbell *et al.* 2005; Ackermann & de Klerk 2002; Jewkes *et al.*, 2003; Strebel, 1996). At the magical level of consciousness, Audrey has emotional AIDS. It is a symbolic Acquired Immune Deficiency Syndrome, where inter-penetration, the give and take between one and other, including sexual relations, are linked to a contaminating event. In South Africa where AIDS is associated with stories of the 'bad black man' contaminating women, Audrey was preparing to meet her 'bad' inner man. Shadow material may be likened to the 'dung' of the *nigredo*. Useful towards transformation of black into gold are moments of meeting the compounds of fear, shame and imagination within human failings.

On one particular day I didn't hear Audrey ring the ship's bell hung at my garden gate. This bell attunes itself to the hand of fate, psyche's laments, making the boundary a Janus gate, looking forward into what is going to happen in the consulting room, and backward to an earlier wound. Eventually Audrey rang the bell sufficiently to be heard.

M: Good you're here . . . wasn't sure I heard your bell . . .

A: I don't like loud noises. Do you mind, I just want to eat a banana.

M: I do mind. (Sipping tea.) It prevents you from telling me what you're angry about.

A: See, see, that's it, you get to have tea, but I can't have what I want.

M: I'm hear to listen . . .

A: I have a sugar problem!!! And I don't like loud noises.

M: You're saying something about feeling weak and the bell . . .?

A: It's like I'm right back (tears) to the first day of primary school . . . really loud bells . . . teacher didn't like me because . . . I was fat . . . everyone came from a rich family . . . except me . . . their mothers wouldn't let them be friends with me.

M: You must have felt very alone.

A: I did, but I learned . . . how to be the smartest in the class . . .

Ridiculed and bullied at school, the bell announced anxiety around not being able to play well with others. She had no memory of people being happy to see her. She didn't know my bell was not from a school but a ship, where it announced *'all on board, time to set sail.'* Including this small fact opened up a chain of associative networks about not being included. In thinking her mind was the only good thing she had, she disassociated from her body, which held the shame of the primal scene, as well as the genetic accident of being darker skinned than other white Afrikaaners. In talking this out she bumped into a link to her worst fear – getting AIDS. Believing God had forgotten her, she fought to be heard. This affect was effective in making her the *penetrator who cannot be penetrated*, an unconscious identification with 'bad black men' of South Africa who inflict women with AIDS. But equally, it is a split with an unconscious concretization to the black women who have been prevented from protecting themselves against contamination (AIDS) and are now labelled 'bad'. At last Audrey could receive interpretation; a personal complex projected into the world, hooked her into a cultural complex of 'us vs. them' (Singer, 2009, pp. 1–9). She began to tolerate a lengthy interpretation without a fight, receiving it in mind and body. In the following days, in an effort to drain herself of the poison, she began to vomit after eating, realizing many of her body symptoms had been brought on by eating food she knew hurt her.

Slowly, the 'bad black man' was allowed to 'come on board' in our sessions. As she learned to speak of him she became more relaxed, and associated him with a street in Cape Town 'where black men knew how to get things done with stealth'. Acknowledging her reliance upon him to protect her and her duty to keep him hidden was easier than talking about herself. In this bridge to her animus there is the opening for empathy towards him, and so her.

Audrey's symbolic AIDS, acquired in childhood, interrupted ordinary relating and trust. Neither the masculine nor feminine was where it *ought* to be to her satisfaction, due to family and cultural complexes at the border of opening and closing between self and other. As Audrey became more tolerant of her own human failing she could allow interpenetration. The sulphur rising no longer inspired borderline features. In parallel, Audrey's dream images turned to love-making. A feast of *coniunctio* began to be a theme, but her primary shame prevented her from bringing these whenever I appeared as a dream figure. This signalled the beginning of a change in the transference, yet something continued to be stuck for her, and in me, to do with feeling aggrieved: *I was failing her.* Audrey's need to judge herself or someone else kept her world in *nigredo* hoping for *albedo*; hoping I would be the better mother, constantly disappointed. It wasn't until she dreamed of me as the analyst who became the accepting 'fairy god-mother', welcoming her to a Christmas feast, letting her eat as much as she liked, without scolding her for bad table manners, could she see how her use of me in the dream turned to denigration – her dream image put me into clothes her mother wore. Later she told me that putting her mother's clothes on people was something she did to keep herself safe. But it never worked.

Concluding thoughts

In their own way each analysand was working through a cultural complex (Singer & Kimbles, 2004, pp. 4–5, 7) of gendered *ought* and *is* notions to connect to the syzygy, the realm of paired opposites (Samuels, 1982: p. 325; CW 9i, paras 193–194). When gender performance is culturally demanded, as with Bob and

Audrey, any differentiation between *what is* and *what ought to be* becomes lost in a blackened body. My way through this has been to question Jungian gender theory 'in the spirit of another Jung; the Jung of the symbolic, the mythic, and the subtle body' (McKenzie, 2006, p. 401).

Post-modernity brings with it new understandings of identity, gender, sexuality, power and resistance. Coupled with advances in social theory in the second half of the twentieth century Queer emerges in personal identification and political organization as non-normative performance in a range of gratifying acts of being and doing. Taken to its fullness, Queer may include any one who in attempting to individuate does not follow the dictates of essentialist cultural gender norms. I propose this is the intersection of convergence and divergence between Jungian and Queer theories. Both value emergence and fluidity as a process towards becoming. Jung's early disposition for gendering opposites, with varying degrees of denigration and idealization, though evidence of extraordinary early work on identifying contradictions in nature seeking reconciliation is underpinned by the mythopoetics of misogyny and female inferiority in the collective unconscious (Hillman, 1972, pp. 215–298).

Through Queer theory we may find inspiration for intra-psychic unions where achieving and nurturing, penetrating and receiving, are normative for performance identity rather than assigning them to gendered bodies; a place where trauma can hide. We need a new language for the tools Jung gave us in anima and animus to address denigration of the feminine: not only in women and connected to feeling states, but in aspects of the masculine and feminine in the opposite gender. We need not one, but many quaternios of reflexive and active energies in dialogue. The androgyne, a union of masculine and feminine which cannot be defined as either, resisting normative gender identity, is the essence of Queer. Understood this way, Queer is in effect the conclusion of Jung's alchemical opus, the Philosopher's Stone.

References

Abelove, H. (1993) 'From Thoreau to Queer Politics,' *Yale Journal of Criticism*, 6.2, pp. 17–27..

Ackerman, L. & de Klerk, G.W. (2002) 'Social Factors That Make South African Women Vulnerable to HIV Infection' in *Health Care For Women International*, 23.2, pp.163–172.

Adler, G. (1961) *The Living Symbol: A Case Study in the Process of Individuation* New York: Bollingen Foundation.

Benjamin, J. (2004) 'Beyond Doer and Done to: An Intersubjective View of Thirdness' in *The Psychoanalytic Quarterly*, 73, pp. 5–46.

Butler, J. (1990/1999) *Gender Trouble* New York and London: Routledge.

Campbell, C., Foulis, C.A., Maiman S., & Sibiya, Z. (2005) '"I have an Evil Child at My House": Stigma and HIV/AIDS Management in a South African Community' in *American Journal of Public Health*, 95.5, pp. 808–815.

Dorn, G. (1602) 'Philosophica Meditativa' collected in *Theatrum Chemicum*, Vol.1, Ursel, 450–472.

Fabricius, J. (1994) *Alchemy: The Medieval Alchemists and their Royal Art* London: Diamond Books.

Haule, J.R. (1984) 'Soul-Making in a Schizophrenic Saint' in *Journal of Religion and Health*, 23.1, Spring, pp. 70–80.

Hillman, J. (1972) 'The Abysmal Side of Bodily Man' in *The Myth of Analysis Three Essays in Archetypal Psychology* Evanston: Northwestern University Press, pp. 215–298.

—— (1989) 'The Yellowing of the Work' in Mary Ann Mattoon (Ed.), *Personal and Archetypal Dynamics in the Analytical Relationship. Proceedings of the Eleventh International Congress of Analytical Psychology, August 28–September 2, 1989.* Switzerland: Daimon Verlag, Einsiedeln.

Hudson, W.D. (1969) 'Introduction: The "is-ought" problem' in W.D. Hudson (Ed.), *The Is/Ought Question: A Collection of Papers on the Central Problem in Moral Philosophy* Glasgow: Robert Maclehose and Co. Ltd., The University Press, pp. 11–31.

Hume, D. (1740/1888/2003) *A Treatise of Human Nature* Mineola, New York: Dover Philosophical Classics.

Jagose, A. (1996) *Queer Theory: An Introduction* New York: New York University Press.

Jewkes, R.K., Levin, J.B., & Penn-Kekana, L.A. (2003) 'Gender Inequalities, Intimate Partner Violence and HIV Preventive Practices: Findings of South African Cross-Sectional Study' in *Social Science & Medicine*, 56.1, pp. 125–134.

Jung, C.G. (1953–1997) *The Collected Works of C.G. Jung*, 20 vols (Eds Herbert Read, Michael Fordham and Gerhard Adler; trans. R. F. C. Hull). Except where indicated, references are by volume and paragraph number. London and Princeton, NJ: Routledge and Princeton University Press.

McKenzie, S. (2006) 'Queering Gender: Anima/Animus and the Paradigm of Emergence' in *Journal of Analytical Psychology*, 51.2, pp. 401–422.

McLean, A. (1981) *The Splendor Solis* Edinburgh: Magnum Opus Hermetic Sourceworks Number 8.

Milner, M. (1955) 'The Role of Illusion in Symbol Formation' in *New Directions in Psychoanalysis* London: Tavistock, pp. 98–124.

O'Sullivan, L.F., Harrison, A., Morrell, R., Monroe-Wise, A., & Kubeka, M. (2006) 'Gender Dynamics in the Primary Sexual Relationships of Young Rural South African Women and Men' in *Culture, Health & Sexuality*, 8.2, pp. 99–113.

Samuels, A. (1982) 'The Image of the Parents in Bed' in *The Journal of Analytical Psychology*, 27, pp. 323–339.

—— (1986) *The Father* New York: New York University Press.

—— (1988) 'Gender and the Borderline' in Nathan Schwartz-Salant and Murry Stein (Eds) *The Borderline Personality in Analysis*. Wilmette, IL: Chiron Publications, pp. 177–232.

—— (1989) *The Plural Psyche* London: Routledge.

Sedgewick, E.K. (1993a) *Tendencies* Durham: Duke University Press.

—— (1993b) 'Queer Performativity: Henry James's *The Art of the Novel*', in *GLQ: A Journal of Lesbian and Gay Studies*, 1.1, pp. 1–16.

Singer, T. (2009) 'A Jungian Approach to Understanding "us *vs.* them" dynamics' in *Psychoanalysis, Culture & Society,* London: Palgrave Macmillan, pp.1–9.

—— & Kimbles, S.L. (2004) *The Cultural Complex Contemporary Jungian Perspectives on Psyche and Society* Hove: Routledge.

Strebel, A. (1996) 'Prevention Implications of AIDS Discourses among South African Women' in *AIDS Education Prevention*, 4, pp. 352–374.

Temple, C. (2002–2012) *Philosophy Index* Online. Available HTTP: www.philosophy-index.com/hume/guillotine/ (accessed 17 February 2012).

Trismosin, S. (1532–1535) *Splendor Soils* housed in Kupferstichkabinett Berlin at State Museums in Berlin. See also Trismosin, S. (1920) *Splendor Soils Alchemical Wanderings*, Introduction by J.K. Theophania Publishing.

Ulanov, A. (1992) 'Disguises of the Anima' in N. Schwartz-Salant and M. Stein (Eds), *Gender & Soul in Psychotherapy*, Wilmette: Chiron Publications, pp. 25–53.

Young, A. (1992/1972) 'Out of the Closets, Into the Streets' in K. Jay and A. Young (Eds) *Out of the Closets: Voices of Gay Liberation* London: Gay Men's Press, pp. 6–30.

13

MASCULINITY AND THE CLAUSTRUM AS SHADOW VAS

Phil Goss

Introduction

'How can I be myself when life won't let me be me?' These words were stuck in my head. They remained stuck there, as one might expect, when my head seemed to be acting as a kind of shadow crucible in which the alchemy of the claustrum could be allowed to work itself through. For Dan, who had uttered these heavy words, the analysis was one more *vas* in which he felt trapped. I guessed he may be wondering: would *I* let him be himself . . .? I will explore how the analysis with 'Dan' (whose analytic journey is a fictionalised example of themes encountered in my clinical work with some men) recreated the claustrum he was caught within. In turn, this will be used to illustrate a discussion on how the struggle to grasp hold of the masculine in order to move towards a freer relationship to life, less contingent upon the permission to be, can be understood alchemically. I will utilise the term 'claustrum' as proposed by Meltzer (2008, p. 1031).

'Claustrum' is a Latin word originally used in neuro-anatomy referring to a layer between a nucleus and other elements collected around it (Jewell and Abate, 2001, pp. 151–283). In a psychological sense, Meltzer (2008, pp. 928–971) applied this to how an infant can get caught in a claustrophobic space between mother and self: stuck 'within' an enclosed space inside an internalised version of mother. Because of disrupted, sometimes pathologically wounding, early experiences in the attachment to mother, the infant unconsciously seeks to inhabit, or 'have' for themselves, parts of her – such as breast, genitals or rectum – while also struggling to moderate powerful drives and feelings towards mother. This means healthy separation and relating can become a lifelong struggle repeated in unconscious process, and replayed in present relationships (to self and others). Feeling trapped, or stuck – in life generally, or in specific relationships – can be one manifestation of this phenomena.

I will explain this phenomenon and its conceptual framework further below, as well as its adaptation to an alchemical frame of reference, where I suggest it can be seen as a 'shadow alchemical vas', where shadow refers to 'the sum of all the unpleasant qualities one wants to hide, the inferior, worthless and primitive side of man's nature' (Samuels *et al.*,1986, p. 138). In alchemical language, the vas, or crucible, was the retort, the vessel in which the chosen substances were mixed together. The aim was to release what was good, new or precious from this mixing process. As 'shadow vas', the claustrum does the opposite – it traps real and potential 'gold' in a self-limiting container.

I will illustrate my theme with examples from fiction, which also highlight how the archetypal workings of the claustrum as shadow vas may get re-constellated in internal process and external experiences for some men. These themes in turn inform a consideration of how the alchemical cycle brings its influence to bear in the development of object relating, giving momentum towards defining a pathway to masculinity which is influenced by gender, oedipal struggles and a prospective search for identity.

The second of these influences will also be considered in terms of 'self as male', for example in how oedipal forces influence Dan's relation to mother and to triangular dynamics. Being caught in the shadow crucible or claustrum is often intimately linked with faulty 'resolution' of the oedipal conflict, leaving the boy and then the man struggling to comfortably locate himself as a distinct individual with the agency to give and receive love in intimate relations. Here, identity as a man, or a person who happens to be male, gets thrown into uncertainty. In this respect, I will draw on some of my own terminology (Goss, 2010, pp. 50–51), which seeks to rework Jung's initial thinking (CW 9ii, paras 24–34) on contra-sexuality (*anima* as the feminine image and influence in men, and *animus* as the masculine image and influence in women), in order to help make sense of these considerations.

On the one hand, I recognise the influence of anima–animus may represent the availability of both feminine and masculine to both women and men as they generate and process experience. However, I see anima as the predominant, unconscious energic influence in men (that is, where animus is available to a man it is via his anima; and vice versa for women) and propose this approach can provide a valuable tool whereby contra-sexual energies enable the spotlight to be turned upon sometimes difficult dynamics within intimate heterosexual relations. Here, there are ways in which the contra-sexual other constellates the projections onto a partner, in turn evoking a complex: a combination of personal and environmental influences framed by an archetypal backdrop, characterised by a powerful emotional tone which grips the psyche and unconsciously shapes attitude and behaviour (CW 8, paras 202–253).

In this respect, where the claustrum of the shadow vas holds someone in its grip, the presence of a 'blackening' anima (or 'thanima' (Goss, 2010, pp. 53–54): anima infused with thanatos, or the death instinct (Freud, 1920, p. 44)) has established itself during pre-oedipal and oedipal development, splitting off the availability of healthy masculine and feminine energies. The alchemy of trying to redefine a sense of the masculine for men is the focus of this chapter, presenting fresh formulations for it arising through a wrestling between 'being male' on the one hand and 'the masculine' (in its real as well as illusory manifestations) on the other. This involves an exploration of meanings derived from alchemical readings of the masculine as distinctions emerge between the imbided social, and embedded archetypal, masculine and the singularity of the individual lived experience of being a man. I trace the uneven but still pivotal alchemical process in a man's analysis and describe how the alchemy between *male* and *masculine* can be loosened and then reconfigured via unconscious process, and be brought into conscious expression.

The value of exploring these processes is threefold: first, it helps us to understand how the alchemy of the analytic process can generate reconfigurations of gendered identity, in this case concerning a heterosexual man, which in turn can operate to free up healthier ways of relating, particularly in the heterosexual relational context. The description of this fictionalised clinical example will help in illustrating the ways the therapeutic relationship can facilitate such developments. Second, this example sheds light on the individuation process, and the degree to which one can look at this as having a 'gendered dimension'. A fundamental question thrown up by this line of thought is: to what degree does a man's 'maleness' influence the nature of his individuation process compared to how a woman's individuation process is experienced and pursued? Here it is important to recognise the plurality of potential ways of being and experiencing which arises from the archetypal roots of our life patterns. Sexuality and gender, as archetypal continuums, throw up an array of possible experiences, desires and relational patterns. Individuation encompasses these possibilities, though it also asks of us that we notice how our gendered identity and experiencing influences how we can more fully become who we are (CW 6, paras 757–762).

In heterosexual relations, while there are undoubtedly huge areas of commonality of experience between men and women, the potential value in trying to distinguish between 'what being a woman is *like*' (Samuels, 1989, p. 297) – rather than 'is' – compared to what being a man is like, has, I believe, its own value. This pertains particularly where, for men, patterns of relating to women and domesticity which can throw up difficulty and suffering – such as avoidance, escape, aggression or impotency (physiological and psychological) – and the quest to address and overcome these, remains relatively unexplored. Rather than pathologising such behaviours as examples of faulty male responses to being partners and fathers, it is worth considering whether or not a heterosexual male individuation path may require a distinctive frame for understanding and working with the ways men can avoid, react against, even reject their prescribed role within the family and home.

Third, the clinical, alchemical and individuation dimensions of working with men who find themselves in the grip of what one might call a 'complex of home' (where home is experienced as an entrapment) has a political dimension. To what degree can men find their place within the conventional, but post-feminist, home? This applies particularly where there are powerful unconscious influences and complexes – one of which is oedipal – at work in their own lives. This question is also pertinent to the wider context of heterosexual relations, parenting and the domestic space hallmarked by some fraught patterns in the westernised world, particularly regarding relationships between fathers, families and home (Lewis and Lamb, 2007, pp. 2–8).

This fictionalised case study throws up questions about what happens for a man when the alchemical process in the analysis reflects what may be a battleground of relational tension with his partner. It also explores to what extent working with unconscious process can enable real relationships – in this case Dan's with his partner and child-to-be – to adjust in order to re-constellate stuck and antagonistic aspects and transform them into something which can be worked with constructively. Politically, this study therefore opens up the vexed area of heterosexual relations by focussing on how a man may experience the movement into full parental commitment when he has unresolved oedipal issues, within a culture where a father living separately from their family home is common. An alchemical perspective may have something helpful to say about the problematics of contemporary heterosexual relations.

The claustrum as a shadow alchemical vas

Drawing the lens back in from these wider considerations, I will now elucidate further the notion of claustrum, as central to understanding the way a man may experience a sense of entrapment, and specifically how the family home may become a 'shadow vas'. By 'claustrum' I am referring to a proposed development on from the term as used thus far in the psychoanalytic world. Developed from Klein's work on the paranoid-schizoid position (Klein,1946, pp. 99–110) by psychoanalyst Esther Bick (1901–1983) on the basis of infant observation (Bick,1968, pp. 558–566), the concept found its fullest explication in the work of another Kleinian psychoanalyst, Donald Meltzer (1922–2004) who emphasised the notion of intrusive identification as fundamental to the formation of the 'claustrum', proposing that in certain circumstances involving the unavailability of 'good enough' relating and care, a young child's unconscious reactions may involve a 'turning within', and the seeking out and creation of spaces inside (Meltzer, 2008, p. 901). As indicated earlier, this takes the form of an unconscious projective movement by the infant *into* an internalised version of the primary object (or most important relational 'other'): mother (usually), or as a part-object, her breast.

Rather than a developmentally healthy episode of primary identification (Rycroft, 1995, p. 137), this means he or she gets stuck in perpetually experiencing their sense of self as being in a constant relation of 'within mother'. In this way, a 'claustrum' – an enclosed and therefore both protective but entrapping – psychic container, is set up. In this, the infant identifies with, and 'inhabits', introjected part-objects – unconscious representations – relating to mother, for example her head, breast, genitals or rectum. As psychoanalyst Roger Willoughby (2001, p. 918) notes, the enclosure created: 'carries overtones not only of a boundaried living area, but also of a certain metaphysical and moral status: sanctity for adherents or narrow-mindedness and delusion (a narcissistic state) for external critics'.

Here, for the infant, relationship is about the secure availability of self-stimulation and self-soothing, elicited by 'being within' the desired but unreliable object, rather than meaningful relationship with a real other. This does not offer genuine growth and maturation, and becomes an embedded identification with experiences of being stuck, or claustrophobically held-in. There ensues an entrenched struggle to free oneself from it, powerfully hampered by the fear of what might be lost in the process: 'The claustrum thus results from a primary object perceived as frustrating and hostile although necessary for survival in relation with a primitive self, dominated by its own fear and intrusive aggression' (Willoughby, 2001, p. 926). In Dan's case, the claustrum he inhabited seemed to be related to mother's head and breast, experienced by the infant unconsciously as: 'the font of knowledge and wisdom' (Meltzer, 2008, p. 1286). Here the child, and then the adult, struggles to find their own truth, their own creativity. Secrecy and avoidance can hallmark their attempt to protect their sense of separate self-hood.

While for the alchemists, the vas was, as described earlier, an *enabling* and *creating* container, the claustrum is a metaphor for keeping what is contained stuck within itself, stymieing growth and development. This kind of unconscious entrapment is so embedded that being inside the claustrum is the norm, a space one will never get out of (supposedly) so one learns to use the experience of being within it to soothe and stimulate oneself, with the masturbatory implications which can go with this. An image which often came to me with Dan reflecting this phenomenon is of a bath which is full of lukewarm water and high, slippery sides you can't climb. Here the wait for help, for meaningful *coniunctio*, is a lengthy, sometimes never-ending one, as the claustrum has 'slippery slides'. Those aspects of psyche striving to experience a sense of separation and autonomously express themselves, find themselves slipping back down into the murky warm waters to fall back into self-soothing and self-stimulation.

Dan recreated the claustrum in many contexts and guises, usually unconsciously but sometimes as a conscious act of defence, such as the efforts to feel separate from the home, outlined below. Better to create his own version of it, rather than being caught out by it creeping up on him and finally swallowing him up. In archetypal terms, Erich Neumann (1905–1960), the Jungian analyst who made a definitive study of the archetype of the Great Mother, described this as a battle to free oneself from the deathly power of the goddess, who is able, like Demeter or Hecate, to close the wombs of living creatures . . . (so that) . . . all life stands still' (Neumann, 1955, p. 17).

Archetypally, to be genuinely released from the clutches of this power, and move from a fused – or 'uroboric' (ibid., p. 172) – state within what Meltzer would term the claustrum, requires the activation of an effective heroic ego state. When this happens: 'Progress to the male consciousness and the autonomy of the spirit-sun requires the "symbolic slaying" of the Great Mother . . .' (ibid., p. 203), which in turn is facilitated by the awakening of the hero, inspired by the availability of 'father' consciousness. This is a similar equation to Meltzer's description of how a degree of release from the claustrum can be fostered. He describes a facilitated process whereby a middle or third way of being emerges for the analysand between a: 'rigidity of avoidance and instability of contact . . .' (Meltzer, 2008, p. 1662), something like the metaphor of a hero emerging within who can move the person towards a freer, less discontinuous, experience of living, and a more genuine and open capacity for relating. In alchemical terms, these observations beg the question: is this a version of the alchemical process which requires escape from, even the breaking apart of, the vas in which men consumed with a sense of entrapment find themselves? Does this require the availability of a sense in the analysis of a healthy *un*-containment alongside the more conventional 'require-ment' of the therapeutic container?

The claustrum as shadow alchemical vas and analytic container

In the analysis with Dan an alchemical process emerged which illustrates the power of unconscious processes, as framed by alchemical language. He seemed to be 'fishing' for a right relation to the masculine *and* the feminine, like in the picture from *Mutus Liber* used by Jung (CW 12, p. 259) where he describes 'Centre, the *soror mystica* with the artifex, fishing for Neptune (animus); below, artifex, with *soror*, fishing for Melusina (anima) . . .'. Something in Dan reached down into his unconscious for tools to short-circuit his mesmerised unwillingness to break free from the claustrum.

Through an opening up to an acceptance of the need for *putrefaction* (CW 16, para. 479) (see Chapter 1) – or dissolution – of some masculine identifications, a *nigredo* (blackening) was arrived at, where identity can become frighteningly elusive when stripped away from gender identification. Both analyst and analysand fell into an abyss of uncertainty, also fed by historical identity uncertainties in the lived experience of the analyst. My experience of 'father-as-absent' further charged this uncertainty, but also proved a gift (Young-Eisendrath, 1996, pp. 33–44) in enabling the empty space we shared to constellate a new sense of 'father' in the analysis, much like Samuels' observations on the way notions of 'father' can be renewed through taking a more open and playful approach to the possi-bilities inherent in the term (1993, pp. 125–148). Here, frames of reference for 'being a man' and 'masculinity' fall into the background as do the less helpful tendencies of the human mind to split reality into familiar, pigeonholed meanings, particularly where these apply to gender (Steinberg, 1993, pp. 12–22).

I will now turn to the analysis and describe how alchemical principles helped make sense of how Dan found his way back from the claustrum of stuck-ness and exile, towards a discovery of the value of relational identity in the crucible of home, the vas of the analysis seeming to enable this enlivening transition. This process will be described here referring to the classic stages of alchemy upon which Jung based his thinking (CW 12, paras 333–341). Four stages broadly capture this movement: first *nigredo*, a blackening; second *albedo*, a whitening; third *citrinitas*, a yellowing; and fourth *rubedo*, a reddening. I will also refer to Jung's application of the cycle to analysis, where he draws on the more specific 12 stages of the *Rosarium* (CW 16, paras 353–401). Here the alchemical couple ('King and Queen') come together in the alchemical vas and journey through the various stages, including *nigredo*, a deadening of relationship, as often happens in a long-term analysis before there is a *sprinkling of the dew* and a 'whitening' begins the process towards a new *coniunctio*. The analysand is helped to integrate *shadow* aspects; freshly developing versions of self can be generated. The analyst is also affected, moved into further development of self by being part of this alchemy.

Nigredo: home as claustrum

In our first session, Dan asked early on if he could open a window (alongside the one I already had on the latch). It was warm, but not stifling, summer sunshine receding into the early evening through the vertical blinds behind me. There were thin strips of light on the wall either side of Dan, framing him and his haunted stare in the empty space between them. Before I had an opportunity to respond he stood up and walked to my right to reach through the blinds and open the second window. He then held the blinds and moved behind them, and I could hear him standing there breathing in and out deeply, as he stood by the open window. This man needed space, and to sense a way of *escape* like someone checking for fire exits in a public building. It did not take long for me to get a strong sense of how this man was 'inside' something, something which made it hard for him to breathe. As the early sessions unfolded, I began to wonder how far, rather than *if*, he might be caught in something deadened and enclosed. I worried this might come to characterise his experience of the clinical container and wondered if the thera-peutic vas might become a representation of the claustrum he seemed caught in. This is precisely what happened, and now I find myself speculating: how much of this was a self-fulfilling prophecy; my claustrum, as much as his?

It was when Dan started talking about the birth of his first child, six months prior to the beginning of our work, that key features of the complexes which were the building bricks of the claustrum began to emerge. The story, told at first by Dan when he stood at the window again in the fifth session (apparently not something he could relate face-to-face to me), was dramatic. Becoming a father had activated a flight reaction in him so strong it had demanded he remove himself from the supposedly life-giving vas of home and the loving partnership which was to bring literally into life the product of that *coniunctio*. The prospect of the arrival of a child seemed only to provoke a powerful feeling of being trapped and a belief he would now be (more) heavily constrained against 'being me'. The arrival of this child meant he would be negated; he would cease to have being and identity. Symbolically, the child would kill him, like Oedipus killed Laius in the Greek myth (Graves, 1990, pp. 371–376). Yet, I sensed there was more to it than this. His habit of going to the window in most sessions, and always towards the beginning (sometimes as soon as he came in the room, sometimes later as if he remembered he had forgotten to complete this ritual) spoke of a yearning for freedom and release. This was evidenced in my consulting room in the way described, and in the way he seemed to experience home as a place of potential entrapment.

His reaction to his wife passing on the news she was pregnant was to affect joy while really, he said, 'I was feeling absolutely horrified, terrified, a feeling of being lost, consumed . . .'. He described sitting slumped on the sofa in the living room after his wife had gone to bed after they celebrated the happy news. Dan said the walls of the room seemed to be moving in towards him, reminding him of a scene from a film from his youth where a group of young people were inside a room doing just that, escaping at the very last minute when the hero outside pressed the switch which stopped them being crushed to death.

The 'hero outside' seemed to be a suitable metaphor, as Dan's driven solution to the problem he confronted was to assume the answer lay outside home, in the wide open space of 'out there' where he could define himself as he wished without being squashed into nothingness by the walls of home. Inside him, caught in the teeth of an apparently devouring, all-consuming 'home complex', the claustrum was suddenly magnified in its power, the walls of the vas threatening to extend upwards to infinity, with no chance of escape.

His reaction in the outer world was to spend lengthy periods of time at work, as well as setting up fictional business trips away from home where he would pretend to be elsewhere in the UK, or abroad, while really he was in a hotel room on the other side of town, watching TV, sitting in a restaurant or drinking in the hotel bar. This projection outwards of the claustrum has a vivid echo in the book *The Best a Man Can Get*, in which the protagonist, Michael, sets up an alternative home with his mates (O'Farrell, 2000, pp. 84–111) pretending to be working away from home, while his wife brings up their young children.

Mythologically, as hinted at already, the pattern behind both examples carries strong hallmarks of the story of Lauis, murdered by Oedipus (Graves, 1990, pp. 371–376), who is unaware the man he killed was his father, and the woman, Jocasta, he went on to marry is in fact his mother. When he discovers these unbearable truths he gouges his eyes out, an act which symbolically reflects the unconscious depths, and extremes of feeling generated by the oedipal complex (Freud, 1924, p. 177). In both cases, whatever conscious and relational factors are at work, the strong reaction to the arrival of a 'third' presence alongside the original couple is translated into a desire for escape, sometimes acted out.

Dan brought a dream. He is at the bottom of a well, which has no water in it, but just thousands of dead insects, mainly flies, which threaten to overwhelm and suffocate him. The parallel with being caught deep down inside of an enclosed space with no apparent escape (just the distant light of the sky at the top of the well to remind the dreamer there is any possibility of an alternative) is obvious, reflecting the enclosing power of a constellated claustrum, infected by oedipal toxicity. Further consideration of the circumstances in the dream elucidate his psychic predicament as well as hints at a possible 'way out' which is not just a blind rush to escape. Manically trying to climb out of the deep well would simply mean Dan falls back to the bottom, injuring himself in the process.

The dead insects, mostly flies, could be looked at in a Freudian way – that is, as a representation of a wish for 'living flies', the zip or buttons on men's trousers, which allow them to get their dick out and deploy their phallic potency. This could be either to discharge unwanted, sometimes toxic, waste; or to penetrate others sexually, particularly, in Dan's case, to be able to penetrate the feminine, in the guise of his partner, without it bringing something 'murderous' into life, as the birth of their child seemed to represent. Now Dan needed to feel his masculinity would not be stolen from him, that he could experience fatherhood as empowering not as a burdensome castrating threat.

The dream set out the problem as one of emasculation via the presence of a new 'third' in his relationship to partner/home. This constellated, *re*-constellated, the enclosing claustrum which had roots in earlier patterns of Dan's development. These became clearer as the analysis unfolded. Shakespeare provides us with a story illustrating the archetypal template of this pattern. In *A Winter's Tale* (Shakespeare, in Pafford, 1962, pp. 1–78), King Leontes banishes his child from the kingdom, preferring to believe he is not his son. He turns his wife into a statue, because unconsciously he experiences the new-born as a threat to his masculine power and autonomy. The special 'good thing' which his union with Hermione, his queen, has produced he feels driven to enviously destroy, projecting his oedipal rage also onto his old friend Polyxenes, who likewise has to flee. His masculinity has become a curse.

However, there is a further clue in Dan's dream as to how he might find the way out of the well: the lack of any water. He is at the bottom of a dried up well lying on a bed of dead flies. For a well to be completely dry implies there has been no water coming up from the spring beneath for some time. Something in Dan has literally 'dried up'. The availability of the water of soul, the flowing desire and search for intimate relations, has atrophied: positive energies provided by life-giving anima energies – which I call *erosima*, once combined with the application of 'eros' energy to the concept of anima (Goss, 2010, p. 47) – are not available. Rather, anima has been deadened – thanima – and the feminine has turned against him to enclose and squash him.

As I mulled over Dan's dream in between sessions, the key to his problem appeared thoroughly alchemical – on the one hand he needed to access the father energy unavailable to him and 'open his flies'. On the other hand, this could only happen if the thanatos – infused anima (which I call the 'thanima') – atmosphere at the bottom of the well could be superseded by the presence of erosima, seeping drop by drop through the walls of the claustrum, moving Dan closer to a *coniunctio*, a fresh 'marriage' of the feminine and masculine within. Jung used the term 'syzygy' (CW 9i, paras 40–42) to describe the archetypal 'ideal' of a yoked feminine and masculine conjunction. Dan did not need the ideal, he just needed a reawakening of life-giving anima to help him turn his masculinity from a curse to a source of embodied potency. As things stood, whatever context he found himself living in would become a claustrum: home as claustrum, and my hunch was: *analysis* as claustrum.

Alchemically, in Dan's case as well as the narratives created by Shakespeare and O'Farrell, there is a powerful reaction against *coniunctio*, a deeply driven need to be away from the vas of intimacy. So how might we further make sense of this analytically, drawing on the wisdom of the alchemists? One frame of reference is Jung's exploration of Mercurius as a masculine-based 'spirit' of movement between opposites (CW 13, paras 239–303).

Jung's exploration offers a descriptive starting point of how the masculine dynamic is archetypally portrayed in myth and story, where the puer, or eternal child as identified by Jung as an important manifestation of the child archetype (CW 9i, paras 259–301), is provided serendipitously with something which enables him to find a way through a crisis helped by a 'wise old person'. This echoes the qualities associated with being 'caught in the claustrum': 'when the hero is caught in a hopeless and desperate situation from which only profound reflection or a lucky idea – in other words, a spiritual function or an endopsychic automatism of some kind – can extricate him' (ibid., para. 401).

Jung draws on Grimm's fairytale 'The Spirit in the Bottle', where a boy tricks the angry spirit Mercurius to go back into a bottle he was imprisoned in under the ground, amongst the roots of the tree. The boy is rewarded by Mercurius with a magic cloth for releasing him once more and the boy and his poor father suddenly have all the riches they need for the rest of their lives (ibid., para. 239). Here is an archetypal template for the alchemical shift needed to free the boy from the claustrum: there needs to be confrontation with 'bottled up spirit' that does not destroy the hero/ego. Through trickery or a re-configuration of power relations there is a 'new deal' with 'spirit' and the archetypal masculine.

In developmental terms, a boy requires a 'good enough' internal father-object, another way of describing how the hero strikes a deal with 'spirit' in the story. A father's penis acts as a bridge (Gordon, 1993, pp. 69–84) out of the claustral, maternal world and towards a freer, more potent 'father' space. Here the emphasis on the need to 'open his flies' in the dream of the well suggested Dan might. He needed to create conditions in which this could happen. Potent 'animus' energies in a man can only be reached via the 'sprinkling of the dew' of erosima – life-giving anima energies – creating receptiveness to the possibilities of the masculine. Dan's anima was in a deep sleep smothering any sense he could define or re-define himself as a father and partner without fleeing the nest.

The sprinkling of the dew: whitening the well

'I love the rain, I love the fucking rain!' Dan's head stretched out of the window. The torrential rain soaked his hair but he was oblivious, as well as to soaking the blind and floor of my consulting room. I went to get him a towel. When I came back he stood with an almost manic grin. I handed him the towel, feeling like a barber who had washed his client's hair and was now preparing to cut it. I noticed a shot of despair run through me – he acted-out in front of me an embedded wish to throw off responsibility for self (and others) and deliriously allow himself to be soaked in unconsciousness. This challenged me – would my own potential to identify with his experience of absent fathering lead me to join him in unconsciousness? Had I colluded by getting him the towel? I realised my anxiety about him potentially 'causing a scene' out of the window, and anger at him flooding my floor, lay behind my move for the towel. However, it felt like a genuine moment of 'containment through connection': a peculiar mixture of uncontained anxiety and a surge of care for him, like a mix of mother and father. He wrapped the towel round his head, quickly sat down and said: 'Ok I'm ready to work now'.

The 'barber' metaphor arising from this moment proved more useful than I first realised. Something needed to be cut away for the new to grow, for erosima to seed healthy locks on his flaky scalp. Unlike Samson, cutting his 'hair' did not represent a diminishment of Dan's strength, rather it was shedding the dead hair of earlier attempts to 'find father' and then 'be father'. His disinhibited 'hair wash' spoke of an unconscious wish to drown in the feminine. We explored the disconnectedness he experienced with his mother: she showed love in unpredictable ways, sometimes showering him with affection like the rain cloud, at other times physically withdrawing when he sought out her touch or warm smile. The forming of the claustrum he found himself in had been a joint effort, a co-construction between his mother's depressed ambivalence about him, and his defence against the pain caused by her 'apple of my eye today, rotten apple tomorrow' stance. He had locked shut the door from the inside rather than put up with the uncertainty of whether she would be there when he opened it. Separation from mother, for Dan, was achieved via deadening feeling, and now thanima was the decisive influence on his sense of self and capacity for relating.

As for his father – he was what Michael and Leontes were for their infants in the stories mentioned above – he went soon after Dan was born. Dan only met him once; his father had visited from the States when Dan was 14. Inevitably, it was an awkward meeting which Dan described as 'without feeling on either side, my father just seemed embarrassed and disinterested', though Dan reported he 'spotted a touch of redness and moisture in his eyes' when they said goodbye. Here again I had to watch my own identification with him, as I too had an 'absent father': I noticed the sting in my own eyes when he said this. I couldn't ponder whether he would be able to use this absence as the 'philosopher's stone' on which to build a new deal with his own fathering potential. Instead our shared uncertainty about how to be father, how to be male, took centre stage and I was as lost in the vacuum between us as Dan.

In that moment we had to 'sink or swim' together, an unnerving pointer to the need to bear un-containment rather than try to shore up the vas. He could see my eyes redden and his eyes bulged in shock before fixing fiercely on the window. As he frowned blankly at the blind I gathered myself, cleared my throat and said

'I wonder what happened there'. He shook his head, stood up, walked to the edge of the claustrum and took a few deep breaths behind the blind.

Yellowing: decaying faulty masculinity and emerging male *jouissance*

In alchemical terms, the yellowing stage is often absorbed into the final 'reddening' phase of the cycle. In this analysis, our shared search for fresh versions of the masculine and 'being male' fit the notion of the sun's emerging at this stage of 'citrinitas'. The masculine needs to be reborn via a new penetration of, and embrace with, the feminine. For Dan and me our mutual uncertainty about how to 'be male' created the space within which erosima could begin and drop the dew of a new relational possibility into the space between and around us. This space in turn continued to oscillate in my experiencing of it from the familiar, stifling, claustrum (alleviated by Dan's trips to the window), to a more chaotic, frightening sense of us being thoroughly open to the (psychic) elements, acted out by Dan's insistence on having the window open, whatever the weather.

Contention about the window helped constellate 'the bad father'. This helped Dan, after a rupture in the work, renegotiate his own relation to father and fathering. A few weeks after the 'hair washing' episode, the heavens opened again half way through the session. Dan could not resist making for the window, with the same wide-eyed expression as before. He ducked behind the blind and moved to fling the latched window open. I reminded him firmly we had agreed he would not do this again after the soaking the room got last time. I heard him hesitating with the latch for a moment, his head still, propping the blind as if pausing to decide whether to burst the claustrum open irrespective of what I'd said, or we'd agreed. I heard the sound of the window swinging open and juddering against the outside wall. I resisted the urge to get up and go to the window; instead, I waited for him to return.

After a couple of minutes he came back and stood in front of his chair, water running down from his head onto the carpet. Another surge of wet emotion ran through me as I saw the boy drenched in his sorrow in front of me.

'No towel this time I guess?' he asked.
I shook my head.

Again he saw the tears in my eyes, shook his head and left, slamming the door angrily behind him.

Fermentatio: the redness of the eyes and a rubedo of maleness

Dan phoned me a month later and asked sheepishly if he could make a further appointment, apologised 'for being an arsehole' and offered to pay for any damage to my furnishings. When we met he said he'd felt intensely angry when I reminded him of our agreement about the window. This was the sharpest of constellations of the claustrum: all the hurt and fury at his mother's ambivalence towards him, and his father's abandonment of him surged through him and exploded in an act of bitter defiance. 'I don't like rules' he said, but 'When I saw your red eyes . . . looked like tears were coming as well . . . it was too fucking much . . . I mean you were telling me what to do, but I could see you cared as well . . . so I had to come back.'

The cycle of abandonment had, if not definitively broken, at least been interrupted. He had abandoned me and the analysis, like he'd abandoned his partner and child-to-be, like he'd been let down and abandoned by his parents. Now he gave himself the experience of return, and considered the possibility that nothing in a relationship has to be final (while both participants live and breathe). It was his turn to well up, and as his eyes reddened he choked out a request to go to the window, then went and stood behind the blind with the window opened carefully by his hands, and cried.

As I looked down and saw a tear from my own eye soak into the carpet, in response to his sobs, I wondered what was left for us to do. Erosima – the life-giving anima – had finally returned, bringing a *coniunctio* with new masculine possibilities, a fresh male *jouissance* – allowing in felt and sensual (including erotic) experience with pleasure or pain, however risky (Lacan, 1991, pp. 89–93) – new ways for Dan to be himself, and to be a father.

To use Meltzer's terminology, Dan had broken through the claustum because of: 'The recovery and renewal of the passionate moment . . .' (Meltzer, 2008, p. 1659). The fracture between us arose from my refusal to let him soak himself, instead giving an experience of firmness, which he had come to associate with 'bad father'. Meltzer describes the conditions needed for 'the passionate moment' as where:

> ability consists essentially in the readiness to try again. This readiness must . . . imply a mutual uncertainty of the reasons of the breakdown in intimacy and a readiness to forgive, both oneself and the other. That, in turn, requires a sophisticated attitude towards pain in which the interest in its meaning exceeds the aversion to its sensual quality, the painfulness of the pain.
>
> (Ibid., p. 1666)

Dan had moved, ready to bear the pain in order to get to its meaning. The reddening of the work, like the reddening of our eyes, had come about by a gradual, at times painful, recognition of our mutual incomprehension about how to break the hold of the claustrum. We shared confusion about how to be male, where maleness requires a performance that is genuine for the man, while also meeting the needs of those dependent on his maleness.

The search for a 'new deal with the masculine: alchemy and Dan's analysis

Dan's new deal with his masculinity and performance as a heterosexual male came about via many twists and turns. Outside analysis, he found a way back to his partner, whose hurt and incomprehension at his behaviour meant he had to work hard to foster possibilities that they, like he and I, could 'try again'. Within the analysis, the fermenting movement towards 'the passionate moment' came about through a letting go of the need to understand, and an acceptance that a cognitive grasp of the heterosexual male predicament – where it generates feelings of being trapped or stuck in relation to family and fatherhood – does not of itself break the power of the claustrum. Instead, the sprinkling of erosima's moisture enables (and is further strengthened by) the gradual awakening of the potent masculine, the 'opening of the flies'. For Dan, his decision to end the analysis once he felt ready (and she had agreed) to return to his partner and their impending parenthood reflected what David Tacey, Professor of Humanities and Social Science at Latrobe University, Melbourne, describes as the importance of 'holding fast to our own authority . . .' (1997, p. 67) as a way of integrating the healthy image of father. Dan got hold of his authority in separating from me, and moving beyond the shadow vas of the claustrum.

Concluding remarks: rediscovering the symbolic language of maleness

In our clinical work, when it came to the 'ascent of the soul', the mundificatio purification helped us discriminate better between inauthentic masculine identifications and something more genuinely felt as *male*, or simply *human*, experiencing. This brought elements of a more authentic language to talk about male experiencing to arise between us, like a male version of Kristeva's unspoken *semiotic* of the feminine (in Kristeva and Moi, 1986, p. 4) which nevertheless fleetingly finds verbal and non-verbal expression. These moments represent the *lapis*, at least a male version of the cosmogonic archetypal human form (CW 16, para. 397) associated with the New Birth at the end of the alchemical process. A deeply felt way of speaking and feeling manifested for Dan and, occasionally, for me. The alchemy of gender throws up archetypal, interpersonal and cultural dimensions. Interplay between male-masculine and anima-animus enables the historical confusion – a rigid yet confused *coniunctio* – between 'male' and 'masculine' to loosen, especially its aggressive and erotic anima elements. This allows a certain amount of reconfiguration of what 'being a man' means. This does not imply there are no 'certainties' or archetypal roots to being male, rather, there is a constant interplay between these and the fluid phenomenological experiencing of being a man.

The alchemical metaphor of the vas, counterpointed by my suggestion of claustrum as 'shadow vas', helps highlight both the psychological and political dimensions of the relationship between heterosexual man/father and 'home'. The clinical example here portrays a way 'home and family' may re-activate the claustrum in some men, unconsciously driving them to seek escape, further exacerbating the collective image of men as less responsible and reliable parents than mothers. This theme raises the question of how differently (or not) women and men who live together experience the container of home. It also begs the question of how men like Dan can come to feel more comfortably contained by home rather than feeling trapped. Here, seeing home as a vas in which the working through of power, and other gendered, dynamics can happen, gives scope for the languages of maleness and femaleness to interplay in a challenging but healthy *coniunctio*.

References

Bick, E. (1968) 'The Experience of the Skin in Early Object Relations' *International Journal of Psycho-Analysis*, 49, New York: APA, 558–566.

Freud, S. (1920) 'Beyond the Pleasure Principle', in *Vol. 18*: *On Metapsychology* Middlesex: Penguin (1987).

—— (1924) 'The Passing of the Oedipus Complex' *International Journal of Psycho-Analysis*, 5, New York: APA: 419–424.

Gordon, R. (1993) *Bridges: Metaphor for Psychic Processes* London: Karnac.

Goss, P. (2010) *Men, Women and Relationships – a Post Jungian Approach: Gender Electrics and Magic Beans* London: Routledge.

Graves, R. (1990) *The Greek Myths* London: Penguin.

Jewell, J. and Abate, F. eds (2001) *New Oxford American Dictionary* Oxford University Press.

Jung, C.G. (1912–1968) references are by volume and paragraph number (other than where indicated) to the *Collected Works of C.G. Jung* (eds Herbert Read, Michael Fordham and Gerhard Adler. Trans.: R.F.C. Hull). London: Routledge.

Klein, M. (1946) 'Notes on Some Schizoid Mechanisms' *International Journal of Psycho-Analysis*, 27, 99–110.

Kristeva, J. and Moi, T. (1986) *The Kristeva Reader* New York: Columbia University Press.

Lacan, J. (1991) *Le séminaire*, Book 17: *L'envers de la psychanalyse (1969–1970)* Paris: Seuil.

Lewis, C. and Lamb, M. (2007) *Understanding Fatherhood: A Review of Recent Research* York: Joseph Rowntree.

Meltzer, D. (2008) *The Claustrum: An Investigation of Claustrophobic Phenomena* Karnac Books.

Neumann, E. (1955) *The Great Mother* London: Routledge and Kegan Paul.

O'Farrell, J. (2000) *The Best a Man Can Get* London: Doubleday.

Pafford, J. ed. (1962) *The Winter's Tale* Oxford: Arden Edition.

Rycroft, C. (1995) *A Critical Dictionary of Psychoanalysis* London: Penguin.

Samuels, A. (1989) *The Plural Psyche* London: Routledge.

—— (1993) *The Political Psyche* London: Routledge.

Samuels, A., Shorter, B. and Plaut, F. eds (1986) *A Critical Dictionary of Jungian Analysis* London: Routledge.

Steinberg, W. (1993) *Masculinity; Identity, Conflict and Transformation* Boston, Mass.: Shambhala.

Tacey, D. (1997) *Remaking Men: Jung, Spirituality and Social Change* London: Routledge.

Willoughby, R. (2001) '"The Dungeon of Myself" The Claustrum as Pathological Container' *International Journal of Psycho-Analysis*, 82, New York: APA, 917–931.

Young-Eisendrath, P. (1996) *The Gifts of Suffering* New York: Addison-Wesley.

14

ANOREXIA AND ALCHEMY

John Colverson

This chapter explores anorexia nervosa through an alchemical lens. Anorexia occupies one end of a spectrum of eating disorders with compulsive eating at the other extreme, and bulimia holding the ambivalent middle ground. While eating disordered individuals often move between different places on this spectrum over time, anorexia is a phenomenon in its own right; demanding attention with the image it presents, the reactions it generates, the near-psychotic distortion of body image, and frighteningly high mortality rate. A long-term study by British psychiatrist Ratnasurya and colleagues (1991) found after 20 years 12–20 per cent of patients had died – half by suicide. British psychoanalyst Susie Orbach (1993, p. 4) argues that 'The starvation amidst plenty, the denial set against desire, the striving for invisibility versus the wish to be seen – these key features of anorexia – are a metaphor for our age.' This chapter will use an alchemical perspective to attempt to understand that metaphor.

Professor Arthur Crisp, instrumental in developing our modern understanding of the condition, argued that it is not an eating disorder in psychopathological terms: rather it is a panic disorder – the onset of puberty creates the panic. Family dynamics and childhood experiences can make many vulnerable to the experience of entering puberty. Young females who go on to develop anorexia attribute feelings of insecurity, panic, and shame to the development of adult body shape and its basis in the female of normal 'fatness' – which can then come to be experienced as 'not owned': alien, dangerous, and an identity challenge. Efforts to control and regulate escalate. The suddenness with which calorie control takes over reflects the profound relief experienced from the reversal of the pubertal process itself. Once puberty is banished, the problems it had prompted are resolved. Thereafter, the individual rapidly develops a phobia of weight gain (Crisp and McClelland, 1996, pp. 3–6).

Anorexia is recognised as being mostly confined to women. Currently only 10 per cent of people suffering with anorexia in the UK are men (Kirby, 2011). Male anorexic patients I have worked with all began bodybuilding in their early adolescence, but were unable to maintain this, subsequently collapsing into anorexic self-attack like their female counterparts. This suggests a wish to suppress feminine characteristics and present an exaggerated masculine to compensate for the lack of an effective masculine in their inner world. This idea is supported by American psychiatrists Pope, Katz, and Hudson (1993, pp. 406–409) who discovered a phenomenon they called 'reverse anorexia' among body builders using steroids, who avoided social contact because they perceived themselves to be too small despite being large and muscular.

The first time I met a person suffering from anorexia was while working as an assistant nurse on an acute admission ward at a London psychiatric hospital. A young anorexic girl was transferred from the local eating disorders unit. She was thin to the point of being skeletal, reminding me of the victims of Nazi concentration camps. She sat beside me and asked me if I thought her legs were too fat, pointing at the thin layer of muscle clinging to her thigh bone. She hated this fat. I remember being stunned at the level of her perceptual distortion. I was amazed she managed to walk around at all, and was struck by the amount of anger her small frame contained behind a seemingly compliant exterior.

The visual appearance of extreme anorexia is shocking, the image of walking skeletons deeply disturbing. Anorexia nervosa involves a denial of need and a vicious, ruthless, attack upon what needs to be nourished within. The image shouts of starvation: the body starves in a literal depiction of their inner regressed reality as a result of sadistic self control.

The roots of anorexia are believed to lie in early attachment issues. Jan Wiener, a London-based Jungian analyst, has suggested in psychosomatic expression (such as anorexia) 'disturbances emanate from a time when sensuous communications between mother and baby can critically affect emotional development' (1994, p. 345). Failed sensuous communications interfere with what American professor of psychiatry Daniel Stern calls the vitality affects of the emergent self (1985, pp. 53–61). The noted French psychoanalyst Joyce McDougall argues this is a preverbal stage of development during which the body itself is used as the theatre of expression (1989, pp. 40, 42). The British psychoanalyst, Wilfred Bion, argued that a mother normally provides an infant with an experience of holding and containment of experiences, which in the early months of life are disorganised and potentially frightening (1962a, pp. 90–94; 1962b). Em Farrel, a north London psychotherapist, argues mothers of future anorexics have a flaw in their ability to provide this. They had often experienced attachment problems with their own mothers, and lack boundaries regarding their sense of self. They use their babies (future anorexics) as appendages and transitional objects to help them negotiate this boundary (Farrel, 2000, pp. 36–38). Jungian analyst J. K. Newman argues, as a result of this initial experience of faulty containment, anorexics do not feel contained in the physical skin of their bodies, which would normally give identity and definition (2006).

Gianna Williams, a consultant child and adolescent psychotherapist working with eating disorders at the Tavistock clinic in London, argues that an experience of merger with mother is created by the mother's use of toxic projective identification. Toxicity coming from a source of nurture leads to confusion in an infant who develops a 'no entry' defence (Williams, 1997, pp. 120–123). The sense of merger undermines the creation of a potential space, which British paediatrician and psychoanalyst Donald Winnicott argued is essential for play and development of symbolisation (1971, p. 128). Although the development of symbolisation continues to a greater or lesser extent, the infant tends to resort to the use of what the British psychoanalyst Hanna Segal called symbolic equations (Segal, 1957, pp. 391–397). These give literal concrete interpretations of phenomena which would normally be perceived symbolically. For example: mother = mater = matter. This use of symbolic equations means the infant's intra-psychic perception of archetypal patterns, described by alchemical metaphors, takes concrete form.

A mother holds the infant's initial projection of the self: on the one hand the archetypal core of the psyche, on the other, its totality. Through this projection mother is given a numinous role. There is identification with mother as a hateful and implacable god, as well as an all giving earth-mother. Consequently there is a rupture in the ego–self axis. The ego, cut off from its source of nurture and support, feels alienated (Edinger, 1972, pp. 38–48). Anorexia involves acting out probably the most powerful envious attack on the self of any psychopathology, due to projection of the negative experience of mother onto the 'fat' of the body. Melanie Klein believed envy has its origin in the regressed fantasy that mother's breast is withholding goodness and keeping it for itself. In fantasy, the infant completely scoops out the breast and fills it with badness (bad parts of the self) in order to spoil mother (Mitchell, 1986, pp. 212–213).

Anorexia and the alchemical process

> Four stages are distinguished characterized by the original colours mentioned in Heraclitus: melanosis (blackening), leukosis (whitening), xanthosis (yellowing), and iosis (reddening). Later, in about the fifteenth or sixteenth century, the colours were reduced to three, and the xanthosis, otherwise called the citrinitas, gradually fell into disuse or was but seldom mentioned . . . the change in the classification of its stages cannot be due to extraneous reasons but has more to do with the symbolical significance of the quaternity and the trinity; in other words, it is due to inner psychological reasons.
>
> (CW 12, para. 333)

With the omission of the citrinitas (xanthosis), the magnum opus (the great work), consists of three main stages: blackening (Nigredo, melanosis), whitening (Albedo, leukosis), and reddening (Rubedo, iosis), through which the primal matter (*prima materia*), which contains all possibilities in a chaotic and unrefined state, is transformed into a state of perfection.

In *Psychology and Alchemy* (CW 12) Jung explores a parallel between the work (opus) of the alchemists and the psychological process of individuation. The metaphorical language of alchemy abounds with references to digestion by acid, vinegar, urine, sea-water; devouring and being devoured as a means of breaking down and facilitating the transition to a new state, generally involving the coming together of disparate parts. In anorexia this is made literal with an anorexic digesting his, or her, own body with stomach acid, lactic acid, and digestive juice. Alchemists would seed the alchemical process with gold – but anorexics through their projection of negative mother, and the envious attacks this involves, are unwilling to invest in their analysis – at least initially.

Anorexics as 'puffers'

American theologian and researcher Karen-Claire Voss argues the adepts understood alchemy as a form of illumination, a means of transmutation, a method for experiencing levels of reality not ordinarily accessible: spiritual and transcendent rather than immanent. In contrast, an alternative form, 'material alchemy', was practised by those referred to as 'puffers'. Originally this term simply referred to their efforts with the bellows to keep the fires going. Eventually, it acquired disparaging connotations between rivalrous groups of alchemists: those who were engaged in mere pseudo-alchemy and whose insights never extended beyond the material, and those who saw the work as a spiritual quest. 'Puffers' maintained the Philosopher's Stone was simply material gold. They were in the work for the money, or to increase the store of scientific facts, or both (Voss, 1998, p. 147). There is a parallel here between the concretisation of the 'puffers' as pseudo-alchemists who miss the point, and anorexics who – through concretisation – miss out subtle archetypal powers of symbolisation, which could provide a way for their individuation to unfold.

Prima materia

From an alchemical perspective the food which the baby receives from its mother can be thought of as *prima materia*, raw material. This makes sense if we think not only about literal food, but also about how initial experiences of nurture result in the establishment of a stable ego–self axis and the commencement of individuation. The perception of the *prima materia* containing 'a treasure hard to obtain' is seen in terms of the ego's relationship to the self. The alchemists saw the process as progressing in a spiral. Alchemical gold or 'the lapis' once obtained was then *prima materia* for a further round of the process. Individuation clinically involves numerous experiences of breakthrough – while 'golden' in their own right, they are not the ultimate goal. An anorexic's experience is quite different. Failures in maternal attitude, holding and containment, and the toxic nature of the nurture the baby receives, results in the individuation process stalling.

Nigredo

The nigredo, the first stage, can be a result of the quality of the *prima materia*, or else produced by separation (solution, separation, divisio, putrefaction) of the

elements (CW 12, para. 334). The experience of mother's toxic projective identifications during an anorexic's infancy creates intensely confused feelings of love
and hatred (massa confusa), and a sense of 'nameless dread' as a result of being
used as a receptacle of these projections (ibid., p. 122). These experiences result
in a 'darkening' of the infant's inner world, from which it tries to defend itself by
splitting (separating) them into good and bad; the badness being experienced as
the self. The nigredo is a dark unrefined state which might be experienced as a
deathly depression, a dark night of the soul. Extreme anorexia is literally death-
like – it has the highest mortality rate of any psychological pathology. Through a
remarkable act of will anorexics attempt domination of their attachment needs.
They are in a constant state of trying to purify what they see as an unacceptable,
hateful, and detestable body – their 'pure' body, devoid of flesh, is a grotesque
concretisation of the alchemical metaphor, a destructive parody. Their frantic
activity, hours spent on gym treadmills or 'power walking', is a manic defence
against inner despair. The 'pure gold' an anorexic seeks is unobtainable, because
of constant projection of what they have alienated onto their body.

Case one: Sarah

Sarah is in her early thirties, the youngest of four children, all girls. Her sisters are
considerably older and all did well academically. She formed the impression as a
child that her parents did not expect her to do so well. Consequently she strived to
excel academically and professionally in a jealous attempt to win their love. Her
anorexia, for which she was hospitalised, developed after the breakup of a
relationship with a man she'd met at university. She'd quickly become dependent
on him, losing any sense of herself. Becoming an appendage replayed early
attachment issues. She felt he no longer cherished her as special, as he did initially.
Since the breakup, six years before analysis, she'd not been in another. She came
to analysis because she was bingeing and vomiting uncontrollably when alone. She
found it hard to focus at work, and despite supportive and understanding bosses,
was ultimately 'let go'. Then she moved back to her parents. While they were
concerned about her, she found them controlling and incapable of empathy –
which led her to weep uncontrollably 'for no apparent reason'.

Sarah was afraid to get better, to return to her flat and professional life, afraid
she would lose the attention her parents were giving her because of her anorexia.
They have a strong work ethic, and in her mind this means she has no intrinsic
value for just being. Being still if only to admire a view is something she can't
allow herself. In an early session she brought this dream:

> I am climbing up the stairs of a hotel. The place is mostly in darkness,
> with poor lighting, semi derelict. After going up and down a lot of stairs
> I eventually come across a stairway to the roof. There I find a huge
> swimming pool the size of a lake. I know this has something to do with
> the breakup of my relationship. I go to find my family to tell them my

discovery, but when I find them they are most dismissive. Later, I am back in the hotel. It is well lit now and in contrast to its previous poor state, it seems to have changed and looks impressive. I try to find the swimming pool again – it's difficult now as everything is so different. When I eventually find the stairway to the roof I discover a great piece of concrete has been put there. It's like a piece of old stone saying 'this is ancient history'.

If the hotel is a metaphor for her body, then it is not something belonging to her. The contrast between the first and second visit suggests her unconscious knowledge of her internal state radically differs from her consciousness of it. The swimming pool could represent the great volume of Sarah's repressed emotions about the breakup of her relationship, replaying her maternal relationship. Access to the swimming pool is concretely blocked by the rationalisation 'this is ancient history', which became a familiar defence as sessions unfolded. The dismissive attitude of her family speaks of her own lack of empathic connection to herself.

After a few months, Sarah began saying she didn't know what to say. On exploring, she explained her fear that I would be annoyed if she wasn't working at the therapy. She had realised she tried to figure out how she should be for people. This is a common experience working with anorexics as they try to determine the persona they should construct to be acceptable: externally they are over-compliant, internally they never comply. Sarah complained it was difficult with me as I didn't give much away. She hated silences.

J: So what happens for you in the silences between us?
S: I feel like I'm in a glass bubble.
J: Is that a familiar feeling for you?
S: Yes. It's there in the background all the time.
J: Can you tell me more about it?
S: Well, it's like I'm the subject of a scientific experiment. I'm in a glass flask – and there's all these people looking at me.

Sarah links this experience to a series of repeated dreams in which she is discovered on the toilet, as if she has been caught doing something disgusting – nobody else does this. She feels deeply ashamed.

J: In terms of what is going on between us here, it seems you are very much on your own – and you have me outside the flask. It sounds very difficult for you because you fear I'm going to judge you and reject you, like you fear with the figures in your dreams. But it doesn't sound like you are getting the support you need, isolated as you are in this glass bubble. What do you think would need to happen between us to allow me to be in the flask with you?
S: Oh that would feel very intimate.

There are parallels here with the hermetically sealed vessel of the alchemists, which contained the opus and allowed the opposites to transform. The Jungian term *temenos* is synonymous with this hermetically sealed vessel. The original Greek word referred to a sacred precinct, a sanctuary, in which a god's presence can be felt. In early development, the infant needs the mother to hold its projection of the self (God image/divine) in such a way. However, an infant 'anorexic' does not experience enough of this positive numinous relationship with mother; she is experienced as a hateful god, and a threat to the ego. Consequently, the *temenos* is not strong enough to hold the process of ego separation from the self, the ego-self axis cannot develop, and the individual remains stuck in an infantile position. Sarah's regression to a dependent position in her last relationship, and her fearful dependency on her parents, speaks of this.

Understandably, Sarah feels alone within the analytic container. The fear of being judged as disgusting is clear in the transference. On the one hand she needs to protect herself from taking in anything toxic from me; on the other hand she fears rejection for having such badness. The toilet dreams relate to toxic negative feelings threatening to spoil the perfect and acceptable persona she wishes to present. Alchemically this is an example of putrefactio, discussed in the next section (see also Chapter 1). The difficulty in taking food via the 'no entry' defence makes it difficult for Sarah to take anything from me. The development of bulimic symptoms suggested that her regressed need for love and nurture could break through this anorexic defence. She binges, generally on foods she considers not 'good', as a rebellion against her anorexic restriction.

An experience of my being in the alchemical container might ultimately lead to the coniunctio which, as the alchemical rosarium describes, is the central stage of the opus (see Chapter 3). Her saying that this would be 'very intimate' suggests a wish for her experience of isolation to be overcome, and a need to be accepted in a symbolically erotic union. But she fears her 'no entry' defence being breached.

Putrefactio

Putrefactio can be seen as a sub-stage of the nigredo, involving an experience of putrefaction which resembles how an anorexic experiences themselves internally (see also Chapter 1). From the alchemical perspective rot facilitates change. This process is fortified by sulphur. 'Sulphur hastens nature towards its decay and thus towards its next season, and so, when things stink, when they yellow with decay, something important is going on, and what is going on is sulphuric' (Hillman, 1991, p. 81). Clinically this might provide a way in, if the patient is open to exploring this experience both in their body and in the transference, as 'putre-faction is itself an awareness; the feeling something is wrong is already sulphur experiencing its wound' (ibid., p. 82).

Alchemists regarded sulphur as coming from the 'fat of the earth'. My anorexic patients often talk of having a 'fat day' in which fear of their bodies being seen as disgustingly obese becomes an overwhelming preoccupation. From a Winicottian perspective, an anorexic's perception of their true self is as disgusting and unlovable, which results in it being suppressed into the unconscious and projected onto their bodies – they have no true sense of self. However, the suppressed true self still craves nurture from mother. There is identification with mother's hateful and rejecting attitude towards this needy regressed true self, a fear of merger with mother, and fear of the loss of any sense of independence this craved-for nurture entails. So hatred of 'disgusting' fat involves a real fear of being overwhelmed by need, threatening to reduce an anorexic to a merged appendage of a poisonous, hateful, and rejecting mother.

As a result of receiving toxic projective identification as an infant, and the perception their authentic identity is unlovable, an anorexic experiences who they are inside their own skin as 'bad'. They fear their own skin is unable to contain this badness. There is paranoia in anorexia: their repellent insides might leak out of the flawed containment of their skin and cause rejection. This experience can turn into a fear of disease.

Case two: Peter

Peter is an anorexic in his mid-thirties. His sense of self-worth depends on his ability to perform professionally and meet unrealistic demands of clients; evenings and weekends are often filled with work. He excelled academically at school, but became fearful of his desk space being invaded. He obtained a first class honours degree at a leading university. However, he believed he had to put so much effort into his studies due to a fear of failure. The degree of his success only meant he hadn't failed. He felt a lack of any genuine concern from his mother who showcased and gossiped about him in an invasive, insensitive, and disrespectful way, unable to understand how he felt. Her narcissistic superficiality excluded Peter from any true intimacy. His father, with a past history of hospitalisation for depressive illness, provided no real support either. He over-identified with Peter's struggles and responded with sadistic bullying.

In our sessions Peter often says he is having a 'fat day' in which he is hyper aware of his body. He will feel others see his body as disgusting and as repellent as he sees it himself. He grew increasingly concerned that something was wrong internally, had a number of investigations which found nothing, yet he was convinced he had cancer. He feels as if there is garlic on his breath: what comes from within is repellent. This was an issue when his wife became pregnant with their daughter, conceived after a third round of IVF. Peter was sure IVF wouldn't work because he is a 'failure'. During the pregnancy he had a number of dreams of their baby being perfect and wonderful, a compensatory contrast to his conscious belief. The child represents the unconscious potential of his self.

Albedo

Matter brought to whiteness, refuses to be corrupted.

(Figulus, 1963, p. 287)

In this alchemical stage the impurities of the nigredo are gradually washed away to reveal a whitened state ready for further transformation. Pursuing thinness is as far as an anorexic gets on the crusade for perfection. In extreme anorexia the body gets covered in fine white hairs called lanugo, an attempt to keep warm when stripped of its natural layer of insulating fat. Alchemically, an anorexic's body attempts to camouflage itself: whiteness without feels radically different from blackness within.

Anorexics, through continued defensive concretisation, seek to rid themselves of vile flesh and leave only the white bones of their skeletons. Through the symbolic equation matter = mater = mother their attack on the matter of their bodies resembles an attack on their relationship with their mothers. The hatred involved is staggering – driven by a fight for separation from a poisonous merger.

The family dynamic of an anorexic as conduit of societal shadow

An anorexic is brought up in a family environment of control in which there are high expectations of performance: Sarah's inability to sit and enjoy a cup of coffee in a café because she is yoked to a family work ethic; Peter's paranoid fears of being a failure through not performing adequately in his academic studies. As the Canadian Jungian analyst Marion Woodman points out:

> the child . . . learns how to perform and has an idealised vision of how he or she should be. Anything that does not fit in with this ideal has to be pushed back and annihilated. As a result, whatever is human in the child, whatever is "dirty" . . . anger or natural joy is blocked and so the child concludes "Whoever I am in the reality of my being is not lovable . . ." natural being is repressed and performance becomes everything. But in pursuance of perfection the much slower, spontaneous, and receptive feminine side, the beat of the earth, the state where you simply are is forgotten.
>
> (1993, pp. 22–23)

In the dominant discourse of western society it is assumed our species is special, the centre of creation. This is a stuck and delusional perspective inhibiting the resolution of the problems it creates. In a similar way the scapegoating of an anorexic, within their family dynamic, gives them a special status which avoids resolution of the psychological problems of the individual family members. Anorexia is a symptom by which the psyche is trying to alert us to the consequences of contempt for a depth connection with our own nature. I suggest the dysfunctional family dynamic of an anorexic acts as a conduit for societal shadow, and anorexic individuals are effectively elected to mirror our societal malaise (Colverson, 2011). An anorexic individual presents an image which can be understood in terms of what the physicist David Bohm referred to as 'explicate'

(Bohm, 1980): an unfolding of a reality which is implicitly enfolded within each one of us: imprisoned in a reality in which we are starving from lack of nourishment due to the rupture in our societal ego-self axis.

The Spirit in the Bottle

In volume 13 of his collected works, Jung relates the story of 'the Spirit in the Bottle':

> A poor woodcutter had an only son, whom he wished to send to school. Since he could only give him a few coins, the boy ran out before the time for his exams and came home to help his father work in the forest. During a rest, he found an immense old oak. There he heard a voice calling from under the ground, 'Let me out, let me out!' The boy dug among the roots and found a well sealed glass bottle from which the voice came. He opened it. Instantly a spirit rushed out, half as high as the tree. The spirit cried in an awful voice: "I have had my punishment and I will be revenged! I am the great and mighty spirit Mercurius, and now you shall have your reward. Whosoever releases me, him I must strangle." This made the boy uneasy. Quickly thinking up a trick, he said, "First, I must be sure you are the same spirit that was shut up in that little bottle." To prove this, the spirit crept back in. The boy corked it and the spirit was caught. But it promised to reward him if he would let him out. So he did, and as a reward got a small piece of rag. The spirit said "if you spread one end of this over a wound it will heal, and if you rub steel or iron with the other end it will turn into silver". The boy rubbed his damaged axe with the rag. It turned to silver and he was able to sell it for a fortune. He could go back to school, and later, thanks to his rag, he became a famous doctor.

> *(paraphrased)*

Mercurius is a trickster figure, a pagan god with a two-faced nature, as the boy in the story discovered. He contains all 'conceivable opposites', and is both 'material and spiritual' (CW 13, para. 284). Ultimately Mercurius represents the 'archetype of the unconscious' (ibid., para. 299) – the self prior to the dawn of consciousness, providing a counterpoint to the self in relationship to the conscious ego – symbolised by the image of Christ as God made man.

The forest in the story can be regarded as the collective unconscious with the oak representing the self. The roots of this oak extend into the inorganic realm, like the self with its roots in the body: 'indeed the body's chemical elements' (ibid., para. 242). Mercurius, as daemon and wild spirit of nature, was originally an integral part of the tree, a nature deity, but became separated through the development of culture and differentiated consciousness. Trapped within the soul of the world – the anima mundi, as symbolised by the alchemical flask – Mercurius now operates at the level of the psychoid unconscious, the interface between the spiritual and material dimension. In his guise as Hermes, this god has a liminal ability which offers a bridge between nature and spirit.

Anorexia as cultural shadow

Robert Romanyshyn, professor of phenomenology at Pacifica Graduate Institute California, argues anorexia is the latest in a series of 'cultural shadows' which overlap each other,

> each figure simultaneously refigures those that have preceded it and prefigures those that are to come. Thus the anorexic for example, refigures the witch, while the witch prefigures in a fashion the anorexic. It is not surprising to discover, therefore, that the first diagnosis of anorexia occurs in 1689 but that the figure does not become culturally prominent as a symptom until much later. The anorexic is already present throughout this shadow history, but her specific moment awaits our own time.
>
> (1989, p. 149)

If the story of the Spirit in the Bottle is a metaphor about the collective psyche of Western society, how has our collective psyche been buried in this way? Anorexia is not just a problem for the individuals concerned, but the image it presents mirrors a societal malaise. Romanyshyn argues technological development has gradually objectified our relationship to our bodies. As a result of this objectification, we developed a dream of using technology to leave mother earth and become immortal, divorced from the reality of our eventual return to her in death. The fly in the ointment is our physical bodies carrying death with us as we gradually decline – and constantly reminds us of our umbilical connection to mother earth. To attain immortality we need to cleanse ourselves of the corruption of bodies – 'our ascent would have to be an act of purification' (Romanyshyn, 1989, p. 29). This is an albedo fantasy, an impossible purification.

Through depending on the light of reason and the masculine dream of escape from the body, the dark feminine side of our collective psyche with its connection to a warm, rich, dark mother earth, hatched fantasies of the demonic. Fear of Mercurius, as Lucifer the bringer of light from the dark depths of the psyche (CW 13, para. 299), resulted in the deaths of approximately 60,000 people, throughout Europe and the American colonies, between 1480–1700 (Levack, 2006, p. 204), deemed to be witches.

The yellowing of society

It is significant that alchemy ultimately omitted the yellowing (citrinitas) as a stage in the alchemical process, a regression from the stability offered by the quaternary of four stages. Citrinitas involves yellowing as a transitional process. The yellowing in citrinitas is achieved by sulphur which is the 'principle which hinders perfection in all its works' (CW 14, para. 138). Perfection is the goal of an anorexic, but if there is to be any movement towards health this is undermined. 'Yellowing rots the perfection of the albedo state' (Hillman, 1991, p. 84). Experienced symbolically, albedo involves a turning inwards, which can result in a mirrored prison of lunar introspection:

> Where white unifies all colours into a monotheism of subjective reflection, the yellow clarification results in a dawning of multiple vision, seeing each thing as it is, beyond subjectivity, and thus bridging to the rubedo's sanguine tincturing of the world out there.
>
> (Ibid., p. 85)

The omission of the yellowing stage of citrinitas from the alchemical opus reflects the alchemists' resistance to going beyond the whitening stage of societal introspection into an extroverted engagement with the soul of the natural world. This is a resistance Western society largely continues. Within society this internal perspective is seen in anthropocentric preoccupations – introspections about the human soul, not the *anima-mundi*: the soul of the world. Anthropocentric perspectives give a sense of superiority and detachment, the yellowing of alchemical sulphur impedes this detachment and distancing (ibid., p. 81). But this feels like a threat to our narcissistic inflation in imagining we are the most important species on the planet.

Yellowing rots our societal hybris and undermines our largely contemptuous relationship to nature. I am talking particularly about this as an issue of Western society, but advances in communication technology mean it is increasingly becoming an issue for the 'global village'. 'Soul and nature are inseparable: anima mundi. It is precisely this fact the yellowing makes apparent and restores . . .' (ibid., p. 91). Returning to the story of the Spirit in the Bottle, Mercurius is trapped in a vessel which represents the *anima mundi*, hidden among the roots of the tree. This can be thought of as the psychoid level of the unconscious – the birth place of the psychosomatic symptom, in anorexia the only means of communication left open to Mercurius. As a spirit of nature it is hardly surprising he would be angry at the way we have treated nature. Jung points out:

> Mercurius, that two faced god, comes as the lumen naturae . . . only to those whose reason strives toward the highest light ever received by man, and do not trust exclusively to the cognitio vespertina *evening cognition – thought in the absence of this illumination.* For those who are unmindful of this light, the lumen naturae turns into a perilous ignis fatuus *something that misleads or deludes, an illusion,* and the psychopomp into a diabolical seducer.
>
> (CW 13, para. 303, my italics)

249

Extreme anorexia reminds us of inmates of Nazi death camps as the holocaust is still fresh in our collective memories, part of our cultural shadow. Anorexia expresses the shadow side of the Mercurius/Wotan/Hermes archetype which our disrespectful attitude to nature channels through the body of an anorexic. Anorexics might then be seen as victims of Mercurius' destructive rage. This seems extreme considering the mortality rate of anorexics, but this is an amoral archetype. Death and murder are part of the natural order. Woodman has pointed out:

> in its worst form, it's what happened in Nazi Germany. They sought to create a race of supermen, and they were guided by an ideal of this kind . . . You can see that with an anorexic . . . She has an image of what her body should be, and treats herself like a Nazi would have treated her in a concentration camp. She kills her femininity in order to force herself into a rigid ideal, which is delusion.
>
> (1993, pp. 22–23)

The Jungian analyst Jerome Bernstein, based in Santa Fe New Mexico, describes his work with people he calls borderland personalities: 'such people . . . are the front line recipients of new psychic forms that are entering and impacting Western psyche. They experience the tension resulting in split-off psychic material reconnecting with an ego that resists and is threatened by it' (2005, p. 9). The borderland personality an anorexic presents is stuck at a level of somatic consciousness (like Mercurius is unconscious from the ego's perspective). Our cultural ego struggles with integrating what an anorexic presents. Bernstein regards the borderland patients he sees as resembling miners' canaries. He says:

> I believe they have been designated to carry reverence for Nature and to carry the anguish and great grief over its plight, . . . (however) canaries as they are used in mines are usually dead by the time their warning is registered . . . In many ways Borderlanders are being called upon to carry a sacrificial mandate on behalf of the western cultural collective.
>
> (2010, p. 10)

There is a parallel between the yellow colour of canaries and the yellowing of society. In extreme anorexia it is the skeletal image of self starvation that screams the warning and many continue to sacrifice their lives in this regard, although there is no conscious connection to the borderland – far from it.

Case three: Tina

Tina complained of feeling as if she has a black hole in her chest like a black hole in space, and she fears it will devour her from within. Her early negative experience of her mother has taken on archetypal proportions, becoming a terrifying destructive devouring monster located in her heart. Tina's early attachment needs are associated with this terror of engulfment: her hunger for relationship and her wish to have these regressed needs met is unconsciously associated with this negative archetypal mother's engulfment – a situation played out in her ambivalent transference relationship.

Tina came to a recent session saying she had to move to New Zealand with her partner, and this frightened her. It emerged she was worried about being amidst so much nature, she felt threatened by it. She brought many paintings to the sessions, painted with an ash and egg amalgam mix, of young women lost in a fog. These images were dark, some very dark, depicting a nigredo state. We explored these images as lost aspects of her inner nature, and wondered if they might relate to her fear of nature. Tina is resisting the yellowing of her subjective experience into a depth experience: an expansive identity and oneness with nature attained through the next and final stage of the alchemical process – rubedo.

Rubedo

Rubedo is the final stage of the alchemical process, a completion of a stage in the individuation process, and birth of a new personality through relationship with the self. Tina's art work suggested a parallel to the myth of the phoenix, one of the symbolic images associated with the rubedo. It symbolises the renewed personality: gold, the philosopher's stone, born of the ashes (*prima materia*) where the process began. Near the end of its life cycle the phoenix builds itself a nest of twigs which it ignites. Nest and bird burn fiercely and are reduced to ashes, from which a young phoenix hatches, reborn anew to live again – a state Tina unconsciously struggles to achieve.

Red blood is also symbolic of the rubedo. Blood is the essential medium for life, but individuals with extreme anorexia look drawn and bloodless. A female anorexic regresses to a prepubescent state; suppresses menstruation, and develops an androgyne body. Her natural sexuality and ability to procreate is stoppered up: like Mercurius in the bottle. With its associated rejection of a mature female body, this is a concrete embodiment of the virgin archetype. This does not necessarily refer to a chaste state, but as Jungian analyst Layard explains, it is the 'the untrammelled law of pregnant though as yet chaotic nature we dub "virgin", and it is the reduction of that chaos which we call Law and Order' (1945, pp. 290–291). From his perspective, anorexics are, at an unconscious level, spiritual virgins, pregnant with nature – but the chaotic and untrammelled 'Law of God' is suppressed by the masculine 'Law and Order' of the Western societal ego via their dysfunctional families.

From an alchemical perspective, the concretisation of the previous stages of the opus continues: cessation of the menstrual cycle symbolises incapacity to engage with the internal masculine (animus). There is no coniunctio allowing the birth of new psychic life, enlightenment, and completion of the opus.

Escaping the beauty myth

The mirroring anorexia provides society shows the consequences of desperation to remain on the surface: a pursuit of physical perfection which results in the 'madness' of self-destruction. This can be seen in the myth of Pandora, presented as a gift to man, but really a curse, a revenge for stolen fire. Her beauty was captivating, but she brought suffering and death (see Chapters 6 and 8). American Jungian analyst and writer Polly Young-Eisendrath explored the myth of Pandora as an archetypal influence both men and women can get trapped by.

> Pandora is a symbol of the power struggles among men and the rationale for oppressing females. Her story – and all its meanings – is a pawn in the struggle for male dominance. Her story says much about the suffering of contemporary girls and women and the unspoken meanings that lie behind the commodity of female beauty. For . . . especially young women, the beauty myth leads to obsessions with slenderness . . .
>
> (2004, pp. 82–83)

In anorexia, this obsession is taken to extremes, and the perception of what is beautiful is distorted; many falling victim to Pandora's gift of death.

Young-Eisendrath argues that men can feel threatened by beauty because it is a power they cannot control: consequently there is a wish to dominate. 'Helplessness in the face of . . . beauty can lead to fantasies of rape and/or to rape itself' (ibid., p. 83), and murder. By extension this applies to our relationship to the beauty of the natural world – and our wish to rape, dominate, and destroy it. The issue is not one of gender, but suppression of the feminine, which anorexia graphically demonstrates. From a Jungian perspective, the boundaries of the self include the natural world, so such behaviour is a terrible envious self-attack as mirrored in extreme anorexia.

In the 'Greening of Spirituality', professor and director of Liberal Studies at the University of Washington Michael Kalton argues:

> the move from inanimate mechanistic cosmos to a living cosmos requires . . . meaning anchored in life rather than mind thus, displacing human consciousness from its privileged position . . . Instead of the typical vertical transcendence of the Greek inspired tradition, the movement of this kind of spirituality is horizontal, perfecting our relationship with the world of life around us.
>
> (2000, p. 195)

The king on top in the rosarium can be seen as a limitation of the alchemical model in this context.

Conclusion

Alchemy provides a valuable tool in recognising the ways in which anorexia involves a stuck individuation process in an individual. Like alchemists, anorexics have the pursuit of perfection as their goal, and I suggest they have also been elected by our societal unconscious to mirror the true nature of our current societal malaise as warning 'canaries'. From an alchemical perspective, the warning they are presenting belongs to the missing stage of the process: citrinitas, a bridge to the development of horizontal consciousness. There is a huge sacrifice involved in their role as society's canaries. I suggest anorexics are the 'gold' Western society is unconsciously sacrificing to seed the process of its individuation.

References

Bernstein, J. (2005) *Living in the Borderland: The evolution of consciousness and the challenge of healing trauma* London and New York: Routledge.

—— (2010) *Borderland Consciousness and the Borderland Personality: The evolution of the Western Psyche's Reconnection with Nature* Unpublished.

Bion, W. R. (1962a) *Learning from Experience* London: Heinemann.

—— (1962b) 'A theory of thinking', *International Journal of Psychoanalysis*, 43, 306–310.

Bohm, D. (1980) *Wholeness and Implicate Order* London, Boston, and Henley: Routledge and Kegan Paul.

Colverson, J. (2008) 'Anorexia and Societal Shadow' Presented at the IAJS Conference: 'Contemporary Symbols of Personal, Cultural, and National Identity: Historical and Cultural Perspectives'. July 3–5, ETH Zurich, Switzerland.

Crisp, A. H. and McClelland, L. (1996) *Anorexia Nervosa: Guidelines for assessment and treatment in primary and secondary care* Hove, East Sussex: Psychology Press.

Edinger, E. F. (1972) *Ego and Archetype* Boston, MA: Shambhala.

Farrel, E. (2000) *Lost for Words*: *The psychoanalysis of anorexia and bulimia* New York: Other Press.

Figulus, B. (1963) *A Golden and Blessed Casket of Nature's Marvels* London: Vincent Stuart.

Hillman, J. (1991) 'The Yellowing of the Work', In *Proceedings of the Eleventh International Congress of Analytical Psychology August 28–September 2, 1989*, Mary Ann Mattoon (ed.), Switzerland: Daimon Verlag.

Jung, C. G. (1953–1977) *Collected Works of C. G. Jung*, 20 vols (eds Herbert Read, Michael Fordham, and Gerhard Adler; trans. R. F. C. Hull). Except where indicated, references are by volume and paragraph number. London and Princeton, NJ: Routledge and Princeton University Press.

Kalton, M. C. (2000) 'Greening Spirituality', In *The Psychology of Mature Spirituality: Integrity, wisdom, transcendence*. Polly Young Eisendrath and Melvin E. Miller (eds), Hove, New York: Routledge.

Kirby, S. (2011) www.disordered-eating.co.uk/eating-disorders-statistics/anorexia-nervosa-statistics-uk/html.

Laylard, J. (1945) *The Incest Taboo and the Virgin Archetype* New York: Spring Publications.

Levack, B. P. (2006).*The Witch-Hunt in Early Modern Europe* London: Pearson Education.

McDougall, J. (1989) *Theatres of the Body: A psychoanalytic approach to psychosomatic illness* London: Free Association Books.

Mitchell, J. (ed.) (1986) *The Selected Melanie Klein* Middlesex, England: Penguin Books.

Newman, J. K. (2006) 'The Skin of the Psyche: The Psychology of Dermatological disorders', *Harvest*, 1, 52.

Orbach, S. (1993) *Hunger Strike* London: Penguin Books.

Pope, H. G. Jr., Katz, H. G., and Hudson, D. L. (1993) 'Anorexia Nervosa and "Reverse Anorexia" among male body builders', *Comprehensive Psychiatry*, 34, 6, 406–409.

Ratnasurya, R. H., Eisler J., Szmukler, G. J., and Russel, G. F. M. (1991) 'Anorexia Nervosa: outcome and prognostic factors after 20 years', *British Journal of Psychiatry*, 158, 495–503.

Romanyshyn, R. D. (1989) *Technology as Symptom and Dream* London: Routledge.

Samuels, A., Shorter, B., and Plaut, F. (1986) *A Critical Dictionary of Jungian Analysis* New York: Routledge and Kegan Paul.

Segal, H. (1957) 'Notes on symbol formation', *International Journal of Psychoanalysis*, 38, 391–397.

Stern, D. N. (1985) *The Interpersonal World of the Infant* New York: Basic Books.

Voss, K. (1998) 'Spiritual Alchemy: Interpreting representative texts and images', In *Gnosis and Hermeticism from Antiquity to Modern Times* R. van den Broek and W. J. Hanegraaff (eds) New York: State University of New York Press, 147–182.

Wiener, J. (1994) 'Looking Out and Looking In: Some reflections on "body talk" in the consultation room', *Journal of Analytical Psychology*, 39, 331–350.

Williams, G. (1997) *Internal Landscapes and Foreign Bodies: Eating disorders and other pathologies* London: Karnac Books.

Winnicott, D. W. (1971) *Playing and Reality* London: Tavistock Publications.

Woodman, M. (1993) *Conscious Femininity* Toronto: Inner City Books.

Young-Eisendrath, P. (2004) 'Myth and the Body: Postmodern world', In *Subject to Change: Jung, gender and subjectivity in psychoanalysis* Hove and New York: Brunner-Routledge.

15

JUNG'S QUEST FOR INDIVIDUATION

Nathan Field

Since his death 50 years ago, C. G. Jung's legacy of psychological ideas appear to have gained in significance. Chief among them are the archetypes, the complexes, and the collective unconscious. In this chapter, I discuss his closely related concept of individuation. Since this topic has already been explored in earlier chapters, I propose to limit my discussion of its meaning to a few fundamental references. Like all other profound ideas, the *principium individuationis* was not wholly new: it already appeared in the writings of the philosopher Schopenhauer, and earlier in those by the sixteenth-century alchemist Gerard Dorn. But Jung added depth and richness to a concept integral to our understanding of human personality. As is well known, Jung's conception differed in important respects from Freud's who envisaged human development as the simple process whereby our rational faculties progressively gained control over our basic instincts. Jung, by contrast, did not regard the ego as the centre of the personality but something he called the self. His view of the self was significantly wider than Freud's as he included in it the collective unconscious which encompasses both our animal instincts and the highest aspirations of mankind. In contrast to Freud's famous aphorism: 'where id was, let ego be', Jung's vision could be summarised: 'where ego was, let self be'.

By locating the self as the centre of the personality, Jung adopted a different development path from Freud's linear concept:

> The way is not straight but appears to go round in circles. More accurate knowledge has proved it to go round in spirals . . . we can hardly help feeling that the unconscious process moves spiral wise round a centre, gradually getting closer, while the characteristics of the centre grow more and more distinct.
>
> (CW 12, para. 35)

One simple point Jung makes clear is that individuation is not to be confused with individualism. It is not about the growth of the ego. 'Individuation does not shut out one from the world, but gathers the world to itself' (CW 8, para. 432). It is not about assertion of the self, but the understanding of the self, the realisation of the self, and the process of integrating and balancing its various oppositional aspects.

These primarily include the balance between male and female elements in both men and women, between their introversion and extraversion, as well as the conscious and unconscious levels of the mind. 'The aim of individuation is nothing less than to divest the self of the false wrappings of the persona on the one hand and the suggestive power of primordial images on the other' (CW 7, para. 267).

Individuation needs to be differentiated from the medical notion of cure. It means more than just getting back to normal. Medicine recognises another more complex path: you may have to get worse before you get better. You may need to reach a breakdown before making a breakthrough. This comes nearer to the path of individuation. Nor should we assume a single breakdown followed by a single, definitive breakthrough, but possibly a succession of crises throughout life, each hopefully reaching a higher state of consciousness.

Jung sought to offer mankind a new approach to life which he called Analytical Psychology, and hoped to validate it by finding it a worthy predecessor. After years of searching, he nominated alchemy. This discipline had been practised for over two thousand years in China, ancient Egypt, and Greece. His explicit reasons for choosing alchemy are given in the Commentary he wrote for a little-known yoga text, *The Secret of the Golden Flower* (Wilhelm, 1957, p. 81). This had been sent to him by his old friend Richard Wilhelm who translated it from the Chinese. The text, as Wilhelm describes it, constitutes: 'a development from the earlier alchemical procedures to produce a golden pill, known as the "philosophers' stone" that would create gold out of baser materials and lend men immortality' (ibid., p. 6).

Alchemy was, on the face of it, a curious choice. In Europe it had fallen into disrepute as a failed attempt to manufacture gold from base materials. Yet two unexpected developments emerged from the alchemists' endeavours. First, alchemy proved to be the forerunner of physical chemistry which thereafter had an enormous impact on human life. Second, the procedures the alchemists followed in their laboratories (described in Chapters 1 and 2) became a process of their own personal transformation.

What the alchemists hoped to produce was nothing less than the Elixir of Life. Their materialistic dreams of limitless prosperity became the age-old, universal, dream of immortality. Physical alchemy became spiritual alchemy. In parallel, Jung's aspiration as a psychotherapist was not only to heal disorders of the mind but to achieve an ever-higher level of consciousness, perhaps even make contact with the divine. Jung knew that alchemy, while arguably a process parallel to Analytical Psychology, was just one of a number of ancient spiritual paths aiming at individuation. These have been called by various names: salvation, deliverance, self-actualisation, transformation, enlightenment. Although each is different, they all point in the same direction – towards the soul, the archetypal, the numinous, the transpersonal, all of which Jung called: 'the spirit of the depths' (Jung, 2009).

The quest for individuation has been pursued primarily in the mystical branches of the great world religions. In Christian, Jewish, and Islamic monotheistic traditions it combines mainly prayer, study, and the practice of sacred rituals.

These are also part of far older Eastern practices – Taoism, Hinduism, and Buddhism – and include Kundalini yoga, tantra, and meditation. Jung was profoundly interested in the almost forgotten religions of Gnosticism, Mithraism, and the ancient Greek and Egyptian mystery cults, which had similar goals. In later life he became familiar with Jewish mysticism, the Kaballah, which contributed much to alchemy. In our era the quest for personal transformation reappears in a wide spectrum of therapeutic practices, thanks in part to Jung's own discoveries.

Deeply as he researched alchemy, he fully recognised this pre-existing diversity of transformative approaches. For example, while characterising the *Golden Flower* as an alchemical text he notes in his Commentary that 'Hindu Kundalini yoga affords a complete analogy.' By this he meant primarily what alchemy called the *coniunctio*; namely the fusion of the male and female archetypes, either inter-personally between a man and a woman, or intrapersonally as in self-realisation. The former is likely to produce a new human life, the latter a transformed personality. Jung's essay 'The Psychology of the Transference' (CW 16, para. 353 ff.) is a masterly exposition of a classic alchemical document, the *Rosarium Philosophorum* (see Chapter 3) which depicts the development of the *coniunctio*, which he regarded as the heart of the individuation process.

Jung's Kundalini case

Since the quest for individuation has been pursued in different ways in different times and places, I propose to illustrate it with a particular case from Jung's own practice. It happens to be not only a rare example of the way Jung actually spoke to his patients but also intriguing in its own right, insofar as his patient produced physical symptoms identical to a classical Kundalini experience.

This remarkable development must have made a profound impression on him, since many references to the case appear in his writings. It is found under the title: 'The Realities of Practical Psychotherapy', presented at a Conference in Amsterdam in 1937 (CW 16, para. 540 ff). He already talked about it at some length in the 1932 lectures given with Professor Hauer, published as *The Psychology of Kundalini Yoga* (1996, p. 104). He discussed the case again in his Tavistock Lectures (1968, pp. 162–164, 168–169) where he describes his patient's dubious sexual reputation and appalling dress sense but said nothing of her mystical experiences. It reappears in CW 9, para. 656; and again in *Two Essays on Analytical Psychology* (CW 7, para. 189). The last two references include mandala paintings this unknown patient produced at the time. Although Deirde Bair's exhaustive biography of Jung (Bair, 2004) refers by name to many of his private patients, no mention is made of this particular case. In response to my personal enquiry, she confirmed she could find none in any text she consulted. The identity of his patient remains a mystery.

Jung describes her as a 25-year-old European woman, born in Java and brought up by an *ayah*. She suffered from a high degree of what he called 'hysterical fever', to the extent that 'when she played the piano, her temperature rose to 100 degrees'

(CW 16, para. 546). Jung was the third therapist she'd consulted, and he began therapy by reminding her of a dream she'd had with each of her previous therapists. It involved her crossing a frontier but getting lost in the darkness. Jung now asked: 'Have you had a dream like that since you have been with me?' (CW 16, para. 548). She gave an embarrassed smile and told him the following dream:

> Once more she was at a frontier station and said she'd nothing to declare. The frontier guard pointed to her handbag and demanded "What have you got in there?" "To my boundless astonishment he pulled a large mattress, and then a second one, out of my bag." She said she was so frightened that she woke up.
>
> (Ibid.)

Jung offered her an interpretation: 'So you wanted to hide your obviously bourgeois wish to get married and felt you had been unpleasantly caught out' (CW 16, para. 159). He said his patient agreed with his logic but produced the most violent resistances against any possibility of wanting to marry. He adds:

> Behind these resistances, it then turned out there was hidden a most singular fantasy of a quite unimaginable erotic adventure that surpassed anything I had ever come across in my experience. I felt my head reeling. I thought of nymphomaniac possession, of weird perversion, of completely depraved erotic fantasies that rambled on and on, of latent schizophrenia.
>
> (CW 16, para. 549)

After this phase he reports the work went dead. But after a month of stalemate Jung himself had a dream: he saw his patient sitting on the topmost pinnacle of a tower, 'golden in the light of the evening sun.' He adds 'I had to bend my head so far back that I woke up in the morning with a crick in the neck.' He realised this dream put his patient 'on the highest peak, making her a goddess, while I, to say the least, had looked down on her.' Jung decided to tell her his dream: 'with the result' he said 'that all her resistances disappeared. But now her real neurosis began, and it left me completely flabbergasted.'

> She developed symptoms (which) . . . were absolutely incomprehensible to me . . . she dreamt a white elephant was coming out of her genitals. She was so impressed by this that she tried to carve the elephant out of ivory . . . soon after, symptoms of uterine ulcers appeared, and I had to send the patient to a gynaecologist . . . suddenly this symptom disappeared, and she developed an extreme hyperaesthesia of the bladder. . . . No local infection could be found. . . . I gave her the task of expressing by drawings whatever her hand suggested to her. . . . Now symmetrical flowers took shape, vividly coloured and arranged in symbolic

patterns. She made these pictures with a concentration I can only call devout. . . . Intestinal spasms then developed higher up, causing gurgling noises heard outside the room. . . . Their place was taken by a strange parasthesia of the head. The patient had the feeling that the top of her skull was growing soft, that the fontanelle was opening up, and that a bird with a long, sharp beak, was coming down to pierce through the fontanelle as far as the diaphragm.

(CW 16, para. 551)

Jung finally told the patient there was no sense in her coming to him, since he understood almost nothing of what was happening to her. 'She looked at me in astonishment and said: "But it's going splendidly. . . . It doesn't matter you don't understand my dreams".' In addition, Jung came across a book on Tantric Yoga called *The Serpent Power* by Sir John Woodroffe (1958): 'To my astonishment I found in this book an explanation of all those things I had not understood in the patient's dreams and symptoms.' Jung proceeds to clarify:

The fundamental idea of Tantrism is that a feminine creative force in the shape of a serpent, named Kundalini, rises up from the lowest chakra, known as the *muladhara*, where she has been sleeping, and ascends through each of the chakras. These are successive centres of power each of which needs to be awakened in the transformational process. The *muladhara* is the lowest and is hypothetically located in the perineal area but is not identical with the bodily organ. This chakra contains the sacred white elephant and its symbol is a simple flower. The next chakra, called *svadisthana*, represents the sexual centre; its main symbol is water or sea . . .

(CW 16, para. 551)

And so Jung proceeds to link his patient's symptoms with each successive chakra:

When the Kundalini serpent had reached the *manipura* centre in my patient, it was met by the bird of thought descending from above to the diaphragm. Thereupon a wild storm of affect broke out, because the bird implanted in her a thought which she would not and could not accept . . . she gave up the treatment and I saw her only occasionally, but noticed she was hiding something. A year later came the confession: she was beset by the thought that she wanted a child . . . this seemed a great let down to the patient.

(CW 16, para. 562)

How this patient could have produced a range of physical symptoms identical to an ancient and very rare enlightenment experience Jung found very difficult to understand. Recognising she could not have read Woodroffe's book, nor heard of a mystical cult like Kundalini Yoga, he attempted to link her symptoms to her early years in Java: 'she sucked them in with her ayah's milk'. Given his belief in the primordial influence on the psyche of one's native soil Jung certainly believed this explanation, and repeated it each time he presented her case. It seems to me more likely that her mystical experience was just waiting to happen; all it needed was the requisite trigger: namely her therapist, Jung.

The Kundalini awakening is now known to manifest in very different ways: unearthly light in the head, heat, visions, ecstatic states, as well as diverse physical disorders (Gopi, 1970; Sanella, 1992). Jung admitted her dreams and symptoms were incomprehensible to him and therefore rendered him incapable of making interpretations. But it is surprising that even after the clarifications in Woodroffe's book, an analyst of Jung's calibre failed to explore her physical dysfunctions, her 'unimaginable' erotic fantasies, her dream of giving birth to an elephant, or even question her comment that 'everything is going splendidly'. How could that be? At least he was able to accept that her body knew something he didn't. Reflecting later on this case, Jung felt his ignorance of Oriental psychology drew him further and further into the analytical process and forced him to participate as actively as possible: 'Mutual unconsciousness', he remarks 'meant mutual identity'. Is he saying an alchemical *coniunctio* had developed between them?

Long before this case, Jung had expressed his conviction that the therapeutic encounter can profoundly affect both patient and therapist:

> often the doctor is in much the same position as the alchemist who no longer knew whether he was melting the mysterious amalgam in the crucible or whether he was the salamander glowing in the fire. Psychological induction inevitably causes the two parties to get involved in the transformation of the third and to be themselves transformed in the process.
>
> (CW 16, para. 399)

No less a rationalist than Freud, for all his hatred of the occult, had earlier acknowledged that one person's unconscious 'can speak' to another (Freud, 1915, p. 3). Two senior British psychoanalysts, Melanie Klein (1946, p. 8) and Wilfred Bion (1963, pp. 31 ff.), each observed the unconscious makes wide use of projective and introjective identifications. This means each party in a powerful relationship can induce unconscious feelings and ideas in the other, often to the detriment of the analysis (Field, 1991, pp. 103–109). By contrast, highly positive, sometimes ecstatic, examples of projective identification can be found outside the therapy relationship, in the mystical tradition. I am referring to the phenomenon known as *darshan* where a guru, such as the Indian mystic Ramakrishna, could confer on a disciple blissful state of self-realisation merely by a look or a touch (Isherwood, 1964). I am suggesting that, in addition to Jung revealing his dream to his patient, his *unconscious participation* in this therapy acted as a type of *darshan* and triggered her spiritual life.

This would account for her joyous response to all her distressing symptoms, her erotic fantasies, and culminate in her simple wish to have a baby. This wish may not have come as too great a surprise to Jung: he had already interpreted her original dream of the hidden mattresses as her wish to get married. Nor would he have found her desire to have a baby – possibly *his* baby? – an incomprehensible idea. Years before Jung had developed a profound rapport with another young woman patient, Sabina Spielrein. One expression of her love for him was her wish to have his child, the child of a man she virtually regarded as godlike, who would father in her a neo-divine offspring bearing the name of Seigfried, Wagner's archetypal hero. As for his Kundalini case, Jung had been already enlightened by Woodroffe that the fusion of the erotic and the spiritual is characteristic of the ancient Tantric path of transformation.

In fact, this conjunction of sex and the sacred is not restricted to the Hindu cult of Kundalini. Jung's dream had compared his patient to no less a figure than the Virgin Mary; Mary's role as the mother of God was central to the cult of Christian devotionalism throughout Europe in the Middle Ages. The analyst Herbert Moller writes:

> The most striking element of this type of mysticism was a decidedly personal relationship with God. Its highest avowed aim was the attainment of unity with the divinity in a glow of feeling (*unio mystica*) and the divinity was expected to respond as a person to the amorous longings of the mystic.
>
> (1965, pp. 115)

The passions that Mary's son Jesus inspired, through his role as a perfect man and crucified god, set the tone of affective mysticism which dominated Christian belief from the twelfth to the eighteenth centuries:

> He came to be presented as the exceedingly handsome and loving bridegroom of the human soul, and the culminating experience was the union of the mystic with Jesus in "spiritual marriage", an ecstatic feeling of the divine presence.
>
> (Ibid., p. 116)

Could Moller be describing here the Christian equivalent of the Alchemical *coniunctio* and the Tantric *kundalini*? Affective Christianity gave rise to a huge mystical literature, much of it composed by men; yet the vast majority of those who had these ecstatic experiences were women. One of these was St. Teresa of Avila who enjoyed frequent states of rapture. With admirable candour she describes a particular visionary experience that attests to the link between the spiritual and the sexual. It began with the appearance of a handsome young angel:

> In his hands I saw a great golden spear, and at the iron tip there appeared to be a point of fire. This he plunged into my heart several times so that

it penetrated to my entrails. When he pulled it out I felt that he took them with him, and left me consumed by a great love of God. The pain was so severe it made me utter several moans. The sweetness caused by this intense pain is so extreme that one cannot possibly wish it to cease, nor is one's soul then content with anything but God. This is not a physical but a spiritual pain, though the body has some share in it.

(Teresa of Avila, 1957, p. 210)

In St. Teresa's vision, the angel's spear penetrated from her heart to her 'entrails' and produced what might be called a spiritual orgasm. Jung's patient described how a bird with a long beak penetrated through the top of her head down to her diaphragm, leaving her with the conviction she wanted a child. Jung called it 'the bird of thought' but it sounds, on the contrary, more like a numinously charged *coniunctio*, unwittingly triggered by her therapy? Might a similar vision have happened to the devout young Jewish wife, known to history as the Virgin Mary, when the Angel Gabriel appeared and made his announcement that God was going to father in her a divine child?

Jung and the numinous

Memories, Dreams, Reflections (1967) – henceforward referred to as *MDR* – was one of the last books to be published in Jung's name. Much of it was written directly by him, but other sections were produced by his editor Aniela Jaffe from material he provided. He describes how in his early childhood he had a dream which preoccupied him all his life. It depicted his discovery of an enormous phallus standing on a throne in an underground chamber: 'it was made of skin and naked flesh, and on top there was something like a rounded head with no face and no hair. On the very top of the head was a single eye, gazing motionlessly upwards . . .' (*MDR*, p. 27).

As Jung came to understand it, this was 'a subterranean God, not to be named'. Throughout his childhood he was troubled by notions of this ambiguous kind of God who also appeared in the following fantasy:

I saw before me the (Basle) cathedral, the blue sky. God sits on his golden throne, high above the world – and from under the throne an enormous turd falls upon the sparkling new cathedral roof, shatters it, and breaks the walls of the cathedral asunder . . . I felt an enormous, an indescribable relief. Instead of the expected damnation, grace had come upon me, and with it an unutterable bliss such as I had never known. I wept for happiness and gratitude.

(Ibid., p. 56)

The language used here sounds like the utterances of a newly saved Christian – but with a very different kind of God: 'the immediate living God who stands, omnipotent and free, above his Bible and His Church . . .'. Even at the age of 12 Jung declared his right to his own God. In the Prologue to *MDR* he writes:

> In the end the only events in my life worth telling are those when the imperishable world irrupted into this transitory one. That is why I speak chiefly of inner experiences, among which I include my dreams and visions. These form the "prima materia" of my scientific work. They were the fiery magma out of which the stone that had to be worked was crystallized.

(Ibid., p. 18)

Here he speaks the language of alchemy, but his inner life could have as readily been understood in terms of Kundalini, Kaballah, the occult, gnosticism, or even shamanism. Even as a youth he recognised that his mother had a pronounced psychic side to her nature. Her whole family, including his maternal grandfather, frequently organised spiritualist séances. As a university student Jung was able to put his cousin Helene Preiswerk into a trance in which she claimed to bring messages from the dead. This material became the basis of his doctoral thesis (CW 1, para. 1). He chose psychiatry as his speciality and obtained a position at the Burgholzli Hospital. His chief, Eugene Bleuler, directed him towards studies then being made on the Word Association Experiment. Within a few years Jung had made an international reputation with his contribution to this area of psychological research.

Bleuler was also one of the first eminent psychiatrists to be attracted to psychoanalysis. Jung became even more enthusiastic than his chief and eventually managed to organise a meeting with Freud himself. Their first encounter has become legendary, insofar as they talked non-stop for 14 hours. It would be no exaggeration to call it 'love at first sight'. The two men rapidly formed a powerful relationship. Freud was impressed by Jung's physical presence, his intelligence, energy, ebullience, and charisma. Jung found in Freud, just 15 years older than himself, the wise 'father figure' he had always been looking for.

Freud's interest in Jung had another dimension. He was deeply concerned that psychoanalysis should not be seen as merely a 'Jewish pseudo-science'. His current circle of psychoanalytic disciples comprised mostly fellow-Jews whose talents he regarded as inferior to his own. Jung, by contrast, appeared to be every bit his equal; a highly regarded scientific investigator from the most respected psychiatric institute in Europe, *and a gentile*. He was just the champion Freud had hoped to find who would ensure the future of psychoanalysis, and was rapidly promoted as Freud's successor. What Freud did not recognise was that Jung already belonged to an intellectual elite, centred in Germany, which for more than a century had been contaminated with anti-semitic attitudes. Neither did he take into account Jung's own immense ambitions, nor his occult preoccupations, which were deeply alien to Freud's scientific convictions. Within just a few years, Freud came to suspect his nominated 'son and heir' harboured secret wishes for his death. Twice he fainted in Jung's company when the topic of his succession came up. When Jung published his first major work in 1912 (which became *Symbols of Transformation*, CW 7) he already knew how profoundly it challenged Freud's own oedipal theory. As Freud realised Jung had become alienated, both personally and professionally, he decided to drop him, as he had earlier dropped Breuer, Fliess, Adler, and Stekel.

Jung's rejection by Freud, although anticipated, had a devastating effect. In spite of his privileged personal life, his wealth, family, and professional reputation, he entered into a long period of what he called 'disorientation':

> At that time, in the fortieth year of my life, I had achieved everything that I had wished for myself. I had achieved honour, power, wealth, know-ledge, and every human happiness. Then my desire for these trappings ceased, the desire ebbed from me and horror came over me. The vision of the flood seized me and I felt the spirit of the depths, but I did not understand him.
>
> (Jung, 2009, pp. 231–232)

Interestingly he did not seek professional help, but chose to heal himself. How he did this is vividly described in the recently published *The Red Book* (2009). This is the source of the extraordinary experiences Jung later described in *MDR* as 'Confrontations with the Unconscious' (Chapter 6). *The Red Book* provides a near-verbatim account of Jung's self-healing procedure. It appears to have begun as a continuation of his lifelong habit of recording and analysing his dreams: now, threatened by a serious breakdown, he consciously chose to 'confront his unconscious' by inducing in himself a type of trance which he later called active imagination. He recorded these 'visions', however bizarre they might seem, chiefly in writing, drawing, painting, and carving. He frequently declared that what he discovered in the course of his journey into the depths was the foundation of his most creative work thereafter. As World War One approached he had a series of spontaneous visions of monumental proportions:

> It happened in October of the year 1913, as I was leaving alone for a journey, that during the day I was suddenly overcome in broad daylight by a vision. I saw a terrible flood that covered all the northern and low-lying lands between the North Sea and the Alps . . . I saw yellow waves, swimming rubble, and the death of countless thousands. The vision lasted; it confused me and made me ill. Two hours . . . two weeks passed then the vision returned, still more violent than before, and an inner voice spoke: "Look at it, it is completely real, and it will come to pass. You cannot doubt this." . . . I thought my mind had gone crazy.
>
> (Jung, 2009, p. 231)

Such visions, as Jung understood them, prophesied the long and bloody war to come. As a psychotherapist, he recognised they also indicated that he himself was 'menaced by a psychosis'. What he feared was the widening of the lifelong split in his personality between what he called 'the spirit of this time' and the 'spirit of the depths' (ibid., p. 231). In Jung they manifested as multiple splits between his thinking and feeling capacities, between his sense of self and his relationship to other people, his sense of time and the timeless, of the material world and the spiritual, everyday reality and visionary reality. These splits exist in everyone, but in Jung they constituted an immense conflict. He knew it was vital he observed these visionary revelations as objectively as he could, to avoid being swallowed up by the unconscious, as he had seen happen not only to his psychotic patients, but to writers he admired such as Nietzsche and Holderlin. At the same time he had to admit: 'I did not consider that my soul cannot be the object of my judgment and knowledge, much more are my judgment and knowledge the objects of my soul' (ibid., p. 232). To whom then must he listen: to the 'spirit of this time' or the 'spirit of the depths'? He opted to go into the depths:

> I knew I had to let myself plummet down into them . . . I was sitting at my desk once more, thinking over my fears. Then I let myself drop . . . I had the feeling I was in the land of the dead. The atmosphere was that of another world. Near the steep slope of a rock I caught sight of two figures, an old man with a white beard, and a beautiful young girl . . . I approached them, as though they were real people. The old man explained he was Elijah, and that gave me a shock. But the girl staggered me even more, for she called herself Salome! She was blind.
>
> *(MDR*, p. 206)

So began Jung's encounter with two archetypes of the collective unconscious:

> Salome is an anima figure. She is blind because she does not see the meaning of things. Elijah is the figure of the wise old prophet. . . . Salome, the erotic element. . . . Soon after this fantasy another figure rose out of the unconscious. He developed out of the Elijah figure. I called him Philemon. Philemon and other figures of my fantasies brought home to me the crucial insight that there are things in the psyche which I did not produce but which produce themselves, and have their own life . . .
>
> (Ibid., p. 206)

I have quoted this last passage because it is precisely what, years later, the psychoanalyst Bion proposed in his notion of 'thoughts waiting for a thinker'. It is an idea profoundly different from the conventional assumption that thoughts can only be *created by* a thinker. Philemon, who represents Jung's internalised guru, affirms for Jung the existence of an underlying, all-encompassing, numinous dimension of reality always waiting to be discovered. Jung had now entered into the heart of his individuation process. It proved to be a long and dangerous journey.

Individuation and some of its deviations

Many women patients found Jung immensely attractive and this presented him, for most of his life, with serious temptations. Even in his early years as a psychiatrist at the Burgholzli Hospital, scandal began to spread about his entanglement with his patient, Sabina Spielrein. She had arrived there as an unmanageable hysteric but, thanks to his treatment, rapidly improved. In fact, she was soon acting as his assistant. Later she went on to become a doctor, and developed into a gifted psychoanalyst.

It was hardly surprising that Sabina Spielrein should fall in love with him. She conveys something of their encounters when she wrote to Freud: 'we could sit in speechless ecstacy for hours' (Carotenuto, 1984, p. 96). This phrase indicates that they could enter into an altered state of consciousness, a type of *coniunctio*, which Sabina described as 'poetry'. It is assumed by many commentators (Bair, 2004, p. 152) that 'poetry' was Sabina's euphemism for sexual intimacy. Certainly they were involved in a love relationship which very likely became sexual, but based on their deep rapport. Alerted to this threatening situation, possibly by Jung's wife Emma, Sabina's mother wrote to Jung saying poignantly he had previously 'saved' her daughter and should not 'undo' her now. His defence did him little credit but the relationship ended soon after.

I would accord even less credit to David Cronenberg who made the Hollywood film *A Dangerous Method* (2011). It does poor justice to the depth and complexity of their relationship. To date there is no specific evidence of how their sexual feelings were enacted (Kerr, 1994, pp. 223–227). That Sabina would have engaged in the perverse gratifications of spanking, which so damaged her childhood, seems a far cry from the two of them 'sitting in speechless ecstasy for hours'. Nor does it seem credible that Jung, whatever his transgressions, would perpetrate the very abuse from which he had helped to heal her some years before.

That said, Sabina was not the only patient with whom Jung became involved. Soon after his final break with her, he formed an intimate relationship with another ex-patient: Toni Wolff. Like Sabina, she became first his assistant and then his mistress. In fact their partnership developed into a type of 'mystical marriage' which lasted 30 years. During all this time his wife felt obliged to allow Toni Wolff to function as Jung's *soror mystica* and second wife. Although Emma Jung contemplated divorce on more than one occasion, she apparently tolerated such treatment for fear that her refusal might again threaten Jung's mental stability (Bair, 2004, p. 321).

Jung himself was profoundly aware, even in his student days, that he had to struggle with the deepest contradictions between his formidable personality and inner fragility. In *The Red Book* he explicitly differentiates between his two warring personalities: No. 1 and No. 2. The first was his worldly, chauvinistic, and ambitious side; the second was irresistibly drawn to the soul, to mystery, dreams, and visions. No. 1 led him to become a doctor, scientist, researcher, a man of property and a man of the world. As a man of the world, he was also an anti-semite and something of a womaniser, since his culture regarded them both as inferior. No. 2 led him down into the occult, the infinite, the land of the dead, and even, as he believed, to God.

Subsequent to his break with Freud in 1912, Jung's years of rivalry with psychoanalysis, together with his personal ambitions, culminated in his acceptance in 1933 of the presidency of the Nazi-controlled General Medical Society for Psychotherapy. It involved him being in contact with all kinds of Hitler devotees. This provoked deep hostility against him, especially in America, which continues to this day. Jung strenuously denied any complicity with the Nazi regime, and explained he had taken the presidential role primarily to protect the profession of psychotherapy, and Jewish psychotherapists in particular. In fact, he did individually help many of them. In later life he showed a deep regard for men like Erich Neumann and Gershon Scholem who shared his spiritual perspective. As Andrew Samuels observes: 'some of his best friends were Jews' (Samuels, 1992, p. 172), yet there is little doubt Jung shared the widespread ambivalence of central Europe's male 'Aryan' population towards Jews – and women.

But it could also be asked: how deeply could Jung's anti-semitism have gone if he could fall in love with a Jewish patient, Sabina Spielrein? Even stranger, when he suffered, late in life, a near-death experience, in which he 'ecstatically' identified with the founding father of Jewish mysticism: Rabbi Joseph Ben Jochai (*MDR*, p. 325). Jung regarded this experience – that he himself was the mystical marriage, the *coniunctio* of 'Tiferet and Malchut', which represent the archetypes of male majesty and female wisdom in the Kaballah – as a major transformational event in his life. It eventually brought him to the reluctant recognition that this Jewish mystical system was in many respects itself the ancient forerunner of alchemy. The Kaballistic scholar, Sanford Drob, observed that: 'near the end of his life Jung himself came to the conclusion that "the Chassidic Rabbi Baer from Mesiritz . . . anticipated (my) entire psychology in the eighteenth century"' (Drob, 2010, p. 5).

Many who knew Jung personally found him healing, optimistic, inspiring, and generous. Others remember him as arrogant, self-obsessed and seductive. This led to his capacity to be charming to someone present but critical of them in their absence. A shrewd and balanced assessment of his personality is included in the book *Feet of Clay* by psychiatrist Anthony Storr. In regard to Jung's inclination to womanise, he comments: 'His narcissistic needs may have made him unscrupulous sexually, but he behaved no worse than many other men who are gifted with great energy and drive' (1996, p. 104).

Though this is hardly a convincing justification, it is a fact that a disproportionate number of outstandingly spiritual and creative men have been even more unscrupulous than Jung. In most cases, their transgressions were kept secret for years, or known only to an intimate circle of adoring disciples. Jung made no secret of his needs by living openly in a *ménage a trois* with his wife and Toni Wolff. Critics hostile to Jung (see Noll, 1967) also accuse him of organising his devotees in Zurich into a neo-religious cult, with himself as their Aryan messiah. Noll's case proved to be both overstated and literally flawed, but Bair's biography reveals many episodes from Jung's mature years where his behaviour is starkly elitist. Even though Jung was alert to the dangers of the guru–disciple relationship (CW 7, paras 262–265), and struggled very hard against his own grandiosity, he didn't altogether succeed.

It is an irony of the analytic profession that its founders – to name just Freud, Adler, and Jung – may have brilliantly analysed themselves but never actually went through the long-term experience of an analysis by another professional. Had that have been available, might Jung have become more whole and less split, more ethical and less deviant, more benign and less driven? Jung chose to heal himself, perhaps to his own cost, but had he not done so, would the following generations have inherited the scientific and spiritual riches this gifted pioneer was able to bequeath? Jung's contribution offers society not only a worthy heir to alchemy, but a new path to all those disciplines that aspire to the higher levels of human consciousness.

In asking the question 'how far did Jung himself travel his own path of individuation?' it must be remembered that he never conceived of it as a quest for moral perfection but for wholeness, self-realisation, and possibly enlightenment. There can be little doubt he achieved a high level of *self-realisation*, both worldly and spiritual. In regard to enlightenment, his personal encounters with the numinous convinced him there existed another dimension of reality infinitely more real than his everyday existence. But enlightenment does not necessarily transform the pre-existing personality, as is evident from the behaviour of all too many gurus, prophets, cult leaders, and would-be messiahs. With all his worldly success on the one hand, and personal enlightenment on the other, it seems to me inevitable Jung was unable to achieve a comparable degree of *wholeness*. Implicit in the idea of individuation is that the more integration we achieve the more we realise the self. But Jung himself understood that to speak of an achievement can be seriously misleading. Individuation is not a fixed state but a fluctuating developmental flow. It may prove to be something we aspire to but can never really achieve, and yet will still be something immeasurably worth attempting.

References

Bair, D. (2004) *Jung* London: Little, Brown.

Bion, W.R. (1963) *Learning from Experience* London: Karnac.

Carotenuto, A. (1984) *A Secret Symmetry* London: Routledge and Kegan Paul.

Cronenberg, D. (2011) *A Dangerous Method* London: Recorded Picture Company.

Drob, S. (2010) *Kabbalistic Visions: C.G. Jung and Jewish Mysticism* New Orleans. Spring Journal Inc.

Field, N. (1991) 'Projective Identification: Mechanism or Mystery?' *Journal of Analytical Psychology* 36, pp. 93–109.

Freud, S. (1915) 'The Unconscious' (Standard Edition 14.) London: Hogarth.

Gopi, K. (1970) *Kundalini* London: Stuart and Watkins.

Jung, C.G. (1953–1977) except where indicated, references are by volume and paragraph number to the *Collected Works of C.G Jung*, 20 Vols (eds Herbert Read, Michael

Fordham, and Gerard Adler; trans. R.F.C. Hull) London and Princeton, NJ: Routledge and Princeton University Press.

—— (1967) *Memories, Dreams, Reflections* London: Collins/Routledge.

—— (1968) *The Tavistock Lectures* London: Routledge and Kegan Paul.

—— (1996) *The Psychology of Kundalini Yoga* (ed. Sonu Shamdasani) London: Routledge.

—— (2009) *The Red Book* New York: W. W. Norton & Company.

Isherwood, C. (1964) *Ramakrishna and His Disciples* New York: Simon and Schuster.

Kerr, J. (1994) *A Most Dangerous Method* New York: Vintage.

Klein, M. (1946) 'Notes on Some Schizoid Mechanisms' *International Journal of Psychoanalysis* 27, pp. 99–110.

Moller, H. (1965) 'Affective Mysticism in Western Civilization' *Psychoanalytic Review* 52B, pp. 115–130.

Noll, R. (1967) *The Jung Cult* New York: Free Press Paperbacks.

Samuels, A. (1992*)* 'National Psychology, National Socialism and Analytical Psychology' Pts 1 & 2. *Journal of Analytical Psychology* 37, pp. 3–28, 127–148.

Sanella, L. (1992) *The Kundalini Experience* Lower Lake, CA: Integral Publishing.

Storr, A. (1996) *Feet of Clay* London: HarperCollins.

Teresa of Avila. (1957) *The Life of Teresa of Jesus* (trans. J.M. Cohen) London: Penguin.

Wilhelm, R. (1957) *The Secret of the Golden Flower* London: Routledge and Kegan Paul.

Woodroffe, J. (1958) *The Serpent Power* New York: Dover Publications.

ALCHEMY

This bird will never fly again:
like snowflakes its white feathers
lie scattered on the grass at sunset.

This boat will never ride again
the wild and foam-crested waves:
its withered boards of silvery wood
barely rise above the bone-white sands
that have filled it to its very rim.

It's ready to set sail now
to take me to the starry clouds.
Will you, beloved bird,
be my spirit guide,
and carry me on soaring wings
to the very edge of time and space,
powered by my dreams,
to that vast, eternal place
of the ever-lasting Now,
right at the centre of the heart of light
where life is love – and love as life
is pouring forth – unending grace –
a waterfall of countless jewels,
blossoming in rainbow hues,
and glitterising all
in paradise regained?

Gottfried Maria Heuer
Tigh Shee, Iona,
15 April 2010

INDEX

Pages referring to figures are in **bold**.

Printed in Great Britain
by Amazon